DATE DUE			

WEST CAMPUS

GAYLORD

Integrated Treatment of
Eating Disorders

Integrated Treatment of Eating Disorders

Beyond the Body Betrayed

KATHRYN J. ZERBE

W. W. Norton & Company
New York • London

For information about permission to reproduce
selections from this book, write to
Permissions, W. W. Norton & Company, Inc.,
500 Fifth Avenue, New York, NY 10110

For information about special discounts for bulk
purchases, please contact W. W. Norton
Special Sales at specialsales@wwnorton.com or 800-233-4830.

Manufacturing by R.R. Donnelley; Harrisonburg
Production Manger: Leeann Graham

Library of Congress Cataloging-in-Publication Data

Zerbe, Kathryn J., 1951–
    Integrated treatment of eating disorders: beyond the body betrayed /
Kathryn J. Zerbe.—1st ed.
          p. cm.
    Includes bibliographical references and index.
    ISBN 978-0-393-70442-6 (hardcover)
      1. Eating disorders–Treatment.   I. Title.
√RC552.E18Z49 2008
616.85'2606—dc22

2007034459

ISBN 13: 978-0-393-70442-6

W. W. Norton & Company, Inc., 500 Fifth Avenue, New York, N.Y. 10110
www.wwnorton.com

W. W. Norton & Company Ltd., Castle House, 75/76 Wells St., London W1T 3QT
9 8 7 6 5 4 3 2 1 0

For Skip
And, as always, for Kelli
with love and gratitude

Contents

Acknowledgments

As this book goes to press, I embark on a new professional journey. After spending nearly 30 years within the protective exoskeleton of academic medical settings, I enter a solo private practice. Arriving at this juncture would not be possible without the guidance and support of many individuals throughout the course of my career. I will always feel enormous gratitude to the Menninger Clinic, formerly located in Topeka, Kansas, where I began my psychiatric studies and clinical practice (1978–2001) and to Oregon Health and Science University (OHSU) in Portland, Oregon (2001–2007) where I continued to teach, practice, and grow at midcareer. At OHSU, I had the opportunity to simultaneously wear multiple hats as professor and vice chairperson in the Department of Psychiatry with joint appointments as professor of obstetrics and gynecology and director of behavioral medicine in the Center for Women's Health; these roles were a deeply enhancing and gratifying experience. To work alongside so many outstanding physicians, nurses, and other professionals was a nonpareil education and reaffirmed my core belief that a truly multidisciplinary, integrated treatment approach is not only ideal for patient care but has much to offer clinicians by way of the emotional sustenance and occupational maturation that only comes about in the context of collaboration, mutual respect and affirmation, and shared values.

Personal metamorphosis, while exhilarating, is also a time of taking stock and facing down fears; each personal and professional transition I have made has given me pause to reflect on the courage and leap of faith our patients and their families take when they begin their therapeutic journey. Witnessing the determination, persistence, creativity, and hard work of those who seek to find and to develop their true self has been a source of joy, inspiration, and great learning over these three decades. I take this opportunity to thank my students and patients, past and present.

A wise mentor once told me that one cannot thank everyone personally when making their acknowledgments; an author also does not wish to leave out anyone who has made helpful suggestions or given advice. She also hopes to be forgiven when an inevitable lapse happens. Nonetheless, there are a number of people who helped this five-year project come to fruition in many different kinds of ways whose contribution I wish to mention.

    Without the initial encouragement and support of Amanda Clark, MD, Dr. Jerry and Karen Fogel, George Keepers, MD, and Dr. Don and Laurie Rosen, a fortuitous career adventure in Oregon that has brought so many unexpected rewards and opportunities for growth would never have occurred. Each in her or his unique way rolled out the red carpet and suggest exciting possibilities that seemed just around the corner. As the book began to take form, a number of friends, colleagues, and students read chapters, made helpful suggestions, shared clinical material, and offered excellent advice, encouragement, and reassurance at just the right moments. I would especially like to thank Melissa Buboltz, MD, the late Marian "Mimi" Butterfield, MD, Leah Dickstein, MD, S. Roy Erlichman, PhD, CEDS, Constance Jackson, MD, Alfred Lewy, MD, PhD, Adrienne Ressler, LMSW, Jillian Romm, RN, LCSW, Julie Rosenberg, MD, Joel Yager, MD, and Nancy Winters, MD. In particular, Carlene Benson, MBA, CPA, urged me to continue on during those inevitable times when an author gets discouraged and fears that 'the duckling will never hatch' because, she insisted, "this is a perspective on psychiatric treatment that must be told." As at so many other times during my life, I am now glad I listened to her advice.

    I also wish to thank the faculty members, candidates, board of directors, friends, and donors of the Oregon Psychoanalytic Center. Witnessing and being a part of a new and thriving educational tradition to teach and to nurture the next generation of clinicians who aspire to practice psychoanalysis and psychodynamic psychotherapy in the 21st century has been one of the other special rewards in moving to Portland. What evolved during my life transition would not have occurred without the warmth and encouragement of all of the training and supervising analysts and their significant others, and one could not ask for a better group of colleagues to learn from and to work with now. I again wish to express profound gratitude to Jerry Fogel, MD, former Director of the Institute, for his unwavering support, multifaceted help during the years of transition, and ongoing personal friendship; Jerry's generosity of spirit, passion for psychoanalysis, and scholarship are invigorating qualities to emulate. I also wish to thank Hal Boverman, MD and David Turner, MD for their expertise in helping me to sort out and work through a variety of perplexing clinical quagmires, and Duane Dale, MD and Lee Shershow, MD for their examples of humane, creative leadership and plain, old-fashioned, hard work on behalf of further development of the Center over the past few years. Ralph Beaumont, MD, graciously encouraged me to go ahead and use his favorite Wittgenstein quotation in the last chapter after we discussed its applicability in a wide range of situations in a faculty retreat in 2005; Ralph is also a trusted confidant when it comes to understanding, coming to grips with, and confronting group and institutional dynamics and seeing how they may play out among individuals.

    I also wish to thank those formal and informal consultants sought out over the last few years in the wider world of the mental health profession who have unselfishly shared their unique perspectives and superb advice on rendering patient care: William Bernstein, MD, Alice Brand-Bartlett, MLS, Bonnie "B.B." Buchele, PhD, Susan Gassner, PhD, James Hancey, MD, Anton Kris, MD, and Irwin Rosen, PhD. In particular, the intellect and wisdom of Jacob Jacobson, MD, touched my life at a pivotal moment of transformation. I would be remiss if I did not acknowledge how much I have absorbed from each of these clinicians that is likely imbedded, but not adequately referenced, in the text!

Few organizations or clinicians can take on the all the tasks required for the successful completion of our work without the ongoing support, professional skills, and sustaining presence of the administrative personnel who work with us. The Oregon Psychoanalytic Center runs efficiently and smoothly in no small way because of the expertise and multiple talents of our administrative director, Susan Dimitman, and continuing education coordinator, Erika Jacobson. With respect to this book and publication of recent manuscripts, I am especially grateful to Oregon Health and Science University for providing secretarial and administrative support. Jacqueline McQuiston did most of the "heavy lifting" on this project even after she received a well-deserved promotion to a management position in another department. I owe Jackie a huge debt of gratitude for her assistance with the myriad of details that go into manuscript preparation and her quick wit, loyalty, and, especially, her kindness. Sheila Andre and Kristen Robbel also provided essential help and remarkable resourcefulness at the initiation and conclusion of the book, respectively. Eleanor Bell, copy editor on my earlier books and papers, once again made numerous, detailed suggestions and gave invaluable encouragement; after all these years working together, she continues to have faith that I will someday master the nuances of grammar and punctuation. Obviously, I feel grateful to each of these professionals for their hands-on contributions and fortunate to count them all among my friends.

Like many authors, I began this book thinking that it would be a relatively simple undertaking. I discovered rather quickly that a psychiatrist at midcareer can still be naïve, idealistic, and overly optimistic, especially when it comes to her own capacity for sustained work on weekends and receiving those essential creative sparks that are keys to any endeavor of this kind. For many reasons I will not belabor, it took several years longer than originally anticipated. I wish to thank my editor at W. W. Norton, Deborah Malmud, for her forbearance, friendship, and perceptive commentary; this book would never have been written if Deborah had not had the initial vision that yearly courses, workshops, and lectures could be turned into a book on integrated treatment and without her prods to keep going and delving deeper in the face of the usual setbacks that confront authors. Andrea Costella and Vani Kannan, also at Norton Professional Books, helped to shepherd the book through the production process.

Transitions also serve as an opportunity to reflect on one's past and to point one forward to the future. My mother, who did not live to see this book to completion, and my late father and maternal grandparents, unselfishly provided innumerable opportunities for education and testing my wings and in whose presence I experienced great love and the gift of being listened to and heard. New and rediscovered relationships ameliorate some of the pangs of loss during middle life and help one to feel vital, grounded, and sane. For this I wish to thank Kay and the late Karl Cooper, Marie Bonville, Monty Hill, Kathy Liddick, John Williams, and, especially, Beth and Dale Holloway. My uncle, Frank "Skip" Schreckengaust, who assumed the role of *pater familias*, has supplied a sense of family continuity, affirmation, joie d'vivre, and inspiration to always keep learning and being productive. His presence has been a special blessing my entire life. Kelli L. Holloway, MD, my muse and "first line editor," was extraordinarily generous with her patience, time, intrepidity, insights, and clinical formulations; she read multiple drafts of each chapter, gently probing to help develop theme and voice while offering her own keen and refreshingly perceptive appraisal of the examples and suggestions I offer to other clinicians. Her luminescence, unfailing sense of humor, selflessness, and loving devotion close the circle that have made this book a meaningful and rewarding endeavor.

Integrated Treatment of
Eating Disorders

Preface

If recovery from serious eating disorders did not pose formidable challenges for patients and clinicians alike, there would be little need for a pragmatic text on integrated treatment. Despite remarkable advances since the early 1980s in understanding the complex causes of eating disorders and the diverse patient populations afflicted with full-blown and subclinical symptoms, only a sizable minority achieves stable remission over time. Moreover, even when control of the manifest symptoms occurs, the individual patient's overall sense of well-being and quality of life is often impaired. Eating disorders have the highest mortality rate of any psychiatric illness and cause significant medical and psychological morbidities in patients who do not succumb. How can clinicians and those in our care maintain a sense of hopefulness and conviction that life can be better in the face of such sobering facts? Is it possible to bring together insights derived from contemporary research and decades of accumulated clinical wisdom to help bring our patients to a higher level of functioning in and satisfaction with their lives and to greater mastery over their symptoms?

These questions were ones I silently reflected on in the early 1980s as I listened to lectures at a conference devoted solely to the treatment of eating disorders. What led me to choose that particular professional meeting was the number of patients in my inpatient and outpatient clinical practice who spoke about their struggle with a wide range of eating disorder symptoms, displayed disappointment when their body did not achieve the cultural ideal or their personal standards, and invested inordinate attention to measuring self-worth by their appearance and external standards alone. Only a minority of women, and many men, escaped the affliction to some degree. The desire to be something or someone different from whom they were usurped other meaningful life pursuits and took an enormous emotional toll on these patients and their loved ones, even though they often appeared blasé or indifferent to their plight.

As an inexperienced psychiatrist who had just completed her residency, I was also struck by the intelligence, aptitude, and oftentimes remarkable personal and professional abilities of these individuals. Still, they relentlessly complained that they were dissatisfied with themselves, regardless of what they were told by professionals or the significant people in their lives. They appeared to center their lives on weighing less or becoming smaller or having a different shape or form, and they would talk about these topics continually and seem to do almost anything to achieve their goal. Of even more concern from a medical perspective was the degree of denial some of these individuals had about the impact of their relentless dieting, bingeing, purging, overuse of exercise, and the like on themselves and their loved ones, all undertaken for the manifest purpose of "not just looking better but being a better, stronger person in every way." When they felt secure enough in the therapy relationship to reveal their deeper concerns and struggles, they often called their eating disorder "my secret monster" or "an alien inside of me who takes over," as if the symptom complex were a disparate, malevolent, ignominious aspect of themselves that they could neither understand nor control. Clues toward helping these individuals overcome the betrayal of their bodies, and of themselves, were what I hoped to glean at this conference and to take back home to put into practice. Spurred by the admonition of one of my great teachers, the late psychiatrist Dr. Karl A. Menninger, to "try to understand and reduce suffering because patients want relief from their emotional pain, not just a diagnosis or a pill," I sensed that despite protestations to the contrary, these patients' symptoms covered an amalgam of inner agonies and interpersonal tribulations that defied easy understanding.

I will never forget the example of one courageous therapist at the meeting who stood up after a particularly elegant research paper was presented and asked the speaker how he could apply the insights derived from that study to actual work with patients. The presenter was flabbergasted but forthrightly replied that she was not sure how that could be done or if that was the intent of her project to begin with—she simply didn't know if her paper had any clinical utility at the present moment. I resonated with the therapist who asked the question, reminding myself that hard science often precedes concrete and reliable application to patient care. Many other presentations followed in a similar vein. Each was methodical, well-articulated, gave salient information about biology and etiology, emerging demographics, and outcome statistics for the suggested focused treatment protocols, but there was disappointingly little information about how clinicians could actually go about working with eating disorder patients and craft a treatment based upon that individual's unique needs and desires. The message that emanated from the talks was a hard one to hear but one that all practicing clinicians must take stock of over the course of our careers: It is no easy matter for those of us who "toil in the trenches" to translate what is found in a study or outlined in a treatment protocol, paper, or set of guidelines and implement a plan of action to match the particular needs of the human being sitting before us in the office.

Nonetheless, the meeting was useful in helping me resolve to try to help my patients, putting what I learned at the conference, and what I was learning from them, into individualized treatment plans that addressed their personal needs for symptomatic relief but did not give short shrift to other concerns, conflicts, and problems with living that beguile all human beings. I continued to long for practical advice and specifics about what to do and what to say next in particular situations! Even though excellent texts and articles were available, it seemed that the authors never had the same struggles that I did with my patients. I assumed I was the only clinician who worried about how to adapt what I learned from a study to a real world clinical situation with a patient, and it made me feel flawed and deficient in comparison with "the experts" who made treatment of eating disorders sound so easy, straightforward, and failsafe. Although supervisory meetings proved quite useful, I also found that even experienced clinicians I knew had not treated many eating disorder patients so there were some limitations to what they could reasonably offer in the way of specifics. This also left me feeling perplexed and often lonely. Nonetheless, I followed their advice of working toward improving my listening skills and found that this tried and true method was helpful in a number of situations. Still, my questions about how to implement a seemingly endless variety of treatment recommendations in individual situations remained unabated. When patients did improve, I wondered what particular interventions and characteristics of therapeutic work had actually helped to turn the tide.

An aphorism touted among the sages is "one teaches what one most needs to learn." Likely you will not be surprised to read that my questions about the treatment of eating disorders led me to become director of an eating disorder inpatient unit for five years; devote a significant portion of my outpatient practice to treating these patients; give workshops, lectures, and write clinical papers, and eventually a book on the topic; and continue to consult with senior clinicians, and supervise psychiatric residents and other mental health professionals who also found themselves treating individuals with similar diagnoses. From these activities one does derive a sense of mastery and satisfaction when others respond to our efforts and offer constructive feedback. An added benefit of teaching and writing is that one is prodded to go further, dig a little deeper, and adapt or modify one's ideas when they just don't seem to fit or be useful. In this book you will hear the voices of my students and patients (always thoroughly disguised, of course, to protect their confidentiality) who have enriched my life by their tenacity, openness, honesty, and optimism in the face of difficulty. Whether sharing their clinical dilemmas or personal histories, respectively, they rarely shirk from the delicate task of letting the one seemingly in charge of the session know when I was simply wrong or off base. They helped, and continue to help me to learn more about the hard work involved in amalgamating the science and art of psychotherapy to craft a treatment that meets the needs and aspirations of an individual struggling with a burdensome assortment of problems at a particular moment in her or his life.

As all clinicians know, the treatment of psychiatric conditions in the early 21st century is quite different from when I began practice in the 1980s. One of the special issues facing those of us who work with persons with eating disorders is how often the safety nets of hospitalization, partial hospitalization, and residential treatment are less available than they were in the 1980s and early 1990s. Managed care and third parties have drastically limited benefits for psychiatric care, despite considerable research that now demonstrates the value for patients who can achieve and maintain target weights or curtail self-defeating symptoms after a sufficient period of time within a safe, containing environment. This erosion of hospital and residential benefits has also shifted a burden to outpatient clinicians who are left to shoulder more responsibility than ever before, often with serious consequences to patients and their families. Even though multidisciplinary involvement is essential for appropriate care and recommended by national and international panels of experts, at times limited funding resources combine with lack of patient motivation to attempt to force the individual practitioner to "try to go it alone." Despite these encroachments, there is reason to be hopeful because new biological and psychotherapeutic methods are being developed everyday. A significant number of patients can and do improve, as I will attempt to demonstrate throughout this book.

A note on demographics: Eating disorders primarily affect women; approximately 90% of patients are female (Andersen, 1990; Hoek, van Hoeken, & Katzman, 2003; Hsu, 1990; Mehler & Andersen, 1995). However, because the prevalence of this disorder appears to be expanding in both sexes, I include both male and female case examples in the text. Most clinicians are well aware that anorexia, bulimia, and all of the subclinical variants of these conditions have been primarily described in North American, Europe, Australia and New Zealand—those Western societies most influenced by media standards and cultural ideals. Recently, more case reports and population studies report an increased frequency of eating disorders in Asia and South America.

In the United States, some reports (Feldman & Meyer, 2007b; Gordon, 2000; Taylor, Bryson, Cunning, Doyle, et al., 2006) suggest that as many as 15 to 20% of college students have overt symptoms of an eating disorder when interviewed. Many of these late adolescents and young adults do not meet formal diagnostic criteria for having a full-blown eating disorder, but they nonetheless suffer a great deal. There is growing evidence, too, that younger children of both sexes are developing symptoms of disordered eating and body image problems at younger ages. This alarming fact ironically parallels the emerging health concern of growing obesity in all age groups, including children. Binge eating also appears to be disturbingly common among ethnically diverse groups.

The lifetime prevalence of anorexia nervosa is usually referenced as 0.5 to 1.5% (American Psychiatric Association, 2000; Herzog & Eddy, 2007); bulimia nervosa is 1 to 4% (American Psychiatric Association, 2000; Herzog & Eddy, 2007) in the Western populations in which demographics and population variables have been studied extensively. However, this statistic does not take into account the considerable number of people who do not have a diagnosable eating disorder but who nevertheless engage in many health damaging behaviors, such as overexercise, purging, laxative overuse, and periods of restrictive eating.

This important epidemiologic issue needs further exploration by researchers in decades to come.

I have tried to write the kind of book that can be of practical help to beginning and experienced therapists of a variety of professional disciplines and theoretical persuasions who are treating a person with an eating disorder. I also hope to reach out to some patients and their family members who wish to learn more about the many facets of contemporary treatment to insure they are getting what they need to get better and to have an improved quality of life. I include numerous clinical examples to illustrate how psychotherapeutic principles and insights derived from biological, cultural, and psychological studies can be applied in session to help patients get to the roots of their difficulties and begin to master them. Although my professional training and clinical approach are based in psychodynamic theory, I also believe that educational, cognitive-behavioral, motivational, and pharmacological advances are essential to a fully individualized, integrated treatment plan. The patient requires technical skills that will borrow and blend from all modalities and therapeutic traditions. In this respect it is reassuring to know, based on relatively recent research data on real world psychotherapeutic practices, that the majority of us therapists actually move between schools of thought and make our own amalgamation (i.e., integration) of interventions depending on the needs of the patient sitting before us in the room. It behooves each of us not to be beholden to one particular school of thought or therapeutic technique so we can remain open minded about the patient's care and so nurture our own growth as clinicians.

This book is divided into three main sections to aid the clinician in formulating and carrying out an integrated treatment plan. The first section describes what transpires during the opening, middle, and termination phases of treatment. This road map helps clinicians gain a sense of where we are and where we might be going next and provides us with some different strategies for thinking about the frequently asked question of "How can I help my patient with this particular area of concern?" Suggestions about how to conceptualize interventions and ways the clinician might go about putting them into words will attempt to partially answer the other common query, "How might I translate this particular theory or technique into my own setting in a way that is user friendly?"

The second section of the book addresses treatment and recovery through the lens of the developmental life cycle. Adolescents, adults, middle aged, and older patients with eating disorders all deal with specific issues depending on the particular phase in the life cycle they are in when they begin treatment, and their therapies must be tailored to their particular developmental path. In each chapter, the biological, cultural, and psychological bedrocks pertinent to the developmental phase under discussion is reviewed with particular application to the clinical situation. In many instances interventions and listening strategies are applicable to more than one phase of the life cycle as will quickly become apparent, but differences are highlighted also to help clinician and patient take stock of how the eating disorder is presenting roadblocks and inter-fering with completion of essential developmental tasks.

The final section of the book addresses some of the special issues clinicians face when treating eating disorder patients. The patient's sexuality often goes unaddressed, even though it is a ubiquitous concern; many patients are often too ill to be able or want to rectify their sexual difficulties even when they intrude into important relationships or the patient's sense of him- or herself. I devote significant attention to the topic of managing transference reactions and the inevitable countertransference responses that arise during treatment because solid footing in these arenas may fruitfully stretch and enhance the emotional worlds of both patient and therapist. A final chapter takes up the topic of how clinicians, patients, and the eating disorder field as a whole assess the outcome of treatment. A strong pitch is made, based on the guiding philoso-phy of this book, that solid therapeutic outcome must be based on more than symptom control alone. Fortunately for all of us, quality of life studies and in-depth patient accounts of "what really worked" for them in treatment are begin-ning to stand alongside the more traditional measures of therapeutic success to help clinicians and our patients look more broadly at what constitutes improve-ment and more closely gage strategies and choice of treatment intervention.

Each chapter begins with two quotations—usually one from traditional psy-chotherapeutic literature and one from the literary or spiritual traditions. I elab-orate on these quotations in the introduction to each chapter and attempt to pragmatically apply them to the treatment of our patients. I have found that therapists benefit not only from the ongoing support of a consultant or super-visor and immersing ourselves in our discipline-specific journals but from the companionship provided by reading widely; the seemingly disparate traditions of contemporary psychotherapy and those wisdom traditions of literature and spirituality have much to teach and to guide therapists that may also be use-fully integrated into the most challenging treatment. Patients with eating dis-orders also yearn for this kind of guidance. As I also hope to demonstrate, our patients' improvement is most robust when they find a sense of meaning and purpose in their lives that enables them to first minimize, and then move beyond, the manifest, inordinate investment they have had with their symptoms. Both patient and therapist can derive inspiration, direction, and holding from the melding of these traditions in the work of treatment with eating disorder patients.

One particular tale informs the suggestions and practical advice offered in this text. The incident occurred a number of years ago when I purchased a landscape painting from an artist whose work I had long admired; having recently completed my own training analysis, I now had some extra money to invest in a different kind of "life improvement" venture by acquiring a piece I found compellingly beautiful. After the negotiations were completed, the artist and I talked about our interests and life dreams. I found myself asking the artist why she chose watercolor as her medium of choice, rather than oil or gouache.

Her reply echoes in my mind when I contemplate how the therapist really goes about choosing a particular way of working or therapeutic technique. Why do we therapists find ourselves being drawn to one school or set of assumptions and then "selecting" from the array of methods and theories available to us that feels "just right" at the moment, perhaps for our entire career? The artist replied, "Kassy, I've found that watercolor is what works for me. I'd like to be able to paint like a lot of other artists. I just can't 'do' oil. I've learned to accept that. I can only paint the way I paint."

What words of wisdom for the clinician to abide by daily! Our patients so easily see through any falsehood on our part. They value and require our authentic voices more than any packaged product or hackneyed, prescriptive intervention. We must paint the way we paint, for ourselves and for our patient, because our best work is truly our art form. No matter how much clinical experience or theoretical expertise one accumulates during the course of a career, I urge each therapist to strive always to be him- or herself. My hope for my readers is to offer a glimpse into the "studio" of one who works daily at practicing and improving her art, to pass on a bit of the wisdom and advice that she has garnered from some of the masters who have taught her, and to express gratitude for the textured professional canvas that allows each of us to refine our craft during the course of our career with the help of the best instructors of them all, our patients and students.

PART I

THE STAGES OF TREATMENT
OF EATING DISORDERS

CHAPTER 1

The Opening Phase

All one can do is to accompany the patient on her journey into the past and support her in the present, in the hope she may learn to exist again.

—Dinora Pines (1993)

Distance doesn't matter. It is only the first step that is difficult.

—Mme. Marie Anne du Deffand (1697–1780)

Embarking on the therapeutic journey with a new patient is a more anxiety provoking experience than most clinicians would ever like to admit to our patients. When the illness has the potential to rob life, as in a severe eating disorder, the apprehension we feel when we meet a new patient and take that difficult first step in treatment ratchets up several notches. "How will I be able to help, to make a real difference, in this person's life?" we silently ask ourselves as we review the history and past treatment endeavors. In an effort to be experienced as constructive and hopeful, we usually go on to recommend some further diagnostic tests or a new medicine or a novel therapeutic technique, all the while aware that the tenacity of most eating disorder symptoms continues to beguile and perplex clinicians despite significant advances in the field since the early 1980s. In this chapter I describe some tools that aid clinicians to negotiate the steps of the opening phase of treatment. These nuts and bolts are designed to help the therapist strengthen a nascent therapeutic alliance with the patient and assist in managing those inevitable feelings of anxiety or disquietude that occur when beginning a new treatment process.

Given the real challenges most clinicians find in treating eating disorders, it is little wonder that most of us struggle to know what it will take to help a particular patient and if we, in particular, have what it takes to do the job. Providing a fully "integrated treatment approach" is a fine moniker for a clinical paper, book, or even research project, but it is always easier to conceptualize or study a subject in the abstract than to put the recommendations into practice in the here-and-now. How can I apply the insights from new research and years of accumulated clinical wisdom to the person sitting right in front of me today? Will it be enough? Is it possible to help her change direction after years of struggle? Is it possible to help him thrive? Will she survive? These are also some of the other questions that haunt practitioners who treat eating disorders and lead even experienced clinicians to turn away from and avoid helping this group of patients.

Nonetheless, the therapeutic journey "into the past" that points toward a less encumbered future that psychoanalyst Dinora Pines depicts is also potentially exhilarating for both parties in the therapeutic dyad because it holds the potential for the human being to be able to "exist again" or, in the case of a person with an eating disorder, to start to live fully for the first time. Taking that initial most difficult step also takes all of the courage and creativity both participants will be able to muster. There is no single recipe for a truly integrated treatment. Although I hope to demonstrate how to put into practice many useful techniques that inform contemporary treatment in this book, nothing works for everyone, as the evolving outcome literature on eating disorders attests (see Chapter 9). Hence, we clinicians must be modest from the get-go about what we recommend and promise to our patients who are willing to embark on their journey of personal discovery, and always be prepared to switch horses in midstream.

Just as every individual has nutritional needs and preferences that are different from those of every other person, so must the therapeutic palate be seasoned to meet the requirements of the individual. In other words, even the most skillful advice, lists of therapeutic guidelines, and overarching therapeutic principles and techniques will serve only as a mere outline in the majority of situations. The most successful practitioners with eating disorder patients always need to tinker with specifics because of our patient's inherent uniqueness.

As in many other domains in life, ultimate truth and a sense of certainty are longed for because they reduce anxiety and make decisions easy. In practice, we clinicians also long for a one size fits all approach, even though we know in our hearts and in our heads that there really can never be one. This fact alone places a great deal of weight and responsibility on the clinician's shoulders to be well versed in a range of therapeutic skills and techniques but beholden to none. Flexibility and freedom to think through clinical quagmires are essential attributes that will help the therapist provide the support in the present, to go the distance that Dinora Pines describes as key ingredients for progress on the therapeutic journey.

Almost by definition, treatment that is integrated is also individualized. Those clinicians who are able to make their own amalgamation of treatment principles based on the needs of a particular patient place that person on the road to greater individuation, one of the long-held, generally accepted, ultimate goals of any therapeutic process. The therapist who is able to individuate is also the best role model for the patient on a quest for greater emotional freedom and self-expression (Daniels, 2001). In so doing, it is incumbent that therapists be authentic. While staying open to new ideas, one must be careful when incorporating something new into our repertoire. Our patients intuitively sense when we are not being real or sincere and even a hint that the therapist's suggestions are not in keeping with her or his true self will be counterproductive. Throughout the book I describe in greater depth why the therapist's authenticity is particularly crucial in work with eating disorder patients and the developmental basis for the common clinical phenomenon of patients going to great lengths to discover "who my therapist is and what she really thinks."

The maxim of the 17th century French literary figure Mme. Du Deffand, cited at the beginning of this chapter, resonates because all of us intuitively know that the first step in any undertaking is always the most difficult. Whether the initial difficulties that we must overcome in ourselves are insecurity, anxiety, lassitude, fear of failure, or simple inertia, most of us do hesitate before jumping off and into something new, different, and challenging. Our reluctance to initiate helps us to more fully empathize with our patients who have their own set of struggles when trying to envision, and then become, themselves.

In the sections that follow, I describe some general techniques derived from contemporary psychodynamic, cognitive-behavioral, educational, and motivational therapies that may be useful to practitioners in initiating and sustaining the opening phase of treatment. Essential biological factors and medical consequences that must be addressed are also reviewed. The clinician can sometimes make use of the physiological consequences of eating disorders to help motivate a patient and must always keep these complications in mind to effectively treat this diverse group of patients. Some relevant research studies are also cited because the factual basis of what we do is often experienced as salutary for both clinician and patient.

Although it may be enticing to see the approaches herein as prescriptive, to view the author as an expert, or to find the formulations or advice to be panaceas, my clinical examples will amply demonstrate how often I have stumbled and been forced to rethink some of my own best advice. Staying open to new vistas on the therapeutic adventure is what is ultimately the major requirement for both clinician and patient who seek to face down a severe eating disorder. When we are able to do that, we might truly be able to say that we have begun the therapeutic journey and are prepared to go the substantial distance that it will inevitably take for our patient's authentic selfhood, minus the eating disorder, to emerge.

BUILDING THE THERAPEUTIC ALLIANCE BY "SIMPLY LISTENING"

The hallmark of the opening phase of treatment is to help the patient tell her or his story. This crucial first step in building the therapeutic alliance with any patient is so self-evident that most clinicians take it for granted: Experienced therapists recognize that the ability to listen well is a fusion of science and art that we work to cultivate during our entire career (Armstrong, 2000; Peebles-Kleiger, 2002; Zerbe, 1999). Fostering a therapeutic alliance with persons with eating disorders is especially challenging because these patients are mired by denial and tend to distort or minimize their symptoms (Casper, Hedeker, & McClough, 1992; Steiger, Goldstein, Mongrain, & Van der Feen, 1990; Steiner, 1990; Troop, Holbrey, Trowler, & Treasure 1994; Vitousek, Daly, Heiser, 1991).

Most of us have had the experience of a supervisor at some point in our career who perceives that we are having trouble with what to say next to a particular patient. The supervisor offers deceptively straightforward advice: "When in doubt, listen, simply listen." The best teachers go on to explain that there are *ways to clarify or query* a patient that move the treatment forward because the therapist is actively working to make sure that what has been said is both received and understood (Ross, personal communication, 1985). This is especially important in the treatment of eating disorders because the patient is likely to have had few opportunities to reveal problems or symptoms as well as accomplishments and goals in an atmosphere of sincere interest and uncritical acceptance. Nevertheless, even the most sensitive and experienced clinicians have difficulty gleaning information with eating disorder patients because their illness is experienced as a vital aspect of their identity to which they cling lest they experience a loss of sense of self (Boris, 1984a, 1984b; J. Russell & Meares, 1997; Zerbe, 1993a, 1996a, 1996b, 2001a, 2007a, 2007b). As Boris (1984a) aptly stated, "What we call their symptoms, they call their salvation" (p. 315).

Even when the patient does reveal her eating disorder symptoms on a structured interview or research inventory, those objective criteria that are crucial for making a DSM-IV (American Psychiatric Association, 2000) diagnosis, are likely to miss the patient's *subjective* experience of what is deeply troubling (Druss, 1995, 2000). Even if we are able to bypass patients' "evasive, defiant, and resistant" and "overcompliant" stance (Vitousek et al., 1991, p. 651) to gather enough valid information to make informed diagnoses, the clinician faces the more formidable problem of getting patients to begin to look at themselves and accept treatment. Because some patients will be in treatment for a considerable period of time before they reveal their symptoms, or they will finally confide that their symptoms are more extensive than they had previously admitted (e.g., purging 10–20 times instead of 3 times per day), clinicians must learn to trust their instincts, continue to probe patients if we fear they are minimizing, and not feel disheartened or embarrassed that we "missed something." Receptivity, gentle reminders about the serious consequences of these symptoms, and a nonjudgmental attitude lay the foundation for the entire treatment, of course, but are also essential for the patient's sense of safety to confide behaviors and symptoms that have been hidden. While the therapist will usually ask direct questions about eating patterns, overexercise or purging, changes in weight,

TABLE 1.1 Beginning a dialogue with the patient

- Has there been any change in your weight recently?
- What did you eat yesterday? Do you miss meals?
- Sometimes a person may feel out of control of their eating and binge on food. Does this ever happen for you?
- Sometimes a person may try to avoid weight gain by vomiting after eating or using laxatives. Does this ever happen for you?
- How much do you exercise per week? Do you ever feel "driven" to exercise more than you should?
- Do others tell you that you overexercise or don't eat enough?
- Are your menstrual periods regular?
- How would it be for you to gain 3 pounds? How would it be for you to lose 3 pounds?
- Do you ever eat because you feel angry, sad, frustrated, lonely, bored, or any other feeling?
- Do you ever feel that when you start to eat you cannot stop?
- Do you eat when you are not hungry?

or menses at the beginning of treatment (see Table 1.1), at any point when the therapist is concerned that symptoms have returned, emerged, or exacerbated, one should ask again. Doing so sends a powerful message of concern and non-judgmentally confronts self-destructive symptoms. Helping a patient embrace the desire to want to make changes and give up self-deception that will gradually bring about personal growth, including the ubiquitous desire to learn "to love and to be loved—and therein to live" (Menninger & Holzman, 1973, p. 182) is a more complicated undertaking than it appears to many persons outside the helping professions.

CULTIVATING YOUR LISTENING EAR

Each person's history is unique; behind every manifest symptom of disordered eating lies a backstory that is waiting to be told. The first step in treatment, therefore, is the creation of a "secure base" or safe haven (Bowlby, 1988) wherein patients may gradually grow more comfortable in sharing aspects of themselves that have stymied personal growth and found general expression in the symptoms of the eating disorder (see Table 1.2). Over the years a clinician develops a greater capacity to "tune in" to those hidden aspects of patients' stories—feelings, memories, and relationships—from childhood to adulthood. The therapeutic self enlarges its capacity to hear and to "connect the dots" of patients' history, thereby giving it meaning.

Just as patients try to sidestep their emotional pain that is difficult to bear—by using defense mechanisms of denial, splitting, dissociation, repression, and projective identification—so do we therapists, even with the desire to help,

TABLE 1.2   The role of the therapist: Opening phase of treatment

- Listen to the patient's story
- Attempt to understand the patient's "theory" of how the eating disorder developed
- Educate the patient about the medical and psychological aspects of the illness
- Recognize the patient's strengths—this counters the experience of shame and personal inadequacy
- Keep focus on the patient. Maintain clear boundaries
- Be aware of the patient's tendency to want to focus on the therapist. Remind the patient that this is "your time"
- Emphasize that making small changes now will later lead to big ones
- Enlist additional support of multidisciplinary team members (e.g., nutritionist, internist, pediatrician, or other primary care provider; family therapist; support group). Avoid the temptation to be the "only resource" for your patient
- If resources in your community are limited, insist that the patient at least have ongoing visits with a primary care clinician (preferably one who has significant knowledge about the physiological consequences of eating disorders)
- Focus on weight restoration in anorexics and low-weight bulimics. Consider pharmacotherapy as an adjunct

signal to the patient that they should not speak about certain ideas or facts that we are not prepared to absorb (Bowlby, 1979). Listening to painful history takes its toll: burnout is commonly experienced among psychotherapists (Grosh & Olsen, 1994). Consequently, therapists tend to keep our distance or inadvertently avoid aspects of the patient's life that are in need of serious scrutiny because we have unspoken fears about the effects of the patient's pain on our lives.* This natural tendency to dodge inescapable disquietude requires ongoing self-examination and unflinching honesty. Yet, even novice therapists who attempt to listen and to understand how the patient's difficulties first developed will usually find a captive audience on the part of the patient. Listening is not only a caring gesture on the therapist's part: it is a transformative experience for the patient. Each member of the therapeutic dyad takes another pivotal step forward in the journey during the opening phase when an aspect of life unrelated to the eating problem makes its way into the dialogue and demands attention. For the patient, the emergence of the true self is being signaled if only we therapists have the ears to hear its whispers.

*The film *Capote* (Miller & Fullerton, 2005) starring Phillip Seymour Hoffman depicts this phenomenon in its chilling subplot. After years of interviewing and coming to understand the life of one of the murderers in order to write *In Cold Blood*, Capote must anesthetize the emotional terror and personal resonance their dialogue engendered in him by turning to alcohol. After completing *In Cold Blood*, Capote never wrote another novel. The movie infers that when one allows oneself to fly close to human tragedy and evil, one cannot emerge unscathed.

Clinical Example

Dr. A., a fourth-year psychiatry resident, made this discovery about the importance of listening in a poignant psychotherapy moment. Much as we all learn from didactic lectures, books, and supervision, there is nothing like a lesson directly emanating from our patient's mouth to make an indelible impression on our minds! Inevitably, our patients are our best teachers, but their commentary is often painful to take in, particularly when they point out a foible or something simple that we blocked out or forgot to ask.

Dr. A.'s patient Melissa had severe bulimia nervosa that came under reasonable control with fluoxetine and some manualized cognitive-behavioral strategies. In the fourth month of therapy, the patient came for a follow-up appointment, and Dr. A. reviewed her response to prescribed relaxation exercises and the homework assignment (Bulik, Sullivan, Carter, McIntosh & Joyce, 1999). Dr. A. observed her intervention in the session.

> I kept wanting to go back and talk about the symptoms that were getting better and the side effects that Melissa was having on the medication I prescribed. Melissa finally stopped me in my tracks by saying, "We might only have 30 minutes, Doc. I'm telling you the medications are okay. My bingeing and purging are getting better. It's my boyfriend I want to talk about today. Don't you people get it? That's what's on my mind now, and I need you to be here for me, to hear what I have to say about him."

Taking to heart the notion that the patient is always the therapist's "best consultant" (Casement, 1985, 2002), Dr. A. sat back and apologized to Melissa. She realized she was not tuning in to the right channel that day. She settled into her chair for the remaining time. "Listen, simply listen" the patient seemed to be saying, and Dr. A. had the humility and the capacity to make a course correction and pay attention!

On the next visit, the patient picked up where she left off. Dr. A. found herself struggling again with a sense that she wasn't working hard enough by "only listening." In fact, the patient was able to describe "some messy feelings" that played a role in her bulimia and relationship problems. At the end of this hour, the patient thanked Dr. A. for being quieter and less directive. Her compliment to Dr. A. was a signal that the patient was growing and expanding her psychological universe because she could now appreciate another person's efforts to help her (Klein, 1957).

Note Dr. A.'s tendency to be critical of herself. We all have a tendency to want to project our inner critic onto someone else, be it our mother, partner, supervisor, or even our patient! Schafer (2003) described in detail the "bad feelings" that we therapists can easily succumb to when doing our work. According to Schafer, patients and therapists alike must encounter and confront envious wishes to spoil good objects, defenses against gratitude and dependence, and sticky attachments to bad feelings. Getting beyond the critical voice allows us to hear our own voice and the voice of the patient more clearly. Discernment of this kind is a salutary event for both individuals in the therapeutic dyad but requires ongoing refinement "to overhear oneself" (H. Bloom 1994, 2000). In this situation Dr. A. had to blend several theories (e.g., cognitive-behavioral, psychodynamic) to reach her patient but it meant facing down a natural tendency to be prescriptive rather than receptive. Dr. A. had to also get beyond her tendency to project her internal self critic onto a supervisor or theory by "overhearing" herself, and thinking it through, and eventually coming to terms with a blend of both listening and providing directives (see Chapter 2) that fit her evolving style as a therapist.

INITIAL ASSESSMENT TASKS

Patients value the capacity of the therapist to tune in to their plight and be emotionally present. Cognitive-behavioral (A. Beck, 1993; J. Beck, 1995; McMullin, 2000; Schuyler, 1991), interpersonal (Weissman, Markowitz, & Klerman, 2000), and psychodynamic therapies (Aktar, 1992; Alexander & French, 1946; Friedman, 1978, 2004, 2006; McWilliams, 1994, 1999, 2004) have a similar starting point that builds on the principle of clarification of the patient's unique set of strengths and difficulties to arrive at an initial formulation of the treatment (see Table 1.3). This formulation will be revised throughout the treatment as more data become available, but these initial tasks enable both participants to clarify the significant issues and scope of the eating problems early on. Many patients are reluctant to engage with the clinician because their symptoms are meaningful parts of their psychic armor (i.e., maladaptive defenses) and because having a psychiatric problem is experienced as shameful and stigmatizing. Both cognitive and dynamic therapies begin to circumvent this resistance by inquiring first about "problem-free" areas of the patient's life.

TABLE 1.3   Initial tasks of the therapist

- Be emotionally present
- Look for paradox of how manifesting a symptom is an attempt to self-heal
- Understand an eating disorder as an attempt to discharge painful psychic states (e.g., sexual or physical abuse, inner emptiness, experience of fragmentation)
- Help patient identify feelings
- Help patients see how they identify with their symptom (e.g., "I'm a bulimic")
- Help patients see how they use symptoms in relationships
- Recognize your own contribution to the therapeutic relationship
- Keep the focus on the patient as an initial way to cultivate the "true self"
- Be aware of patient's inauthentic compliance or pseudo-alliance (i.e., "false self")
- Look for opportunities to recognize and applaud spontaneous, genuine reactions of patient (i.e., true self functions)

It is important to find a way to acknowledge the patient's strengths. Some treaters simply do this verbally but it is usually better to make the message concrete by helping patients to make a list of what you are to discuss.

Some experienced therapists decry this maneuver as idle chit-chat that is too "supportive" but others find that they gather important clues about the patient's functioning that will be employed later to jump-start and to maintain the treatment at crucial junctures. For example, are patients able to see some islands of strength or is their sense of inferiority and shame so great that they will need confirming evidence of their worth? One may go on to ask patients to talk about the "how, what, and when" of their troubles. At this early stage it is essential to actively engage the patient by rephrasing what is said to make sure you "have got it right." Patients are usually quick to let you know what you have not got right, and in so doing provide you with more important data about their lives, or a specific aspect of their set of symptoms. Perhaps even more importantly, correcting the therapist is a deshaming experience for the patient who likely enters treatment feeling quite demoralized.

As a general guideline, the more a patient edits or corrects you, the better! It is a sure signal you are creating an ambience of safety and humility that enables individuals to speak their own truth. I conceptualize this maneuver in the opening phase as asking patients to describe their "theory" of what underlies their illness. This is not a new idea. For centuries the most experienced clinician/educators have repeatedly reminded students that if one listens carefully to patients long enough, they invariably tell the professional exactly what their problem is (Tables 1.2 and 1.3 list ways the therapist may help develop the alliance in the opening phase).

THE PATIENT'S THEORY OF THE ILLNESS

Since the late 1970s, eating disorder patients have been described in the professional literature as "being alexithymic," meaning they do not have the ability to have fantasies or name feelings (Battegay, 1991; Garfinkle & Garner, 1982; McDougall, 1989). For this reason, some clinicians tend to avoid asking about the nitty-gritty details of the personal history because of a perception that the patient will not be able to say much that is meaningful. This is often borne out in practice because, as noted, patients have psychological needs to keep their issues secret. There are ways to circumvent this so-called "alexithymia" that serve to mobilize the patient–therapist alliance. One way is by asking patients to tell you about their ideas of how their illness began in the first place and what their understanding is about what might be keeping it going. In this way you implicitly encourage them to elaborate their personal narrative while explicitly exploring their understanding of how the manifest problem began (Spence, 1982). The aim is to help patients see early on that they are more than a mass of symptoms and that they have self-knowledge that they can and will build on to thwart the eating disorder.

Clinical Example

In the initial interview, I routinely explain that during my years in practice I have learned that people have a pretty good idea about how their problem began and some idea of what might keep it going. I then specifically inquire, "What is your theory about how your eating disorder got started?"

The case of Tina, age 16, is illustrative of what happens when this question is posed in an initial consultation. At the time I met this delightful but treatment-refractory adolescent, I was in the uncomfortable position of being the consultant to an experienced and successful multidisciplinary team of eating disorder professionals. They were at their wits end with Tina because she seemed to refuse all of their attempts to reach out to her. Although I knew I had no magic up my sleeve that would transform Tina's engagement with the team, I assumed that they had already done some significant preparatory work with her.

In any case, the onus fell on me to try to see if the impasse could be overcome. The dialogue between Tina and me evolves as I make course-corrections based on her feedback about what I have understood and failed to understand about her illness. Note the rephrasings that are deliberate attempts to prod Tina to be clear and explicit about her life experiences. Maneuvers such as this support the patient's nascent sense of self and help her to go further in providing details that will point toward greater self-understanding.

K.Z.: (Summarizing the first part of the hour) We've talked some about school and that you like history the best of your classes. You've filled me in a bit on your family and why they made you come to this center for help. Am I right in saying that it is still a little scary to be sitting here and talking to yet another mental health person?

Tina: It's not as bad as I thought! Maybe a little scary.

K.Z.: Well, I am glad that it is going better than you anticipated! I think it might be hard to be answering so many questions.

Tina: That part is OK so far. It's kind of fun.

K.Z.: (Playfully) I'm glad that if you have to be here in the middle of the afternoon it is at least a little fun. I do have another question for you and it may be a hard one.

Tina: (Playfully) Go for it, doc.

K.Z.: Over the years patients and students have taught me a lot. Sometimes I've found that people who come to see me have a good idea of how they got the problem they have. They seem to have a "theory" of why they got an eating disorder, for example. Tina, do you have some ideas about how your eating disorder came to be?

Tina: That's an easy question!

K.Z.: Easy? Really! Tell me how.

Tina: When I was a kid, say 6 or 7, my Mom and I would go to the drugstore all the time. She was heavy and bought all kinds of books and magazines on how to lose weight. Whenever we talked, like after I got home from school, it was almost always about dieting and how to lose weight.

K.Z.: So you learned about losing weight from those books?

Tina: Not exactly. I did go on diets with my Mom, to keep her company. I just got better at it than she did. My eating disorder is my Mom's therapy.

K.Z.: Your mother's therapy? You mean that you are trying to help or to fix your mother by being better on diets than she is?

Tina: That's part of it. It's also the way we have time together—working on the diets and exercise and all of that. We've stopped talking about diets since I got anorexia, and now I don't know what we can talk about.

K.Z.: I bet that makes you feel pretty lonely.

Tina: No. It makes me sad.

Tina is unusually reflective for a 16-year-old in this first consultative hour. She has acquired these skills by "being her mother's therapist." She has also been in a treatment center, and as I pointed out to her team, their hard work had set the stage for her important revelation to me. Tina's situation, however, is not unique. Individuals like Tina grow up overly sensitized to the needs of their parents, behaving as if they were the parent, primary caretaker, or even therapist in their family of origin (Miller, 1981).

In *Prisoners of Childhood: The Drama of the Gifted Child and the Search for the True Self* (1981), psychoanalyst Alice Miller explained how people like Tina grow up to feel empty, false, depressed, futile, and lacking in the sense of vitality that one sees in the presence of a fully individuated human being. Observe how Tina revealed that her after- school talks with her mother were not about her; they were about her mother. What does this tell us about the kinds of difficulties Tina will later have in talking about herself and taking part in her treatment? As Miller further described:

> Narcissistic cathexis of her child by the mother does not exclude emotional devo-
> tion. On the contrary, she loves her child as her self-object, excessively, though
> not in a manner that he needs, and always on the condition he presents his
> "false self." This is no obstacle in the development of intellectual abilities, but
> it is to the unfolding of authentic emotional life. (Miller, 1981, p. 14)

The manifest alexithymia of a person with an eating disorder may be indicative of the loneliness the patient experienced as she attempted to accommodate to the parents' needs. She attuned herself to her mother and thus failed to develop her own voice—her authentic self. The developmental circumstances of these patients may preclude them initially from being able to speak about their feelings and inhibit them from living a vital life devoid of eating pathology. Usually it will not hinder them from beginning to tell us their story if we are tactful and meet the patient on her or his own emotional turf.

In entering into the patient's world by asking how they have come to understand the development of their illness, we embark on some additional initial steps of the journey that Dinora Pines (1993) described because we are stepping into the patient's past.

Patients like Tina will also attempt to take the focus off of themselves and to put the focus on the therapist (Zerbe, 1993a, 1993b, 1995b, 1995c, 1996b, 1998, 2001a, 2001b). They are more comfortable in the role of "mother's confidant" because this has been their primary role in their family to this point. When engaging the patient by helping her tell about her theory of how she developed her illness, therapists must also be aware of ways the patient will return to old modes of interaction by trying to turn the tables on you! Helping the patient focus on *her needs* and not what she perceives are the therapist's needs or wishes for her will be an ongoing challenge to the treatment. At this initial point we are demonstrating to the patient that the therapy hour is her time and her space, a crucial message that will inform all other sessions by explicitly conveying that it is she and not her mother who will be attended to by our therapeutic stance of listening and responding (Armstrong, 2000). In the opening phase of treatment, the patient's tendency to take the focus off of herself can be partially confronted by segueing into educating her about the cultural, biological, and psychological aspects of her eating disorder (see Chapters 4, 5, and 6), and giving thought to the developmental issues the individual should be working on to be fully engaged in life.

THE ROLE OF PATIENT EDUCATION

Providing the patient with information about the effects of starvation on the body, the medical complications that arise in each body system, and some of the cultural, family, and individual issues that underlie eating disorders, is another key component of the opening phase of treatment. (see Table 1.4 for a list of medical complications to review with patients and their family members to help underscore the seriousness of eating disorders). In some respects, relegating patient education to the opening phase is an artificial boundary. The clinician will continue to educate the patient about the illness and the toll it takes on her life throughout the entire treatment and the patient will gradually be able to understand and take responsibility for this array of potential, life-threatening consequences. The opening phase is the appropriate time, however, to authoritatively launch discussion of the biopsychosocial nature of eating disorders, convey an appreciation for the complexity of the illness, empathize with the hold the illness has on the patient, and spell out its life-threatening impact. For example, a patient who has already experienced some of the medical complications of an eating disorder will likely take more seriously the mortality statistics and long-term disabling nature of osteoporosis or infertility than a patient who has not yet experienced some of the physically compromising sequelae (see also Chapters 5 and 9).

TABLE 1.4 Medical complications of anorexia and bulima nervosa

Cardiovascular system
- Orthostatic hypotension
- Arrhythmias
- Peripheral cyanosis
- Sudden cardiac death
- Bradycardia (<60 beats/minute)
- Cardiomyopathy (e.g., purging from syrup of ipecac)
- Edema
- Congestive heart failure (e.g., after rapid nutritional refeeding

Pulmonary system
- Pneumomediastinum
- Pulmonary edema (secondary to congestive heart failure)

Metabolic system
- Hypokalemia
- Hyponatremia (rare)
- Increased serum amylase
- Increased blood urea nitrogen/cholesterol
- Hypomagnesemia
- Hyperphosphatemia (bulimia)
- Hypophosphatemia (anorexia)
- Metabolic acidosis (laxatives)
- Metabolic alkalosis (vomiting)

Gastrointestinal system
- Dental caries
- Parotitis/hyperamylasemia
- Abdominal pain
- Bloating/early satiety
- Constipation
- Diarrhea (e.g., laxative abuse)
- Esophageal or gastric dilation or rupture (rare)
- Pancreatitis

Endocrine system
- Increased growth hormone
- Increased cortisol
- Decreased triiodothyronine (T3) and thyroxine (T4)
- Osteopenia/osteoporosis
- Cold intolerance/hypothermia

Gynecologic system
- Amenorrhea/dysmenorrheal
- Infertility
- Decreased estrogen/testosterone
- Decreased libido

Neurologic system
- Seizures
- Ventricular enlargement
- Brain atrophy

Musculoskeletal system
- Osteopenia/osteoporosis
- Generalized weakness

Hematologic system
- Acanthocytosis
- Mild anemia (e.g., normochrome/normocytic; microcytic/hypochromic)
- Folate deficiency
- Iron deficiency
- Low white blood cell count
- Low erythrocyte sedimentation rate
- Thrombocytopenia

Dermatologic system
- Dry or brittle skin
- Dry or brittle nails
- Callus formation on finger/hand from vomiting (Russell's sign)
- Lanugo hair
- Thinning scalp hair
- Loss of subcutaneous fat
- Pretibial edema with hypoproteinemia
- Irritation at corner of mouth
- Increased bruisability

Because knowledge increases personal power, the underlying message the therapist needs to convey to the patient in the opening phase is one of assuming more control and responsibility for one's life. Indeed, good outcome may be predicted in individuals who demonstrate self-directedness; some patients take to a brief treatment protocol like a duck takes to water (8 to 24 sessions), making use of patient education, self-monitoring, challenging automatic thoughts, facilitating role changes and transitions, and developing a relapse prevention program (Bulik et al., 1999; Joiner, 1999). When patients are in the initial stage of the treatment and may be less motivated than in later stages to do some of the necessary psychological work, a focus on helping them learn as much as possible about the disorder attacks the major resistances to engaging in treatment indirectly. This is a deliberate stance. As noted, for the person with an eating disorder, the symptom has become a core piece of identity that will not usually be given up easily. Education works subliminally to unify the patient and therapist as they join forces to battle the symptoms without directly challenging entrenched coping strategies.

The question becomes how we best educate our patients in a cost-effective and time-efficient manner. Most residential treatment programs have a series of educational sessions devoted to key aspects of eating disorders; the majority of patients ideally take part in each lecture or discussion at least once during their stay. In outpatient treatment, the onus falls on the clinician to cover all the bases and provide materials. It is highly recommended that the clinician give each patient a handout, developed by the clinician, at the conclusion of the initial evaluation (see Appendix A for a "Sample Therapeutic Handout" you might use or adapt for your practice). Not only is the handout a cost-effective tool in giving essential education to the patient but it enables you to assess motivation and readiness to engage when you review what the patient has learned from the first prescribed homework assignments (A. Beck, 1993; J. Beck, 1995; Geller, 2002; Geller, Cockell, & Drab, 2001; Miller & Rollnick, 2002; Zerbe, 2002c).

From a psychodynamic perspective, a handout that one gives the patient to take home and look over also serves as a transitional object (Winnicott, 1953/1971); a token from the therapist's office signifies your desire to help and to make symptoms more manageable, and, most importantly, that the patient is never alone with the symptoms without something to think about or to do. Some excellent autobiographies written by patients in recovery inspire hope while recounting some of the hurdles in getting better (see Appendix B for a noninclusive, annotated list of self-help guides, first person accounts, and workbooks with exercises to address body image that can be used to engage the patient). Clinicians have also written texts for a popular audience (Crisp, Joughin, Halek, Bowyer, 1996; Mitchell & Willard, 2003; Schmidt & Treasure, 1993; Treasure, 1997; Zerbe, 1993/1995) that detail medical and psychiatric comorbidity, family dynamics, trauma, substance abuse, cultural underpinnings, and the like that can be used as inexpensive and time efficient educative tools (also see Appendix B for an abbreviated list of some useful professionally authored references that will be helpful to patients).

When a patient handout or text is "prescribed," it is essential that the clinician check back with the patient to clarify and answer questions, in part to get the patient's perspective on the text. In this way, crucial historical information and insight into the patient's functioning can also be gathered. If the patient is able to constructively critique or even disagree with what they read that the therapist has recommended, a clinician can be reasonably optimistic that this patient has significant ego strength that can be built on to take the next steps in the process. After all, the patient is already trusting you with her "real self." The patient is not "left alone" with more than can be managed, a frequently heard indictment of family members who "saw but did nothing about" the manifest problem. Therapist involvement in the educational process is also essential to make certain patients are absorbing correct information and applying it to their own situation.

If the patient does not complete the homework, exploration of the resistance is required. The homework assignment may not meet their needs; it may also be that the patient is not yet ready to do it for intrapsychic reasons that are essential to understand. Discussing the reasons for not doing the assignment may lead to more "therapeutic gold" than if they finished it, because the therapist is sure to learn more about the patient's real feelings and experience. Herein lies still another opportunity for the clinician to "step into the patient's shoes" and begin to discover and cultivate the true self.

Patients inevitably share what they know with each other, and much of it is simply misguided or wrong. For example, misuse of syrup of ipecac originated with and has been perpetuated by women who want to lose weight, even though purgative measures do not help weight loss. Unfortunately, patients also learn from the misadventures of others, and many sufferers now also take advantage of chat groups and Internet websites espousing the "glory" of having an eating disorder. As much as possible, it behooves the treater to ask how the patient is getting information and learn what the peer group may be conveying about the problem. Fortunately, most published accounts of those who have sustained and recovered from a serious eating disorder actually help motivate the individual to stay involved in treatment and provide healthy models of identification for those embarking on the road to recovery.

DISCUSSING THE EXPERIENCE OF CONSCIENTIOUS OBJECTORS AND OTHER SURVIVORS OF STARVATION

In this early stage of treatment, it is crucial to educate all patients who have an eating disorder about the psychological and physical experience of malnutrition and hunger. In addition to reviewing the seminal findings of Dr. Ansel Keys (Keys, Brozek, Herschel, Mickelsen, & Taylor, 1950), patients may find that reading books about survivors of starvation will inspire them and also

TABLE 1.5 Psychological experience of hunger among conscientious objectors

---

- Thought about food constantly
- Experienced pervasive and omnipresent sense of hunger
- Lost interest in activities except when related to food (such as discussion of family recipes)
- Became sad, irritable, demoralized, apathetic
- Cut food into little bits, played with food, and talked about food constantly
- Lost sense of humor
- Making decisions became harder; intellectual capacity declined
- Became physically weak
- Libido declined
- Social interactions decreased

Source: Keys et al. (1950)

enable them to learn from the experience of others. Sometimes patients will rapidly identify with the physiological feelings of a somatic "hunger that is more than normal hunger" described in these accounts (Guetzkow & Bowman, 1946). At other times, patients utilize a tragic memoir or novel (Anonymous, 1995; Frankl, 1963; Keneally, 1982) as another initial step toward shifting their attention away from investment in their body image and the eating disorder and engaging in more meaningful personal activities, such as political involvement or returning to school.

Even in situations where a patient is not profoundly underweight, the investigation of human starvation undertaken by Keys et al. (1950) at the close of World War II is important to review with every patient. This study demonstrated the psychological effects and physiological changes in each of the 32 conscientious objectors who voluntarily underwent 24 weeks of markedly reduced caloric intake. Table 1.5 lists the physical and emotional effects on the volunteers that can be reviewed with the patient.

Remind your patients that during the recovery period, these volunteers "made up" for their significant weight loss (25% of their starting weight) by eating up to 10,000 kcal per meal. It took four to six months for weight to return to normal, but the psychological recovery took much longer. The length of time spent attaining psychological recovery after starvation is important to point out not only to patients with anorexia nervosa but those who struggle with bulimia nervosa and binge eating disorder. Those who attempt to lose weight by going on diets often do themselves more harm than good because they get caught up in a vicious circle of losing and then regaining weight that is hard to break (Herman & Polivy, 1980, 1998; Polivy & Herman, 1999). A person who gets very hungry is likely to more than make up the calories at the next meal and then feel guilty about the results.

ENGAGING THE PATIENT BY RECOGNIZING STRENGTHS

Why do people who can benefit from the various forms of contemporary psychotherapy avoid seeking it out? Stigma is a most formidable foe for anyone who needs or desires help for an emotional problem. In the treatment of eating disorders, the clinician is likely to discover significant degrees of bingeing or purging, physical or sexual trauma, inadequate coping patterns, or a sense of personal failure. Indeed, during the opening phase additional queries should be made to fully assess the extent of impairment and threats to life the patient harbors in addition to the eating disorder (see Table 1.6).

Do not be surprised if you learn only later about some of these facts, regardless of how tactful you are or what incentives you give for accurate information (Vitousek et al., 1991; Zerbe, 1992a, 1993a, 1993b, 2007a, 2007b). Patients guard their secrets tenaciously because they protect "from intimacy while helping manage intolerable affects" (Russell & Meares, 1997, p. 692). Maintaining secrets also engenders a feeling of control and hostile compliance, aspects of a false self system that are indicative of disruptions in normal development (Lazerson, 1984; Lerner, 1993; Russell & Meares, 1997). Integrated treatment requires empathy, limit setting, and a full array of therapeutic opportunities through the middle phase to address these resistances and to aid patients in finding their "true self" (Winnicott, 1960/1965). In the meantime, treatment will not be successfully initiated unless the sense of shame that accompanies pertinent historical facts and difficulty experiencing pleasure (e.g., masochism) is confronted first. Engagement in treatment can sometimes be catalyzed by helping the patients name their strengths, but this feedback is always better when specific as opposed to general (e.g., musical ability; devotion to pets) (Swann, 1996).

To counter demoralization and the sense of personal inadequacy the patient feels, enlist patients' observing ego by asking about what they consider to be their personal strengths. Writing them down on a sheet of paper alongside the therapist's own observations of strengths is an affirming step that builds rapport and is reinforcing during times of expectable setbacks. Be generous with what

TABLE 1.6 Additional assessment issues

1. Refusal to maintain weight at 85 to 90% of ideal weight, despite physician counseling
2. Significant impairment in work, school, or family functioning
3. Comorbid psychiatric problems (e.g., depression, obsessive-compulsive disorder, bipolar disorder, anxiety disorder, dissociative disorder, personality disorder)
4. Comorbid substance abuse
5. History of physical or sexual abuse, including rape
6. Family history of eating disorder or other mental health problem
7. Life-threatening medical complications and/or suicidal potential
8. History of excessive exercise or "addiction" to physical activity

you see as assets. For many individuals who have been inadequately mirrored within the family of origin, hearing positive qualities about themselves may be a first. However, patients can also feel easily patronized by therapists who innocently attempt to find out and list personal strengths as a way of making a connection. It is usually prudent to let patients take the lead and then see if they agree with your observations. Again, a dialogue that is rich with "back and forth" flow in the conversation reinforces individuation and, from the patients' perspective, your capacity to hear their voice or the first whisper of the true self.

The therapeutic process can also be moved forward by explaining how the eating disorder has been a crucial way of coping with life. Although obviously a maladaptive strategy and life-threatening disorder that will be deconstructed more thoroughly throughout the next two phases of treatment, one can say at this opening phase that the eating disorder has been a good friend and a most reliable source of comfort to the patient up to this point. Underscore that the strengths you listed together will be called on to defeat this longstanding way of dealing with life to build a stronger sense of the "true self" (Winnicott, 1960/1965). The long-held psychotherapy technique of explaining the psychiatric problem by drawing a physical analogy to medical illnesses such as diabetes (J. Beck, 1995; W. Menninger 1937/1967, 1938/1967; Weissman et al., 2000) is also deshaming and enlists the patient's cooperation.

If the patient is reluctant to engage in the exercise of listing strengths and weaknesses, one might strategically turn to one of the published autobiographical accounts (see Appendix B) and have the patient read it and list perceptions of one of the writer's strengths. How is the story like one's own? What makes it different? In essence, the therapist is catalyzing the patient's therapeutic work by utilizing the confessional of another person first, much as happens within support groups or formal group therapy sessions.

This kind of "building our strength by proxy" is a human activity most of us can relate to in some form. Who has not walked away from reading a biography or novel where the principal character has performed admirably, if not heroically, and garnered incentive and rejuvenation to carry on in his or her endeavors? This need for what psychoanalyst Heinz Kohut called a "mature selfobject experience" is ongoing for human beings throughout the entire life cycle; when human beings can make regular and sustaining use of these selfobjects, they are well on their way toward psychological health (Kohut, 1984). In effect, patients who can exhibit a reliance on a mode of support outside of their eating disorder for self-regulation are moving forward on the road to wellness. Therapists may choose to share at this early juncture something they learned or felt moved by in their own life. Telling a bit about a book, play, or movie that has had a positive impact on the therapist's life is self-revelatory in a limited, but facilitory way. Again, the aim is to jump-start the treatment by an overt deshaming maneuver that implicitly states that the patient is human, not alone, and capable of finding and drawing on resources in the external world that the treatment will build on gradually.

FOCUS ON THE PATIENT

Axiomatic in each major psychotherapeutic tradition is the therapist's interest in, and focus on, the patient. In cognitive-behavioral psychotherapy, focus is implicit when goals and objectives are discussed, and the patient is asked at the end of every session to give feedback about what was and was not accomplished (J. Beck, 1995; Leahy, 2003). Those who espouse motivational strategies attempt to ferret out exactly where the patient is in the process of wanting change. These explicit techniques enhance confidence by reflecting back to the patient what has been said and pointing in a direction about where the dyad may be along the path toward making significant shifts (Geller, 2002; Geller, Brown, Zaitsoff, Goodrich, & Hastings, 2003; Geller, Cockell, & Drab, 2001; Geller & Drab, 1999; Jordan et al., 2003; Miller & Rollnick, 2002). Psychodynamic psychotherapists build the therapeutic alliance by making clarifying statements to the patient, picking up on important affects and even nonverbal cues, and helping the patient make sense out of their world by interpretation (Aktar, 1992; Kramer & Akhtar, 1992; McDougall, 1989; McWilliams, 1994, 1999, 2004; Rizzuto, 1988; Schafer, 1983, 1992).

In the treatment of eating disorder patients, keeping the focus on the patient is much easier said than done. Because these patients are exquisitely sensitive and usually quite bright, they pick up cues from the therapist's surroundings and often have an uncanny ability to "tune in" to the therapist's vulnerabilities and preferences. Unwittingly, patients will attempt to derail their own process by making the therapist's needs or goals the issues. Again, the dynamic found usually resides within the family of origin. The patient has been the one who has done the listening rather than been listened to (as in the example of Tina). This process, called parentification or depersonification, begins when a caretaker has the conscious or unconscious need to also be taken care of (Rinsley, 1980, 1982, 1989) and lacks the psychological resources necessary to take care of the child.

The causes underlying this parental failure are numerous. Sometimes the primary caretaker feels neglected by a spouse or has had insufficient nurturing by his or her own parents when growing up. One cannot give to another person what one does not have within oneself or did not receive at home. The original caretakers found a captive audience in their child, our patient-to-be. Emotions and needs are deposited into another person (sometimes via the defense mechanism of projective identification) who absorbs and then attempts to metabolize the feelings of the adult (Bion, 1965, 1967, 1974, 1977; Klein, 1957).

Keeping a deliberate focus on the patient does not preclude occasionally sharing a vignette from the therapist's life or giving voice to a point of view regarding one of the patient's decisions; it does demand attunement to the multifarious ways patients may entice you to step out of the role of therapist because of crucial historical antecedents in their own lives. An integrated treatment approach necessitates that clinicians cut across theoretical boundaries and be a bit more "real" in the treatment, a development point of view I make use of throughout this text. However, one must be judicious and careful about what one chooses to share in each phase of the treatment. The clinical example of Marjorie is illustrative of how a patient may unconsciously attempt to shift the focus to the therapist in the opening phase and what can be learned from redirecting the flow of the therapeutic conversation.

Clinical Example

Marjorie is a 41-year-old graphic designer with a history of anorexia nervosa that began when she was 18. Maintaining stable, but low body weight for her age and height (BMI = 19), she was finally able to return to work she enjoyed after she completed a residential program. She wanted to begin a more intensive psychotherapy process and sought initial consultation. Even in this first session of the opening phase, Marjorie demonstrated some characteristics of the false self compliance alluded to earlier as she sensitively attuned herself to the environment, and possible expectations, of her therapist.

Observing that the psychiatrist's office contained some prints of Impressionist artists, Marjorie left the evaluation session with this question on the doorknob, "I notice you tend to like French artists. Have you ever been to Paris?" Caught off guard by Marjorie's exit line (Gabbard, 1982), I responded affirmatively, only to be inwardly self-critical later about my breech. I wondered why I had not followed my usual style and replied that I would like to hear more about her questions in the next hour.

On one level, the rationale for placing the question back on the patient stimulates the patient to do the work and to reveal more about herself. Why is she curious about this particular aspect of the therapist's life? One might reasonably also consider other factors in the subtext of her question: What is the boundary Marjorie is testing? Were Marjorie's parents responsive to her questions, or did she feel she always needed to show interest in others and not herself? Is Marjorie commenting on just the art, or is she really wanting to address a deeper issue about the evaluation experience or her perceptions of the therapist (e.g., early transference experience)? Does she simply need to see if the therapist is willing to engage with her in a human way, indicating that her early life may have been lonely and devoid of people who engaged in friendly back and forth conversation? The possible psychodynamic meanings that may underlie a patient's questions are limitless.

In the treatment of eating disorders, the rationale for focusing on the meaning of the question is crucial. In this case Marjorie was attempting to see what I was interested in to avoid coming closer to her own thoughts and feelings. As we were later to discover, Marjorie spent many hours during adolescence alone in her room; she felt estranged from both parents. As she went on to describe her adolescent period of self-discovery, she told me that her mother was absent from her because of illness. When Marjorie and her mother were able to sit together and talk, the conversation nearly always focused on the litany of medical complaints that the mother had and the various physicians who were involved in her care.

Marjorie decided to enter psychotherapy at this time because she still attempted to regulate her misery by continued intermittent periods of self-starvation. She had little sense of her own inner needs and aspirations even though she was also married and a mother. It made her extremely anxious to talk about herself for very long, and she sometimes felt guilty about taking my time to explore her issues.

In a session that followed the one I described above, I asked Marjorie to tell me why she wondered about my choice of pictures and made a tentative interpretation that she was both "trying to find in Dr. Z. a more alive and available mother" while she was simultaneously attempting to "turn the tables" from herself and onto me because she felt "more comfortable and normal when she was listening to the other person" (e.g., her mother).

An interpretation of this dynamic serves additional educational needs. To avoid making Marjorie feel embarrassed for being "found out," I explained that I thought it was difficult for her to allow her thoughts and feelings to come up naturally in the session. I explained that in this new relationship of therapy, she did not have to expend energy or time focusing on me as she had her mother. I also said that talking about herself would not be easy but as she became more comfortable sharing her true feelings, we would know we were on the right track. Her longstanding pattern had been a safe way for her to have some contact with her mother, and she and I were not going to dismantle it quickly.

Alerting oneself to how patients may attempt to deflect attention away from themselves and onto the therapist helps keep the focus on the patient and builds the therapeutic alliance. The new experience of being with one who wants to listen will often be anxiety-provoking for the patient who is more able to listen than be listened to. Hence, it is important for the therapist to explain the rationale for keeping the patient's issues in the forefront. Because the symptoms of the eating disorders shrouds the human need to be heard for one's unique "feelings, needs, and competencies" (Lerner, 1993, p. 268), it becomes crucial for the therapist to model an accepting approach with the patient. Pointing out the patient's accurate observations, or even answering a direct question, may be the most important way that the therapist can begin to recognize strengths and let the patient know that it is fine to observe, to question, and to make inferences—even about the therapist! However, to get the most therapeutic mileage, the clinician will likely want also to explore where the questions come from before answering, at least most of the time. This tack also "keeps the focus" on the patient, not the therapist.

CULTIVATING THE TRUE SELF

The term *true self* was coined by D. W. Winnicott in 1960. He used this phrase to contrast with the *false self*, which he used to describe those aspects of the infant's being that are forced into compliance when the primary caretaker is unable to sense the baby's needs and decode her "spontaneous gestures." A true self is capable of genuine spontaneity and joy in living. The true self in each of us seeks opportunities for safe emergence when we can be ourselves. In the case of eating disorders, a true self may actually be hidden or defended by false-self compliance. When the patient begins to share with us some of her "secret life" or tell us about her "theory of illness," she has the opportunity in the treatment to get beneath her defenses and "tell it like it is or was," thereby revealing and developing the inherent potential and aptitude of the true self enveloped in the personal historical recitation (Spence, 1982).

My colleague, Adrienne Ressler, LMSW of the Renfrew Center, has found an ingenious way of getting at this true self early in treatment and keeping the focus on her patient (Ressler, personal communication, 2006). She asks, "Tell me what it is like to be you?" or "When you walk into a room, what does it feel like to be you?" By these sensitive and thoughtful questions, the patient is given an opening to express what it is like to be their genuine, true self, even if that means sharing painful memories, self-disparaging feelings, or a sense of inadequacy in the presence of others.

RECOMMENDING SMALL STEPS

Because the eating disorder symptom is imbedded in the patient's identity, the thought of giving up the symptom can obviously be terrifying. These patients have little idea of who they are or who they will be without their false eating disorder self. Although particularly relevant for patients with anorexia nervosa, this clinical phenomenon is also observed among those who are bulimic, obese, binge eat, or whose addiction to food may unconsciously "strengthen their insufficient self" (Battegay, 1991). The eating disorder never constitutes one's entire being, no matter how pervasive its manifestations; the healthy islands of self that can be located in the opening phase should naturally expand as treatment proceeds. The challenge in the opening phase is to help the patient take initial steps toward greater health when just below the psychological surface lies so much that is unknown, and thereby potentially derailing.

Moreover, underweight and overweight persons may *appear* to look and be polar opposites, but patients in both groups have more in common than preoccupation with body image. Both have fears of being "fat" or "thin," an apparent paradox that signifies an aspect of their psychological struggle with body image. The defining word is *fear*. The clinician's ultimate task centers on deconstructing what the elemental fears are all about in the individual situation; the first and most difficult step is always trying to help patients acknowledge that they are afraid of something, albeit an obscure, indefinable, onerous, mysterious "something."

In anorexia nervosa, the patient may be trying to shed pounds to "kill off" a hated internal object, such as the mother. In this instance the false self is actually searching for a psychological condition in which the true self is safe to emerge, even if it means destruction of the total self (Winnicott, 1960/1965a, 1972; Zerbe, 1993a). The individual who binges or simply overeats may be attempting to fuse with an internal object to find warmth, safety, and psychological nourishment that was lacking in childhood. In this scenario, the false self system is built on identifications and unhealthy destructive defenses (Aktar, 1995; Winnicott, 1960/1965a). In both situations, treatment that addresses only the symptoms often fails in the long run because the deeper needs for establishing a consolidated sense of self and developing new object ties that are less threatening and ultimately more satisfying are not met (Galatzer-Levy & Cohler, 1993). The clinician is in the perilous spot in the opening phase of having to begin somewhere to establish psychological safety while restoring physical health. Our task centers on helping the patient to take the first small step that will ultimately lead to subsequently larger ones.

Some clinicians adroitly engage patients and their reluctance to change by telling them stories, usually tales loaded with psychodynamic significance. One personal favorite that I borrow from my colleague Dr. Arnold Andersen (1994) is "The Door and the Carpenter's Plane." Andersen, a Professor of Psychiatry and Director of the Eating Disorders Program at the University of Iowa, has written a veritable treasure trove of stories that have been published in *Eating Disorders: The Journal of Treatment and Prevention*. He explains to patients that their problem is much like a door that sticks to the frame. The solution is to take out a carpenter's plane and shave off a thin layer from the top of the door. Although this story can be applied to a variety of clinical situations, in the treatment of eating disorder we want to help patients to be less fearful at the beginning about initiating change. For example, gaining a few pounds is a relatively small step with significantly high yield in helping to mobilize healthier coping strategies in anorexia nervosa. Likewise, bulimics may find it *possible* to wait a few more moments before they purge; from this beginning step they find they can delay longer and eventually curtail their purging episodes. In each situation the patient learns that big changes begin with small ones. But they avoid the internal threat of moving too far, too fast.

Andersen reminds his patients that he is "suggesting you use a carpenter's plane, not a hatchet. I'm suggesting you shave the door a bit when it's sticking, not blow-torch the door" (p. 273). Not only does this story address the cognitive-behavioral principle and motivational strategies of making change seem realistic and possible, but it supports patients who infer that the treatment process will take something precious away (e.g., the false self) before there is the necessary ballast for a new self to form. As treatment proceeds and the patients find new objects with whom to identify (Galatzer-Levy & Cohler, 1993) in treatment and in life, and further discover that the human environment can provide both interest and unconditional acceptance, they are more likely to shed the "psychological skin" of their eating disorder behavior.

Clinical Example

Lola is a 27-year-old graduate student in biochemistry who grew up in a household where her parents continually fought, except when her father was berating Lola about her weight. Throughout her adolescence Lola displayed a pattern often found in the history of eating disorder persons: Numerous fluctuations in weight brought on by yo-yo dieting. When Lola finally began to see a therapist, she had struggled with very low weight for 14 years. Her parents were furious with her and threatened to pull out the financial support for graduate school because they still accused her of being "too fat." This "real world" event only increased Lola's resistance to heeding her therapist's suggestions to see a nutritionist. She refused to begin to eat adequate meals so that her studies would go better. Lola and her therapist could not arrive at an agreed on target weight.

Lola correctly read the inference from her therapist: To get better you not only have to gain weight but you will have to defy your parents by acting in ways of which they do not approve. Naturally, her parents were displeased with some of the reality factors inherent in a graduate student's life, including their daughter's decision to come home less frequently. Not only was Lola genuinely interested in her research and designated career path, but she also began her first serious romantic relationship with a medical student. She was demonstrating that she could take steps away from her parents and meet fewer of their demands but Lola was not yet prepared to fully assert her independence.

Sensing Lola's fear that too much was being asked to be given up at once, her therapist explained,

> I think that you are afraid that treatment is trying to take away your anorexia because in each session you come in and you tell me you want to quit despite the obvious progress you are making in asserting your independence. You will stop struggling with your weight and eating only when you are ready. Can we work toward agreeing to help you get to a slightly higher weight—say about 4 pounds more than you weigh now? Even if it isn't what you and I know is an ideal, can it help you get started? If you can put on a few more pounds and maintain that weight for a few months, you'll find that you'll be able to sleep better and that studying will not be so much of a struggle. You'll also have more psychological energy to do the important work regarding boundaries and limit setting with your parents that we've discussed.

In this case, the therapist made an offer to compromise with what she knows is Lola's "ideal weight." Years ago, when I worked in residential treatment, I would have been critical of Lola's therapist. Most treatment centers were stringent about getting the weight gain up and insisting the patient maintain it. Inpatient treatment and intensive partial hospitalization do provide environments where there is greater safety in executing refeeding and more can be expected from patients in facing down their symptoms. They have more support from around-the-clock staff, and symptom control is deemed necessary for getting privileges. Nowadays when most treatments are outpatient, it becomes more important for therapists to know when they must hospitalize a patient because of refractory, dangerous medical symptoms and when we have leeway to negotiate.

Lola's therapist dodged a potential trap by her intervention. By avoiding an unnecessary battle over weight at this time, she encouraged the patient to care for herself in a mature and competent way. Unlike the parents, the therapist's investment was not in making Lola do something that was not yet on her emotional timetable. True self functioning was implicitly encouraged. Lola's safety was the chief issue. Masochistic submission to the therapist's ideas would undermine the ultimate therapeutic goals. Experience teaches the importance of negotiation and flexibility in helping patients learn to manage their symptoms, but at no time is this more crucial than in the opening phase of treatment.

The technique of "taking only one small step at a time" addresses another key factor that has emerged in research studies evaluating the most effective "ingredients" in the therapy of eating disordered persons (Dare & Crowther, 1995; Dare, Eisler, Russell et al., 2001). The research of Christopher Dare and colleagues at the Maudsley Hospital in London demonstrated that the therapist and patient should have treatment goals that match. According to these findings, it is essential for patient and therapist to experience themselves as being "on the same side" during the treatment. When the patients in the research protocol wanted to maintain low weight or avoid solving real life problems related to work, leisure, and relationships, those therapists who made conditions of treatment the giving up of the manifest problem had unsuccessful outcomes.

Another crucial caveat emerged from this body of work. Even for those patients for whom treatment went well, "cure" was not achieved at termination. The patients were doing better in terms of management of their eating disorder symptoms and quality of life. The researchers believe that the establishment of a working relationship that minimized the chance for the therapist to be seen as a "persecuting, intrusive parent of an infantilized, resentful but ostensibly compliant, good little daughter/patient" (p. 297) launched patients on paths where noxious feelings, rejections from the past, unhealthy coping patterns, and damaging interpersonal relations were attenuated. Hearing and understanding were found salutary and potentially life saving, but in the majority of individuals residual symptoms remained even after intensive individual or family therapy. These findings serve as reminder for both therapist and patient when treatment is initiated. We must expect and be able to tolerate "less than perfection" in ourselves and in our patients who are likely to improve significantly but not as totally as we might imagine. Nonetheless, we must never underestimate inroads that can be made in overcoming serious, pernicious, and life-threatening eating disorder symptoms, and the value of improving quality of life and attenuating symptoms (see Chapter 9).

WORKING WITH A MULTIDISCIPLINARY TEAM

The treatment of a patient with a severe eating disorder should occur within the context of ongoing, supportive multidisciplinary team work. The team members should include, but not necessarily be limited to, a primary care physician who takes care of medical needs; a nutritionist; an individual psychotherapist; a family or group psychotherapist; and a psychiatrist or nurse practitioner who prescribes psychotropic medication. Sometimes these roles can be blended, such as when a prescriber is also the individual psychotherapist. Watchwords in the treatment of a patient with an eating disorder remain "never go it alone." Each team member must have a comprehensive view of how eating disorders are treated and be prepared for ongoing learning by reading, attending conferences and workshops, and partaking of consultation and supervision, including peer supervision. Being part of a multidisciplinary team helps the clinician avoid burnout and the tendency to fall into the all too common clinical trap of trying to become the patient's rescuer or savior.

The recommendation to be part of a multidisciplinary team is made much more difficult in an age of managed care and third-party payers. Residential treatments have diminished in number since the mid-1980s (Zerbe, 1992a, 1996a, 1996b, 2001a, 2007b; Zerbe, Marsh & Coyne, 1993). Even some severely emaciated patients are given only one to two weeks to hit an acceptable target weight—clearly an impossible goal lest the patient be thrown into cardiac failure or some other physiologic peril. It would seem that third parties would also rather pay for correction of the multifarious medical conditions that arise as a consequence of bulimia than address the problem through parity for psychological services. Nonetheless, state-of-the-art, integrated treatment necessitates that the patient have multiple persons involved in the treatment. This approach carries significant psychological and structural benefit for the patient.

As noted, eating disorder patients enter treatment with a paucity of ego resources. The structure to the ego provided by having different clinicians filling individualized roles approximates the role differentiation found within a prototypic family setting. Moreover, when the patient is upset or angry with one of the treaters, the patient has other individuals to turn to for support. As in families where a child commonly asks the other parent if he does not get his way with the first parent, so eating disordered patients tend to pit one treater against the other out of a developmental need. It behooves the team members to have frequent, brief contacts to make sure all are "staying on the same page" and are in general agreement with the goals and objectives of the treatment.

Being part of a multidisciplinary team also protects you from the patient's unconscious efforts to place you in the role of the "good object" by saying or implying that "you are the only treater who can really help me." This omnipotent defense on the part of the patient derives from early developmental failures that must be worked through over time. It resonates with some of our own defenses as therapists to not only do a thorough job but to succeed where others have failed. No therapist can avoid a portion of the "omnipotent defense" at least some of the time, or we would eschew working with challenging situations. But we must be aware of it in ourselves to help the patient achieve healthy ambivalence and be able to take the developmentally appropriate step of getting support from more than one person. Soon enough all therapists fall off our pedestals. We all fail and have shortcomings. The patients also have a developmental need to be angry and disappointed with us and to work through those feelings, learning in the process that they will not be abandoned for their negative feelings.

Sometimes a recommendation for hospitalization, residential treatment, or a structured outpatient program must be made before the patient can reasonably collaborate in psychotherapy. This is particularly true when patients have (1) maintained a dangerously low weight for years and are unable or reluctant to tackle the issue on their own; (2) have a severe comorbid psychiatric problem such as alcohol addiction, substance abuse, severe depression, or complicated PTSD; (3) pose significant medical risk, for example, multiple emergency room visits for an arrhythmia secondary to hypokalemia (Becker, Grinspoon, Klibanski et al., 1999; Kinoy, 2001). In the initial phase, I usually explain to patients or their family members the conditions under which hospitalization or residential care will become mandatory. As a customary procedure, I work only as a member of a multidisciplinary team until the patient has made sufficient progress with nutritional management and self-destructive enactments (i.e., they are well into the middle phase of their treatment).

At the very least, every patient must commit to having ongoing, regular visits with a primary care physician and a nutritionist. A release of information should be signed so that contact can go back and forth. For the psychotherapist the need to talk with collaborators may conflict with requirements for confidentiality. Most patients are actually comforted by the notion that their treatment team members are interested enough in their welfare to discuss their case from time to time. Reinforcing exactly what will and will not be shared protects the boundaries of the therapy. Because family members can sometimes be intrusive and disruptive, I prefer to involve a family/marital therapist adjunctively and to emphasize the need for patients to have their own, safe place where confidentiality is sacrosanct unless there is a medical or suicidal crisis.

Considerations for Pharmacotherapy

In the opening stage of treatment, treatment focus is on weight restoration for the patient with anorexia nervosa and the normalization of eating patterns for the patient with bulimia nervosa, binge eating disorder, or obesity. There is general agreement that the goal of the treatment for the anorexic patient should be restoration to 90 to 95% average body weight (a rather amazing goal for those patients who enter treatment at 55 to 80% or below average body weight). Some evidence supports the fact that restoration of menstrual periods points to a better prognosis in the female patient who has been amenorrheic for some time.

Many patients will find that gaining weight outside of a residential program is difficult, if not impossible for them to do. Research demonstrates that patients may need as many as 3,000 to 3,500 or more calories a day to initiate weight restoration; some males may require 4,000 calories or more (American Psychiatric Association, 2006; Kaye, Gwirtsman, Obarzanek, & George, 1988; P.S. Mehler & Andersen, 1999; Yager, Devlin, Halmi et al., 2005). For individuals who have seriously restricted eating to as few as 500 to 800 calories a day, this is an enormous amount of food. Most patients will need to begin their refeeding program with a goal of gaining 1 to 2 pounds per week in an outpatient setting or 2 to 3 pounds per week in an inpatient setting. Usually this goal entails increasing calories at a rate of 100 to 300 calories per day. Daily calories can be decreased as weight moves toward the normal range.

Until weight is restored, psychotropic agents have little if any positive effect in the anorexic patient. New medications are now in the pipeline that may help stimulate appetite. Currently, no single psychopharmacologic agent has been demonstrated to be satisfactory as a sole or even primary treatment for eating disorders. Fluoxetine appears to have some success in preventing relapse in weight-restored anorexic patients and decreasing the frequency of binge episodes and self-induced vomiting in patients with bulimia nervosa. Normal weight bulimics and patients with binge eating disorder may be started on medication during the opening phase (see Chapter 2 for specific recommendations) but require regular follow-up and a stable therapeutic alliance to receive optimal benefit.

Finally, those patients who present with a comorbid psychiatric problem (e.g., depression, anxiety disorder, bipolar illness), benefit from pharmacotherapy for that problem. Getting the Axis I condition under control may help the patient engage in treatment for the eating disorder. Because only a minority of patients improve solely with pharmacotherapy, it is prudent to emphasize in the initial stage of treatment that the complex biological, psychological, and social underpinnings of eating disorders make it unlikely that medicine alone will suffice.

ADDITIONAL TREATMENT CONSIDERATIONS

In coming for help, patients demonstrate that despite formidable odds and tenacious symptoms, their goal is to make life changes and to seek self-enhancing experiences. Creating an atmosphere of safety in the opening phase sets the stage for those essential later steps toward self-realization. Psychoanalyst Karen Horney believed that self-realization (analogous here to the concept of true self) necessitated "giving up a sense of magical powers, self-idealization, and illusions of perfection." Although Horney was speaking in *general* about the costs to the individual in maintaining a false belief in his or her own perfectibility, her comments are apt for the *specific* problems of those who face a severe eating disorder. In the opening phase, a sense of self and personal growth are facilitated "by conveying to the patient the fact that he is engaged in a final battle and in showing him the odds against which, and the aims for which, he is fighting" (Horney, 1950, p. 362). The therapist serves as a formidable ally in the struggle by decisive and authentic involvement when these "first steps" in treatment are undertaken.

1. Enhance the patient's sense of safety by encouraging the telling of personal history and finding out the patient's "theory of illness." Because the eating disorder is the symptomatic tip of the iceberg, the clinician will discover many clues to understanding the adaptive life context in which the symptom emerged and is maintained.

2. From a biological perspective, focus on weight restoration (for anorexia) and educating the patient about the medical effects of the eating disorder (all eating disorders) in the opening phase. Discussion of the medical repercussions of eating disorders is a crucial aspect of patient education that can motivate and support the patient in the "final battle" waged against the eating disorder.

3. Try to ensure that the patient experiences you as being "on their side." Research has demonstrated that the establishment of a good working relationship with the therapist derives from building on small steps that lead to significant changes over time. Eschew the role of the "ultimate" authority and embrace a more egalitarian perspective.

4. Be part of a multidisciplinary team. Insist on the bare minimum of collaborators (i.e., nutritionist, primary care clinician) who have experience in treating eating disorders. Some patients will resist the team concept, insisting that you are the "only therapist" who can or will ever help them. They may even refuse to take your suggestions to involve other treaters. Avoid colluding with this idealization.

5. If patients have severe medical difficulties or are not able to get their weight up to a mutually agreed upon goal, recommend hospital, residential, or a structured outpatient program. Those programs that incorporate supervised, structured mealtimes may be the only way in which normal eating patterns and getting weight to target can be established. If third-party payers do not heed your recommendations, urge the family to seek legal advice or write their state insurance commissioner (see Chapter 3).

6. Build the therapeutic alliance in the opening phase by conversing with patients about their interests or creative pursuits. This affirms to the patients that you are there for them and that they are "more than just an eating disorder." It also prods them to move a bit further in sharing their inner feelings, another step along the road toward self-actualization (e.g., formation of a true-self).

7. Keep the focus on the patient. Avoid being a "blank screen" but maintain firm boundaries. Remember that eating disordered persons have often grown up in families where they were emotionally required to be exquisitely sensitive to the needs or demands of other family members. They have real

questions about how other families function and how one makes friends. In the opening phase, in particular, sharing a bit of one's own perspective or personal interests can facilitate therapeutic dialogue. Therapeutic spontaneity when judiciously applied maintains the therapeutic frame and serves the best interests of the patient.

8. Identify triggering events or experiences that lead to a recrudescence of symptoms or to changes in motivation. Listening carefully to these occurrences helps cement the therapeutic bond because it eschews facades and the belief in "magical cures." It counters the patient's false belief that perfection is achievable and points the way to realistic change that will occur only over time.

CONCLUSION

Helping patients with a severe eating disorder enter treatment and begin to work effectively is labor intensive. Because the eating disorder is a treasured piece of the patient's psychological armor, it will not be given up quickly; indeed, in the opening phase of treatment, clinicians can expect that most patients will maintain secrets about the nature of their self-starvation, modes of purging, comorbid psychiatric problems (e.g., extent of depression; addictions), and awareness of emotional pain. Empathy and tact are essential attributes for the clinician to maintain, but even the most astute clinician can expect to be surprised by the range of difficulties and dilemmas that are often withheld by the patient who has not yet secured the safe haven to share such "secrets of the self."

The first line of treatment is thorough medical evaluation and nutritional stabilization. Because no biological panacea has been found for these conditions, psychotherapy remains a mainstay of contemporary treatment. In the opening phase, the therapist's stance is to listen well and to empathize. The patient's task is to be able to be with the therapist, telling one's story as openly and honestly as possible. Although the tasks of listening well and empathizing persist throughout the treatment, they predominate at the beginning of the work because the patient is still grappling with how to be a patient and to feel safe with the treater. Both therapist and patient must be prepared to feel "bewildered, disappointed, and discouraged" because these are the inevitable "growing pains" inherent in taking charge of one's own life and assuming responsibility for oneself (Horney, 1950, pp. 362–363).

Collaborative work in the opening phase is only the first step in the patient beginning to find the true self. The false self system that has heretofore been the patient's refuge will be faced down only as the patient derives a sense of mastery in the "other than eating disorder" world. Patients in the opening phase of treatment may appear to comply with treatment while, in reality, defeating or undermining it. As the false self system is challenged, however, the patient becomes more real and involved with the therapist. The therapeutic journey will be launched, and the opening phase ended, when the therapist observes that the patient is symptomatically improved with respect to the eating disorder. The patient is also likely to become more challenging or express negative feelings about the treatment or the therapist. This seeming paradox may feel more like a kick than a forward step for the therapist, who has been there through the good times and the bad, but it also exemplifies that the patient is moving toward a more integrated sense of self.

CHAPTER 2

The Middle Phase

Few psychiatrists would disagree with the saying attributed to Jesus in the *Gospel of Thomas:* "If you bring forth what is within you, it will save you. If you do not bring forth what is within you, what you do not bring forth will destroy you."

—Elaine Pagels (1979)

A principle governing human life could be formulated in the following words: only the true self can feel real.

—D.W. Winnicott (1965a; 1988)

All actions and decisions carry the potential to extinguish the true self. This is even more apparent with the symptoms that are the hallmark of an eating disorder. As therapist and patient successfully traverse the opening phase of the treatment with the difficulties of becoming acquainted, finding a comfort zone, establishing boundaries, and solidifying the safe space to tell one's story, the pair find themselves traveling along the road into the middle phase of therapy. While the time frame for each phase of treatment is unique for every patient, the middle phase is heralded by a sense that the work is deepening and becoming more difficult. Therapists in the middle phase are called upon to use an array of tools and techniques to assist the patient in working through islands of resistance that inevitably arise when a person begins the search to find her or his true self.

The middle phase of treatment is usually the longest and most precarious segment of therapy because it reveals developmental aspects of the true self that come about only gradually and with significant effort. Core issues that compose a human life (see Chapters 4, 5, and 6) must be addressed. Destructive features of the illness must be confronted and overcome so that the individual is free to "bring forth what is within" that is ultimately more healthy, healing, and life-affirming. To find the real, the patient must face down what others, including the culture at large and one's loved ones and friends, might define as "ideal." The individual must also embrace the notion that body and mind will change during the life cycle, and denial or neglect of this natural ebb and flow can be perilous.

How intriguing that branches of contemporary belief systems (e.g., philosophy, spirituality, psychotherapy) converge in their emphasis on this "individual search for an enlightened consciousness" (Pagels, 1979, p. 24). This radical notion embraces a worldview that the authentic reference point for action is the individual whose essence must not be usurped by the dictates of any group or person; following the crowd leads only to a distortion or inversion of what it means to be truly human (Kierkegaard, 1940/1962; J. Klein, personal communication, 1969). Those qualities that imbue the individual with strength of character derive from one's personal history and must be cultivated over one's entire life. Patients who choose to undertake the journey to discern what is true and real for themselves are bound for difficulties and hard questions along the way. Who am I? Where am I going? What do I want to do with my life? These are only a few of the queries posed by the person in search of their true self that are frequently heard by the clinician in the middle phase of a longer-term and exploratory treatment.

Personal knowledge of this kind cannot be found by following the dictates or criteria of any secular or religious authority (D. Cooper, 1997; S. Cooper, 2000). To determine what is real, true, and unique, each individual must engage "in a solitary, difficult process . . . against internal resistance" because a counterforce propels each of us toward a "desire to sleep or to be drunk—that is, to remain unconscious" (Pagels, 1979, p. 126). All of us must also fight internal forces that would have us blindly follow the convictions of others rather than sort out our own values, beliefs, and destiny. One of the beauties of being a therapist is the gift our patients offer us by inviting us to join them as guides on this solitary path toward becoming more familiar with themselves, their roots, their difficulties, and ultimately their strengths and creativity. As they grapple in their inner aloneness with what have been encumbrances to development, we are companions on this journey. The therapist as "guide and companion" becomes much more visible and relied upon during the middle phase.

The lifelong process of bringing forth what is most truthfully and sincerely one's true self enables us to empathize with those who have difficulty paying attention to what is real and the toll that destructive psychological symptoms take on body and soul. In particular, those who rely primarily on a false belief that a particular weight, appearance, or body image will "save them" must discover at some point its lethal potential. They must find out who they really are— and who they really are not—without relying on their symptoms and external pressures of the world around them for self-definition. In the middle phase of treatment, the task of therapist and patient centers on sorting through the multifarious forces that have shackled self-development while straddling those features of individuation and maturation that always accompany a person on what will become a lifelong journey toward greater personal autonomy and discovery.

WHAT SHOULD HAPPEN IN THE MIDDLE PHASE?

The hallmark of the middle phase of treatment is the establishment of a durable therapeutic alliance. This can be observed in the process of the work of the patient and therapist talking. They speak with greater ease and expand upon issues that have caused distress (Novick & Novick, 1998). Although there is no simple definition of a successful therapeutic alliance, in general there is a sense that the patient and therapist are united in the task of talking about difficult, painful issues even in the midst of negative transference (see Chapter 8). Feelings of safety and comfort may also broaden even as the work probes more deeply or becomes more difficult. Ironically, the patient is likely to have some exacerbations with respect to their eating disorder symptoms; even in "good times," there are likely to be ongoing struggles with symptoms of restriction, bingeing, purging, and the like. However, in a general sense, the patient will demonstrate greater motivation for ongoing psychological work and personal development if treatment is going well during the middle phase.

In actuality, the boundaries between the opening and middle phases are not as clear as they may appear in a textbook. The vast majority of eating disorder patients continues to work on the amalgam of issues already described in the opening phase throughout their entire course of recovery. Additionally, given the tenacity of most eating disorder symptoms, many patients may curtail their starvation, purging, bingeing, or overexercise for brief periods in each phase of treatment, only to have the symptoms reappear or to "mutate" to another form. As contemporary research has identified (Milos, Spindler, Schnyder, & Fairburn, 2005; Thompson-Brenner & Westen, 2005a, 2005b, 2005c; Westen & Harnden-Fischer, 2001), more than 50% of eating disorder patients will migrate among various eating disorder diagnoses. Diagnostic stability as well as stable remission rates are low among eating disorder patients, and the majority maintain some difficulty with regulating food and body image even after longer term treatment (see Chapter 9).

The clinician may expect that the biological and psychological factors that lead to the eating disorder are ultimately more important than pinpointing a precise diagnosis of anorexia, bulimia, or eating disorder not otherwise specified, which is subject to change by minor fluctuations in body weight or eating behavior. Although clinician and patient alike hope that symptomatic periods will lessen and finally abate, the therapeutic alliance is best judged by the ongoing collaborative work and feelings of accomplishment that reflect that the patient is thinking on her or his own and has a healthier self-concept. From these accomplishments, a consolidated sense of one's true self emerges. The patient will ultimately have more sustained control of symptoms because they no longer serve their self-protective function. Free to shed the skin of the eating disorder, the patient has more energy to creatively engage in the world and participate in meaningful, intimate relationships.

By expanding on the core features of the middle phase of treatment that are outlined throughout the chapter, one gleans a sense of what connotes the deepening of the therapeutic process that enables both clinician and patient to navigate murky waters. Clinical examples in this and later chapters will explore the key issues and conflicts that ensnare the patient. We therapists find ourselves getting pulled in a variety of directions and need to attend to our countertransference responses (see Chapter 8). We even find ourselves cast into roles with the patient that we had not otherwise anticipated. The patient who is able to successfully traverse this pivotal phase experiences significant gain in quality of life and sense of well-being, including significantly greater control over the eating disorder.

Unfortunately, a vast majority of patients never get to the middle phase of treatment. Reluctance to engage with the therapist, limitations by third parties (e.g., insurance limitation or other financial issues), and lack of family support may play significant roles (see Chapter 3). The savvy clinician always looks beyond those manifest, reality factors and into the patient's deeper psychological difficulties that may also stand in the way. Because the eating disorder behavior is ego syntonic, the patient experiences fragmentation when it is relinquished. To some extent this fragmentation must actually occur before the false self system can give way to a more stable sense of the true self; what may be temporary setbacks and relapses are often experienced by both patient and therapist as discouraging and frustrating.

Although manualized treatment protocols and behavioral controls may also help patients recover symptomatically, they often also fall short of fully helping patients reclaim their body and develop a true self. As the patient (and family members who are supportive of the treatment) continue to more forward in the therapeutic process, their motivation will be both tested and potentially strengthened by reviewing sobering outcome studies (see Chapter 9). Just as in the opening phase of treatment, it continues to be important to provide patients with new and ongoing research data regarding the impact of their eating disorder on quality of life as well as mortality and morbidly statistics. Repeating the data, facts, statistics, and outcome studies in all phases of treatment is important, but as the patient grows and changes psychologically, the capacity to hear and to make use of the information expands. Having knowledge of this kind may be frightening; however, by utilizing it one hopes to motivate and guide the patient to feel less helpless and fearful and more powerful and able to fight back. The data may also be used to secure additional benefits from third parties and attain a sense of mastery (Zerbe, 1996a, 1996b). Family members can be very supportive and add to the reinforcement needed in working with third parties and joining the ongoing battle against the illness.

A comprehensive, individualized treatment program is labor intensive, financially expensive, and requires enormous commitment on the part of both patient and the clinician. Together we enter the new world of self-discovery to enhance life and face down death. Treatment of this type has as its main goal the full immersion of the individual into the cycle of life. The patient must learn crucial, new life skills. They must negotiate their autonomy while making and maintaining meaningful connections with others.

Integrated treatment in the middle phase is not beholden to any one particular theory; indeed, what seems to be most important over the long haul is not the particular school or training that the therapist has had but rather the willingness to go forward with the patient, paying close attention to development of self as the treatment proceeds. For those patients who have suffered from abuse or have had a paucity of healthy relationships, new modes of relating must be practiced.

The therapeutic alliance during the middle phase is a joint creation during which both therapist and patient will need to weather periods of doubt, disappointment, difficulties in communication, and resistance, but they will also experience satisfaction, accomplishment, and joy. Psychoanalysts Novick and Novick (1998) write, "working well together is incompatible with sadomasochism" because it "provides an experience of competence" and "motivates further collaborative work" (pp. 832–834). The eating disorder patient who successfully navigates the middle phase will be less self-destructive and more able to partake of love and work, leading to greater life fulfillment.

BLENDING COGNITIVE-BEHAVIORAL AND PSYCHODYNAMIC PRINCIPLES

Cognitive-behavioral and psychodynamic principles are more easily blended in the treatment of eating disorders than at first recognized. In part, this arises because many cognitive-behavior principles are actually derived from psychodynamic ones (McWilliams, 1994, 1999, 2004). The crucial ethical value is always tailoring the treatment to the needs of the patient (Zerbe & Fabacher, 1989). Just as contemporary philosophers, ethicists, and theologians (Armstrong, 1993; D. Cooper, 1997; Smith, 2001, 2003) are struck by the similarities in the truths and values espoused by disparate wisdom traditions, so psychotherapeutic principles converge in manifold ways that are readily discerned. Psychological truth springs from a common root but has no one master.

In Table 2.1, I list some of the most common issues and the role of the therapist in helping the patient negotiate "the middle phase" regardless of the therapist's theoretical background or preferred treatment modality. I believe that cognitive-behavioral and psychodynamic conceptualizations address common problems encountered in the middle phase by similar means but different names (see Table 2.2). For example, after a binge it is quite common for a patient to have catastrophic thoughts. Tending to see the world in black and white, the patient believes that she is worthless, on a downward spiral, and incapable of righting her behaviors, so she gives up. Every clinician recognizes the pattern. This kind of perception often leads to the vicious circle of purging to

TABLE 2.1   The role of the therapist-middle phase

- Address the patient's inner critic (i.e., punitive superego)
- Contain and silently process the patient's "emotional wave"
- Promote autonomous behaviors while recognizing ongoing dependency needs
- Encourage power and competence in activities
- Validate the patient's personal authority
- Promote intimacy in nontherapeutic relationships
- Set limits and know when to be a "bad-enough" object
- Discuss and deconstruct the meaning of food and eating
- Focus on body image issues
- Tolerate open conflict in the therapeutic relationship
- Help the patient grieve the symptom

TABLE 2.2   Cognitive-behavioral and psychodynamic approaches to self-criticism

Cognitive	Psychodynamic
<ul><li>Address tendency toward catastrophic thinking</li><li>Point out tendency to minimize and magnify</li><li>Discourage maladaptive behaviors by redirection and affirmation</li><li>Confront personal discounting and tendencies toward thinking in absolutes</li><li>Label feelings/look at exaggerated beliefs</li><li>Learn modes of tension reduction (i.e., deep breathing, progressive relaxation)</li></ul>	<ul><li>Confront "shoulds," "oughts," "musts"</li><li>Enhance awareness through self-reflection</li><li>Enhance ego strength through reflection and gentle confrontation</li><li>Promote a more "benevolent superego"</li><li>Use transitional objects and other self-soothing tools</li></ul>

get rid of the "badness," "yucky feelings," or sense of self-hatred; remorse and humiliation routinely follow. A vicious cycle of bingeing and purging may even evolve into a more protracted stalemate, and patients are unable to take their rightful place at the smorgasbord of life.

Cognitive-behavioral therapists intervene by helping the patient confront catastrophic thinking and the tendency to think in terms of absolutes. Psychodynamic therapists characterize a similar intervention in terms of enhancing the capacity for the ego to come to grips with implicit self-devaluation by reducing a harsh, punitive superego that punishes the patient for any mistake. With each modality the aim is to foster greater control of the eating disorder over time by reducing the patient's experience of internal self-hatred and defeatism. Interestingly, contemporary research of the cognitive-behavioral mode validates the concept that a lack of self-worth results "in the adoption of extreme measures either to lose weight or to keep from gaining weight" (Byrne & McLean, 2002, p. 27) which feeds into the vicious cycle of binge eating and purging and becomes self-perpetuating. Hatred of one's body is one manifestation of an overactive superego that when untangled and confronted in psychodynamic work furthers enhanced self-esteem and a greater sense of freedom.

WORKING WITH INTERNAL SELF-CRITICISM

One pitfall of catastrophic thinking and extreme self-criticism is the tendency to keep dangerous secrets. For example, patients may hide the number of binge/purge episodes out of a sense of shame or guilt. They mistakenly believe they are losing the war of symptomatic control if they make even one mistake. To enlist the help of the patient's benevolent superego (Alpert & Spencer, 1986; Horney, 1970; Paris, 1994; Sandler, 1987; Schafer, 1960), psychodynamic therapy formulates how the patient must become aware of "shoulds, oughts, and musts." These issues, while present in the opening phase, will be more thoroughly addressed as greater reflectiveness and insight is gained during the middle phase. The therapist who keeps in mind that the patient can be his or her own worst critic enables the patient to make significant strides in ego development and a sense of self.

The therapist can begin to help the patient challenge the inner critic by posing questions like, "Why are you being so mean to you?" or "Who am I hearing in that self-critical voice?" In cognitive-behavioral terms, evaluating and challenging negative thoughts and belief systems enables the person to face down cognitive distortions. The tendency to minimize one's strengths, magnify one's faults, think in all-or-nothing terms, and overgeneralize is gently confronted to enhance awareness of emotions and evaluate automatic thought patterns (J. Beck, 1995; Leahy, 2003). The challenge for the therapist arises not only in seeing how similar the theories are but framing the intervention so a particular patient can work with her or his inner critic in a manner that ultimately helps empower the patient and strengthens the nascent sense of self (see Table 2.2 for a comparison of how cognitive-behavioral and psychodynamic therapy conceptualize and deal with the inner self critic). Ways in which cognitive and psychodynamic principles may be integrated are demonstrated in the following case example.

Clinical Example

Anton is a 38-year-old geologist and assistant professor of metallurgy at a community college who has struggled with bulimia nervosa since his teens. Despite notable professional accomplishment, Anton returns home at the end of the day and purges to "get rid of the sense that I am so worthless." Few colleagues in Anton's workplace suspect his eating difficulty even though he is thin and regularly excuses himself after faculty meetings or informal get-togethers in order to purge. Not surprisingly, this patient is also addicted to exercise; he runs several hours every day, and he is never satisfied that he "has done enough or is good enough."

Anton insightfully recognizes that a core issue for him is self-esteem management (Bloom, Kogel, & Zaphiropoulos, 1994; Byrne & McLean, 2002). He resonates with the therapist's observation that from childhood well into adulthood, he was never able to please his father, a successful attorney. Although Anton's father recognized his son's brilliance, he also demanded that he become a physician even though Anton's interests lay elsewhere. Anton had significant resolve to defy his father and follow his own life course, but not surprisingly this took a hefty psychological toll, particularly related to guilt when it came to asserting himself and attempting to become "his own man." On a conscious level, Anton believes he is responsible for letting his father down; on a less conscious level, he is angry and frustrated with a father who has been experienced as "impossible to please." For Anton, the binge/purge cycle has become a "habit," as he calls it, in which he rids himself of a myriad of affects. His "best buddy" (e.g., bulimia) fills "an empty hole" inside him that longs for love and self-acceptance while serving a secondary purpose of ridding himself of the "worthless feelings" of disapproval, loneliness, and rage.

In Anton's situation, cognitive-behavioral principles may be successfully employed to categorize thoughts and feelings that lead to binge–purge episodes. Homework assignments help him to confront catastrophic thinking while offering an opportunity to recollect exactly what goes through his mind (i.e., thoughts, feelings, and memories) before he purges by overexercise or vomiting. Reviewing the homework further gives him the sense that he and the therapist are working together (i.e., the pleasure of accomplishment that signifies a good working alliance in the middle phase). Even before putting into place a specific relapse prevention plan (i.e., a structured activity or group meeting to go to immediately after a meal), part of the ongoing homework assignments require Anton to think about how his father might annoy or criticize him. The therapist also suggests ways for Anton to counter those thoughts with positive affirmations. In psychodynamic terms, this process enables the patient's ego functions to expand, permitting the patient to more logically think through self-defeating patterns and his unconsciously directed punishment for defying his father. He is using his secondary thought process to counter self-punishment; his bulimia is partially understood as aggression turned against the self derived from guilt for fear of paternal disapproval and fear of his father's retaliation for following his own path.

Anton's tendency to magnify and internalize self-criticism and minimize what he can accomplish on his own is thrown into bold relief by the homework assignment. His pattern of other forms of internalized self-criticism—his tendency to always think what he "ought" or "must" do—is counteracted by the self-actualized experience of speaking openly with the therapist and following the homework assignment. By doing what he can, his ego strength grows and his internalized, harsh superego gradually becomes a bit kinder. Indeed, the capacity to be kinder to oneself eventuates over time in a deeper capacity to demonstrate concerns for others, another goal of treatment shared in most therapeutic traditions.

After such a prolonged course of bulimia nervosa, it would be unreasonable for the therapist or Anton to expect that his symptoms would easily abate. He has already had several attempts at treatment. Each failed because of lack of motivation and aggression turned inward toward the self. As his binge–purge episodes lessen in frequency, he is able to function better at work and enjoy his personal life. For the first time, he experiences joy. It is crucial that the therapist be prepared to accept "less than perfection" and model that doing just a little better is "good enough." This tack is also useful for therapists who have a tendency to demand rapid results, reflecting our own punitive superego functions.

Because of the potential lethality of eating disorders, we therapists also become mired in the trap of "ought, should, and must" out of an excessive need to help or rescue the patient. We expect early and long-term symptomatic control from our interventions. Just as the therapist must help patients work with their superego expectations, so the therapist must be ready to accept improvement, not perfection, from our patients. That is, we must model a healthy superego function. Recognizing that success usually builds upon success, the therapist must be vigilant about any tendency toward discounting and minimizing progress on the patient's part and on our own. This permits the patient to identify with the benevolent and loving aspects of the therapist's own superego, thereby reducing the tendency toward self-punishment. Behaving more kindly toward oneself serves as a most healthy model of identification for the patient.

CONTAINMENT: THE THERAPIST'S SILENT TOOL

The concept of containment was developed and elaborated by psychoanalyst W. R. Bion, a student of Melanie Klein, and has been extensively applied by contemporary clinicians (Ferro, 2002; Ogden, 1979, 1982, 1986, 1989; Schafer, 1997). It is one of the most useful tools in the eating disorder therapist's repertoire, as I have already and will continue to demonstrate in several more clinical examples. Like other treatment principles discussed throughout this volume, containment is much easier to conceptualize as an abstract principle than to actually master in a given session. I will also describe why this is the case and offer some advice about how the therapist can more effectively sit and process affects, maintain a sense of equanimity in crises, and, in a general sense, decrease the fevered pitch and anxiety that inevitably find their way into treatment hours with eating disordered patients.

The therapeutic maxim, "Just don't do something, stand there" (Titus, 1982) will be powerfully and repeatedly emphasized as we seek to understand how containment and silent processing are reliable resources to draw upon in life-threatening psychopathology, such as an eating disorder (Gabbard, 1989; Grinberg, Sor & deBlanchedi, 1993; Mitrani, 1995, 2001; Zerbe, 1993/1995a, 1993a, 1995b, 1995c, 1996a, 2007a). We will also find that adequate containment of a patient's anger, anguish, malcontent, or other disruptive affects is often a signal that something very useful has transpired in the treatment (Epstein & Feiner, 1979). That is, change within the patient is foreshadowed by the therapist's realization that he or she is "holding" and containing more of the patient's anguish via projective identification. In the middle phase of treatment, therapist and patient will be able "to generate an *increase in meaning* rather than leaving the degree of meaning as it was" (Ferro, 2002, p. 35). In this phase, the "receptive capacity" (p. 63) of the therapist will very gradually enable the patient to tell and find new meaning in her or his narrative, always "encouraging and taking a keen interest in it—while remaining *conscious* that there is also another level to the story and that a long road must be traveled over a prolonged period of time to bring the two levels together" (Ferro, 2002, p. 32). Containment during the middle phase supplies the space for the emergence and further mental processing of the life stories that have been long suppressed.

Containment is a "dynamic notion" of "thoughtful emotionality and emotional thoughtfulness" (Alvarez, 1992, p. 52) that occurs within the therapist. Psychodynamic theorists have likened this process in the therapist to the state of reverie that occurs within the mother with her baby. The mother feels the infant's distress that is projected from the child onto her but she is able to contain it, eventually returning it to the infant in a modified form. This process, which soothes the baby, is analogous to what happens in treatment with patients who have difficulty knowing, verbalizing, and modulating affect. Our patients inevitably draw us into their emotional worlds as they tell their stories. Getting caught up with emotions of the individual are utterly human qualities but often cause an array of inner disturbance in the therapist.

We therapists often become critical of ourselves when this happens. The norm in such circumstances is to wonder how we can be better at what we are doing and to suppress our own and our patient's experience by talking too much or making excessive interventions or taking emotional distance. Silently processing our thoughts, ideas, affects, memories, and all the bits of history that pass through our minds, but trying our best not to act on them, is what we mean by "containment." It may appear that we are "doing nothing" (Gabbard, 1989) but in actuality we are doing quite a lot. Like the mother of infancy, we are processing what we hear and what we think to eventually help the patient "take back" or "return in modified form" (Alvarez, 1992, p. 53) what the patient has deposited in us.[1]

In lectures to professional audiences, I make use of a PowerPoint slide of several ancient, hand-woven Indian baskets to illustrate and to concretize several aspects of containment. Just as each basket is a different size and design, so each clinician will "hold" a patient's material differently. Just as no two people remember the same details of a story or interpret a movie in exactly the same way, so each clinician hears details of the patient's story with different ears. The therapist's first task lies in being a "good enough container" to receive as much as possible of the patient's range of hopes, fears, and desires until the patient is sufficiently ready, having successfully transformed personal raw experience, to take some of those parts of themselves back as their own (Grinberg et al., 1993).

In terms of the therapist's experience, what gets deposited into the basket is unique in every therapist–patient dyad. The kinds of therapeutic "raw" material that are deposited into the basket include painful emotions, vignettes of personal history, deep questions about the meaning and direction of life, and reactions to everyday dilemmas in personal relationships. Note that the Indian basket is semipermeable. It allows some contents to easily leak out, but others to be held in. The container of the therapist, being human, will also be able to catch some contents better than others. Some material won't be caught at all. Thus, therapists always glean different messages and meanings from the same case material. We learn from each other when we take part in workshops, seminars, or supervisory sessions that force us to "hear the different language" of another person. We grow because others inevitably "catch" something we totally missed! The other person has heard a nuance—or contained an emotion—that totally passed us by, and what they have perceived helps the patient's message or story to make more sense! Hence, nothing succeeds in keeping a clinician humble like regular review of one's work in supervision.

In any human relationship that is intense and intimate, one can and will be swept away by feelings from time to time. The opposite can also occur as we seek to protect ourselves. Sometimes we avoid, retreat from, or close ourselves off (as if in a cocoon) from the powerful feelings that are stirred. One fundamental problem in human nature, and certainly for therapists, is that our containers can fill up more rapidly than we would like—and it becomes hard to listen, hard to take another person's woes, joys, and discoveries seriously.

---

[1] Therapists who champion the work of Harry Stack Sullivan and contemporary relational theorists will note that the process of projective identification is roughly analogous to Sullivan's concept of the "contagion effect" (Sullivan, 1953, 1956). Years before infant researchers actually demonstrated how easily babies attune themselves to the affects and emotional states of their mothers, Sullivan described how feelings between mothers and their babies can be "contagious." Likewise, anxious patients tend to provoke anxiety in their therapists, and vice versa (Zerbe, 1990)!

Consider, for example, how you can suddenly and sometimes even out of conscious awareness tune another person out. Try to take note of why this happened. Were you bored? Annoyed? Moved to tears? Preoccupied by a personal issue of your own?

Beginning to "tune in" and get curious about those times when you want to listen but find you just can't has much to teach about our capacity and lack of capacity to be receptive to others. Having a talent for listening well is one of the most frequently cited qualities of the best therapists when surveys of patient expectations are quantified and studied (Norcross, 1996). When a patient pays you the compliment that you "listen well," remember that this is a quality you may have a natural propensity for, but one you also have worked hard to develop over the years, and one that even master clinicians must work hard to maintain.

IN WHAT WAYS WILL CONTAINMENT HELP?

The process of containment is an essential intervention because it ultimately helps patients gain respect for themselves, their lives, and their dilemmas. This intervention, based on psychodynamic understanding, does not negate the use of other treatment modalities, including restoration and maintenance of adequate weight by means of good nutrition, exercise, medication, and judiciously employing cognitive-behavioral strategies to gainsay maladaptive patterns of coping. It can, however, occur only when there is enough time and space for the personal history to unfold.

Given the restrictions on time that therapists now face in a managed care environment, one might structure most sessions in the middle phase to review the cognitive-behavioral exercises or educational homework exercises for a minority of the time (say 20–25%) and leave the major part of the time (75–80%) to helping the patient tell and process her or his narrative (see Table 2.3 for a list of cognitive-behavioral components). In my experience, patients can and will quickly and successfully do some of the necessary exercises that lead to behavioral change that are recommended in manualized treatment, so long as the therapist *reviews the homework* at some point during the session. This leaves more time (albeit there is probably never sufficient time) for patients "to bring

TABLE 2.3 Cognitive-behavioral therapy: Some components of care

- Provision of cognitive-behavioral conceptualization
- Provide ongoing patient education about the illness
- Facilitate self-monitoring of affective states that lead to maladaptive behaviors
- Teach meal planning and stimulus strategies
- Encourage cognitive restructuring
- Facilitate development of coping skills
- Discuss problem solving and give examples

forth what is within them" so that a growing understanding can develop between therapist and patients about the multifarious reasons the eating disorder has taken such a hold on them.

As patient and therapist talk together about elements of the patient's dilemma, the patient develops a new language. Slowly, aspects of the personal story link together—as if they were beads on a silk thread—and connections between elements of the past begin to take on meaning for the first time. One's personal history, including but not exclusively related to the eating disorder, begins to make sense and become understandable (Spence, 1982; Stone, 1961; Westen, 2000). There will be additional examples of this process in each chapter of this book, but at this point I suggest a way that the therapist might listen, especially during the long middle phase.

Because the therapist does not react in a negative way but rather welcomes the strong emotions and painful parts of the story, patients grow in their capacity to take themselves more seriously and to contain their emotions. In so doing, they discover the courage and curiosity needed to make the commitment to face life; as a deeper understanding and appreciation of the self takes form, the patient is able to make more life-affirming decisions that abet or face down the eating disorder. When one welcomes into the therapeutic office the "inner disturbance" of the eating disorder, one conveys that there is meaning in the symptom that can be understood over time (Rothstein, cited in Zerbe, 2007c). Psychoanalyst Bion believed that this process of transformation is similar to the work of an artist who is able to take "an experience, felt and described in one way," and describe it in another (Bion, 1965, p. 4). In this way, too, the best therapists are artists. By interpretation and development of metaphor, we help those in our care describe their experiences in a new way and thereby creatively transform and master even the most vexing problems.

The pediatrician and psychoanalyst D.W. Winnicott had other words of wisdom for psychotherapists that approximate this concept of containment. He advised that one simply "stay awake and alive" during the therapy process (1958a, 1965b)! It seems like a benign intervention that is easy enough to do. Why did Winnicott stress this point about "staying alive?" Surely most of us don't begin a therapy hour preoccupied with our mortality or anticipating our death! Winnicott was going beyond the stance of listening well and zeroing in on the intense reactions, including hatred and malevolence, which the patient may also project onto the therapist.

This can be overt, as when a patient repeatedly gets angry or simply thwarts every intervention the therapist makes to help gainsay the eating symptomatology. The thwarting of the therapist's benevolence also can occur more subtly. The patient may seem to comply but turns right around and defies the most judiciously derived treatment plan. When pouring out one's heart and sharing tales of deprivation, abuse, or even simply misattunement or disappointment, the patient cannot help also pouring repellent material into the "container" of the therapeutic relationship.

Later in this chapter, I describe how the therapist can manage the seemingly intractable pull on the part of some patients to be a "bad object," and in Chapter 3, I review the most insidious, ultimately self-defeating patterns of negative therapeutic reactions that result in premature treatment termination. Here I describe the more typical daily challenge for the therapist to contain and process difficult material and the beneficent results for the treatment when the patient can "own" and work through negatively charged affects, like hatred and aggression.

All of these factors make it difficult to "stay awake, attuned, and alive" — that is, to really listen to a patient's story. How much easier it is to write a prescription, to suggest some therapeutic exercises or activities, or to have a prescribed set of questions than to actually attend to another person's imbroglio. Containment permits the therapist to be receptive to the patient's need to be followed along the path of telling her story. But beware. There is also an emotional cost to the treater. By receiving "the emotional wave" (Ferro, 2002) of the patient's communications and helping transform the material into manageable feelings and stories, we make ourselves available for the emotional needs and demands of the narrator.

Containment helps both parties in the dyad link *the beads of the life story together, the active work in making the beautiful Indian basket.* Like the actual mother, the therapist's employment as container and metabolizer of affect is temporary. Our goal is always to become unemployed by our patient. The work of therapy is to help the patient become her or his own container, the unique vessel that "holds" the inner, emotive contents of the individual life. Improved capacity to own and process one's affects is the beginning of the work a person must do along the path of self-discovery that ultimately is the final arbiter and champion of the life force that gives birth to the true self.

DEALING WITH THE DIALECTIC OF AUTONOMY AND HEALTHY DEPENDENCY

Traditionally psychotherapists were taught that a central task of treatment was helping patients achieve "full autonomous functioning" by moving through the longitudinal steps of the separation-individuation process (Mahler, Pine, & Bergman, 1975). This goal, while helpful to the patient in some respects, is actually impossible to achieve in reality because all humans are also social beings who oscillate between needs for connection and separateness. The capacity to smoothly move between the two states depending on the requirements of the particular circumstance is significantly impaired in patients with eating disorders. The ability to negotiate the dialectic between autonomous functioning and connection is another central concern for the patient and therapist to address in the middle phase of treatment (Alpert & Spencer, 1986; Aronson, 1993; Balint, 1959; Masterson, 1981, 1983, 2005; Masterson & Lieberman, 2004; Modell, 1993; Novick & Novick, 1996; Searles, 1986; Stiver, 1991). This capacity is required for work, school, running a household, maintaining friendships, and developing intimacy.

Persons with eating disorders may experience pride about the control they command over their bodies by restricting, vomiting at will, or exercising for hours. Their sense of self-control and autonomy derives from the inordinate value they place on maintaining the manifest symptom that provides a sense of power and competence and enables them to feel safe and separate from the whims of other people. They must come to understand that this notion of personal autonomy is fictitious and destructive; autonomy must coexist with a healthy sense of dependency. This understanding is championed by the ongoing dialogue between patient and therapist, the setbacks and gains throughout the process, and by gradual growth of trust and capacity to be vulnerable in the safe setting of therapy.

Healthy relationships provide a sense of security without a need to cling or to be clung to. Therapists must be attentive to the issues of "optimal distance" and make use of opportunities such as vacations, unexpected interruptions, or a change in plans, and pay attention to what occurs between sessions to begin a discussion about the dialectical needs for closeness and autonomy. This focus helps patients learn that they, too, can experience "growth in connection" (Gilligan, 1982; Jordan, Kaplan, Miller, et al., 1991; Wallerstein, 1986) while concomitantly discovering that they can function independently in the world.

ENCOURAGING POWER AND COMPETENCE IN ACTIVITIES

To underscore the autonomous strides the patient is making, the therapist can attain significant therapeutic leverage by the technique of "communicative matching" (Masterson, 1981, 1993, 1995). This process of mutual cuing is roughly analogous to Kohut's concept of mirroring. Masterson demonstrated the educative value of communicative matching in treatment by pointing out how the therapist builds upon the patient's openly discussing "general and universal" (Chatam, 1985, p. 398) interpersonal situations, feelings, and conflicts that arise as the patient begins to individuate. It is very important to note when a patient spontaneously brings up a new interest. For example, in the middle phase, you will know you are moving ahead when a patient brings a book or a creative project to the session or begins to speak about a new interest or hobby (e.g., politics, gardening). When you ask a question or two about the patient's choice and explicitly give permission to say more about it, you facilitate growth of the self. These events are particularly important to underscore when they involve activities not related to eating or cooking because they signal that the patient may be moving out of the world of the eating disorder.

Moreover, when the patient has had a dearth of persons who were fully invested in their growth, the newfound interest is another test of the therapist's conviction regarding the patient's finding the true self. "Can you be involved enough to see and to hear what I'm doing yet allow me to have my own subjectivity and choices?" the patient seems to be asking between the lines. By staying attuned to those implicit and explicit changes that signal growth, the therapist demonstrates that the patient's desires are not only tolerated but welcomed. The fear that the therapist will turn away is disconfirmed. The patient is hoping that you will see what has not been seen before, particularly in her or his desire to have a full life and is encouraged when you follow their lead. This intervention of "asking about the obvious" is often a missed opportunity when we cling to a notion that our job is to be the wise one with tools or answers or that a therapist should never gratify a patient's wish, particularly the wish to be noticed!

These sorts of tests are likely to be repeated over and over again during the middle phase of therapy. Tact and technique merge as the therapist notes the change brought about by asking simple questions or making statements about a new interest. Within the healthy connection of the therapeutic dyad, autonomy is facilitated by showing interest in new activities that the patient is trying out. Another straightforward intervention one might also employ to further the dialogue during the middle phase of treatment encourages further ego growth by posing a simple, clarifying question. Simply inquire, "Can you expand on that?" and listen for what happens next. We therapists also tend to miss the opportunity because our own superegos chide us with internal criticism such as "It's just too basic" or "I'm not being active—or brilliant—enough. I'm not earning my fee." Again, communicative matching is another form of not doing something "big" or momentous in the moment but its impact is felt over time.

Attention must also be paid to giving patients a sense of "optimal distance" (Balint, 1958/1987; Swift & Letvin, 1984; Tustin, 1990) lest they feel that the therapist is too close and not giving them enough emotional space in which to grow. As described in Chapter 1, particularly where the child has been forced to attune to the psychological needs of others, the patient is always looking closely for any signs that the therapist will put her or his own psychological needs first. Comments that seem to be made off the cuff but demonstrate the patient's sensitivity to the surroundings, such as interest in the therapist's family or the way the therapist dresses, may also be deeper communications about the patient's early attunement to caretakers. Such patients will find it difficult to think their own thoughts or to make autonomous actions without taking into account what they perceive or fantasize others, especially family members or the therapist, want them to do.

Hilda Bruch (1973, 1974, 1978, 1988) described this phenomenon among adolescents with anorexia who struggled with feelings of engulfment in their families (see Chapter 4). These adolescents do not experience self-initiative. Clinical experience since the mid-1970s confirms Bruch's point of view and demonstrates that this type of problem can occur during the entire life cycle, not just among adolescents (see Chapters 5 and 6). In essence, the patient-to-be is put in the unconscious role of being the primary caretaker's "best friend or therapist." The caretaker relies on the patient for emotional support, physical comfort, and sometimes even physical gratification. Often the caretaker's motivation is unconscious; she or he is not trying to be malevolent or preoccupied with self but is acting on needs for gratification or support that were not met in the person's own childhood or are not being met in their adult environment. The effect on the patient leads, however, to great difficulty in understanding that legitimate dependency needs can be met without damaging the other person. The following clinical example is a case in point.

Clinical Example

Mercedes was 18 years old and in college when she began psychotherapy after a six-year course of anorexia with bulimic episodes and self-cutting. Mercedes believed that her symptoms improved after her parents' divorce when she was 16. Prior to that time, "All I can remember is how they fought all the time, my mother cried, and dad would storm out of the house like a 2-year-old." Mercedes's mother never remarried. From her daughter's recollections, this mother talked about her loneliness and misery with little pause. Mercedes's mother refused to engage in individual or family therapy despite the recommendation of the family physician, but she did permit her daughter to see a nutritional counselor in high school when her weight dipped and the patient stopped menstruating.

In the initial intake with the nutritionist, Mercedes said that her mother was "just too embarrassed to talk about her problems with her friends." Mercedes's mother turned to her daughter and the two would chat for hours about her mother's feelings of betrayal by the patient's father. The mother tried to provide her daughter with a great deal of nurturance—such as helping her with schoolwork and developmental issues—and did so in many respects. Mercedes had friends, took dance lessons, and enjoyed playing with her pet ferrets. Difficulties arose in late adolescence when school activities and wishes to date precluded the patient from being available to her mother. Mercedes's mother was not overtly destructive, but the patient felt guilty about participating in her own age-appropriate activities because, "Mother always wanted me to stay home, watch TV, and go shopping with her. I feel so guilty and sad when I say no. I just gave up."

This kind of example is not uncommon. Mercedes's nutritionist repeatedly recommended that the patient have the additional support of therapy. This nutritionist wisely resisted the role of being pulled into the role of omnipotent caretaker. When she realized early on that Mercedes's problems were greater than the ongoing check-ups for her weight and meal plans she provided, she flatly told the mother that she would terminate if other resources were not utilized. These resources included regular visits to a primary care practitioner for added support and reinforcing the seriousness of the eating disorders. Forming alliances with an individual, family, and group therapist were paramount steps for a fully integrated, multidisciplinary treatment. Some family members are so threatened that they will not heed this advice, but the nutritionist's firmness, combined with solid experience in the eating disorder field, brought out the constructive side of the mother who did want to see her daughter mature normally. The mother agreed to the cadre of treaters from various disciplines that proved to be of great benefit to the patient, the family, and, in this case, the nutritionist.

Mercedes closely observed her individual therapist for any waning interest when activities, school, or friendships were mentioned. The therapist pointed out that the patient seemed to stay on guard to "figure out what you really would like me to do." The therapist's sensitivity to these maternal transference issues later enabled her to gently wonder and later confront Mercedes for not permitting herself greater leeway in age-appropriate activities in college.

In essence, the therapist formulated that the patient needed to have a safe connection where she could also experience herself for the first time as an autonomous person who did not need to care for the mother. In the transference, the therapist became the mother who needed care. Mercedes also needed the therapist to show interest in her new activities, including romance. There is always a delicate balance in finding the correct mix between encouraging activities and new interests in the therapeutic relationship and taking a more neutral wait and see position; one does not want to be too eager in applauding independent functioning lest one inadvertently push the patient in a direction that seems to please the treater but is false for the patient. The therapist must always silently ask: How do I maintain a sense of closeness and interest and still give my patient the space needed to choose?

Posing this question silently allowed the therapist to point out and name the crucial affects—anxiety and betrayal of mother—that Mercedes had when she seemed to do anything that signaled her desire for autonomy and true self functioning. The therapist also wondered with the patient if this might be related to a need to stay close to her mother and avoid making age-appropriate steps toward individuation because she was afraid to disappoint her mother and to leave her alone.

This more general dynamic was then tied to the eating disorder as a reliable, but ultimately unhealthy, way for the patient to, as she put it, "find my own space and place." By not eating, she stayed the little girl whom she assumed her mother desired. But her life-threatening anorexia was also a way to, albeit unconsciously and spuriously, aggressively attack the inner mother to promote survival (Zerbe, 1993/1995a).

VALIDATING PERSONAL AUTHORITY: PROMOTING INTIMACY

Attachment theory is the most thoroughly researched area of psychodynamic psychotherapy (Allen, 2001, 2005; Fonagy, 2001; Fonagy, Gergely, Jurist, & Target, 1999, 2002; Schore, 2001; Schore 2003, 2005; Stein, Fonagy, Ferguson, et al., 2000; Stern, 1985). Interventions based on its application are becoming more frequently utilized in clinical work to help patients validate their authority by "knowing what is on their own mind." When one is confident that one knows what one is feeling or thinking, intimacy in relationships is more easily achieved because one has developed a sense that one's personal ethos and boundaries can and will be maintained when one expresses oneself. In essence, one embraces the power to say "no" or "yes" based upon one's own judgment and needs. Opinions and desires of others are valued (or else one would be totally narcissistic) but one does not cave because of the will of another. This is the antithesis of what happens to the maltreated child or adult who believes she or he is subject to the whim of the abuser. Tragically, the history of many patients usually verifies that they were not heard, and when they enter treatment they have little belief in their personal authority or sense that they can effect positive change in their lives. What can we learn from the lives of resilient people who have been maltreated to apply to the lives of our patients who are in similar jeopardy? The majority of eating disorder patients have a disturbed or insecure attachment pattern. The high frequency of sexual abuse (see Chapters 4, 5, 6, 7, and 8) among bulimic patients is another indicator for the need to repair faulty attachment patterns.

In a review of 763 pediatric analytic cases at the Anna Freud Centre in London, psychoanalysts Peter Fonagy and Mary Target (1996) found that children who grew up in severely traumatic environments had a higher quality of life and resilience after the trauma if they had acquired a capacity for "primary reflective functioning." These researcher-clinicians suggest that other therapists apply this developmentally based research to help patients verbalize inner states and break down anxiety into small entities, thereby increasing the capacity to think clearly. This process, nowadays often referred to as "mentalization," is a function of the prefrontal cortex, which helps the patient regulate her or his emotions while considering (often unconsciously) one's own and the other person's mental state (Bateman & Fonagy, 2006). Helping the patient to (1) separate reality from fantasy, and (2) delay gratification when appropriate, are all touchstones of the technique of mentalization (i.e., primary reflective functioning). This process enables our patients to "lift inhibitions on mental functioning that in turn make access to the emotional world easier" (Fonagy & Target, p. 68).

The treatment of the children in this study took quite a long time but the subjects demonstrated considerable gains in the capacity (1) to think about cause and effect; (2) to sustain mental images of themselves and others; (3) to establish some give and take in relationships; (4) to develop a capacity to delay gratification; and (5) to hold opposing ideas in mind. The patients learned the qualities necessary to sustain a healthy emotional life. While the subjects did not have an eating disorder per se, they came from disturbed, traumatogenic environments. The results of this work demonstrate that progress can be made in helping individuals develop tools that foster intimacy and autonomous functioning simultaneously. Despite the significant psychopathology that the subject of the research brought to treatment, marked improvement occurred, but it took considerable time and effort on the part of the therapists in the study.

Clinical Example

Carmen is the younger of two daughters in a Hispanic family. For as long as she can remember, her mother has been preoccupied with Carmen's weight. Now 20 and a college junior, Carmen reports that there was little physical affection in her home; her parents always seemed preoccupied with acquiring more land to expand the family business. Although Carmen was only slightly below target weight, she knew that it was in her best interests to gain. She began therapy in her senior year in high school, made significant headway that year and graduated, and returned to see her therapist during semester breaks and summer vacation. When she returned at the end of her current academic year for additional psychotherapy, she explained that it seemed that her mother "got on my case—again—about eating. She told me that it would be better if I had anorexia than be fat." Carmen was now restricting more than ever before and was now at only 85% of normal weight for her age and height.

In fact, Carmen's mother was slightly underweight herself. In family sessions with another clinician on the multidisciplinary team, she admitted that what Carmen had reported in individual sessions was true. In grade school, this mother sent her daughter off with no breakfast and only one-fourth of a sandwich and one-third of an apple for lunch. She regaled Carmen with comments at dinner such as, "Go ahead and eat all of that, but you're going to get fat," even before her daughter had finished her plate. Cookies, candies, and sodas were simply not permissible except for special occasions like a birthday or Christmas. Again, Carmen's mother's intentions were not meant to be as hurtful as they might appear. She worried that her daughter would face additional discrimination if she were overweight. "Remember your heritage, daughter," she pleaded because "you're already at a disadvantage being dark. What man will want you if you're fat, too?"

The islands of gustatory deprivation, verbal reprimand, and projected self-hatred and racism contrasted with extraordinary parental care and generosity in other ways. Carmen was given piano and guitar lessons, sent to the best private schools, and had closets full of toys and clothing even though her family was not wealthy. Carmen's pediatrician kept excellent records, which when reviewed by the psychiatrist on the team indicated a number of mother–infant feeding problems from birth onwards. The physicians suspected but could not be sure Carmen's problems were of psychological origin that began with a mother who obsessively worried about her baby's "fat" (Winters, 2002). Intensive family therapy, individual psychotherapy, and nutritional counseling were indicated in helping reverse this patient's and her mother's preoccupation; obviously, both needed education and understanding to counter the unwitting trauma the mother was perpetrating on her daughter.

Carmen's recovery was complicated because, like many people, Carmen's mother was reluctant to engage in her own treatment process. Again, her mother did not mean to do harm. As she explained in one powerful family session, "How will this child do if she isn't thin and beautiful in the world? Have you read Nancy Friday's *The Power of Beauty* (1996)? Just try to get ahead without a pretty face! Naomi Wolfe may say beauty is a myth, but it isn't." She was referring to Naomi Wolfe's (1991) classic study, *The Beauty Myth*.

An intensive day-hospital program augmented with patient education groups; three daily, supervised meals; art, music, and supportive group therapies; and individual counseling provided the safety net for this patient. Knowing that it would be difficult for the patient to reverse her eating patterns without the support of her mother, because of feelings of disloyalty, the therapist decided to supplement the therapy by providing a transitional object (Winnicott, 1963/1965a) of recommended readings about recovery from an eating disorder after completing the residential program (see Appendix B for suggested titles). She gave her the list and a patient education handout in addition to a small stone from her personal collection so that Carmen would feel connection in between sessions.

Carmen's therapist also thought it wise to break the sessions down into "manageable" steps that occurred more frequently but were for briefer periods of time. She had the patient come to her office, at first for 20-minute periods three times weekly, increasing to 30 minutes three times weekly, and finally increasing to three 45-minute periods after 18 months. Because of the mottled attachment pattern in childhood and adolescence and the lack of soothing that Carmen felt, her therapist made use of brief telephone and e-mail (Aronson, 1996; Yager, 2003) contact when the patient returned to college. Both patient and therapist kept a notebook recording these communications and reviewed them in the sessions to make sure important issues did not go unaddressed.

In this context, the therapist conceptualized her role as the "available maternal object" who helped the patient mentalize during and in between sessions. Carmen was challenged to consider the circumstances and reasons why her mother was so concerned with body image and to think about the impact those ideas had on Carmen's development of an eating disorder. By the telephone, e-mail, and frequent face-to-face sessions, the therapist was helping Carmen become more alert and aware of her own subjectivity, own those actions and behaviors that impacted her well-being, and develop a sense of self-continuity. The initial short sessions aided Carmen in affect regulation. As she expanded her capacity to "listen to herself," she was also able to "sit with" her feelings longer and become interested in how they changed and the circumstances that impacted them (i.e., conscious perception of her own mental functioning). Because Carmen had a reasonably secure family attachment in her infancy, these straightforward interventions led to an enhancement of mentalization and an increase in control over self-destructive restriction within 18 months. The therapist was applying the research of Fonagy and other researchers in attachment theory, to help the patient hold the "opposing ideas" of her love for her mother along with a recognition of her mother's own eating and body image problems to arrive at an enhanced capacity to think her own thoughts (e.g., reflective functioning) and make more realistic decisions about her eating.

LIMITING SELF-DESTRUCTIVENESS: THE IMPORTANCE OF BEING A "BAD ENOUGH OBJECT"

Therapists frequently will be called upon to set limits on a highly resistant eating disorder patient's self-destructive behavior. On those occasions when one must confront the multifarious tolls of the symptoms, the therapist is actually being placed in the role of the "bad object" who will often be perceived as stern, frustrating, and rigid. My former colleague, training and supervising psychoanalyst Dr. Irwin Rosen of Topeka, Kansas (1993), derived the term *bad enough object* from the work of psychoanalyst W.R.D. Fairbairn. Having worked in the C.F. Menninger Hospital with highly masochistic children and adults for more than 50 years, Rosen, like Fairbairn, was struck by the need of some individuals to cling to their bad objects even as they were offered the experience of kinder, more thoughtful ones by the staff members of the residential unit.

One wonders why abused or maltreated people have such difficulty in letting go emotionally and psychologically of the person who abused them. I often tell my students that we therapists would all be out of business if some of the excellent self-help guides that are available at any library or touted as the latest fad on television were all that individuals needed to deal with longstanding characterlogical patterns. I take solace in the fact that in the final decades of his career, Sigmund Freud wrote extensively about the tenacity of symptoms to endure despite the ministrations of the doctor or the person's conscious will to let go of someone we know is not good to or for the patient. He called this tendency the "adhesiveness of libido," observing how common it is for lovers to stick like glue to the beloved object once it gets going (Freud, 1937/1964a). Especially if the beloved is hurtful or rejecting it may be especially hard to let it go because each of us maintains a measure of "adhesiveness" within ourselves.[2]

---

[2] I cannot resist the temptation of mentioning that romance novels, movies, and television soap operas put this propensity of the human spirit to use every day for fiduciary reasons: What compels better than a tale of unrequited love and obsession with a rejecting beloved? Why does this theme sell and keep on selling? Is it not that we all can easily identify with the poor soul who cannot resist the allure of getting caught up with someone or something despite how bad he, she, or it may ultimately be? This tendency for "libido to adhere"—to stay stuck in love despite its sometimes painful consequences—is a romantic dynamic that partakes a bit of the "bad object" experience. You don't want to let it go and you cannot let it go until you face off with your own internal bad objects. Hence, most romantic fiction ends with a transformation of the lover who finally "sees the light," leaves the "bad" one behind, and takes up with a better, "good" object." But the process takes time, is usually torturous, and is frequently humiliating to the one filled with passion. After all, only in a movie like *Moonstruck* (Jewison & Stanley, 1987) can Cher slap the enraptured lover played by Nicholas Cage on the face and say, "Snap out of it!" and have it work.

Fairbairn expanded on Freud's notion, theorizing that by holding onto a bad object tenaciously, individuals avoid loss. In essence, the individual internalizes bad objects because this is the only object they have. The bad object is the "only game in town" (Fairbairn, 1943/1952; Grotstein & Rinsley, 1994; Rosen, 1993; Sutherland, 1989) for someone with a history of neglect or abuse. Building on Fairbairn's early conceptualization, Rosen believes that individuals who hurt themselves such as by an eating disorder or other self-destructive symptoms hate in order to stay connected to any object. In essence, our patients are attempting to recapitulate in the relationship with the therapist what they had in their early life; they must recover in us the original, "bad object" and find a way to attenuate the experience in order to get better (see Chapter 8).

Some eating disorder patients do not believe you care for them and will not listen to your advice unless you are "bad enough." They are in great need of what Fairbairn called a "homeopathic dose" of the bad object experience from their treater. As one of my long-term bulimic patients remarked after I refused to continue her outpatient psychotherapy until she got better control of her symptoms by entering residential treatment,

> At least I knew you worried about me when you finally put your foot down. You didn't go on a tirade like my parents did when I was a kid but I knew you were pissed when you said "no deal! You have to get refed in a safe place!" I sometimes think I want you to get angry with me and see if we can both survive.

All clinicians who treat eating disorders will recognize this kind of plaintive cry that is heard over and over again. The patient is clearly challenging the therapist to set a firm limit and not to be swayed or seduced by pleas to cast a blind eye to the eating disorder symptoms. This crucial step in helping the patient learn to self-regulate, draws on the therapist's capacity to be the "bad enough object" who is not afraid to set limits and back them up. For example, one might use a therapeutic contract that details what steps will be taken if certain behavioral controls cannot be achieved on an outpatient or day hospital protocol. The therapist will need to follow through on the stipulations in the contract and demonstrate to the patient that implacable, self-destructive sadism toward the treatment will not be tolerated. Thus, be sure to think carefully as to the content prior to proposing it and base the contract on what the patient can actually achieve (i.e., at times it is imperative to include termination as a criterion, but on other occasions this could backfire or lead to further sabotage).

Again, this intervention style of firm limit setting is employed by different schools in the treatment of eating disorders. For example, relapse prevention methods and all behavioral controls can be understood as providing the patient with small but crucial homeopathic doses of bad objectness. Patients feel guilty when they believe they are getting too much of a good thing from their treaters, and they inevitably idealize those whom they believe possess goodness they lack.

TABLE 2.4 Therapist's ability to be "the bad object"

- Counters self-destructiveness and masochism
- Helps patient know that therapist will not permit treatment sabotage
- Allows expression of hostility, but only to a point
- Counters greed and envy of therapist who may be perceived idealistically
- Lets patient know that therapist will not be destroyed or robbed of goodness if anger is expressed
- Promotes integration of good and bad internal objects within the patient

Excessive greed and envy are countered when the therapist sets limits because you demonstrate that you are not afraid of your aggression. You inevitably become less idealized when you call upon this aspect of your real self as you see the patient through the crisis (see Table 2.4). Fairbairn (1943/1952) wrote that it is only over time that bad objects are released and lose their terror. Patients must become familiar with their own "bad-objects," especially aspects of their internalizing anger and rage. In prescribing that "homeopathic dose" of bad-object experience, he concluded that "they are cured by the hair . . . of the dog that bit them" (p. 80). One can thus be prepared for some contentious times between patient and therapist in the middle phase as the experience of having and being a 'bad object' is worked through.

Perhaps most importantly, the patient senses that the therapist permits the display of hostility and self-destruction—but only to a point. Repeated self-sabotage in the way of self-destructive symptoms is inevitably experienced by the therapist as a form of defeating the treatment, leading to a feeling of being persecuted. This stirs inevitable countertransference anger and a sense that one is being invited into a masochistic submission (see Chapter 8). Knowing when to take a properly timed stand, and to do it with firmness, promotes integration of psyche and soma by new identifications. By becoming "the bad enough object," the therapist refuses to replay the sadomasochistic relationship the patient had with a primary caretaker that originally led to the dissociated psyche and soma and internalized aggression which eventuated in the eating disorder.

DECONSTRUCT THE MEANING OF FOOD

Most clinicians will at some point in the treatment need to discuss dietary intake and other specifics related to nutrition. These kinds of educative discussions are essential but incomplete in scope. For example, opportunities to see the more symbolic, unconscious, but highly meaningful ideas the patient has about food are often missed unless the therapist is willing to probe a bit further. With patients who have eating problems, I liken discussions about food to working with dream material. Just as I may ask a patient to elaborate further on what comes to mind about a dream image and to follow that associative

TABLE 2.5   Deconstructing the meaning of food

- Food is a symbol. Work with it as if it were an element in a dream
- Food stories contain the patient's history. Listen for how individual psychology is embedded in stories about eating, food preparation, withholding of nurturance
- Food is a source of communication. Be prepared to talk about food as you do any other experiences
- Food is a test. Have food available if patient is hungry; be willing to talk about the patient's fantasies of the therapist's use or misuse of food
- Food is fuel. Remind patient of the biological reality of how they must sustain life and challenge a tendency to be counterdependent by not eating or caring for the physical self

process in order to gain greater understanding of the patient's inner world, so do I ask patients to tell me what comes to mind about a particular food, choice on the menu, memories of breakfasts and dinners at home or lack thereof, and what the patient may fantasize that I do or don't eat. The results of these associations and stories often lead to rich material and an enlivening of the therapeutic process in the middle phase (see Table 2.5).

For example, in 2001 I reported (Zerbe, 2001a), a case of 40-year-old physician treated in expressive psychotherapy who had a protracted course of anorexia. One day this patient arrived for her session totally depleted and exhausted from work. She mustered up the courage to tell me she felt as though she were "starving" and asked if I had anything in my office that she could eat. I happened to have a chocolate bar handy and asked if she would eat it. Her horror that I actually kept candy bars in my office led to many productive sessions where she compared and worked on how I was different from her mother who deprived her of chocolate and other foods. Having placed me on a pedestal for the first two years of treatment, finding out that I actually ate—let alone would partake of a forbidden food—was the first hint of an emerging important, negative and deidealizing transference that we were able to elaborate as the treatment progressed. Suffice to say that I believe that the same issues would have been played out with other kinds of material, but in this case a discussion about chocolate and eating brought a highly forbidden topic right into the room. Indeed, just as Sigmund Freud (1900/1964b) found that taking the dream images of the patient seriously was the royal road to an understanding of unconscious processes, so for the eating disordered patient, the role food has played in life is one path to grasping important aspects of the psyche and character armor.

Another touching vignette from the same patient, some months later in the treatment, adds some additional spice to the story. Off and on throughout the treatment the patient would engage me in a form of play by talking about food. We were able to discuss the multifarious meanings of food in her life, including ways that she had experienced each of her parents as withholding in parental nurturance. What was particularly conflictual for this physician was that she had also gleaned so many positive personal attributes and anchoring ideals from each of her parents. Like her, they were generous, invested in learning and education, and highly ethical individuals. Unfortunately for all concerned, conflicts about expressing love and sensuality were projected onto the patient. The patient's mother would even lock up food and worried that her daughter would get fat if she ate too much. She did not trust her own or her daughter's capacity to self-regulate. In the transference, this patient also tested me repeatedly to see if I would "keep the goodies locked up" as her mother did.

One Monday morning after a difficult weekend where the patient had been on call and worked through the night, she walked in for her session and announced, "I smell a sandwich!" She caught me totally off guard as I rarely carried my lunch to work but had on this particular day. The sandwich she smelled was actually concealed behind my desk and contained in a closed plastic container. The patient's attunement to the aroma of food, highly suggestive of much psychological yearning and need for nourishment, allowed her to zero in on the fact that some concrete sustenance might be present in my office.

She courageously asked if we might be able to actually eat something. Given her state of emaciation, I agreed. I recalled the classic case of Freud (1909/1964c) who fed his patient the Ratman when he was hungry. I made an on-the-spot determination that the patient should eat some of the sandwich in the session because she was overriding so many internal prohibitions to let me know she was starved. She was also obviously testing to see if I could be different from her mother and let her have something to eat. Therapists who treat patients with eating disorders will frequently talk about similar "feedings" in their practices, but there is scant literature on this topic (Bloom & Kogel, 1994a, 1994b; Davies, 2004 are two notable exceptions).

Once again, this action led to many productive hours that encompassed the meaning not only of this "feeding" but additional stories about the patient's history as they related to food. For example, she struggled to go out with friends or to date because she knew she would have to eat in front of people. The fact that she had "caught me" having both chocolate and a sandwich in my office were glimpses of the "real Dr. Z. who actually eats" that we also discussed. Discussion of body image, gluttony, competition, internal regulation, and parenting came to the fore, all through the elaboration of the metaphors and stories surrounding foods, eating, and recognition of our mutual needs to eat.

ADDRESSING BODY IMAGE

Verbal therapies are necessary but often insufficient in helping eating disorder patients address their body image concerns. Recommending that patients address self-care by learning to modulate their exercise with the help of a personal trainer, going to a massage therapist where they can experience self-touch, learning about body boundaries and function in dance classes, or attending group therapy that focuses on body image issues (Cash & Pruzinsky, 2002; Freedman, 1989; Kearney-Cooke & Ackard, 2000; Kearney-Cooke & Isaacs, 2005) are quite useful methods that can be selected to address this problem. They are experienced as supportive and facilitating in the middle phase of treatment when the patient is moving ahead with greater autonomy and has established a strong treatment alliance.

Experiential treatments (Hornyak & Baker, 1989) such as biofeedback, music and dance therapy, psychodrama, family sculpting, and art therapy are specialized procedures which, when worked with by experts, can and do have substantial impact on helping the patient integrate body and mind. Outcome research for these ancillary methods is limited and may always defy the established methodology and gold standard of the "double blind, placebo" controlled trial. However, patients attest to their value, particularly when they also partake of group or individual sessions that enable further verbal processing and augmentation of what transpires in the body work.

Nonverbal modalities enable the patients to recognize, express, and be less fearful of internal feeling states leading to greater self-regulation and psychosomatic integration. Like verbal therapies, they also help the patient honor their subjective narrative, particularly when the therapist is able to make salient interpretations of the patient's emotional life and counter life-threatening problems by prescribing life-enhancing activities. Art and music therapy, psychodrama, and some kinds of body image work are often done in groups, thereby helping patients to learn to interact and socialize while they receive more accurate perceptions about their body from others in the group. Relaxation therapy, biofeedback, and other hypnotic techniques are particularly useful in helping promote a healthy self-image because the patient is encouraged to visualize a healthy body, alter body image distortions, learn greater sensitivity to hunger and satiety, and modify bingeing and purging behaviors (Pettinati, Kogan, Margolis, Shrier, & Wade, 1989). Axiomatic in body image work (Cash, 1997; Cash & Pruzinsky, 2002) is the notion that the patient has a stable alliance with the therapist that has flourished as a result of other modes of psychological work. Focus on the body inevitably raises issues of comparison and competition with respect to the bodies of others, which must be systematically addressed so that the patient develops a sense of greater mastery of her feelings of inadequacy or jealousy. Sometimes regression occurs when body image exercises are undertaken; therapist and patient need to be aware of the high risk/high gain nature of delving into the arena.

With respect to the individual psychotherapy relationship, the patient may be helped to see how she has abdicated personal responsibility for her body by gorging on cultural symbols and messages. Advertising images, the diet mentality, and a host of other cultural symbols strip a sense of agency from the individual when they feel that they must fulfill a cultural ideal of having and maintaining a particular kind of body image (Bloom, Gitter, Gutwill, Kogel et al., 1994; Orbach, 1978). Sometimes food has been misused because it is the only form of body control the patient felt, and the individual psychotherapist is in the position of helping the patient deconstruct how the culture at large and family relationships, in particular, may have imparted a false notion of control to the patient (see Chapters 4, 5, 6, 7, and 8 for more extensive reviews of cultural issues and research into their impact).

Exercising frenetically to feel alive, purging to evoke action from the therapist, avoiding eating to push a treater (or significant other or parent) away are just some examples of maneuvers that patients use to defend themselves from what they perceive as another person's ownership of their body. As noted, this may reflect a real or imagined parental overinvestment in the patient's bodily functions, such as when the body was thought to be the possession of the parents when the child was growing up. The patient must be helped to understand how the eating disorder paradoxically hurts the body while it remains the most precariously held mode of self-possession.

Welcoming the patient's stories about the body image into the treatment for verbal exploration may uncover a belief on the patient's part that one or both parents were insufficiently concerned about the individual's psychological growth (i.e., real self) and unwittingly indicated to the child that they were an extension of the parents. Self-care, which includes care for the body, necessitates that the patient move away from impinging cultural and familial messages. These messages must be brought to consciousness and worked through in the middle phase of treatment by encouraging the patient to look at those internal conflicts and core deficits upon which their eating disorder is based. Group therapy modalities are particularly useful in helping patients address individual issues and parse out underlying cultural messages. Psychodrama and family sculpting may help the individual to "gain access to hidden parts of the self" (Callahan, 1989, p. 106) and "experience, practice, and strengthen the healthier aspects of the self" (p. 106). They may also explore the societal expectations concerning thinness and its numerous ramifications (i.e., sociodrama). Regardless of the specific technique that is used, the patient must find ways to uncover the effects the cultural messages have had on her or his individual mind and attempt to generate constructive ways of coping with them at this stage in the treatment in order to arrive at a healthier sense of body image.

Clinical Example

Jasmin is a 35-year-old former dance student who made significant progress with controlling bingeing and restriction in therapy. Deciding that it was time to get "back into the groove of dance" and "finally deal with my feelings of all the others being thinner than me," Jasmin's therapist referred her to a therapeutic dance class. When areas of competition arose, the therapist normalized the experience. The body image work also enabled the patient to acknowledge waves of feelings in her body and about her body. In her individual process Jasmin worked on the common preoccupation of eating disorder patients that "everyone in the group has an eating disorder." Her therapist pointed out how often this thought crossed her mind and the energy she used in looking closely at others, always wondering, comparing, and thinking about the emphasis they placed on their bodies. Jasmin's therapist commented on how these preoccupations kept the patient from doing what she loved in dance and diverted her attention away from developing her true self.

VALIDATING PERSONAL AUTHORITY:
TOLERATING CONFLICT OPENLY

Contemporary society idealizes technical, scientific, so-called "objective" scholarship. This worldview neglects the subjective importance of the individual narrative. For an eating disorder to be faced down individuals must find a way to appreciate themselves, their relationships, and their world; that is, they must come to believe in their own personal authority and have it validated. As a first step, this personal authority must be validated in the therapy. The conceptual guideline is to help individuals to embrace their inner voice and their own search for the truth. Patients must be encouraged to become experts in their own experience.

Theoretically speaking, this point of view reflects contemporary developments in ethics, philosophy, feminism, theology, and psychodynamic thought. Self-examination is a theory of liberation for both men and women because it values subjective knowledge that can only be gleaned by an appreciation of one's inner voice and an appreciation of what in-depth exploration offers an individual. Those clinicians who share a reverence for hearing the voice of the true self are pari passu inviting the individual to validate her personal authority. Obviously, treatment techniques that evolve from this point of view are not prone to emphasize rigorous experimental design or quantitative measures of clinical efficacy. Rather, data is synthesized from unstructured interviews and by encouraging the patient's narrative to illuminate existential experience (see Chapter 9). Theoretically, openness to the meaning and value of one's world increases awareness of an appreciation of that very world, leading to enhanced personal growth and new capacity to face down the eating disorder. In effect, the patient is encouraged to become her own "inner expert" on "an individual search for enlightened consciousness" (Paglia, 1992). Some of the practical tools a therapist might employ to help develop the individual's unique voice are listed in Table 2.6. Once again, these suggestions are commonly recommended guidelines from different psychotherapeutic models that should be integrated into the treatment in the middle phase because they focus on development and growth of the self and not merely control of a symptom. They pose additional reference points for the therapist who values the importance of welcoming the eating disorder into the room to *understand* its value and meaning and not *just* provide interventions that implicitly say to a person, "Stop this. It's bad for you."

TABLE 2.6 Practical tools for developing one's own voice

- Use the conversational paradigm of individual, group, and family therapies
- Encourage expression and development of personal narrative in letters, journals, poetry, essays
- Name affects with patients. Sometimes have a patient keep a "feelings journal" or jump start work on feelings by having them write down reactions they observe in a character in a movie, book, or play
- Recognize and mirror patient's strengths
- Encourage growth and expansion of knowledge, especially in areas that are different from those of the therapist (e.g., communicative matching)

Clinical Example

Shane is a 30-year-old graduate student who entered therapy for dysthymia, binge drinking, and subclinical bulimia nervosa (e.g., activity disorder) after he gave up his career aspiration to become a professional wrestler. Shane's parents divorced when he was 5 years old and he resented how he was placed in the caretaker role for his 2-year-old sister. According to Shane, his parent's arguments and physical fights led to his feeling that "I was always in the middle and even had to keep them from killing each other twice." His feelings of rage went underground to some extent but were effectively sublimated by his excellence in sports.

When a series of injuries forced Shane to forego his dreams, he sought solace in alcohol, promiscuous sex, and food. Ill equipped to mourn the loss of his "first love," wrestling, Shane enacted his suffering through his self-destructive behaviors, a signal that he clearly needed help. Like many patients with subclinical eating disorder symptoms, Shane's symptoms came under rather rapid control in the context of cognitive-behavioral techniques and reassurance from his therapist. Within months he was tapered off antidepressant medications without any recrudescence in his symptoms, but he remained committed to coming to weekly psychotherapy "just to talk things over and think that somebody is there, on my side."

Much of the first two years of therapy was spent hearing about Shane's disappointment in how neither of his parents were there for him from a psychological standpoint. Grateful that his father was able to lend financial support as he now undertook graduate school, Shane resented the fact that his father "comes to me for advice. I thought it was supposed to be the other way around."

Three years into treatment, Shane is faced with a new dilemma. His paternal aunt wants Shane to leave graduate school for a semester in order to provide care for his father who has just been diagnosed with a rare blood disease. The father's medical problem is not immediately life-threatening but Shane feels the pull from his inner critic to leave his own career trajectory to meet his aunt's demands. He is also resentful of even the hint that he should give up his plans. From Shane's point of view, life has already been unfair and forced him to relinquish too much; he has had to fight his way back from depression, an eating disorder, and other behaviors that did not serve his long-term self-interest. In the dialogue that follows, Shane and I attempt to sort out the nature of his conflict so that he can make his own decisions (e.g., assert his personal authority) without returning to self-destructive behaviors.

> *Shane:* My aunt called yesterday. She's trying to make me feel guilty about not just stopping everything and going there to take care of Dad. I was proud of myself. Not only did I tell her "No" but I didn't do any of the self-destructive things that I used to.
>
> K.Z.: Like drinking or purging? (Clarifying how he might have relapsed and welcoming a discussion of these behaviors into the room if that needs to occur)
>
> *Shane:* Yeah. I talked to my girl friend instead. And I thought a lot about the position my aunt and my father might be putting me in. My girl friend is really curious about the discussions that you and I have. She listens like you do and gives me feedback. She's very supportive that I'm not quitting grad school to do what my aunt says I should do.
>
> K.Z.: Sounds like you feel you have two people in your court now—your girl friend and me—but it must be hard to keep your own countenance when there is the competing pressure of your aunt and your sense of responsibility for your father (mirroring his turning to others for support and using his own mind as positive adaptations and islands of psychological growth).
>
> *Shane:* I know that what I can give my father has limits on it. He should have more friends than he does that are in his age group. He shouldn't rely on me, but then that's what my parents always seem to do. They relied on me to take care of Ella (his sister) and to some extent, even them. You and I know that's why I'm behind in getting my graduate degree. I could be finished by now if I could have given up wrestling earlier (note Shane's greater sense of personal authority and capacity to reflect on the past).
>
> K.Z.: But first you had to work through your dream of being in professional sports and then we had to work on your dream of not having a perfect family (emphasizing mourning work that has been accomplished).
>
> *Shane:* Do you think I'm doing the right thing, Dr. Z., to not dash off every weekend or even to stop my studies to take care of Dad? I know you're fond of quoting that passage from Hamlet, "To thine own self be true. . . ."
>
> K.Z.: It's always easier for the therapist to quote something from literature than for the person in the other chair to actually do it. I think that what

you are saying in reminding me of the quote is that it is very hard to be true to oneself. I actually think that you are trying to find an important balance by not giving up on your own aspirations or goals but still showing loyalty to your father by your calls to him and your obvious concern (clarifies conflict for further working through).

Shane: (brightens) In spite of everything, I still love my dad.

K.Z.: Of course you do, Shane. We only get one father and one mother and it is a sign of your maturity that you love each of them (and your aunt, too) in spite of their flaws. On the other hand, your knowledge of yourself seems to be saying that it is also important to follow through on your career plans. After all, actualizing those goals now is what is helping you to get beyond your symptoms (helping process the affect he has while encouraging growth and recognizing strengths because they were not mirrored in the family of origin).

Shane: Like I said, my girl friend is curious about what we talk about in my sessions. Do you think I should tell her?

K.Z.: I think that's very much up to you. Just like you must define the boundary about how much you give to your father, so you will need to test out how much you feel comfortable sharing with your girl friend about your therapy. There aren't any hard and fast rules about how to be true to yourself when it comes to that issue (validating personal autonomy to make his decision while acknowledging importance of new support system and relationship with girl friend).

Shane: I like having a space where I can think about the choices. I don't have to decide this minute what I will say the next time she and I get together (new capacity to think and wait and not act on impulse).

In this treatment segment, Shane is finding new abilities to give voice to his own personal narrative and life dream. He recognizes that he has silenced himself in the past through his eating disorder and other psychological problems; he is recognizing the price that his family dynamics play but he has moved beyond the stance of having his parents assume blame for his difficulties. He is taking responsibility and thereby moving forward in his search for a more defined sense of true self.

Yet, exercising a sense of agency is not without cost. Shane must deal with the inevitable conflicts that occur within intimate relationships. In particular, he is struggling with how much to "give" his aunt, his father, and even his girl friend. The therapist's role in these circumstances is to acknowledge the distance the patient has come, clarify and witness his efforts in finding self-definition, and acknowledge the loyalty bind within which he finds himself. Note how the dialogue with the therapist asserts the restorative power of helping the patient find his own voice by validating his right to make his own choices while continually pointing out the conflicts in which he finds himself mired.

GRIEVING THE SYMPTOM

For the eating disorder to recede in psychological importance, the patient must develop the capacity to mourn. This crucial psychological skill enables the individual to move through the stages of life in order to accept those "necessary losses" (Viorst, 1986) that herald inevitable change. As a treasured piece of the patient's identity, the eating disorder must be given up for the patient to be able to embrace the true self. While the therapist must also spend time helping the patient discuss real and perceived losses that accompany every individual in the course of life (e.g., death, breakup, career setback), special attention must be given to what it means in order to move forward when an entrenched symptom or pattern has helped one cope with life.

Depending upon the comfort zone of the therapist, many different techniques can be used when helping the patient to mourn the symptom. For example, conceptualizing the problem from an interpersonal therapy perspective (IPT), views the state of moving from having an eating disorder to not having one as a role transition. Using a Gestalt framework, the therapist might ask the patient to concretize and externalize the manifest symptom by seating it in a chair. The patient speaks to their symptoms, says goodbye to them, or even has a funeral. Obviously, group therapy and experiential therapies can all be adapted quite specifically to address the concept of mourning the eating disorder; for example, some group or psychodrama therapists also partake of the notion of "having a funeral" for the symptom and asking each of the participants to eulogize their symptoms. Feedback about what life will be like without this treasured, precious, reliable coping strategy can be given and group members can support the grieving member. Regardless of the modality that is chosen, emphasis should be placed on helping the patient recognize the complex emotions they have about losing the symptom. Obviously, this is also good practice for the ongoing life experience each individual will have in working through inevitable loss and change. There are always parts of our old life we miss even as we seek to embrace our new one.

The therapeutic procedure embedded in "grieving the symptom" encourages the patient to turn to other human beings rather than the eating disorder to fulfill needs. Like any grief process that follows death or life transition, a block in mourning the process impedes forward movement in the developmental life cycle. What is needed most urgently when the patient begins the mourning process is the ongoing atmosphere of acceptance and a safe place to express one's feelings.

The late Dr. Mary Cerney, a pioneer in the study of grief therapy at the Menninger Clinic, cautioned therapists that anxiety and anger are expectable companions of all grief. It behooves clinicians to pay attention to both the realistic and unrealistic anger that patients have toward their eating disorder symptoms. Cerney also advised clinicians to have their patients speak directly to the subject of the loss in the consultation room and to visualize "saying goodbye" to the loss outside the actual therapy hours (Cerney, 1989; Cerney & Buskirk, 1991). This sage advice can and should be taken regardless of the favored techniques of the therapist. A brief visualization or meditation exercise can be a required homework exercise that facilitates the process of letting go. (e.g., you might ask the patient to surround the symptom in light and walk away from it; you might suggest a ritual that might be performed).

Helping people manage issues of loss and grief are central to all religious and therapeutic traditions. The loss of a destructive symptom is obviously very different from losing an actual loved one, but the principles of working with grief are similar. In large part, an individual who grieves must recognize, own, and resolve feelings of anger. Avenues for the healthy expression of this and other affects may be found in individual or group therapies. In contrast to the usually sanctioned advice to perform rigorous exercise or activities to alleviate grief, the eating disorder patient does not have the carte blanche for participating in these activities for the obvious reasons. Hence, our general tact must be to help our patient verbalize, accept, and learn to cope with difficult feelings in the here-and-now in order to grow. "Grief must be shared to be born" is the oft-quoted maxim that encapsulates the therapist's major role at this point in the middle phase of treatment. Once again, a painful experience for the patient is being welcomed into the consultation room for discussion and processing. This is in a sharp contrast to our current cultural tradition that appears to have less time and space for honest expression of grief, or well-meaning people who say, "You have to go on" or "Keep that stiff upper lip."

PHARMACOLOGICAL CONSIDERATIONS

Clinical and control trials have produced a small but significant body of evidence that demonstrates that pharmacological treatments when combined with psychotherapy are superior to pharmacotherapy alone (see Jimerson, Wolfe, Brotman, & Metzger, 1996; Mitchell & Selders, 2005, for succinct reviews). Given the complexity and refractory nature of eating disorders, the clinician can reasonably hope that medication will help improve the condition but rarely produce "cure." Under the best circumstances, medication should only be prescribed as a treatment adjunct after a solid therapeutic alliance has been established (Hamburg, Herzog, & Brotman, 1996). On some occasions a trial of a new medication may be employed to sidestep patient resistance, such as when a therapeutic impasse occurs or if the patient or family members convey a sense of defeat or hopelessness. At those times it may also be useful to review options for therapeutic modalities that have not yet been tried but have demonstrated benefit in trials; for example, cognitive-behavioral therapy, interpersonal therapy (anorexia), dialectical behavior therapy (bulimia) (Jarman & Walsh, 1999; Mitchell, Hoberman, Peterson, et al., 1996; Thompson-Brenner & Westen, 2005b; Walsh & Devlin, 1998). This approach may imbue a sense of hopefulness and willingness to hear the patient on her own terms while modeling a sense of openness to help the patient find what will work for her.

In the middle phase of treatment, the therapeutic alliance has been established to the extent that the patient will more easily ask questions about medication. The patient will also have more energy to do his or her own research and will frequently bring the results of literature and Internet searches to the attention of the therapist. Patients should be cautioned to question the information they learn about a medication because as yet no pharmacological panacea has been identified. As with other psychiatric disorders, a flurry of excitement about a particular medication is often followed by a relatively slow reappraisal of its usage over time. From a psychotherapeutic perspective, the patient who is better able to assess critically what she or he hears is demonstrating increased ego autonomy, healthier coping skills, and advancement along the road toward a healthier sense of true self.

Anorexia Nervosa

Many different classes of medications have been studied but found to have limited benefit over the long term course in anorexia; that is, first and second generation antipsychotics, tricyclic antidepressants, monoamine oxidase inhibitors (MAOIs), and selective serotonin reuptake inhibitors (SSRIs). In one double blind, placebo controlled trial, fluoxetine was found useful in maintaining body weight in weight restored anorexic patients (Kaye, Nagata, et al., 2001), but this finding has not always been repeated (Strober, Pataki, Freeman, & DeAntonio 1999; Walsh, Kaplan, Attia et al., 2006). In general, patients do not respond well to antidepressant medication when they are malnourished and underweight. The dosage of fluoxetine (40–60 mg per day) used to help stabilize weight recovered patients is higher than the dosage used for depression. The action of this SSRI in the treatment of anorexia nervosa is unknown, although it likely modifies diverse neural networks and synaptic pathways at the cellular/molecular level, ultimately effecting change in stress mediated responses and brain morphology (Reid & Stewart, 2001).

Since the 1960s, antipsychotic agents have been used empirically to reduce the delusional-like cognitions that anorexics experience toward their body and food. In fact, at one time anorexia nervosa was conceptualized as a monosymptomatic hypochondriacal delusion, making the use of antipsychotics appear rational, logical, and scientifically sound. However, in the majority of controlled trials, agents such as chlorpromazine, thorazine, pimozide, and haloperidol did not show positive benefits over placebo; moreover, their side effect profile (e.g., tardive dyskinesia, seizures) made them poor choices except in chronic, refractory patients who did not respond to any other form of therapy.

The second generation antipsychotic agents have a more tolerable side effect profile and have been demonstrated to help some anorexics gain weight. While controlled trials are still ongoing and additional research is needed to confirm initial research, the second generation antipsychotics (e.g., olanzapine, quetiapine, risperidone) have been found to reduce fat phobia, unrealistic evaluations of size and weight, and distorted body image in small cohorts of patients (Boachie, Goldfield, & Spettigue, 2003; Powers, Bannon, Eubanks, & McCormick, 2007; Powers, Santana, & Bannon, 2002). For example, in a series of 20 patients (Powers et al., 2002) 14 of 18 had significant weight gain using olanzapine; 3 of the patients had full weight recovery. Powers cautioned that her findings about the medication might be inflated because the patients also took part in "medication adherence groups" where nutrition, family education, principles of cognitive treatment, and facts about anorexia were taught. As in all studies where more than one therapeutic intervention is made, the clinician always asks the question that Powers reminds her readers to ask: Which therapeutic adjuvant made the difference or was there something about the combination that worked synergistically?

While not all of the case series of olanzapine and risperidone have had positive outcomes, the majority of reports to date indicates at least modest weight gain (in the 2–5 kg range) and enhanced self-esteem, reduced obsessionality and compulsive activity, and improved body image (Barbarich et al., 2004; Fisman et al., 1996; Mehler et al., 2001; Newman-Toker, 2000; Schwam et al., 1998). In one case study of four children, olanzapine was well tolerated when used proactively (dose = 2.5 mg) for weight restoration (Boachie et al., 2003). Some clinicians refrain from using risperidone because of its effects on the electrocardiogram and the potential for exacerbating compromised cardiac function.

Neither estrogen nor bisphosphonates have a role in the management of anorexia nervosa. Most women whose weight is restored and maintained will regain normal menses; their bone density will also improve, although probably not return to the normal range. Estrogen also causes bone growth plates to close prematurely in adolescent females (Golden, 2003; Odivina et al., 2005). Finally, artificially inducing menses by giving estrogen may reinforce a patient's denial of her illness.

Appetite stimulants such as cisapride and zinc have not been consistently found to be therapeutically useful. Some studies in the literature attest to their value, and sophisticated patients are likely to ask about them because the media (including women's magazines and the Internet) raise awareness of their use. Other complimentary medicine modalities have been touted as helpful, but as yet no substantial body of research substantiates their regular use (e.g., acupuncture; somatic integration or massage therapy for sexual abuse victims).

One therapeutic caveat stands out among all others when treating anorexic patients with medication: Beware the potential for life-threatening side effects, especially when the patient is very low weight. For example, lithium carbonate is potentially toxic to patients who severely restrict food intake or who induce vomiting or abuse laxatives or diuretics. Controlled trials of tricyclics (TCAs) and monoamine oxidase inhibitors (MAOIs) have significant side effects and limited benefits in terms of weight gain and measures of psychopathology.

Given the high suicide rate among the anorexic patient population (see Chapter 9), special care must be undertaken when trying these agents or any agent with a black box warning. They are generally not recommended. Other agents such as clonidine or the antimanic agents have minimal, if any, clinical use in anorexia unless one is treating a comorbid psychiatric condition.

Because multiple neurotransmitter systems are likely to be altered in patients with anorexia, peptides such as neuropeptide Y, leptin, vasopressin, and corticotropic releasing factor may prove to be fruitful means of intervention in the 21st century (see Chapter 5). Theoretically, agents that act directly or indirectly on the brain's satiety centers will hasten weight restoration and be well-tolerated physically and psychologically by patients (Maj, Halmi, Lopez-Ibor et al., 2003). However, given the complex cultural and psychological underpinnings of anorexia, it is unlikely that a "magic bullet" will emerge in the foreseeable future that eradicates the internal angst and despair most patients experience when they are given the opportunity to tell their story.

Bulimia Nervosa

Antidepressants (e.g., TCAs, MAOIs, and SSRIs) are all moderately effective in a substantial number of bulimic patients. While SSRIs are the most frequently used front-line medications for the disorder, the selective norepinephrine uptake inhibitor reboxetine which is not yet available in the USA (dose = 4 mg/day) has demonstrated benefit in a small sample of outpatients (Fassino, Abbate-Daga, Biggio, Garzara, & Piero, 2004). Depressive symptoms, improvement in global functioning (GAF), and lowered drive for thinness and body dissatisfaction are found in both drug categories (Fassino et al., 2004). To date, fluoxetine is the only Food and Drug Administration approved medication for bulimia. Evaluated in two parallel, multicenter, double-blind, randomized, placebo-controlled trials, it is usually prescribed at doses of 40 to 60 mg/day (Goldstein, Wilson, Ascroft, & Al-Banna, 1999; Romano et al., 2002). Citalopram has also been found to reduce bulimic symptoms in one small (n = 37) randomized trial (Leombruni et al., 2006).

In bulimia nervosa there is a high placebo response to any medication. Patients must be told that in the trials that have been performed, sample size is limited, length of the trial is generally short (1–3 mos), and drop-out rate is considerable. Yet some general guidelines are emerging in the literature. Although psychotherapy is generally better accepted by patients than pharmacotherapy, antidepressant therapy is an effective adjunct in many situations and can on occasion usher in full remission (Bacaltchuk & Hay, 2003; Walsh et al., 2000). The opiod antagonist naltrexone has also been cited in limited trials to diminish binge eating in bulimia and eating disorders not otherwise specified, but toxic effects on the liver can hinder its usefulness (Marrazzi, Markham, Kinzie, et al., 1995; Marrazzi, Wroblewski, Kinzie, & Luby, 1997).

A subgroup of patients with comorbid cluster B personality disorders and impulsive traits do not respond as well to SSRIs or other medications. In one study, methylphenidate (Ritalin) in doses of 15 to 20 mg day was useful to bulimics with cluster B personality disorders who responded poorly to psychotherapy and SSRIs (Sokol, Gray, Goldstein, & Kaye, 1999).

Tricyclic antidepressants (i.e., imipramine in doses up to 300 mg/day; desipramine up to 300 mg/day) reduce binge eating and preoccupation with food while improving global functioning in control trials (Agras, Dorian, Kirkley et al., 1987; Barlow, Blouin, Perez, 1988). Treatment benefits subside when medication is discontinued. Debate continues about whether or not these medications have a specific antibulimic effect or actually reduce bingeing and purging by decreasing depression. It appears that antidepressants may help patients by several mechanisms, including treating the underlying depression, reducing hunger and increasing satiety, reducing core symptoms, or reducing sensitivity to stress. In practice, a brief explanation of the potential mechanisms of action and the rationale for considering one particular agent (e.g., the patient's side-effect profile and individual history) helps establish a collaborative relationship and a firm therapeutic alliance (Powers & Cloak, 2007).

MAOIs have been less systematically studied in the treatment of bulimia nervosa than tricyclics and SSRIs. In the controlled trials that have been done, phenelzine has been found to reduce bingeing by at least 50%. On the other hand, meclobemide, an MAOI type A selective and reversible inhibitor, was not found effective. Bulimic patients may struggle to comply with the MAOI diet, and consequently, physicians will have less opportunity to use these agents. However, in a reliable patient who has not responded to other agents, an MAOI may be worth a trial.

The anticonvulsant topiramate has demonstrated efficacy but as yet is an off-label treatment for patients who binge. Susan McElroy, Professor of Psychiatry at the University of Cincinnati and a world expert in topiramate's use in bipolar disorder, reported that the number of weekly binges dropped and significant weight was lost at one-year follow-up (median final dose = 200 mg) (McElroy, 2003). Topiramate has also been shown good efficacy for outpatient weight management in a review of obese binge eaters (Hoopes et al., 2003).

Recently the antiemetic, selective serotonin receptor antagonist ondansetron (dose = 4 mg three times daily to start and increasing to 24 mg/day in divided doses) has demonstrated initial effectiveness in a few short-term clinical trials (Faris et al., 2000; Fung & Ferrill, 2001). The clinician who prescribes these medications may need to intercede with third parties to cover the patient's medication because they are (1) still deemed "experimental" and (2) expensive. Many investigators believe that novel antiemetics show promise in the treatment of bulimia.

For some patients the effect of the medication is experienced as a turning point after years of struggle. Exacerbation of binge–purge behavior occurs when medication is discontinued. Practically speaking, this often means keeping the patient on medication for months if not years. Preliminary evidence as well as clinical experience currently converge on maintaining the medication at the lowest effective dosage that substantially reduces core bulimic symptoms. As noted, treatment approaches that combine medication and psychotherapy are superior to single treatment approaches.

Other typical agents (e.g., trazodone, mianserin) are effective but not recommended as first-line agents. Bupropion (Wellbutrin) is contraindicated because of the reports of seizures in patients who have eating disorders (Horne, Ferguson, Pope et al., 1988). Carbamazepine and lithium are not recommended because of their potential toxicity.

Bright light (10,000 lux) was found to reduce binge frequency in a group of 16 bulimic subjects by 50% (Sullivan, Bulik, Fear, & Pickering, 1998). The researchers in this study underscore that the results are not as dramatic as results for patients receiving a combination of an SSRI and cognitive-behavioral therapy. Light therapy may hold promise for some bulimic patients who do not respond to other treatments or who are prone to binge eating in winter (Braun, Sunday, Fornari et al., 1999; Lam, Goldner, Solyom, & Remick, 1994). Interestingly, carbohydrate cravings, an increased desire for food, and depressed mood are commonalities of bulimia and seasonal affective disorder. It is speculated that bright light, which is a safe, effective, and inexpensive treatment for a subgroup of patients with these disorders, may have a modulating effect on serotonin transmission. Carbohydrate craving is related to deficits in serotonin or defects in its normal metabolism or transmission. In some bulimic patients bright light might be a useful adjunct to drug therapy or CBT.

Binge Eating Disorder and Other Eating Disorders Not Otherwise Specified (EDNOS)

SSRIs are the pharmacological agents of choice for binge eating and other subclinical eating disorders which are subsumed under the rubric of EDNOS in the DSM-IV (Carter, Hudson, Lalonde, et al., 2003). As a general point of reference, the third edition of the American Psychiatric Association's "Practice Guidelines" for the Treatment of Eating Disorders (2006) states that subclinical cases be treated similarly to cases that meet full diagnostic criteria. No formal statistics exist on how many "subclinical" eating disorder patients inhabit North America or Europe, but when one talks to practicing clinicians one is led to believe the eating disorder continuum is extremely common. The "Practice Guidelines" take this "real world" perspective into account when they advise a conservative course when treating the binge eating because it may curtail worsening or avoid chronicity.

Interestingly, despite the frequent side effect of weight gain when SSRIs are used in the treatment of depression, weight loss has been demonstrated when this class of medications is used in binge eating disorder. Orlistat, topiramate, and sibutramine have also been employed with some success in reducing binge frequency but to date the number of randomized trials is small. Each may produce modest weight loss but have unwelcome side effects. Caloric restriction, exercise, and behavioral modification can also produce weight loss but in the majority of persons it is not sustained. Regulation of energy balance may present another potential target for intervention in the future (Badman & Flier, 2005) and aid patients in their struggle with overweight induced by binge eating.

A MIDDLE-AGED PSYCHOANALYST LEARNS SOME NEW TRICKS

As I have already alluded to and will develop further in later chapters (see especially Chapter 8), nothing takes the place of psychotherapy for the clinician or patient who wants to grow and develop her or his true self. From a well-timed interpretation or confrontation, we all learn so much about ourselves, but friends and loved ones also often make observations about us that even the most astute analyst or therapist will miss. In part this happens because these people experience our flaws in "real time," have to contend with our most annoying behaviors in the "real world," and live and work with us in our "natural environment." I remind colleagues of all levels of experience that we get valuable insight and critiques in our daily lives, usually given to us by a scrupulously honest and courageous friend, partner, or spouse, who cares enough to tell us a difficult truth if we only have the ears to hear it.

Although friendship can never replace or be equated with what we derive from working with a therapist, our closest relationships do have some of the same therapeutic elements in them that can teach us much about ourselves, life in general—and even elements of the therapeutic process. Psychoanalyst Karen Horney termed the growth we all receive by experiencing daily life and listening to the perceptions of those close to us "the psychotherapy of everyday life," and she contrasted this with the painstaking insight and interpersonal skills an individual gleans from undertaking psychotherapy with a professional.

An example from my life taught me a great deal about the value of Dr. Horney's observation; sometimes only a cherished friend can bear witness to and then comment on some "necessary corrections" or "rough edges" that need to be attended to for our lives to run a smoother course.

My "forever" friend, Carlene Benson, of Kansas City, an MBA and CFO for a not-for-profit agency, might well have been a therapist had she not chosen a career in finance. Carlene is quite self-effacing but she knows when to be firm and make a tactful comment that needs to be said. One day we were sitting in my living room talking as my pet Schnauzer and Lakeland terriers boisterously played and rough-housed. To my mind, the dogs were simply being their "true canine selves" that demand continuous attention. In an effort to cover their grating behavior as they jumped, raced, and begged for pats and treats, I said they were just "being their adorable, mischievous, rambunctious, canine selves." Carlene wryly quipped: "Yes, there is something uniquely determined about the terrier breed . . . But, Kassy, I have to honestly tell you that these two critters seem to be the stereotypical pets of a psychiatrist in a *New Yorker* cartoon. If they had hands instead of paws, and if you had a piano, they would be sawing the legs off!"

I took this as a gentle hint that it was perhaps time to get some counseling from a local "dog whisperer." Obedience sessions seemed necessary for the terriers to settle down and for me to learn some new tricks to help lead the pack. From working with a skilled animal behaviorist, Camilla Welhaven of Portland, Oregon and making notable, rapid progress, I gained even more respect for what behavioral therapies offer. I take this example as an opportunity to not only remind readers of the chances our lives provide us for opportunities for growth from many unsuspected sources, but to once again point out some of the overlapping methods in all schools of therapy.

First, Camilla took a very detailed history of the actual behavior problems the dogs had (e.g., barking all the time, lunging on their leads, and ignoring commands). Indeed, she was so empathetic while getting the history that I felt immediately helped simply by sharing my story. Camilla never appeared shocked by any problem with the pair, so the natural tendency of the client to be embarrassed or feel ignorant was minimized. For example, she would often make some of those well-timed empathetic "oh my's" and "uh huhs" we therapists of humans are known for; she also asked questions to clarify just what the pets were up to and implicitly signaled that she had heard a lot worse. This also worked wonders for decreasing my anxiety and incipient shame response. Then she began to break down suggestions into very simple steps and had me write them down for later use (i.e., my homework assignment). Afterwards, Camilla had "the family" practice our lessons together.

When the dogs did better at a particular task (such as having Miles, the Schnauzer, sit at the front door, not lunge or bark when the bell rang, and only then receive his treat), I watched her say "good boy" and give him a pat on the head. He appeared to respond to the positive affirmation and mastery of task as much as getting his treat. I will never know for sure, however. As the lessons progressed and the tasks grew more complex, we all actually moved out of doors. I noticed how freely Camilla gave praise. "Good job, Sophie (the Lakeland)," "Good job, Miles." "Really good job, Kassy (me)."

As the classes continued, I had more opportunity to pause and reflect on Camilla's interventions and subtle ways of helping her clients. I recalled how momentarily proud I felt by the affirmations she gave me; I wondered about how often we psychotherapists miss the opportunity to encourage patients who are on their own forward momentum and mastering something they didn't believe possible when we withhold positive commentary. I gained additional respect for behavioral therapies, because I witnessed and was the recipient of substantial gains in skills that when applied in a different context can help people with an array of issues.

I take this opportunity of "the process" with Camilla, animal behaviorist, to review therapeutic commonalities and to summarize some of the major techniques frequently and repeatedly employed in the first two phases of treatment: (1) Taking the patient's story seriously (in this case, the owner); (2) empathizing with that individual's difficult life situation; (3) giving hope that progress can be made; (4) assigning homework and making a written plan; (5) underscoring how even little changes will take practice in order to cement new patterns; (6) emphasizing that these small changes can lead to bigger ones over time if one keeps trying and practicing; (7) affirming the changes that are made by showing delight when the subject (i.e., dog and owner in this case) arrives at a new level of mastery.

I conclude this final example in the chapter with some follow-up. Sophie and Miles continue to do better with their behaviors, albeit with occasional relapses. Carlene and I continue to have a close friendship despite the physical distance of 1,800 miles; the telephone is a great invention through which we have, as she puts it, "regular and essential brain cleanings" wherein we assume the mutual role of listener and "truth sayer" for each other. Camilla Welhaven, bless her canine-adoring heart, remains on retainer for the household for those occasions when Kassy or the dogs need a "booster" or "adjuvant" session described for other purposes throughout this book.

ADDITIONAL TREATMENT CONSIDERATIONS

Eating disorder symptoms diminish during the middle phase as the patient finds new ways of addressing key symptoms, interpersonal concerns, and psychological pain and conflict. Essentially, this work enables the true self to emerge. Therapeutic relationships are a vital avenue for the patient to experience a sense of personal satisfaction and competence (Novick & Novick, 1998) outside of the inherently self-destructive eating disorder symptoms. Gaining a sense of autonomy and mastery in collaborative work gradually helps the false self system to recede, because one must also struggle with life's inherent ambiguity and conflict. While working together in this phase should bring satisfaction to both therapist and patient, there are inevitable disappointments. One grows and tests one's wings during times of success and failure. When subjective knowledge is valued as it is in therapy, one gradually learns to forgive others for their failings. Paradoxically, autonomy and personal authority are enhanced when healthy dependency needs are also met. The dialogic nature of the therapeutic relationship enables the restorative power of the individual's unique voice to emerge.

Therapeutic activities that may enhance progress during the middle phase include:

1. Encourage the expression of the patient's personal narrative and creativity by writing letters or poetry, journal keeping, or making works of art as supplements to the therapeutic process (Rabinor 1991). The "conversational

paradigms" of individual, group, experiential, and family therapies promote the development of one's unique voice where the body has heretofore been the mode of expression and communication (McDougall, 1989).

2. Spell out to the patient that when relapses or other dangerous behaviors occur (e.g., severe self-cutting, suicidality), more structure is required. If the treatment is disrupted by an exacerbation of symptoms, renegotiate the therapeutic contract. While regressions are expectable in treatment, both patient and therapist must have a sense that the work is moving forward, positive internalization is occurring, and life is becoming more satisfying. The clinical maxim that "the patient must always need the therapist more than the therapist needs the patient" applies particularly in those situations where the therapist may feel held hostage by the patient's unrealistic demands (e.g., after hours phone calls; rejection of therapeutic interventions; unremitting symptoms despite time, patience, and insight).

3. Model healthy self-regard and self-care. Help the patient to get to know how the healthy parts of themselves are battling with an internal enemy (Fairbairn's "bad object"). Set firm boundaries, particularly when symptoms exacerbate. Knowing when to take on the role of "bad object" not only ensures patient safety but enables the patient to face down their own sadomasochistic tendencies.

4. Renegotiate the therapeutic contract as the patient consolidates her sense of self. Expect more from the patient who is able to take better care of herself than she did at the beginning of the treatment. When symptoms are sufficiently under control and the patient has a nascent sense of the emergence of the true self, help the patient to mourn what the symptoms have meant.

5. Help the patient discern how his hypertrophied investment in an ideal body and perfection of self led him to eschew real mastery, autonomy, and control in more life-affirming realms. Unraveling the ways in which the search for an ideal self and an ideal body were driven by the ineluctable need to separate and individuate from faulty cultural institutions and outmoded family patterns promotes consolidation of the true self.

6. Encourage the patient to see how she deprives herself of healthy interactions based on fear and outmoded behaviors. Giving credence to the need for interdependence in relationships that are neither psychologically nor physically traumatic conveys the therapist's soberly optimistic attitude that a stormy past can be weathered, the eating disorder can be faced down, and a healthier, more resilient sense of self can be found.

7. Engage the patient by talking about the meaning of food and eating in their lives. Avoid the temptation to see food as a four-letter word that can never be broached from a psychological perspective. This topic is often neglected in therapy but when it can be explored the patient reveals much about their psychological life. Stories about food and how it was used or misused in the family of origin shed light on core deficits and conflicts that the patient holds about nurturance, autonomy, and self-care.

CONCLUSION

Conceptualizing the major issues that occur in the middle phase of treatment aids the clinician as he or she walks with the patient on her journey. Psychotherapy is rarely a linear process in which the patient makes consistent gains without regression. In most cases the patients will make some forward strides and then plateau for a while in order to consolidate gains; in the majority of situations, small increments of progress will be followed by a backslide in either eating disorder behaviors or in another life domain. These occasions can be discouraging for both patients and therapist but a quotient of optimism may be maintained by pointing out to patients that lasting changing will occur, albeit incrementally, and almost always with difficulty.

In the middle phase of treatment, patients may complain that they are "always going over the same issues, round and round" and the clinician may silently share a similar sense of battle fatigue or ennui. At these times one is buttressed by the clinical wisdom that analogizes therapy to a spiral and not a circle. With each rotation around the spiral, one goes further and delves deeper. Observe how concerns may seem similar over time but new understanding and enhanced mastery occur with each circumlocution. The more one goes over the same material, and in many ways deepens one's appreciation of it, the more likely one is to have attained a sense of how multidetermined every problem in life inevitably is.

During these "plateau times" in the middle phase, therapists are most challenged to value our work and to remember that while much may not seem to be happening on the surface, containment and silent processing are ongoing. Thinking through some of the issues that are yet to be tackled—such as helping the patient attain greater intimacy in her personal life, feeling less ashamed of her healthy dependency on the therapist and others in her circle, and mourning the role that the eating disorder has placed in her life—serve as a "mental tickler file" for the clinician who must always keep in mind important issues that are yet to be discussed and worked through.

Being human, patient and therapist alike would sometimes like to see the work as further along than it may be. Unfortunately, patients may also need to interrupt the work in the middle phase because of financial pressures (i.e., third-party limitations) or internal prohibitions and conscious reluctances to push further. In these situations therapist and patient can take solace in the fact that a solid piece of work has been done and that at some future point the patient may want to do more. When treatment is conceptualized as a "chapter" of a person's life, implicit permission is given to the patient to honor and conclude the work that has been done and to reopen the book at some future point.

Goals during the middle phase are usually achieved in subtle ways. Like our patients, we therapists must also deal with our inner critic who is rarely satisfied with residual symptoms or an improved but far from perfect life at work or at home. A more realistic goal is to help the patient achieve an enhanced capacity to cope with the vicissitudes that confront all of us in life. Development of the "real, true self" that psychoanalyst Winnicott pinpointed as the goal of treatment is a lifelong project that requires acceptance of flaws, imperfections, and work left undone. And, just as Winnicott also described the "good enough" mother as the primary object or caretaker who imperfectly meets the needs of her child, therapist and patient must accept imperfection in each other and the work they do together.

The work of the middle phase can be simultaneously empowering and sobering as both therapist and patient face the illusion that a perfect, symptom free, pain free existence is just that—an illusion. We must welcome "being wrong" in the consultation room and make course corrections based on the patient's critique, sometimes at several points during a given hour. A poignant aspect of the middle phase necessitates that both members of the therapeutic dyad confront the exigencies of life that face us and, to some extent, become more comfortable accepting our limitations. We must recognize what we can and cannot accomplish or "bring forth" in one session, one treatment process, or in one lifetime. Ironically, this process of pruning enables one to bring forth and to grow what is most true to the self and force down and weed out what is false. The personal knowledge that supports the development of the true self will provide nourishment as the therapeutic journey enfolds, and the patient discovers that life can become "plenty good enough," indeed.

CHAPTER 3

Termination

The only part of the world that is wise about the proper time to push the young out of the nest are the birds, and even they take a calculated risk. But they're willing to do it.
—Elvin Semrad (cited in Rako & Mazer, 1980)

Realize that no matter how wonderful a situation may be, its nature is such that it must end.
—Dalai Lama (2002)

Little has been written about the termination phase of treatment for eating disorder patients. This likely reflects the fact that a significant number of patients have a relatively brief course of treatment that focuses primarily on symptom control. At least 30% of patients who enter treatment appear to respond to a short-term, behaviorally based treatment, get well, and move on with their lives (see Chapter 9). These patients leave treatment with an important set of tools for keeping the eating symptoms at bay (e.g., self-monitoring skills, affect regulation, relapse prevention methods), and the therapist and patient are likely to have spent less time discussing their relationship and the meaning of the treatment structure in the patient's life. In the termination of such a structured, short-term treatment, the final phase involves reviewing essential skills but puts less focus on process and assessment of what treatment and life goals were met or left unfinished in the therapy.

Limitations by third parties also may interfere with the treatment relationship so that issues usually addressed at time of termination are neglected. While termination ideally ushers in "the final stage of therapy" where "the eating disorder patient does not experience termination of therapy as she experienced separations in the past" (Kearney-Cooke, 1991, pp. 313–314), because "new internalizations" have taken place, to date research has not demonstrated the length of time or the process by which these new capacities to self-soothe and to become more autonomous and functional take place. The criteria for and timetable of termination with eating disorder patients are often left to the judgment of the therapeutic couple themselves if third parties (e.g., insurance companies, managed care personnel, family members) do not prematurely intervene. Under more ideal circumstances, clinicians may reasonably contemplate the factors that should be considered essential in concluding treatment and be prepared to mull over when the patient has truly reached "maximum clinical benefit." We must concomitantly question ourselves about the myriad of issues that might get in the way of timely termination and healthier separation.

For those of us who have done longer-term work with patients (i.e., from nine months to five or more years), experience reveals that in residential, hospital, and outpatient settings, both the therapist and the patient may resist ending treatment. As the late psychoanalyst and professor of psychiatry Dr. Elvin Semrad of Harvard University amusingly observed about the ambivalence when launching a child (or patient) from the protection of a safe haven, one must take a calculated risk when the fledgling is pushed out of the nest (Rako & Mazer, 1980). Given the array of psychological difficulties, psychiatric comorbidities, and potential lethality that affect eating disorder patients, it may be more difficult for therapists to take this calculated risk of suggesting termination because we fear an exacerbation or recrudescence of eating disorder symptoms. Additionally, having established an intimate bond with our patients over time, neither we nor they may want to bring to an end the one-time phase appropriate therapeutic symbiosis that launched and sustained the clinical process.

Adapting the humorous bumper sticker, "Insanity is hereditary: parents get it from their children," one might say that we therapists are prone to "catch the virus of therapeutic infinitude from our patients." While their symptoms may keep them from fully engaging in life and following through on the thousands of beginnings and endings inherent in living, so may we therapists avoid the losses and mourning that are inevitable when saying goodbye and seemingly pushing the fledgling out of the nest and into the world (Schlesinger, 2005).

Therapists who find themselves reluctant to let go must heed and find balm from the counsel of His Holiness the Dalai Lama who recognized that even the most wonderful life situations do come to an end. Living with this fact is made more difficult for therapists who idealistically and omnipotently wish to see our patients get "weller than well" (K. Menninger, Mayman, & Pruyser, 1963) before considering the therapy as completed. Not unlike a parent who is conflicted about the child who packs up to leave home to go off to boarding school, college, a new job, or a committed relationship, to make mistakes and face problems on his or her own, therapists can be reluctant to see our patients terminate out of fear of potential backsliding or unfinished therapeutic tasks. We may rationalize that they are not ready to go yet, and they may even agree that they are not able to meet life's challenges. While this is no doubt always true to some extent, therapists cling to fears about patients' futures out of their own separation angst. It then becomes difficult for us to hear when the patient

TABLE 3.1 The role of the therapist: Termination phase

- Review the entire course of treatment
- Underscore progress patient has made
- Help patient explore and honestly describe what treatment did *not* accomplish that she or he expected when it began
- Continue to elicit feedback of the patient's experience of therapist, especially noting disappointments, ambivalence, negative transferences, and anger
- Normalize the experience of letting go of and mourning the therapist
- Remind patient that coming to therapy was a part of their life's structure. Help patient adapt to "life without therapy" by asking what he or she will put in its place
- Explain concept of "treatment chapters." Give explicit permission to return or to seek other kinds of treatment or a different therapist in future
- Leave plenty of time to "say good-bye"

tells us that she has had enough therapy, is better, and wants to move on and try things on her own (Schlesinger, 1996).

Knowing when to stop is a matter of therapeutic judgment; emphasis must be placed on hearing and tuning in to the often subtle message that the patient is ready. It goes without saying that family members, the patient, and the therapist would like treatment to conclude with the eating disorder symptoms under perfect control, never to return again. In the majority of cases, this will remain an idealized fantasy and unachievable end point because many patients can get better but do not end therapy with perfect symptom control (see Table 3.1 for some likely reactions to ending and why more research should be done on this topic).

On the other hand, it is reasonable to expect that symptoms will be in much better control, the patient will have an improved attitude about what support systems will keep the symptoms in abeyance, and she or he will be able to use an assortment of concrete behavioral tools to continue to confront the symptoms (see Table 3.2 for a list of tasks that therapists should keep in mind while negotiating this phase with the patient). Patients must also have new psychological capacities to be able to take on the life tasks crucial to the developmental phase they are in to be considered fully ready to end therapy (see Chapters 4, 5, and 6).

Research suggests that patient and therapist should decide together when optimal improvement has been achieved at this particular phase in the patient's life (Firestein, 1978; Kupers, 1998; Wallerstein, 1986). The art of saying goodbye in therapy includes the capacity to differentiate between treatment goals and life goals (Ticho, 1972). When those obstacles that impeded the patient's full participation in the developmental life cycle (Erikson, 1950; Wallerstein & Goldberger, 1998) and that have significantly impaired quality of life have been surmounted (e.g., treatment goals), the patient is in an infinitely better place

TABLE 3.2 The therapist's termination tasks

- Focus on separation; remember that regression in the service of separation-individuation is the norm, not the exception, during termination phase
- Work with any relapses in symptomatic behaviors
- Help patient to maintain focus on termination even when relapses occur
- Understand backslides as an expectable consequence of moving toward termination
- Provide additional educational or cognitive/behavioral adjuvants, especially when relapses occur
- Emphasize difference between *treatment goals* and *life goals*
- Seek consultation for any therapeutic impasse; recognize that some patients may only be able to separate or terminate by devaluing or becoming angry with the therapist
- Remember that some patients are not able to terminate (i.e., "lifers"). This is not a failure of either patient or therapist but a manifestation of psychic structure, interpersonal need, or premorbid psychiatric illness
- Help patients and their support systems to accept future or ongoing therapeutic contact if there becomes a need

to make use of her inborn capacities and talents to chose what she wants to do and to be (life goals). Drawing upon Erikson's (1950) attribution to Sigmund Freud that the healthy human being is one who is able "to love and to work," I believe that the patient with an eating disorder is most ready to terminate when she or he is able to gainsay self-destructive eating symptoms, is able to care for himself and experience intimacy, and to enjoy his work and play. The patient also needs to be able to "listen and give a voice" to the true self, which the eating disorder has effectively silenced and precluded him from meeting his life goals (Kearney-Cooke, 1991, p. 315).

THE TIMING OF TERMINATION

When therapy is open-ended and arbitrary limits are not imposed by third parties, physical relocation, or other variables, the therapeutic couple must arrive at a mutual decision based on their judgment that optimum improvement has been achieved. Even when the therapy has gone on for years, it is wise for both parties to consider the current process as "only one treatment chapter" (Buchele, personal communication, 1995) because the patient may wish to continue at some later point. All treatment relationships are born and bred at a particular period of an individual's life, and the exigencies of personal development, as much as an exacerbation of symptoms, may catalyze a need for a patient to return for additional therapeutic work. This advice should be one of the explicit tasks of the therapist to underscore during the termination phase (see Table 3.2).

The common psychotherapeutic maxim, "The treatment is really not a treatment until it ends," reflects the clinical wisdom of how easy it becomes for some treatment relationships to continue indefinitely. There is a hazard in a gratifying therapeutic relationship that the work can "take the place of life" (Kupers, 1988; Schlesinger, 2005). Though the therapeutic couple may have a good sense that there has been significant improvement, they may avoid broaching termination because (1) separation is painful; (2) the intimate bond formed between therapist and patient is unique and gratifying to both; (3) fantasies develop that the results will not be long-lasting or will disappear after separation; and, in particular, (4) conflicts always ensue when acknowledging improvement, giving up the sense of loss of one's "old identity," accepting good things, and moving forward (see Chapters 7, 8, and 9).

Most studies of therapeutic outcome of eating disorders have looked primarily at the control of symptoms at the end of a period of treatment as a measure of good outcome (see Chapter 9 for a critique of this outcome literature). Certainly, therapist and patient must acknowledge that significant inroads in symptom control of disordered eating, excessive concern over body image, episodic bingeing and purging, and any form of self-vilification are made before one can be considered recovered and ready to end treatment. Operationally, however, other indicators may also point the way toward the time when termination should be considered. Notably, the patient's actual physical appearance is likely to have changed significantly. She or he will no longer be emaciated, appear sickly, or have some of the telltale signs of bulimia such as chipmunk facies or Russell's sign (see Tables 1.4 and 1.6). They will have more energy for life and appear happier, enthusiastic, and serene. They will be less likely to make the body a focus of their lives; for example, you will hear much less about the sense of "feeling fat," wanting a tummy tuck or other surgical procedures, and needing to exercise frenetically to "stay fit" or "take off inches" or "be strong." These differences may not have been totally extinguished but they will be fewer in number.

Even though many of the *external circumstances* under which patients enter treatment may not have changed, they will have a greater sense of resiliency when tackling stressors such as interpersonal conflict or a setback at school or at work. Their coping mechanisms will be expanded and recast; they have likely weathered some relapses in their symptoms without becoming demoralized. Indeed, the capacity to think about how one will deal with a relapse in the eating disorder or in another life domain is still another additional positive indicator of the significant work already done in treatment that leaves the therapist with a sense that termination may be in the offing (see Tables 3.1, 3.2).

After patients have completed a significant portion of psychological work, they have greater clarity in assessing the toll the eating disorder has taken on their lives and have an improved capacity to deal with painful feelings about their past. They are then in a better position to do the work of mourning. The story that the patient constructs of her or his life will have greater coherence;

there will also be fewer secrets held (e.g., the eating symptoms; comorbid psychological problems like alcoholism; knowledge in the family that the patient possesses but is not supposed to reveal), because the patient no longer needs to stay "hidden but in plain view" (see Chapter 4). Making sense of one's life includes understanding one's past and being able to forgive flaws, inadequacies, and even maltreatment rendered by others. One is also able to own one's own flaws and not simply see the worm in the other fellow's apple (e.g., projective identification, externalization, displacement).

All-in-all, eating disorder patients who are ready for termination will have accomplished much in the therapy process beyond control of their symptoms alone. In the best of scenarios, they will embody the capacities for healthful living that the late William Menninger termed the *criteria of emotional maturity*. This does not mean the person will be a perfect specimen of psychological health; even the idealization of what treatment can do must also be worked on for therapy to be considered successful. William Menninger's more benevolent and realistic list of criteria of the emotionally mature individual remain benchmarks for termination of treatment of eating disorder patients today (Menninger, 1964/1967). Consider whether or not your patient (1) is now able to function under difficult circumstances; (2) has attained a degree of flexibility and can weather change; (3) is relatively free of tensions and anxieties; (4) has the capacity to give rather than receive, and, what is more, enjoys being "a giver of good things" to others; (5) has friendships and generally gets along with others; (6) handles hostility and guilt more constructively than in the past, and more crucially; (7) has an expanded capacity to love.

Because psychotherapists tend to be our own sternest critics, one professional hazard that we face as termination nears is our professional satisfaction or dissatisfaction with our patient's accomplishments. Even as we are witness to the transformations that occur within the therapy process, so are we reluctant to hear our patients say either directly or between the lines that, "I've had enough therapy, for now."

As during other treatment phases, a good supervisor or consultant may play an essential role in helping the therapist recognize that the patient is now ready to leave because of her or his "flagging interest in treatment in favor of life outside" (Schlesinger, 2005, p. 118). Emotional maturity will signal a readiness to take the developmentally appropriate step of ending the treatment. As noted, this will manifest itself in the eating disorder patient's internalization of some new capacities to soothe the self and exercise her or his personal power and secure sense of the true self by leaving. Even though a desire to hang on to old ways will persist and the patient may avoid being pushed from the nest, she or he will have less fear in the future. Still, this is a time of complicated and inevitable emotional responses.

The struggle that both therapist and patient have in letting go may lend itself to feelings of anxiety, grief, and mourning, frequently cited affects in professional papers that address termination. While these feelings of loss, sadness, and

TABLE 3.3   Reactions frequently encountered during the termination phase

- Grief and sorrow
- Pride and achievement
- Competence and pleasure
- Excitement about moving on
- Separation anxiety
- Separation rage
- Disappointment and sadness
- Numbing (e.g., the avoidance of sadness or other feelings at the loss of therapy)
- Loss of energy, exhaustion (because of the psychological work of mourning)
- Fantasies and/or dreams of birth, rebirth, loss of control
- Fear or sense of vulnerability
- Acceptance of one's finitude, eventual death
- Conflicts acknowledging improvement, gains during treatment, and other successes

the desire to remain connected certainly occur for both participants, research on psychotherapy patients during the termination stage also demonstrates that positive feelings such as joy, pride, and a desire for new experiences are just as frequently encountered (Roe, Dekel, Harel, Fennig, & Fennig, 2006). One must encourage patients to speak to both sides of this complicated equation as they end the treatment (see Table 3.3).

In particular, therapists who are more satisfied with the outcome of treatment tend to elicit more positive responses from their patients and feel a greater sense of pride and accomplishment in their work. The research on termination has demonstrated that disappointment and other powerful feelings of regret or loss at termination must be reckoned with, including the loss of the meaningful relationship with the therapist. Those clinicians who support the patient's practicing of independence are able, however, to reflect positive gains made during the therapy; they are not envious of the patient's new feelings of competence, and this engenders a greater sense in their patients that "the therapy was helpful and that it led to positive change" (Roe et al., 2006, p. 79). In essence, while the task of the termination phase must include helping the patient accept loss, limits, and the pain inherent in any important separation, the positive reactions of pride, pleasure, excitement, eagerness, and gratitude must also be given their due by conscious recognition by both therapist and patient of the genuine transformation that has occurred.

Echoing Herbert Schlesinger's (1995, 1996, 2005) well-honed clinical advice that it is the therapist's duty to help the patient survive a positive change because owning one's progress and growth is always more difficult than it may appear, termination must be met with shared pleasure in what has occurred. Acknowledging therapeutic success engenders higher expectations in life as both quantitative and qualitative termination research studies of diverse patient populations reveal. As Roe and colleagues (2006) described, based on their own open-ended queries of 84 persons who terminated psychotherapy:

> A central factor contributing to positive feelings about termination was the actual implementation of a self-made and initiated decision that held the personal meaning of independence—the ability to end therapy. Participants frequently perceived this as an achievement that echoed the progress they made in therapy moving toward greater autonomy. The act of ending therapy was frequently experienced as therapeutic in itself. (p. 76)

I have found that a sense of humor is one of the best indicators of the patient's improvement. With new energies and perspective now available, the patient is able to stand back from their troubles and poke fun at themselves and at the therapist. This healthier channeling of the aggressive drive

> allows us to face reality and yet respond as if it were a game. . . . It (i.e., humor) can deflate without destroying; it can instruct while it entertains; it saves us from our pretensions; and it provides an outlet for feeling that expressed another way would be corrosive. (Vaillant, 1993, p. 73)

Ironically, when our patients can lampoon us, they are signaling that they have internalized the therapist as a good object.

Clinical Example

Shelby, a 40-year-old physician recovering from a long history of anorexia (see also Zerbe, 2001a), got quite a charge out of hearing my stomach rumble in the middle of one midmorning session and teased me about my own *internal hunger*, a term we had used to talk about her symptoms and early life experiences. Shelby also knew I had spoken about psychophysiological reactions in the therapist publicly so as to give others implicit and explicit permission to own foibles, countertransference reactions, and our own physiological states that may arise spontaneously during treatment.

As the treatment proceeded, this brilliant woman could sometimes bring me to tears by her imitations of me and impersonations of some notable authorities in her subspecialty who were also known to me. The capacity to "turn the tables" on those seemingly in the chair of authority was only one of Shelby's creative gifts as a raconteuse, but it only came alive as her physical condition improved.

Buttoning up her own voice and point of view as a child as her family of origin stayed glued to the television set or read books, Shelby was now taking stock of what had led her parents to stay silent, aloof, and seemingly self-involved. She now looked at the multiple roots of their dysthymia (i.e., she mentalized and mourned), and she had become less fearful of her anger and speaking her truth to me, albeit through the healthy medium of humor.

TASKS OF TERMINATION

Once the patient and therapist have decided that it is time to terminate, a date should be set. While patient and therapist have likely talked about the ending of therapy many times during the course of treatment, it is the actual setting of the date that makes the end real. As noted, the patient is likely to have a range of emotional feelings as the distinct issues of termination are worked through, and the therapist should keep these in mind so as to leave no stone unturned concerning the varied and unique affects that arise and are exposed within an individual as the process draws to a close.

The process of termination inevitably awakens feelings of separation anxiety, and consequently, regression in symptomatic behavioral patterns often occurs. If there is a recrudescence of eating disorder behavior or other self-destructive patterns, the patient and therapist may become unduly alarmed and avoid following through on the date they have set. While the actual date should never be set in stone (e.g., can be moved depending upon the therapeutic requirements), the therapist who recognizes that some regression is an inevitable part of termination is better equipped to help the patient accept the backslide, see it as a likely temporary phenomenon, and use it for additional therapeutic work. This is also a good time to underscore how future upheavals in life may exacerbate symptoms and to discuss the conditions under which the patient should reenter therapy or find other avenues or adjuvants for support.

Termination is also the only time in psychotherapy where one has an opportunity to look at what the structure of treatment itself meant to the patient. Whether the patient came several times a week, weekly, or even monthly, the very fabric of having ongoing meetings provided a psychological exoskeleton for the patient. Prepare the patient for this aspect of termination by exploring what other avenues of support (e.g., structure such as a volunteer job, hobby) she or he will rely on. As previously stated, sometimes the investment in life itself has become such a powerful force that the loss of the treatment structure will not need to be made explicit to the patient. The therapist will be listening for the many details of life that are taking the place of the therapy (e.g., new interests, friendships, marriage).

What follows below is a section of dialogue between a patient and me as the termination phase begins. Although an unanticipated turn of events has catalyzed the separation process, Jacqueline exemplifies many of the changes and growth surges one might listen for, and how a therapist might comment on some of these expectable issues brought about by her decision to leave treatment now. Her readiness to examine ways she has grown and even "moved beyond" her therapist in what is a crucial life domain for her might conjure up guilt about doing better. The therapist must also be prepared to address these conflicts directly or, in this case, by the metaphor of the patient's favorite hobby.

Clinical Example

Jacqueline is a 29-year-old administrator who decided to take a job in another city and pursue her lifelong dream of returning to school to get her master's degree in public health. Although Jacqueline never had to be hospitalized for anorexia, nonpurging subtype, which "morphed" into overt bulimia for five years, she experienced significant medical consequences (e.g., periodic hypokalemia; dysmenorrhea, osteopenia). She profited from group and individual sessions in her community. In fact, over her five years of outpatient treatment, Jacqueline was able to decrease the frequency of her individual therapy from twice weekly to once weekly sessions and had terminated from her therapeutic group 18 months before she decided to leave town. She then established ancillary supports by joining a reading group and made many friends as manifest symptoms diminished. She continued to see her primary care provider, a nurse practitioner with experience in treating eating disorders, thrice yearly for routine follow-ups. Jacqueline refused to take psychotropic medications because she insisted she wanted "to do the work by myself with the help of my team," and she surprised all of us who worked with her by rapid improvement in symptom control and eagerness to work on psychological issues that beguiled her.

Jacqueline is one of those hard-working, engaging patients whose motivation for change has helped her withstand any tendency to relapse over the past three years. She continued to work on many different psychological issues in order to insure her quality of life (see Chapters 5 and 9). As she gets ready to embark on a new professional direction and end the therapy, she makes some direct appraisals of where she has been and where she understands herself to be going.

After a few moments of catching up on what has gone on the week before, Jacqueline spontaneously turned her attention to aspects of her eating disorder. This therapeutic dialogue shows us some expectable termination issues.

> *Jacqueline:* It's interesting to me that I don't get so upset anymore. Things that used to stir me up at work happened this week. I didn't get angry. I didn't purge or restrict. I feel calmer.
>
> K.Z.: Might you say that you can better soothe yourself?
>
> *Jacqueline:* Exactly. It puts me in the mind of when I was a kid and could run home when I was upset and talk to my mother although she has been dead for years now. Those were the best times I ever had with her.
>
> K.Z.: It's almost like you can call upon a mother inside you when you are

upset or troubled and not have to turn to overexercising, throwing up, or even getting silent and going into your shell (internalization of a soothing object).

Jacqueline: You might find this really silly, but now when I get upset I just go home and work in my garden. I haven't told you yet but this year I plan to see if my green thumb holds out by planting *Euonymus fortunei* (better coping skills and self-soothing).

K.Z.: I've never even heard of that flower.

Jacqueline: (laughing) It's not exactly a flower; it's a shrub! I get a kick out of being able to teach you something that you obviously know absolutely nothing about.

K.Z.: You're taking a lot of pride in what you are learning and doing. (mirroring and communicative matching). You are finding that you can use your hobby to deal with everyday problems on the job. That's so much better than turning to the old symptoms! (Therapist comments on healthier defense mechanisms while including observations that there will be ongoing issues to deal with in life, at work, or school.)

Jacqueline: I am excited to get started with school and the new job. I know that they are both going to be challenges, especially doing both at the same time. That's new for me. It seems strange that I feel so happy and yet also a little sad because I know I won't be seeing you. I am really going to try and go it alone for a while and not get another therapist unless I feel I have to. (inevitable sadness about growth and ambivalence about change)

K.Z.: Letting go in therapy often comes with a mixture of emotions. You are excited but at the same time you are grieving our relationship and all that you are leaving behind. You are anticipating having lots to do that will fill up your day and give you structure that will help take the place of our work. (normalizes termination feelings)

Jacqueline: This is making me think about how I felt when my mother died. Even though I know you are not dying, it's not like I'll just be able to come in and tell you what is happening or what I'm doing. Do you think we could talk on the phone every now and then? I could drop you a card. (termination brings up earlier losses)

K.Z.: Of course we can certainly discuss that. I would like to hear how things are going and I don't have any problem with infrequent contact. But I also think we need to hear how some of the feelings of loss and letting go are coming back, reminding you of the death of your mother. We have to take these feelings seriously. Letting go in here brings up your prior experiences with loss—maybe not only your mother's death. It's not unlike what we have talked about so much in therapy: Present sometimes repeats the past. (More working through of current loss is an opportunity to reexamine earlier losses.)

EXPECTABLE REGRESSION AS TREATMENT ENDS

When one considers the impact of expectable regression and the need to think through what the loss of treatment means, the therapist is also prompted to review the relapse prevention plan and use any educational or cognitive-behavioral adjuvants to gainsay recrudescence of symptomatic behavior (Schlundt & Johnson, 1990; Westen, 2000; Zerbe 2007b). Reviewing the course of the treatment provides an opportunity for both participants to acknowledge what has and has not been achieved. If either the patient or the therapist is still beholden to unrealistic idealization of what therapy can accomplish, the opportunity for exploration of disappointments and failures must not be missed. On the other hand, when one is able to acknowledge the ambivalence, ups and downs, positive achievements, and work always left undone, the greater the opportunity for the patient to realistically grieve the treatment and proceed with her or his life.

Emotional closure of this type has been shown to have a profound impact on physiological as well as psychological variables. People who can express their feelings have been demonstrated to have improved immune functioning, greater capacity to begin and be satisfied with new jobs, and thrive in interpersonal relationships. When anger and hostility are not worked through, there are social and occupational consequences and a greater propensity toward stress related illnesses. Mutative factors which derive from the the expression of emotion are essential to healing and working through disruptions and loss (Goleman, 1995; Pennebaker, 1991, 1997; Edelman, 1992).

With so many tasks to keep in mind, it behooves the therapist to make sure that plenty of time is left to say good-bye. Clinicians have long noted that the same issues are present on the last day of treatment as on the first. This has led most authorities to note that termination, while a significant phase of the treatment process, has similar thematic content to the opening and middle phases. Bringing the patient back time and time again to the importance of "saying good-bye" keeps the mourning process undeniable but expressible.

Those individuals who cannot endure the pain of separation may abruptly and permanently interrupt the treatment without saying goodbye. In the majority of situations where patient and therapist have worked well together, the dynamic impact of the termination process will be felt by waves of sadness and grief and an expectable oscillation between affects, in particular anger, joy, pride, and regret (see Table 3.3).

As the agreed upon date of termination neared, Jacqueline continued to review a range of feelings about the treatment process and what she had gained. Sensing that her feelings were "laundered," meaning all too positive, a decision was made to gently confront Jacqueline with what she might be disappointed about in the therapy and try to tune in to expectable symptomatic regressions, frequent as they are after a termination date is set.

Clinical Example

Jacqueline: I was talking to Lance (her boyfriend) the other day. He tells me that he thinks I am an entirely new woman and gives my treatment, meaning you, the credit. He is helping me get ready to move and I am so excited that he will be able to come for weekend visits at least every month until he finds a job that suits him in the city. I know that during the week I will be too busy with work and school to think about him much. I have never been so excited in my life and I think I owe it all to you.

K.Z.: That sounds like a lot more credit than I deserve. I bet it makes you angry at both of us. After all, Jacqueline, you've done the work! (confronts the idealization and explicitly permits expression of negative feelings about the therapist)

Jacqueline: It's time to turn the tables on you, Dr. Z. You would tell me if I said such a thing that I was "getting defensive." When I think about all the things we have been through together—my refusing medication and your tolerating that discussion, the times that I would get so mad at you that I would just walk out of your office and slam the door, and the sense of hopelessness that I had of ever taming that ferocious Godzilla of an eating disorder—I can't help but think of you as some kind of magician or miracle worker.

K.Z.: Jacqueline, I am glad you are reminding us both of some of the difficult times. This "miracle worker" could make you quite angry when she pushed you to take the medications or didn't say what you appeared to need at the moment. (helping her acknowledge the therapist's inevitable lapses)

Jacqueline: Yeah, I guess you weren't so perfect after all. The difference is that now I can go home and complain to Lance when I think you are off base. I couldn't then. In the past, I'd just get frustrated and walk out or let you have it.

K.Z.: You let me have it and, let's face it, I couldn't always fix it. We both had to work hard to tame Godzilla. I do wonder as we get ready to say goodbye if you have some disappointment about some things that we could never "magically fix" or put together again. (encouraging her unabashed appraisal of what she didn't get from therapy that she may have wanted, consciously and unconsciously)

Jacqueline: Maybe so. Especially with my dad. Sometimes when I am with Lance I remember how you and I so often talked about how my dad and I just never connected. I worried that I wouldn't know how to talk to a guy because Dad and I were so distant. Yet I feel this yearning, this love when Lance and I are together. We looked up at the sky the other night and he told me about Cassiopeia. As good as it felt, as safe as he makes me feel when we are together, it also feels so strange because I never had any moment like that with my father.

K.Z.: This "Kassy" couldn't pull out of the hat a good relationship with a father that Jacqueline always wanted. (Picking up on the innuendo of the therapist's nickname [i.e., Cassiopeia] that ties the interaction between Lance and Jacqueline to the therapist directly. The therapist then uses the story as an opportunity to highlight the deidealization that is occurring and the patient's sense of earlier loss.)

Jacqueline: (more soberly) Maybe there is more stuff in that "black box" of me that I need to look at. It did help to talk about Dad, but you really couldn't make it the relationship that I wanted it to be. It helped me when you suggested that I read Jane Fonda's autobiography *My Life So Far* (2005) because she talks so much about her father and their problems. But my story is different from hers. She grew to love and understand her dad. I envy her that.

K.Z.: It's a big step when we can acknowledge envy or jealousy of what someone appears to have that we don't. Maybe most importantly, I couldn't make that particular story of yours have a happy ending. Knowing that it is hard to face disappointments and leaving at the same time, I have wondered if things are always going as well as you tell me they are, especially with your symptoms. (confronts gently the tendency to make the ending sound "too good to be true")

Jacqueline: I haven't wanted to tell you but I have been restricting a little bit more and purging, too. I don't think it is out of control but it is definitely worse.

K.Z.: That kind of recurrence of symptoms is not uncommon when you are getting ready to terminate. I know that you will be tempted to feel that it is a sign of failure. I am really proud that you can tell me about it. (normalizing while encouraging truth telling)

Now let's look at ways that we can ratchet up your relapse prevention plan and maybe get some of those symptoms under better control. You have already taken the most difficult step, Jacqueline. You have told me about the relapse. You have also been brave enough to tell me about the ways in which our work together has been disappointing to you. (preparation for cognitive-behavioral adjuvants; see Yager, 2007a, 2007b).

WHEN THIRD PARTIES DISRUPT TREATMENT

Most therapists and many patients and their families have had the experience of being told when to end treatment by a third party. Since the mid-1980s, insurance carriers and managed care companies have arbitrarily put a limit on the number of inpatient days and residential days, outpatient sessions, and medical and psychiatric conditions covered by a policy. Increasingly, patients also fear garnering a psychiatric diagnosis lest they face the additional stigma of being denied medical insurance or a disability policy down the road. One result of the incursions by third parties is the genuine limitation that patients and those who care for them face in securing adequate treatment.

Some tenacious individuals have prevailed in securing necessary benefits despite significant odds. Occasionally an invested clinician has been able to wrangle sufficient benefits in a particular case. Persistent family members and patients have also sought legal counsel to fight for benefits that they are entitled to because of the understanding under which they bought the policy. In other fortuitous circumstances, an employer has "gone to bat" and prevailed upon the company's insurer so that the loved one has been able to receive the necessary treatment (see Zerbe, 1996a for a case in point).

Unfortunately, these scenarios occur more commonly for diseases such as cancer, kidney failure, or severe injury than they do for psychiatric illnesses, particularly an eating disorder. Despite all of the known medical and psychiatric risks that can occur (see Chapter 1, 4, 5, 6, and 9), a psychiatric illness is still not always viewed as a "real disease." Until parity is legislated, and enforced, and loopholes are closed for psychiatric conditions, all too often treatment will be terminated prematurely (i.e., before the patient has achieved significant symptom control and is fully engaged in living their life; see Chapter 9 for a critical look at what constitutes "good outcome" for an eating disorder).

Before the clinician goes along with the limitations imposed by any third party, steps must be taken to insure that the patient, family members, and managed care personnel be given all of the facts. For risk management purposes, it is incumbent for the clinician to document the imminent dangerousness (i.e., suicidality or homicidality) and the potential short-term lethality and long-term medical and psychiatric complications of eating disorders. In particular, in patients who have anorexia nervosa, the sixfold increase in suicide must be noted, even though the reasons for this tragic outcome in these patients remain unknown (Hsu, 1990). After all of the pertinent information has been explained and fully documented to all involved in the clinical record (i.e., patient, family, members of multidisciplinary team, managed care personnel), some carriers will automatically launch an appeal process if benefits are denied.

Providing pertinent scientific papers and published expert opinion is yet another intervention that the clinician may use to underscore the gravity of the patient's particular situation and educate those in the decision-making process about the complexities and consequences of the eating disorder. At the very least, I recommend that clinicians keep a file of published papers that summarizes such issues as medical complications, mortality statistics, and long-term outcomes, in addition to the latest edition of the American Psychiatric Association's "Practice Guidelines" (2006) to eating disorders. The materials may be faxed or sent by registered mail to the insurer. In these ways, the clinician is doing all that he or she can do to help inform and educate those in a position to grant benefits or waive restrictions. These individuals often have limited experience with psychiatric diagnosis and, what is more, may be unaware of the full range of issues that accompany eating disorders.

By so doing, the clinician is advocating for her or his patient. I also recommend that whenever possible, the patient take on the fight with the third party for their treatment. Some patients or invested loved ones have secured significant additional benefits by writing letters, seeking legal counsel, calling or writing their insurance commissioner, state and federal representatives, and the like. Such steely steps auger for a better long-term prognosis, of course, because the patient is taking responsibility for her or his own life, has moved away from a position of denial of the illness, and is able to externalize (or project) the heretofore self-directed aggression onto a new "bad object." Most of us who have treated eating disorder patients since the 1990s have been deeply moved by memorable situations in which the patient, a spouse, or a parent has been able to turn the tide on their or their loved one's own behalf and taught us an important life lesson about standing up to tyranny, taking back our power, and going after what we need to make our lives better and more satisfying (Zerbe, 1993/1995a; 1996a; 2001a).

The downside of directly tackling a third party is that it is all too easy to up the ante psychologically and make someone or something other than one's self "the designated enemy." For patients to heal and to have a healthy, successful termination, they must be able to own their own aggression and express anger, particularly when it has gone underground and been displaced onto the manifest symptom of their self-destructive eating disorder. While the therapist must support and champion the patient and the family's actions in securing benefits from third parties, we must also be mindful so as to not collude with the human tendency to make "the other" into an enemy. This splitting maneuver can quickly turn on us when we ourselves do not accede to the patient's demands (e.g., setting a target BMI; saying "no" to a request). It behooves us to bend over backwards to help the patient be fair to all parties with whom they have a reasonable disagreement and to understand the position that another human being is in (e.g., case manager). This also helps build the patient's capacity for empathy as much as it eschews the tendency to make "an evil empire" out of an insurance carrier.

Because treatment scholarships and very low cost care are only occasionally available, clinicians who treat eating disorders must have at their fingertips a range of community resources, low fee clinics, and an ever expanding set of bibliographical and Internet references, should treatment be artificially interrupted by a third party for financial reasons alone. The insurer may express the view that medical necessity is not met (as frequently happens when weight or laboratory values are normal), and in these situations it is also incumbent for the clinical team to *educate* the insurer as to how many eating disorder patients may appear to be healthy or "in control" when they are not. Some clinicians also make it a priority to take one or two very low fee cases into their practice. This is more difficult to do with an eating disorder case than a medically stable depressed or anxious patient, unless the eating disorder patient has access to ongoing medical backup (e.g., laboratory studies, primary care clinician, medical hospitalization if severely ill).

To avoid unwittingly traumatizing the patient, sufficient time must always be given in order to say good-bye, particularly when extenuating circumstances beyond the patient's or the clinician's control interfere with accomplishing more work. Even though such premature terminations cause significant anguish for both therapist and patient, it is important to remember that therapeutic work can be done until the final hour. At the very least, the patient has the opportunity to practice a healthier way of leave taking and acknowledging limits. Clinical trials of time limited psychotherapies have also clarified that sudden, significant gains can be incurred by means of brief "treatment chapters," so long as therapist and patient are realistic about limitations of time, have clear goals, and express mutual respect for each other (Malan & Della Selva, 2006; Schlesinger, 2005).

Clinical Examples: Positive and Negative

Joshua, age 21, was referred by his outpatient therapist, sports medicine physician, and primary care clinician to a residential treatment setting for evaluation of severe, refractory bulimia. A gymnast since his early teens who had high professional goals for himself, Joshua angrily entered residential treatment for the first time at age 18 for severe cachexia secondary to overexercise and restrictive eating. He improved considerably and was discharged to the same outpatient team where he remained in recovery until the present episode of a severe relapse. This episode was precipitated by the breakup of a serious romance and rejection from graduate school. Joshua had developed the true self function of deciding upon a professional path; he completed his RN but wanted to become a nurse practitioner and eventually practice in a sports medicine clinic or in private practice with athletes. He was devastated when he failed his first attempt at admission to a topnotch program for his master's in nursing during the same week his girl friend ended their relationship.

On several occasions during the first three months of this current residential treatment, episodes of gradual refeeding and educational group therapies led to improved psychological functioning, but Joshua's insurance carrier tried unsuccessfully to pull the plug on treatment. Fortunately, Joshua's father was squarely in support of the treatment and his son's psychological development. Although proud of his son's notable athletic achievements and desire for additional academic accomplishment, Joshua's father was realistic about the potential lethality of his eating disorder and sought legal counsel when the insurance carrier threatened to stop treatment.

This father's employer backed up the father: Human resource personnel opposed the insurance carrier's denials because they had purchased the particular policy with an understanding that there would be mental health coverage. Their challenges eventually carried the day. As Joshua improved and was discharged from residential care and entered partial hospitalization and eventually was followed only by his outpatient multidisciplinary team, the insurance carrier again threatened to curtail benefits. Joshua's father and the team members worked in tandem to send letters and pertinent journal articles about medical consequences and long-term lethality to those in a position to deny benefits.

Each time the team and the father fought back as a united front, benefits were reinstated. However, Joshua was his own best advocate. On several occasions he wrote to the case manager at the insurance company about his need for treatment, including his understanding of the expectable ups and downs that he was having.

Joshua's case is notable for the difference that positive, tenacious efforts can make with a third party when one has the backing of the patient, a concerned family member, legal counsel, the organization or business that buys the policy, and knowledgeable treatment personnel who are willing to advocate and not take an initial "no" for the ultimate answer. By standing firm and repeating that they were not trying to be threatening, simply insisting on what was their due, those in Joshua's court reframed the issues to be about Joshua's care. They underscored the extensive therapeutic literature on the morbidity and mortality of eating disorders. They successfully argued that the dollars saved by the successful treatment would be cost effective in the long term. I have described elsewhere another case of how patient and therapist can work together with managed care personnel to secure additional treatment benefits based on emerging data about the cost effective nature of psychiatric care for a range of emotional disorders (Zerbe, 1996a).

Madeleine, age 15, was admitted to an inpatient unit after nine months of severe, restrictive anorexia nervosa. One of the antecedents of this patient's eating disorder appeared to be her parents' marital separation. Within the structured environment of three meals a day, an enriched activity therapy program, and individual and group therapy sessions, this adolescent gained weight quickly. In art therapy, she began to cut out pictures of the latest movie icons and pop music stars and put them on the walls of her hospital room.

At a family conference, the social worker and treating psychiatrist reviewed Madeleine's progress. Both of her parents came to the "family week" sessions and appeared to be pleased with their daughter's progress. They were actively engaged and interested in the educational and therapeutic meetings held. Treatment team members were taken aback when Madeleine's father called and said he would no longer support treatment and would take his daughter home the following week.

This father complained that his wife "felt lonely" without Madeleine at home. They viewed their daughter's newfound interest in boys, as evidenced by the pictures on her wall, as salacious and destructive. In this case, at least part of Madeleine's plight can be understood as that of the parentified child who must fulfill the psychological needs of one or both parents. Treatment team members were left to work through the loss of the patient after repeated telephone conferences and expressed concern about potential regression went unheeded. Termination was instituted by a third party, the parents, who in all other respects seemed to provide caring and structure for their child.

Angelica, age 60, began psychotherapy for bulimia nervosa and a history of domestic violence. Divorced for 15 years, she was alienated from her daughter and two sons who sided with their father, even as they recognized that his verbal and physical abuse had led to the demise of their parents' relationship. Angelica's therapist quickly formed a bond with this patient despite the unusual circumstances under which the treatment began; the patient's wealthy brother and sister-in-law told Angelica that they would only attempt to rectify the alienation that "you have created with your children" and "continue to subsidize your apartment and hobby of animal rehabilitation" if she would capitulate by beginning therapy.

The savvy therapist established a contract wherein the brother paid for the twice to three times a week sessions (because of the patient's financial limitations) but knew in advance that there would be no sharing of information in order to protect Angelica's confidentiality. According to Angelica, her brother, "has tried to interfere with my treatment before" and "always wants information about me, just like he did when I was a kid and even a married woman." Angelica's history of trauma was extraordinary; despite significant professional accomplishments and superior intellect she could not function at a job because of severe anxiety. The therapist learned over a period of two years that this patient attempted to "treat" her anxiety, traumatic memories, and sleep disorder with alcohol and her eating disorder. However, when Angelica came to the sessions, she was always sober and the therapy led to surprising shifts in the eating disorder behavior and in Angelica's personal life. For the first time in many years, she began to work as a dental assistant, joined two groups for spiritual development, and began dating a widower.

Angelica's brother learned of his sister's romance by chance. While there had been no history of overt incest in this family, Angelica's therapist certainly wondered why her brother seemed so threatened and angry about a new development that would give his sister a new opportunity for improved quality of life and greater independence from him. The brother was of a different religious faith from Angelica's new partner, and the potential for an exogamous marriage with the widower may have been one factor that had bearing on his reassertion of control. He once again pulled the plug on payment for therapy as he had done in the past when his sister improved.

At the time of termination, Angelica did not have funds to continue, even though she had found this episode of treatment extraordinarily useful. She told the therapist that their years of work together had been "like going to graduate school, writing my thesis, and completing it." She decided that she would take a break from the treatment and not capitulate to her brother's demands to see someone else he had found and "approved of" for her. She joined two local support groups to address her addictions and began classes to convert to her partner's religion.

After six months, Angelica recontacted her therapist. She decided to return to weekly sessions, which she could now afford, having made some necessary adjustments in her lifestyle. The additional structure of working a few additional hours on the weekends in a bookstore increased her feelings of autonomy. She no longer took any financial help from the brother. The therapist made a significant reduction in her weekly fee, and the work continued unabated for two years, at which time Angelica married the widower and moved to another state.

In this unusual termination scenario, individuation from the family of origin was facilitated by an untimely rupture of the therapeutic bond. At the time of the first termination, Angelica poignantly told her therapist,

> I think I am actually ready for a sabbatical because of the work we have done. I am angry with my brother but I can understand that his own conflicts and emotions must be getting in the way (i.e., Angelica exhibits empathy and capacity for mentalization of her brother's plight). I have relied upon his financial help way too long, but now I don't have to because I feel that I have hope for life, and my symptoms are under much better control (i.e., greater autonomy and sense of self). Besides, what about the old adage, "living well is the best revenge?" (a healthier, non-self-punitive expression of aggression)

The therapist was moved by the patient's increased ego autonomy and her ability both to reflect on her brother's state of mind (i.e., primary reflective function), and to find other sources of emotional sustenance (i.e., newly achieved healthy dependency on her chosen life partner and support groups).

DISAPPOINTING TERMINATIONS

Clinicians who treat eating disorder patients are likely to experience a significant number of situations where treatment may get off to a good start and then abruptly end. On other occasions, the treatment may be going along for years, often with the expectable ups and downs of any process where difficult issues, negative transference, unresolved traumas, and unconscious repetitions from the past, are worked on. Then, the process gets derailed and despite work by both parties, the decision is made to interrupt with the current clinician, or transfer to another therapist, or simply curtain treatment altogether.

In the professional literature it is much more common to present cases of so-called treatment success than treatment failure. In controlled trials of medications, for example, negative results seldom make it into the research literature. In psychotherapy journals and books there are some notable exceptions, but for the most part we clinicians would much rather talk about the patients we help than the patients we may feel we do harm to or who leave treatment in an unsatisfactory mode or with a chip on their shoulder.

In these circumstances we feel disappointed, confused, bewildered, and often self-accusatory.

Where have we gone wrong, we ask ourselves? Sometimes therapists will call upon a trusted colleague to help sort out the details. I spent over 20 years of my career at the Menninger Clinic in Topeka, Kansas, and there I learned that even the most experienced and respected therapists had disappointing terminations of this kind. When these proverbial treatment stalemates occurred, staff members called upon esteemed faculty members to help us process through some of these most challenging situations that would leave us feeling impotent, smarting, and sometimes reeling with anger. Usually the patient would demand transfer to another multidisciplinary team in the hospital or insist upon beginning therapy with a brand new psychotherapist. This would frequently leave the current team members or psychotherapists questioning their own competence at the work and feeling extremely self-critical.

In Chapter 2, I cited the work of my former teacher, Irwin Rosen who, as the Director of the Adult Outpatient Department at Menninger for many years, was one of the most frequently sought after senior clinicians in such situations. The therapist or a team were being put in the unenviable position of being "the bad object" (see Chapter 2). Dr. Rosen had both an intuitive and theoretical understanding of what it feels like for the therapist to be devalued, mortified, and insulted even as one is trying one's best to do good. After he reviewed the details of what may have sent a particular treatment off track, Dr. Rosen would also help the treaters involved in the case look at what had been achieved during the period of time the patient and the individuals involved had worked together (Rosen, 1982–1990, personal communications).

Dr. Rosen would often evoke the metaphor of the treatment journey when he told the patient, the therapist, and the team members the following parable:

> You have all come a certain distance on the road together. Now it seems that your roads must diverge. The paths you have walked together have been important and you may look back on it in years to come and see it differently than you do now. It appears that you have gone as far on your journey together as you can for now.

With this sage advice, Dr. Rosen was empathizing and engaging the benevolent superego of the treatment staff (or the therapist) because only then could we begin to look more closely at what we might later be able to do differently.

Dr. Rosen might then go on to offer a didactic explanation; the patient had a need to make us into the "bad object." He might also comment on how some of Freud's patients were "wrecked by success." Our patient was simply unable to take advantage of what the psychotherapist or treatment was offering. In most cases, the clinicians could then arrive at some possible hypotheses about the dynamics in the individual's life that led to the stalemate or "treatment wreckage." Still another way to understand these kinds of abrupt terminations results from "relinquishing the self-sustaining but intensely conflicted" bond with an early caretaker. This leads to "intense anxiety and frequent depressive affect . . . the groundwork is laid during separation-individuation which is made especially difficult by the particularly close and ambivalent tie of the child to the mother" (Levy, Seelig, & Inderbitzin, 1995, p. 653). In other words, some patients will have struggles taking in the metaphoric "good fuel" of a particular treater at a given time because of early, profound difficulties in attachment. In other situations, our consultant helped us sort out our countertransference "blind spots" or "dumb spots" that got in the way of going further with the patient on her or his journey (Bernstein & Severino, 1986).

The important thing for all readers to remember is that treatment failures happen to all of us. Rarely does one therapy process take care of every psychological need, especially in the case of a severe problem such as an eating disorder. As more therapists write about their personal treatment experiences (Daniels, 2001; Guntrip, 1975; Little, 1990), we learn more about the inevitable gaffs, issues left untouched, and need for new and different therapeutic experiences, even among the well-known and revered in our field. From reading and listening to what seasoned psychotherapists do to further one's own personal therapeutic work, the clinician can more easily embrace the fact that no treatment "does everything" and what may feel temporarily disappointing with a patient may bring forth fruit down the road.

Dr. Rosen's comments resonate on a deeper level now as I am further along in my professional development, and have weathered my share of personal and professional losses and transitions. Few people accompany each other all the way along life's journey; roads inevitably depart. When psychotherapy reaches a stalemate, it is essential for the therapist to take stock of those "blind spots" and "dumb spots" that get in the way of going further with the patient; it is just as important to avoid a quest for therapeutic perfection.

Termination in such circumstances may feel as much of a failure to the patient as it does to the therapist. Given that the curative factors in any psychotherapy process remain unknown to us, so do the deeper reasons for what may cause a treatment to go off-track and be deemed unsuccessful. The therapist is left holding the bag or trying to contain and process what might have gone better. This is always a useful exercise, and particularly so when one has a trusted consultant or supervisor with whom to go over the case material in depth (as I suggest in almost every chapter!).

One is forced to appreciate something novel or challenging and "learn from our mistakes" (Casement, 2002). On the other hand, given the vicissitudes of life itself, and what we know of the value of multidisciplinary work and integrated treatment, individuals do have the capacities to get new and helpful things from different individuals with different personalities and skill sets. Hence the benefit of suggesting transfer to another therapist of different sex, personality, training, or theoretical point of view. Although the students I train seldom believe me when I first tell them this fact, I have also had to eat more than my share of slices of humble pie when I have passed a treatment process that bottomed out with me to a resident or other junior colleague and just sat back and watched as that therapeutic dyad process went swimmingly! What may be perceived as a treatment failure or stalemate in the short run may ultimately benefit the patient as the following case examples from my practice attest.

Clinical Examples

Patrick was a 21-year-old son of a prominent author who began treatment for substance abuse, bulimia nervosa, attention deficit disorder, and "feelings of failure in everything I do." This young man made considerable progress with twice weekly psychodynamic psychotherapy and medication management to the point of returning to college and getting a job to partly support himself rather than turning to his family for emotional and financial sustenance. Patrick seemed to be making extraordinary gains in coming to understand that he had different talents from those of his idealized father who, in the fashion of a narcissistically brilliant and self-preoccupied overachiever, had never paid very much attention to his only son.

With the eating disorder, substance abuse problem, and attention deficit disorder well under control with supportive interventions and medication management, Patrick was actually doing quite well in school and at his job when, like his complaints about his father, he became extremely devaluing of women. Specifically, he began to miss sessions, castigate the therapist for being repeatedly off base, sarcastically comment on the treatment frame (i.e., need to pay for missed sessions), and so forth. Although I confronted Patrick about these behaviors and noted the change in our former working relationship, he became all the more mistrustful and seemingly "wrecked by his success." He called and said that he would no longer be coming for sessions but would get his medication from his primary care doctor. Although I urged a brief termination process to say good-bye, even if it were for just a meeting or two, Patrick refused.

In this case, it seemed as though treatment might have done Patrick more harm than good; he had exchanged what he called his "miserable symptoms" and his self-abnegation for the narcissistic personality attributes that mirrored what I knew from hearing about his father. In fact, what was particularly troubling was the sense that Patrick had "morphed" into a version of his father.

Despite what I felt were my best efforts to get Patrick to look at what was happening to him and how he was ultimately undermining himself, Patrick was unreachable by me. Left feeling that the treatment had created a monster, I was reminded of Freud's sobering admonition that psychotherapeutic results can initially appear to be too good to be true. In Patrick's case, this resulted in greater difficulty in establishing and maintaining a masculine identity than I had heretofore imagined. Perhaps a male therapist would have had better success in helping the patient establish healthier identifications and work through characteristics of his sadistic, narcissistic father. With a female therapist at this point in his life, Patrick had to assume the role of an "uber-man," who like his father, consciously, pretentiously, and argumentatively, enjoyed spoiling relationships with women.

Irene, a married, childless, 40-year-old dentist who came to thrice weekly psychotherapy for four years was able to curtail abuse of over-the-counter diuretics and prescribed thyroid medication, exercise addiction, and periods of self-starvation. This treatment incorporated aspects of a "corrective emotional experience" (Alexander, 1956; Alexander & French, 1946) wherein Irene would bring pictures from her childhood, draw and create collages of her emotional experience to share, and later invited the therapist to office openings and family events (which I chose to analyze but not to partake of).

For the duration of our work together, Irene wondered if she would ever be able to leave treatment because "you are like the mother I never had." In fact, Irene's mother had died when she was a child and we spent much time working on the multiple reactions and suppressed, angry feelings she had for her mother for dying. These could never be expressed directly in the family of origin but were very much alive in the transference relationship with me (see Chapter 8). I came to believe that this would likely be a treatment that would go on for many years because Irene, now clinically stable, seemed to be deriving great benefit by coming, talking, and processing her life that was becoming more full. For example, she and her husband were considering expanding their family by becoming foster parents (see Chapter 5) or by adopting rescue pets. These activities appeared to represent a positive identification wherein she could now mother as she felt cared for in the treatment; her greater vitality and vibrancy seemed to be promoting sublimation of earlier aggressive energies directed against the self in her eating disorder.

Imagine my surprise when Irene walked in one Monday morning for her regular hour and began shouting about what she was not getting from the therapy that she felt she needed. All of a sudden, and without any warning, I became a very bad object. A consultation with a trusted colleague helped me to see that this was a necessary development in the treatment, and I pursued the path of trying to help Irene express her feelings as fully as possible. Not surprisingly, some of her eating disorder symptoms recurred. Even though I thought we were working well with both the symptomatic expressions and dynamic meanings behind her relapse, Irene began to insist that she was "going nowhere" and requested referral to another therapist.

In what felt like a cruel blow, she was particularly apt to zap me where it hurt: She read widely in the field of psychodynamic psychotherapy and began to tell me that supportive and expressive therapy had no value for her. She wanted cognitive-behavioral therapy (CBT). Even though I had included aspects of CBT, interpersonal therapy (ITP), and psychodynamic principles into her treatment, pointing out these facts only made me feel defensive, seemingly "full of yourself" to her, and added to the belief that "coming to see you is throwing good money after bad." Eventually, I could see no way out of what was quickly becoming a therapeutic stalemate and advised Irene to seek treatment with a cognitive-behavioral expert, leaving the door open for continued expressive treatment down the road with me or (more likely) someone else.

Agnes, age 25, was referred for consultation because her cognitive-behavioral psychotherapist felt she might need hospitalization. This patient had also struggled with anorexia nervosa since age 15 but had made notable progress with the referring clinician. Nonetheless, she never achieved more than 85% average body weight and was amenorrheic and osteopenic; her husband of two years complained of sexual difficulties in the marriage and threatened to divorce Agnes unless she "could get it more together and be a better partner." Agnes entered the hospital and achieved a stable BMI in three months.

For over a year Agnes saw both the cognitive-behavioral therapist and me for weekly outpatient psychotherapy sessions after discharge from the hospital. The cognitive-behavioral therapist is a psychologist in my community whom I deeply respect. We communicated weekly. He continued to address issues related to the patient's manifest symptoms, but we both began to focus independently on masochistic patterns in the marriage. We repeatedly suggested a marital process for the couple which Agnes apparently welcomed but her husband refused. Both of us therapists began to wonder who really held the power in this family and the meaning behind the need for such interpersonal misery within this couple.

Why did they remain married if they were so unhappy? What role was Agnes's eating disorder playing in keeping her in an asexual role that also helped her husband in some unknown way? If he was unwilling to get into therapy, would persistent but low-intensity confrontation eventually help Agnes to see how he might be needing her to stay in the "sick role" because he had more psychological difficulties than were overtly apparent?

As Agnes began to consciously entertain these questions with our joint and concerted efforts, her husband "decided" to take a job in another city and the treatment ended. We were left to wonder if this occurred only for external reasons or, more likely, because of unconscious needs on the husband's part to interrupt the treatment based on anxiety he had about what would happen if his wife truly improved, became more sexual, and was a more available and emotionally healthier partner in the marriage (see Chapter 7).

I choose not to elaborate on my hypotheses about why these "disappointing terminations" ended in the way they did or at the time they did other than what I include in the examples themselves. My hope is to convey by these personal examples that none of us is immune from situations in which (1) we would welcome a better termination and (2) have processes suddenly go sour. Readers are left to speculate for themselves what might have happened and why. In describing interventions where I was totally off base or by including some cases of my own that did not conclude positively or even with the feeling I had done my best work, and much was left unresolved, I hope to convey that we so-called "experts" who write, teach, and consult have our share of failings and failures. A workshop participant years ago put what I am trying to get across in this book best: "When you tell us about your cases, your glitches, and your goofs, it makes me feel less bad about my own. It also makes it easier to get back on the horse and do the work I like doing, Kassy."

At those moments I am reminded of another teacher from Menninger, the late Dr. Peter C. Novotny. Dr. Novotny was the kind of clinician who was always learning new techniques and principles to help his patients improve. He was a psychoanalyst, but he had incorporated behavioral techniques and was an expert in Bowen systems theory. From these diverse perspectives, he reminded his students that when a treatment appears to hit a roadblock, "it only means that you can't go any further *now*. In a year or two, you may have the skills to help this particular patient or someone similar" (Novotny, personal communication, 1981). This benevolent but true advice serves clinicians well because it leaves the future open for both therapist and patient.

SATISFYING TERMINATIONS

Termination involves the reliving, reworking, and taking stock of the ground that has been covered in the previous therapeutic work. This facilitates the mourning process; it provides new opportunities for the patient to look at what has and has not been achieved. Feelings of loss, separation, and abandonment inevitably arise. Patients have a new opportunity to talk about what has positively unfolded. Sometimes the patients will even note changes observed in the therapist over a period of time and thereby once again demonstrate new abilities to speak truth to power, a notable quality of the expanding "true, real self."

The timing of termination can take both participants by surprise; the amount of work seems to be "enough already" and the process feels like it has "jelled." In effect, the patients got what they came for and are prepared to push forward on their own.

Eloquently expressed by psychoanalyst Martin Silverman (1987), patients come to treatment ready to establish

> wishfully passionate, but disappointing, dissatisfying, insufficiently fulfilling, and even painful relationships with the key persons of their past (and with the present) lives within which their core problems formed. They do this not only in a quest for mastery and for a hopefully new and better outcome but also . . . in the hope of obtaining active control over what they previously had experienced passively and helplessly. (p. 285)

When those self-defeating tendencies that block patients from realistic ambitions and obtaining satisfactions and achievements are relinquished, they are ready to give us up. However, the beauty of growth has the potential to upset the applecart.

Even change for the better is experienced as a threat to the self and to one's autonomy; termination implies that the patient may still be ambivalent about her or his growth but is able to withstand, anticipate, and to come extent, embrace it. Because fear of change is never totally resolved, in part because life itself is so unpredictable, still another criterion for termination is the patient's acceptance that these fears of progress are "universal and ubiquitous" and in the future, "[changes] will come about only through his own initiative; change requires personal effort" (Castelnuova-Tedesco, 1989, p. 112). In essence, patients give up the fantasy of the therapist's perfectibility, magical and omnipotent control of the change process, and they take on more active roles in their lives. As in the case examples that follow, patients are more able to deal with anxieties that accompany success in the many forms it will appear in their lives. The patient is less fearful about opening their eyes and ears to life because they are less self-protective and "grasp that both influence and actual change . . . are essential for growth—and if it is to occur—for cure" (Castelnuovo-Tedesco, 1989, p. 116). They are sometimes even able to grasp and comment on real and perceived changes in their therapist.

Clinical Examples

Kate, now 32 and the mother of three adopted children, made the decision to leave treatment when her husband took a job in another city. This particular termination was also prompted by my decision to leave the setting where I worked to move to another state. In a sense, there was a mutually agreed upon time to terminate based on each participant's reality factors. It was unlikely, because of the changes in location, that Kate would ever be able to have another "treatment chapter" with me should she desire one.

Kate's therapy had naturally decreased from thrice weekly during the four years of intense work to less frequent weekly or even twice a month meetings. Her eating disorder symptoms were in complete remission, and she was experiencing much more of a fulfilling life, even though conflicts with her husband over money, household chores, and discipline of the children led her to take couples' classes at her church and to eventually embark upon a mutually agreed upon couples' therapy process.

During the termination process which took six months, Kate and I reminisced about the ups and downs of our work together. This patient reviewed how she worked through her dream of achieving her doctorate because the course work of an intense professional training program would be so taxing as to likely lead to a recrudescence of symptoms. She also was thriving in her role as "stay at home mom." These decisions also reflected considerable growth in boundary setting within the family of origin. Kate's academic achievements had been quintessentially important for her father and mother, and they had pushed her early on to take on various projects and activities to reflect well on them and fulfill their dreams. Now at a weight that allowed her to menstruate and was considered healthy for her age and height by her primary care physician, Kate and her husband were undergoing fertility testing because they wanted to have a biological child. Kate also worked on many fears of her sexual responsivity (see Chapter 7) during the course of her individual and ancillary group and couples' therapy processes.

As the individual therapy neared conclusion, this patient became unusually silent and reflective during several sessions. I sat back and tried to give Kate the space she seemed to need to address the important affects of sadness, joy, abandonment, and anger that might be just below the surface of her conscious thoughts (see Table 3.3). When she did speak, Kate demonstrated by her stories many of the components of therapeutic change that will be described in later chapters of this book. She exemplified a new capacity to think her own thoughts, put her history into words, express how important people affected her, set better boundaries without getting overly, viciously angry, and express love, care, and pride in her family. In essence, she was taking her place in the adult life cycle and was fully engaged in facets that make up a life well lived. She had friendships, a primary relationship, and took pleasure and found meaning in the raising of her children.

I decided to intervene after several days in which Kate's silence seemed to fill up the room. I commented on Kate's unusual quiet demeanor and thoughtfulness. I wondered if Kate was reviewing in her mind all of the changes that occurred in our five years of work together.

After a long pause, Kate leaned forward and retorted, "I know I have improved a lot in this treatment and I am happy for it. But Dr. Z, do *you* realize how much *you* have improved over my years of therapy?" I laughed out loud and asked her to elaborate. Kate was eager to share the ways in which she had watched me grow in technical abilities such as listening better, not jumping to as many conclusions, and staying involved but not overly involved when she made decisions on her own. In these ways, Kate demonstrated not only a newfound capacity to speak her truth but the consolidated ego strengths necessary to be oneself and speak from a perspective of autonomy.

Sheena, a patient whose problems with binge eating and obesity I describe further in Chapter 5, made enormous headway in three years of once weekly individual psychotherapy in developing her true self. While she recognized there was additional internal work for her to do, she was now at peace with her full figure and was able to do substantial self-reflecting and self-analysis on her own. She spoke with the therapist about returning for treatment at such times that she might need a "tune up," but she was also looking ahead to having "free space" in which to do self nurturing. Sheena was planning yoga classes, spirituality courses, and spending quality time with her family.

Like most patients, Sheena actually thought about terminating long before she ever brought it to the therapist's attention; when she finally did, she was anxious and embarrassed because she thought that the therapist might think that she was "crazy" for wanting to do more self-nurturing activities on her own. Interestingly, the therapist had witnessed quite a bit of growth on Sheena's part and had silently considered broaching termination. The therapist immediately recognized the patient's defense as one of fearfulness at the usual abandonment concerns that come up when termination is broached.

In a maneuver that simultaneously lightened the mood in the room and clarified the reasons for engaging in therapy, the therapist reminded the patient that when she started she worried that the therapist was "crazy" herself when she told the patient that the work would not be about losing weight or reading self-help books but rather about understanding the meaning of food in the patient's life and cultivating a state of mind so that eventually "food would be simply food." In the early metaphor about food, the therapist went on to explain that if therapy worked the way it should there would be a large space inside the patient to enjoy life and self-enhancing activities.

The therapeutic couple looked at how these goals had been accomplished. The therapist was also able to point out and support the patient in her decision to begin the termination process. In Sheena's case, decreased anxiety to look at this natural ending as one of closure and not permanent separation from the therapist was helpful. She requested to come back quarterly for "check-ins." Now supported in the psychodynamic and cognitive behavior literature, these "booster" or "adjutant" sessions help patients see termination as merely a conclusion of a treatment chapter. The patient is given explicit permission to return if and when she wants more help. Sheena confirmed the clinical wisdom of this approach by saying,

> It helps me to feel that I can come back when I need you. It also helps me to know that you support me in not doing the therapy "forever." It's like you understand that I need "space" to do other activities in order to enrich my life and cement what I've learned here.

ADDITIONAL TREATMENT CONSIDERATIONS

Ideal terminations of psychotherapy allow the patient and therapist sufficient time to reassess the work they have done together. Traditionally, psychotherapists tried to focus the patient's termination work on issues that are always left unresolved or undone at endings, but contemporary research indicates that patients also be given ample opportunity to express how they have benefited and grown in their process. Because termination is a real loss for both patient and therapist, preparation time and attention to feelings must be given to work through this essential human experience which will recapitulate other losses. Paradoxically, termination is also a new beginning for both participants in the dyad, especially when significant gains on the patient's part can be recognized and the quest for perfection can be relinquished.

Psychoanalyst and novelist Allen Wheelis spoke eloquently to these central points in his classic monograph *How People Change*. While acknowledging that our efforts as therapists can ameliorate suffering and augment a sense of safety, they do not provide the patient with a life as if we lived "in the kingdom of heaven." Rather we strive to assist our patients to achieve a capacity to live life so as "to deal better with emerging conflicts which will never end so long as we live" (1973, p. 114). According to Wheelis, the individual who undertakes the journey of self-transformation will be able to "handle some things better, to suffer less" (p. 107) with the realistic knowledge that the true self "must bear responsibility all the way" (p. 102). This magnamous but sober view allows the therapist to reckon with the fact that we can help the patient to make significant gains that will always be, nonetheless, limited.

Even in the most successful treatment, termination will pivot on a sense of the "partial and provisional" (Wheelis, 1973, p. 106) nature of all change. Having garnered a sense of greater wisdom, both participants in the dyad will be pleased with what has been accomplished but realistic about how perfection can never be achieved; goals should include a modification of a harsh superego, contentment that the process has been "good enough," and a capacity to love so as to "think not of all or none, sick or well, miserable or happy, but of more or less, better or worse" (Wheelis, 1973, p. 106). Management of the termination phase requires the clinician to assess and to review a number of essential therapeutic life tasks, a potential list that is enumerated and expanded are below:

1. Underscore how the patient's functioning has improved and be specific about areas in which you both can agree on areas of progress and better life adjustment. If the patient's anxiety increases about functioning on her own, abandonment depression may be stirred and must be worked through. Setting a date and sticking to it whenever possible provides support for the patient's separation–individuation process, which was likely stymied during crucial developmental periods (see Chapters 4, 5, & 6).

2. Allow the patient the leeway to suggest the time for termination and adopt a "weaning schedule" if it fits their needs. Reconsider the date if the patient has a significant relapse or regression (e.g., suicidal ideation, severe restriction and weight loss, excessive exercise, purging, misuse of substances). In the majority of cases where essential therapeutic progress has been made, the patient will have new capacities for "self-righting" (Lichtenberg, 1988; Lichtenberg, Lachmann, & Fosshage, 1992, 2002). Individuals who achieve this capacity will be able to accept and expand upon positive changes in the self and in their external conditions, demonstrating that they are now capable of overcoming developmental lags on their own. Watch for this capacity to self-right after a temporary backslide because it heralds a step "that has not been taken or a normal experience that has been absent [that now] becomes possible" (Lichtenberg, 1988, p. 186).

3. Take the opportunity to review the entire treatment history keeping in mind (a) the patient's capacity to cling less to old patterns of adaptation

and defense, particularly the eating disorder; and (b) the ability to construct a coherent life narrative. Making sense of one's life story (i.e., personal narrative) is the most important factor that has been shown to prevent relapse (Malan & Della Selva, 2006). The individual who is ready to terminate will have less self-directed aggression, which will likely result in (c) greater capacity to express affects, particularly anger; (d) less need to protect others, especially the therapist, against whom a variety of affects may be directed; and (e) enhanced capacity to find realistic gratifications and less guilt about enjoying them. The patient may also have greater capacity to express in words and through self-observation those causes that led to her or his eating disorder; self-defeating patterns will be significantly minimized. Physiologic illnesses tied to the eating disorders also improve when individuals can relive their trauma, express unconscious anger and grief, and assimilate previously overwhelming feelings consciously in the therapy process (Luborsky, Singer, & Luborsky, 1975; Malan & Della Selva, 2006).

4. Give patients an opportunity to think about their life goals and help them separate the longer term goals from the more immediate treatment goals. Those patients who have not been given the emotional space in their family of origin to feel they can function on their own will need to be given more of a push to look at and proceed with their life goals; all patients will likely test the therapist about letting go and owning their autonomy during the termination phase. Consider countertransference reactions carefully (see Chapter 8), particularly if there is an excessive need to hang onto a patient or to feel a sense of pathological guilt or shame that not enough work has been done.

5. Look for an increased tolerance on patients' part to experience uncomfortable affects such as envy, grief, love, or hate and a lessening of pathological guilt and shame. The literature on termination has grown since the mid-1980s and now eschews an ideal of a "fully cured" or "totally well" human being, even in situations when the individual does not enter treatment with the full array of medical complications and ego deficits that may accompany an eating disorder.

In considering the criteria for termination, an affirmative answer to the question, "Can this patient, given all her or his strengths and limitations, and the reality situation in which he or she lives, manage better and more successfully than before the start of treatment?" usually marks readiness for ending. In contemporary treatment, one might conceptualize the ending as a treatment chapter that is completed but the door for further work is always left open. The patient may return to you or to another therapist should a need arise. Perhaps one way to answer the question of whether or not a treatment has been fully successful resides within the patient who will feel more open and less ashamed about getting help in the form that they need after any given episode of therapy and be able to directly express or hint about this possibility in the termination phase.

CONCLUSION

Termination will inevitably awaken feelings of loss for both the patient and therapist. These feelings will, even in the best of circumstances, complicate the process of letting go of each other. The capacity to bear this mourning will demonstrate newfound capacities of the patient to withstand psychological pain and become more intimate with one's self and others.

As therapist and patient review the entire treatment during termination, even if it has been a short period of therapy, previous losses of the therapist's and of the patient's will come to mind because the ubiquity of mourning is an experience that must be worked on throughout life. The termination phase of psychotherapy is yet another opportunity to practice, become more familiar with, and gain greater capacity for dealing with significant losses over the life cycle. As in all circumstances when one must let go of an important relationship, it is also a time to celebrate the positive qualities of that relationship and to look forward to what may lie ahead for the individual.

In preparing individuals for death, the Dalai Lama advises that one be as awake and alert as possible so as to experience the present moment as fully as possible to learn, to transcend, and to move forward. The termination of psychotherapy requires the same focused attention on the connection between participants up until the last session in order for both therapist and patient to be fully alive and respectful toward what the process has and has not meant to each of them.

This advice is particularly apt for eating disorder patients who have walled off so many aspects of their affective states and disconnected from their bodily selves. As the quest for perfection is given up in a course of a less than perfect treatment, new capacities to more freely experience life emerge. The patient may more readily take on "greater responsibility for what we have been, are, and will become" (Wheelis, 1973, p. 170). The greater resiliency born of a successful psychotherapy will allow the individual to "undertake only to do what he can do, to handle something better, to suffer less" (Wheelis, 1973, p.107). It will not deprive the patient of ongoing conflicts, failures, and losses. It will, however, provide a protective barrier against those crushing life forces that have heretofore almost extinguished the patient's life.

Termination of psychotherapy provides patient and therapist with a new opportunity to look at and conclude their work together, not as a fixed end point but as a leap into the unknown. Like a baby bird mentioned in the epigraph who may be reluctant to be pushed out to begin its first flight, the person with an eating disorder is ready to leave the clinician's nest when he or she has the energy and physical capacity to do so (i.e., symptoms are primarily resolved). The therapist will have helped prepare the patient to embark on her or his life's journey despite the ambiguities and losses inherent in human life (i.e., have greater adaptive defenses and interpersonal resources to cope with change). The patient will be ready to take on those risks that a full life inevitably brings (i.e., the eating disorder no longer protects the patient as an adaptive strategy from living or making changes). With greater zeal and energy to take on those essential life tasks that lie ahead, the individual can be said to be embracing a new beginning even as the endpoint of the chapter of psychotherapy nears.

PART II

TREATMENT OF EATING DISORDERS OVER THE LIFE CYCLE

CHAPTER 4

Adolescence

Many young people feel just as I did, hopeless and empty, not knowing what to do with their lives. . . . My alienation took the form of sleeping all the time, bulimia, and deep conventionality. Drugs, acting out, drinking, and driving too fast are escapes other young people turn to in order to feel they actually exist, in the absence of a sense of self.

—Jane Fonda (2005, p. 111)

These deficits in the sense of ownership and control of the body color the way these youngsters face their problems of living, their relationships to others. . . . The eating function is misused in an effort to solve or camouflage problems of living that appear otherwise insoluble.

—Hilde Bruch (1973)

In 2005 actor Jane Fonda's compelling autobiography *My Life So Far* was published. In addition to revealing the trajectory of her fascinating, multifaceted career in film, the antiwar movement, the fitness industry, and, currently, philanthropy, she draws her reader close by her intimate, frank, and often heart wrenching descriptions of the underbelly of success that the public rarely sees in the life of a celebrity. Her memoir is laced with gripping stories of the glamour of growing up in the limelight as the daughter of the beloved Henry Fonda. A pall was cast on Jane Fonda's life by her mother's suicide and her longing to acquire love and recognition from her father. Although considered beautiful and brilliant by others in adolescence, she believed that any "imperfection centered on my body. It became my personal Armageddon, the outward proof of my badness: I wasn't thin enough" (p. 84).

Jane Fonda goes on to explain how important it was to her father that "Fonda women" be thin. She confides that by her teens, "the only time my father ever referred to how I looked was when he thought I was too fat" (p. 84). Not surprisingly, this dynamic played a role in how Jane, like other Fonda women, developed a severe eating disorder. In documenting so vividly her battle with bulimia that lasted for five decades and by describing the family and cultural conditions that gave rise to her problem, Fonda provides an inestimable public service in raising awareness about the longevity and personal toll of having an eating disorder. She starkly tells her readers: "I betrayed my body even though my body never betrayed me."

In adulthood Fonda learned the necessity of taking personal responsibility for her plight in order to rise above her adolescent travail. Like millions of other individuals who begin to restrict in early adolescence in order to gain family or peer approval, Fonda suggests that striving to please her father, who demanded that the women he cared for be thin, was the primary cause of her eating disturbance. What began as an effort to win affirmation and to shore up a feeble sense of identity and self-worth became a fixture in her adult life. Fonda admits to difficulties in making the developmental transition that adolescents must make in order to grow; instead, her eating disorder provided "reassurance" (Bruch, 1988, p. 151) and a solution to insoluble dilemmas that enabled her to "exist, in the absence of a sense of self" (Bruch, 1988, p. 167). The quest for love and mirroring from her aloof, charismatic father played a pivotal role in a life overtaken by periods of self-restricted dieting, purging, and other self-destructive behaviors. Jane Fonda was eventually able to surmount many of these problems and come to greater peace in her relationship with her father before his death. Through psychotherapy and confrontations with herself, she grappled with what Bruch refers to as the potential "sinister fate" of her severe eating disorder by becoming "aware of and by harnessing a sense of her own role" in its perpetuation and building actual "substance and worth" that was not moored to "the strain and stress of a superstructure of artificial perfection" (Bruch, 1988, pp. 167, 168).

Isn't it remarkable how the opening quotation from both Hilde Bruch, the psychiatrist long considered to be one of the greatest teachers and innovators in the treatment of eating disorders, and Jane Fonda say almost the same thing, in many of the same words, but from the different points of view of clinician and patient? Common truths often spring from the same well. As one who suffered from a severe eating disorder, Fonda's adolescence is a wrenching profile not unlike Bruch's many clinical examples found in her professional papers and books. However, there are some notable differences. Only a few of Bruch's patients were in professions where one's appearance mattered so much as it does for actors, and they were also largely from middle-class, not exceptionally well-to-do families. Bruch also found that the majority of her patients struggled with the thorny issue of mother–daughter enmeshment. A father's role in the normative separation-individuation process for girls in adolescence is only occasionally mentioned. However, the need for positive mirroring and understanding from caretakers (including parents, grandparents, friends, and eventually one's partner) of the unique talents and attributes one brings to the world are found to be essential components of progress and recovery by both authors.

While the actor and psychiatrist describe opposite sides of the same coin, one representing the sufferer's perspective and the other a clinician's understanding of what this disorder is about, they do provide several essential, overlapping, and compelling insights. Often eating disorders become an attempt to solve problems of living that perplex young people as they transition from childhood to adolescence and into early adulthood. The individual who does not begin to discover a stable sense of who she or he is during this developmental period is inclined to engage in forms of self-destructive behaviors that do violence to their changing bodies.

Therapists who aspire to helping patients master eating disorders in order for them to come into their own by forming a healthier sense of self must be prepared to weather many a stormy sea. In order to conceptualize an integrated, developmentally based treatment plan, and navigate the therapeutic waters with an adolescent patient, one must keep in mind the multiple currents of the individual and family dynamics; an emerging knowledge of genetics and neurobiology; the impact of caretaking during early infancy; the plasticity of the adolescent brain; and the cognitive transformations that begin in puberty and will continue throughout adulthood. The core concepts to keep in mind when embarking with the adolescent eating disorder patient is the rapid and inexorable changes in body and self that mark puberty. This phase in the life cycle normally places inordinate stressors on many individuals and their families who were safely encased in predictable patterns and roles prior to the hormonal, sexual, educational, and peer influences that may appear to come about overnight. For the eating disorder patient, in particular, a return to childhood may feel like a welcome refuge as the body begins to change in unpredictable and often unwanted ways. Those activities and relationships, which under the best of circumstances provided a sense of safety, begin to crumble as the adult world of sex and new responsibility beckons.

In this chapter I review some of the traditional and fresh perspectives that are informing a contemporary understanding of eating disorders in adolescence and apply them to clinical practice. As in the other chapters that look at treatment needs based on the *developmental* stage of the patient, I approach the task by taking into account biological, cultural, and psychological perspectives that will influence how an integrated treatment plan is formulated for an individual patient.

I begin with a cursory summary of some important research findings that suggest that *some* eating disorders begin in infancy because of severe psychopathology on the part of primary caretakers. I then move on to other considerations that will influence the pragmatics of treatment of the adolescent, attempting to synthesize this biopsychosocial perspective to outline some "high yield" interventions that can be put into daily use in clinical practice. Key to informing the establishment of a secure therapeutic frame will be the clinician's silent question: What convergence of factors led this patient to derail her growth by the development of her eating disorder and what protective functions, if any, might the eating issues serve in shielding the teen and her family from the inevitable pangs of growing up, moving ahead, eventually leaving home, and establishing a sense of self?

WHEN MISATTUNEMENT IN INFANCY PLAYS A ROLE

In her pioneering study of the psychological growth and development of 36 children over four decades, Sylvia Brody (2002) and colleagues made in-depth assessments of the parent–child bond from infancy through adolescence and into adulthood. Brody's longitudinal research began in the early 1950s at the Menninger Foundation in Topeka, Kansas. As part of the orginal work of Sybil Escalona on child temperament, maternal behaviors, and infant mental health, Brody was in the fortunate position of observing her subjects from birth to age 30. These data are rarely available in case reports or other kinds of scientific writing and thus a unique close-up view is provided by a highly skilled team of infant and early childhood investigators. The direct observations and research findings of children and parents were documented on film, through interviews, and by extensive diagnostic psychological testing.

Brody's work demonstrated the "elemental need for whole-body safety" that infants derive from "maternal behaviors of touching, holding, carrying" and posited a primary "biological need for social attachment [that] precedes a need for oral and stomach satisfaction" (Brody, 2002, pp. 6–7). From observing the mother–infant interactions over time, Brody and other attachment researchers since the mid-1970s (Brazelton, Tronick, Adamson, Als, & Wise, 1975; Emde, 1983; Fonagy et al., 2002; Main, 1995; Stern, 1985) have established beyond doubt that "attachments to human persons are stabilized or diversified in the first year of life" (Brody, 2002, p. 11), and that "The importance of infancy lies in being a prologue to acquiring knowledge of earliest sources of mental peace or conflict" (Brody, 2002, p. 17).

The Infancy Research Project led Brody to some startling and unexpected conclusions regarding the development of severe anorexia and body image distortions, which she thoroughly describes in her book *Anorexia Nervosa: The Hunger Artists* (2002). Two subjects (whom Brody calls "Ariel" and "Helen") did not receive much succor or soothing from either their mother or father when they were babies. Brody traces the psychogenic causes of anorexia in these two people from its earliest roots in their infancy through adolescence and into adulthood. She suggests that in *some* patients, parental failures and misattunement in early infancy and into childhood may actually lead to anorexia and other psychological difficulties, such as regulating feeling states, body image, and physiology.

According to Brody, the mothers of Ariel and Helen "never expressed affection, or pride, or sympathy, or tenderness, or good humor" (p. 133) to their daughters. These mothers also appeared withdrawn and unhappy. The subjects' fathers appeared self-confident but were, in fact, disinterested and autocratic, never showering their wives or children with love or nurturing. Brody sees the early feeding problems that the girls exhibited as being derived from how the parents controlled or withheld food. Brody believes these failures in attunement were the *forme fruste* of the later eating disorder.

By adolescence, Ariel and Helen were turning aggression inward, but as babies they had already lost a capacity for spontaneity and appeared dejected. They clung to transitional objects, had difficulties feeding and being soothed, lacked a sense of curiosity and joy, and experienced developmental delays in language acquisition and motor activity. Brody was awestruck by the conspicuous neglect of both sets of parents despite the observation that "both girls had discernible longings [to believe] that they were cherished" (Brody, 2002, p. 170). Brody further concluded:

> Among infants with experiences like these, disenchantment with the hope of receiving and giving affection can set in before the first year. The loneliness, the absence of physical, sensory, and affective assurances of love, and the persistent screaming throughout their infancies appear to have been remote causes of their anorexia in adolescence in that they set the stage for the children's feelings of despair. . . . The external sources of their fears lay in their parents' inability to interest themselves in the ways of children, their lack of freedom to create emotional ties to their children, or to hold back their aggressive demands on them. (p. 180)

This research is important for therapists to consider when thinking through the repertoire of interventions needed in a particular situation when primary attachment is disrupted and ongoing affection and soothing ministrations were not afforded. While the majority of psychotherapists are now conversant with John Bowlby's theory of attachment and the research that has followed from it, Brody's work directly assesses the infancy and developmental patterns of two people who developed anorexia and comorbid psychopathology. It augments what clinicians already know about attachment based therapies and is essential to recall when discouraged. The disturbance may actually arise in or from early parental failure, leading to the patient's later wishes for death, denial of dangerousness, and severe rebelliousness, and the "triumph of rage" (pp. 187–205) as found in the case histories of Ariel and Helen. This kind of "psychological desolation" will require ongoing "protection and containment" in the therapy to reverse the early developmental failure (see Chapters 1 and 2).

From early childhood onward, Ariel and Helen had significant distortions in their body image, manifested hyperactivity, and the need to be in control, and were ascetic and depressed. By adolescence each girl engaged in life-threatening anorexia, had few healthy identifications with any adult, demonstrated little capacity to resolve inner conflict, and displayed unstable, primitive psychological defenses. Brody demonstrated that underlying the adolescent anorexia in these two subjects lay emotional deficits and conflicts that originated in infancy but were also exacerbated in childhood by ongoing misattunement and emotional abandonment within the family of origin. From this highly documented work she found why, in adulthood, the eating and body image problems persisted. Ariel and Helen continued to suffer enormously. Their problems centered on dysregulated feelings and maintaining stable attachments. Most importantly, Ariel and Helen yearned to be loved.

Practicing clinicians will quickly see that Brody's research extends Hilda Bruch's (1973, 1978, 1988) pioneering hypothesis regarding the development of eating disorders in adolescence as being due to family enmeshment. Both have significant implications for our daily work. Bruch believed that family enmeshment and the mother's difficulty letting go was the root cause of anorexia. Brody's work suggests that in some cases the problem goes back to infancy. Both women saw how when the developmental needs of the individual are not met in the early environment, the individual will have many problems with regulating emotional states and developing a sense of self. Each vantage point takes a developmental point of view that shows why subtle change usually occurs over time and is never solely about eating or weight regulation.

Both Bruch and Brody's work, when taken together, help the therapist grasp some pragmatics about working with our patients and why it takes time. As Bruch (1988) herself observed, psychotherapy is "the first time that somebody had truly 'listened'" (p. 74) and "is often a slow process of ups and down" (p. 201). At times we are likely to be working with a very early problem that began between caretaker and child in infancy; when "upbringing did not foster clear and independent observation and thinking" (Bruch, 1988, p. 155); only a longer treatment that provides plenty of direct feedback, confronts the patient's self-deception, examines "erroneous conclusions," and reinforces "honest self discovery" (pp. 46–47), will help the patient "begin to trust her own thinking" where her or his "own feelings and wants are recognized and validated" (p. 156). Not only will patients need help in negotiating the ongoing steps of separation-individuation, but they will also have needs in developing modes of self-care and self-regulation. Therapy must aim to help patients find ways to go beyond their "rebelliousness," desolation, and denial of danger and find a way to live inside their own skins, protect themselves, and begin to find fulfillment in life.

Additional data emerging from the fields of cognitive neuroscience and attachment theory also support Brody and Bruch's contentions. Family-based education, cognitive-behavior, and psychodynamic issues detailed in the remainder of the chapter are designed to help adolescent patients gain new strengths, including the capacity to mentalize. It will be just as important for clinicians to allow into our consultation room "angels in patients' nursery" in addition to any ghosts or devils of misattunement, maltreatment, and abuse that are in their history (Lieberman, Padron, VanHorn, & Harris, 2005). Resiliency and mastery of a severe symptom may be fostered by helping the patient recall and identify those "benevolent past experiences" (Lieberman et al., 2005, p. 516), which always also occur between parent and child, even in the most odious of family circumstances. Fortunately for therapists, the overwhelming majority of parents want and do provide many good things so that exploring those "'beneficial cues' and other protective childhood memories may be especially valuable in creating a therapeutic space that maximizes the potential for growth in parent-child relationships" (Lieberman et al., 2005, pp. 516–517).

The parent may not have to bat 1,000 to have many winning seasons with their child and even hit some home runs and grand slams that in treatment will bring forth joyful and happy memories. As Lieberman et al. (2005) noted, the essential therapeutic position, also informed by state of the art infant research,

> gives equal importance to supportive early memories and to memories of conflict, abuse, or neglect . . . cultivating a frame of mind where joy, intimacy, pleasure and love are considered to be as worthy of therapeutic alteration as negative experiences can be of great assistance in personality momentum toward psychological health. (p. 517)

Perhaps the more complex and rich portrait that the adolescent creates about their parents, by giving focused attention or simply permiting these positive images to come into the hour, facilitates the integration of good and bad object representations over the longer term. One result of these more "humane and flexible perceptions" (p. 517) surely is the capacity for individuals to forgive, an attribute and ethical value that will be called upon repeatedly in adulthood to live within intimate relationships and the contemporary workplace. Sylvia Brody hints at this important achievement when she cites the Hindu proverb, "If we take vengeance for vengeance, then vengeance never dies" (p. 171).

ESTABLISHING AN INTEGRATED PERSPECTIVE WITH FAMILIES

Integrated treatment includes explaining pertinent facts about the illness to patient and family that takes into account the multidetermined nature of symptoms. In the 1970s, psychiatrist George Engle described how mental disorders are best understood and treated by emphasizing the biological, psychological, and social underpinnings of any psychiatric illness (Engle, 1977). Engle was actually building upon the work of Sigmund Freud who conceptualized all illnesses as overdetermined in nature and coined the term *complemental series*, meaning that for every patient the constitution (i.e., genetics, temperment, neurobiology) and psychological and social dynamics must be taken into account in treatment.

Freud's early views and Engle's later articulation are now taken as givens by contemporary scientists and mental health clinicians (Marcus, 2004). Fortunately for clinicians in the 21st century, a rapprochement is occurring in psychiatry and psychology that may help to heal the split between those who would understand and treat an illness *only* biologically or *only* psychologically.

This body of work asserts how those genetically encoded, built-in biological capacities are essential in helping the human learn and adapt in the world. That is, although human beings are neurologically prewired in a fixed way that helps us learn, our brains are also flexible so that we all can and do make adaptational changes in the course of life (Silverman, 2006). Even though the genome determines in a species-specific way the neuroarchitecture present at birth, experience also shapes and modifies the brain. Gary Marcus (2004), a researcher at New York University, shed new light on the old nature–nurture controversy by articulating how professionals and those interested in brain-environment interactions must,

> take insights from the genome and use them to revamp our understanding of nature, of nurture, and of how they work together to create the human mind. . . . We are more than anything else, born to learn. . . . Nature bestows upon the newborn a considerably complex brain, but one that is *prewired*—flexible and subject to change—rather than *hardwired*, fixed, and immutable. (pp. 11–12, also quoted in Silverman, 2006, p. 899)

The fact that genes are not static in their expression is good news for practicing clinicians and those we seek to help in our work. When informing our patients and their families that eating disorders likely arise from a variety of genetic, biologic, social, and individual psychological variables, we must refrain from being overzealous in attributing the illness to any one cause. A humble and judicious approach not only shows the patient what we do not as yet know, but it helps destigmatize the illness. Engaging the patient and family members in treatment occurs while reviewing what we do know in a supportive, educative manner that eschews blame or finger pointing (Crisp, 1995; Marx, 1992). After all, shame and guilt are already keenly felt even before one seeks treatment; who among us has not benefited ourselves from sharing Harry Stack Sullivan's maxim with a patient that "we are all more simply human than otherwise" as a way of modifying embarrassment and angst?

When patients and family members are helped to understand that the illness is likely to derive from a confluence of factors, they are also less likely to feel singled out or held totally responsible and thus are more ready to engage in treatment. By the same token, when some of the neuropsychiatric and genetic factors are summarized, some family members may be prone to misconstrue or overinterpret the data by thinking that the illness is so biologically determined that nothing can be done in the environment to help remediate the problem. One never wishes to promise more than one can offer. One hopes that family members will be able to take on their share of responsibility to help support the individual and make environmental and family shifts that need to occur for a felicitous outcome (see Table 4.1 for a list of suggestions to keep in mind and offer to families when setting up a treatment plan).

For example, asking family members to refrain from making disparaging remarks about the body and to partake of regular family meals are staples of

TABLE 4.1 Tips to address with parents about coping with an adolescent's eating disorder

Don't	Do
Don't put emphasis on child's weight or appearance	Ask about nutritional intake and what happens at family meals as part of a routine assessment
Don't put the child on a diet or tell the child she is fat. This message encourages dieting, which leads to some cases of bonafide eating disorders	Encourage families to aim for weight within healthy range rather than placing a child on a diet
Don't discount the emphasis society places on beauty and body image	Advise moderate exercise, low fat foods, and having the family meet at a mealtimes at least several times per week
Don't expect the child to be open about the eating problem if parents (who are important role models) are secretive about their eating problems	Make discussing weight at mealtimes a taboo subject
Don't turn to your child for comfort for your emotional needs. Seek out a friend, spouse, partner, or individual or couples therapy to avoid placing an emotional burden on the child	Encourage parents to help a child develop sources of self-esteem that do not depend on appearance alone. In particular, help child cultivate positive "self-talk" that helps him or her face down negative stereotypes or self-recrimination
	Help parents increase media awareness in their child
	Help child to find role models other than unrealistic, ideal stereotypes of a perfect body
	Set a no-tolerance policy at home for teasing about weight or body in the family
	Remind parents that their eating attitudes and body image have an impact on the child. Ask parents how much they focus on body image, food issues, weight in their family-of-origin. Do any other family members have an eating disorder?
	Remind parents that they must be vigilant about relapse in their child (e.g., weight loss; missing food in the kitchen; overexercise; bathroom use after meals)

contemporary treatment that necessitate a change in how some families operate. Parents of adolescents may also have to face down their own denial of the illness, need help in navigating the health care system and advocating for the child, and learn to be vigilant about any tendency toward relapse (Lock & Le Grange, 2007). A nonjudgmental, empathic approach on the part of the clinician paves the way for further emotional exploration of the meaning of the symptom and allows the clinician to offer some concrete advice to the family (see Table 4.1). Adolescence is the time, as psychoanalyst Erik Erikson suggested over 50 years ago (1950), when identity consolidates in order for the individual to be able to carry forward into adulthood with the tools to make autonomous decisions and forge intimate relationships. The patient's individualism and the family's deeper appreciation of some of the cultural and biological issues will be fostered by reviewing some of the findings that are summarized below.

CULTURAL CONSIDERATIONS

The incidence of eating disorders appears to be increasing among children and adolescents. What is particularly alarming is the serious impact that these disorders have on physical and psychological development. Since the early 1990s, serious efforts have been made in some school systems to prevent these problems from ever developing. Despite the importance of these programs, eating disorders continue unabated and cast a pall over a period of the life cycle that should be free of pervasive media influences, excessive competition among youth, and overemphasis on how one looks or dieting.

Recent polls indicate that nearly 20% of students at universities believe they have an eating disorder or have had one at some point in their lives; the rates of middle and high school students experiencing these symptoms continue to rise. Reports offer global statistics that as many as 25 to 50% of students report occasional self-induced vomiting or binge eating. Dieting is nearly ubiquitous among girls and adolescents, with as many as 75% skipping or avoiding meals to take off weight. Paradoxically, the number of students who are overweight or obese and binge eat also continues to rise, portending a major public health problem to come. Most unfortunately, the great majority of adolescents receives no intervention or preventative efforts whatsoever. Because siblings and caregivers are also negatively impacted when an adolescent develops a full blown eating disorder, the full public health impact of anorexia, bulimia, or binge eating disorder is likely to be an underestimate of an extensive, costly amalgamation of medical, psychiatric, and social maladies.

The reactivity of adolescents to media pressures had been postulated for at least three decades before the pivotal investigation on the media-naive population of Fiji. In the late 1990s, television was introduced to Fiji for the first time. Over 60 adolescent females participated in a study that assessed television's impact within a month of introduction and after three years. This first naturalistic experiment documented how quickly media exposure has an impact on a young woman's desire to emulate a television star's shape and weight. According to the investigators, there was a "dramatic increase in disordered eating attitudes and behaviors in this peer environment following prolonged television exposure," which represented an extraordinary cultural shift, given the previously strong cultural sanctioning of robust appetites and body size among Fijians" (Becker, Burwell, Gilman, Herzog, & Hamburg, 2002, p. 513). Prior to the change in media, Fijians were not concerned with becoming or looking too thin; body aesthetic ideals shifted so quickly that instead of being considered an insult to look slender, and potentially unhealthy, it became flattering to notice weight loss or appear thin like a "sexy" Western television star (Becker et al., 2002; Becker, Burwell, Navara, & Gilman, 2003).

While this research raises concerns about those media that "may act as catalysts for other social and mental health problems among youth in developing societies and elsewhere" (Becker, Burwell, Gilman et al., 2002, p. 513), "girl culture" in contemporary Western culture drives home the message as never before that what girls "look like is more important than who they are" (Steiner-Adair & Sjostrom, 2006, p. xii). Books to help parents communicate on a variety of issues that impinge on the adolescent psyche, including beauty standards, fashion cliques, and weight are bestsellers (Greenfield, 2002; Pipher, 1994; Wiseman, 2002). Manuals are becoming available to assist adults who work with girls and adolescents on these issues; in Steiner-Adair and Sjostrom's (2006) innovative prevention program to help teenage girls address key concerns related to their bodies and self-image, hundreds of suggestions are made to help leaders and teachers tackle the issues that these girls now struggle with daily. A list of the section and subsection titles that must be taken up with girls to prevent eating disorders and result in "sustained positive changes in girls' knowledge about health, nutrition, weight and puberty" (p. xi) is a veritable education on the range and depth of concerns young people must deal with in contemporary culture.

For example, Steiner-Adair and Sjostrom advise an eight-unit program to tackle issues such as fat myths, politics of the body, personal and media values, ways to affirm oneself and one's body, and physical and psychological nourishment. Based on their results in 40 pilot site schools, these research-clinicians have not only developed a hands-on, practical manual with plenty of user-friendly handouts to help girls and teens cultivate their own "call to action" and provide tips for parents, but they determined from their follow-up that this was the "first prevention program of its kind to effect sustained positive changes in girls' body image, body satisfaction, and body-esteem, important risk factors in the development of eating disorders" (p. xi). The topics clearly delineate the pressures adolescents are under today that were not there in previous generations. During the first and second wave of feminism, "not even an ounce of prevention" of this kind was ever taught in schools because it was thought irrelevant or unnecessary. The conclusion that new avenues for women's empowerment, career choices, and success would lead to less focus on beauty and body ideals turned out to be a totally false and overzealous repudiation of "the power of beauty" (Friday, 1996).

Niva Piran, Professor of Education at the University of Toronto, has been involved in prevention of eating disorders for over 20 years. Employing a feminist-informed model, Piran advocates a group model where "from a discussion of body shape, bodily functions, and expectations of one's appearance, the dialogue is transformed into a discussion of power and voice" (Piran, 1996, p. 326). Given that her intensive and long-term involvement using feminist counseling for health promotion occurred in a residential dance school, her results that validating, supporting, educating, and helping young women attend to relationships and develop their voice are most impressive.

In her approach, Piran also emphasizes that those often neglected topics of "positions of power, gender, race, and other social barriers" (p. 331) be brought into the room and spoken to directly. Her more recent work with educators (Piran, 2004) enlists those on the front lines in the classroom to expose youth "to a critical examination of the social forces that disrupt children's and adolescents' connection to their body so they can be able to provide alternative perspectives and experiences to their students" (p. 6).

Certainly, evolving studies like the one on the Fijian adolescents, and historical reviews that provide extensive commentary on these contemporary issues like Brumberg's *The Body Project* (1997), or *Fasting Girls* (1988), should be included in the curricula. Moreover, these same educational tools and strategies need to be more thoroughly presented and absorbed by parents in concentrated efforts to provide "some special relief or protection from the unrelenting self-scrutiny that the marketplace and modern media both thrive on" (Brumberg, 1997, p. 197).

BIOLOGICAL CONSIDERATIONS

The Role of Genetics

Family and twin studies suggest that in many cases of eating disorders heredity plays a role. Anorexia nervosa has a concordance rate of nearly 70% for monozygotic twins and 20% for nonidentical, dizygotic twins. Bulimia nervosa also shows a higher concordance rate in monozygotic twins than dizygotic twins. Anorexics are more likely to have a first degree relative who is also anorexic. Patients with anorexia, binge–purging type, and bulimics have more first degree relatives with a mood disorder than normal controls. In addition, bulimics have the additional vulnerability of higher rates of substance abuse in their families of origin. However, it is sometimes difficult to tease out how much a parent's eating disorder or eating preoccupation may influence a child's development of her own, often unrecognized, eating disorder or body image disturbance.

Since the 1980s, population studies have demonstrated a substantial role for genetics in the etiology of anorexia by comparing the incidence of the disorder in monozygatic and dizygotic pairs of twins. In the 21st century, this research continues to evolve and this work may eventually lead to innovative treatments. For the time being, reviewing the heritability factor in *some* eating disorders may be helpful for patients and their family members because it is simultaneously deshaming and depathologizing.

The rationale for including a short summary of this research in this chapter is twofold. First, the association and linkage genetic studies have primarily compared prepubertal and pubertal females. It is now believed that when at the onset of puberty estrogen genes are activated, the higher levels of estrogen may influence the transcription of the 5-HT2A receptor gene. Both may be involved in the mediation of basic affects (e.g., anxiety, depression) or personality and temperament traits (harm avoidance, perfectionism) that are common among patients with anorexia (Klump & Gobrogge, 2005). These molecular genetic studies have also demonstrated that in families with adolescents with restrictor-type anorexia, high levels of obsessionality and the drive for thinness could be linked on chromosomes 1, 2, 10, and 11. Different regions of the genome may yet be found "to be important for a range of eating pathologies" (Klump & Gobrogge, 2005, p. 544) even though larger sample sizes of subjects and shared databases among researchers are needed to confirm results and to identify and elucidate the function of genes that influence the neurobiological mechanisms that can lead to eating disorders.

Family members can also be told that studies of monozygotic and dizygotic twins demonstrate the significant genetic influence in girls who appear to have their eating pathology activated during puberty, likely through a complicated cascade of biochemical changes that occur during the transition from childhood to adolescence and are regulated by a variety of genes (Klump, McGue, & Iacono, 2002, 2003). In these cases it appears that the shared environment of the twins was important in prepuberty. However, at puberty genetic influences trumped the environment demonstrably. Again, the possible role of ovarian hormones, primarily estrogen and progesterone, activated during puberty under the aegis of the genetic endowment, may play a defining role. Although other biological systems such as the hypothalamic-pituitary axis and stress hormones may play contributing roles, fluctuations in estrogen and progesterone modulate food intake during the human menstrual cycle and lately play pivotal roles in appetite and weight regulation.

Estrogen has been known for decades to influence eating and feeding behaviors; moreover, men and prepubertal females are much less prone to developing an eating disorder than a pubescent female. The working hypothesis that can be shared with family members is that genes activated during puberty, and hence "out of the direct influence" of the family may play a decided, if not definitive role, in their loved one's restricted eating (Keel & Klump, 2003; Klump, Wonderlich, Lehoux, Lilenfeld, & Bulik, 2002).

One potential downside of this explanation could be that loved ones and the patient will make use of the genetic explanation to avoid taking a deeper look at compelling cultural influences and individual psychological issues that

must also be addressed for comprehensive treatment; the adolescent's psychological growth will be challenged on the way through all of the entanglements,
losses, and potential for positive change that are part of this "second individuation"(Blos, 1969). On the other hand, this evolving genetic research will also
provide insight into why females may have increased vulnerability to eating disorders at puberty and the complex interaction of genes and environment. That
is, additional understanding of genetic susceptibility to environmental factors
will shed light on why some individuals react to environmental stressors while
others do not. The patient's genetic makeup may activate the many as yet
unknown neurobiological systems to cause psychopathology based on an external environmental pathogen beyond the individual's conscious control (Caspi
& Moffitt, 2006).

The Role of the Brain

The dorsolateral prefrontal cortex of the adolescent's brain is still immature;
this is the last part of the brain to undergo myelination; connectivity between
different regions of the brain has not as yet fully developed. Some of the problems adolescents have in making good decisions, weighing the consequences
of their actions, and regulating their impulses and actions may arise from immature brain functioning and the impact of fluctuating hormones on their less
than fully developed neurological systems. Because eating disorders in adolescents may arise from the complex interaction of genetics, hormones, environment, and the underdeveloped prefrontal cortex, they may pose particular challenges to treatment because the adolescent has not yet developed the
neurophysiological or neuroarchitextural capacity to regulate their emotions.
"We do not yet know what the specific impact of having an eating disorder has
on the maturing brain but we do know enough to say it has a very negative
effect," notes pediatric and adolescent neuropsychologist Bonnie Nagel, PhD
of Oregon Health and Science University, an expert on the way substance
abuse effects the developed brain (Nagel, 2007, personal communication).

In all likelihood, cortical and subcortical changes in the brain are as likely
to result from eating disorders as they are from schizophrenia, attention
deficit hyperactivity disorder, William's syndrome, and substance abuse
(Sowell, Peterson, Thompson, et al., 2003; Toga, Thompson, & Sowell, 2006).
Documented changes in the size of the thalamus, midbrain, and pituitary gland
run parallel to deficits in cognition in some eating disorder patients. Of even
greater concern is the neurochemical, hormonal, and functional abnormalities
in these patients which may negatively impact an array of neurological
processes overtime, including interruption of myelination, decreased synaptic
density, and impaired or mottled dendritic pruning. Even though longitudinal
studies do suggest that overall brain volume returns to normal after weight gain,
there is cause for concern that cognitive and behavioral changes that are not
easily remediated, if at all, arise from the impact of eating disorders on the

brain's maturation (Katzman, Lambe, MiKulis, et al., 1996; Katzman, Zipursky, Lambe, et al., 1997).

Any assault on the already immature prefrontal system may impact the individual's mirror neuron system. Neuroscientists have only recently discovered the vital role that the mirror neuron system plays in interpersonal relations, complex social behaviors, and the ability to empathize. An individual with a highly impaired mirror neuron system (e.g., autism) may have difficulties understanding metaphor, reading the emotional state of another person, and observing and learning sophisticated tasks. Deficits in the mirror neuron system may contribute to problems internalizing the psychotherapist, although the relative plasticity of the brain assures that development and maturation can and do occur throughout life. Indeed, neuroscience perspectives are a boon for clinicians because "the most salient environment leading to brain growth is the relationship with caretakers" (Pally, 2000, p. 208). Even deficits from early trauma or pathological attachment patterns like the ones already described earlier, while difficult to change, may be ameliorated over time when the "implicit/nonverbal modes" and "explicit/verbal modes" enlarge the patient's capacity for "matching and distress regulation" (Pally, 2000, p. 234) that engage both *conscious* and *subconscious* brain mechanisms simultaneously.

Applying this fascinating and rapidly expanding amalgamation of neurological data to daily clinical work is another matter altogether. I asked my colleague, Leeza Maron, PhD, a neuropsychologist at Oregon Health and Science University, to suggest some "high yield" neuropsychological principles to augment treatment with adolescents who have an eating disorder. Considering the additional potential impairment on the developing brain by nutritional, hormonal, and stressful disruptions that accompany an eating disorder, Dr. Maron advised: (1) Set small, achievable goals. Because eating disorder patients tend to set very high goals, be sure to inquire, "What will it be like to meet that goal? What will it be like if it doesn't work out?" This gives the patient an opportunity to plan and figure out what they will do next or if they have a setback. (2) Monitor affect and teach affect monitoring. Develop a plan the patient can put into effect automatically if she or he is overwhelmed. Tell the patient that, "No one has the brain resources we need when we are 'stressed out' to think it through." In this way, the therapist is engaging a metacognitive ability. In essence, the prefrontal lobes are being "exercised" to plan and abstract *before* a problem happens. (3) Cultivate imagery and visualization of problems. In the brain, thinking is akin to doing (mirror neuron activity). Review progress and what to do in the future and witness the shift in responsibility and enhancement of those metacognitive shifts that happen for the patient. (4) Be sure to emphasize progress over time. It is easy for the patient to miss the strides she is making. Reflecting on progress also helps the patient use the tools in the future by enhanced planning; primary reflective capacity becomes further cemented in the brain. (5) Remind the patient that developing a new behavior is always a trial-and-error process. The experience of "success" may be different from what the adolescent planned in the here-and-now. This technique aids the patient in being sturdy when disappointments come and opens a pathway for evaluating strides from new angles (Maron, personal communication, 2006).

The Role of Temperament

Anorexic patients phenotypically express these genetic, neurobiological vulnerabilities in their temperament. Several recent studies have linked the anxiety, fearfulness, rigidity, and perfectionism of anorexia nervosa to obsessive compulsive disorder (OCD) and obsessive compulsive personality disorder (OCPD) (Serpell, Livingstone, Neiderman, & Lask, 2002; Klump, Bulik, et al., 2000). Unlike OCD or OCPD, anorexic symptoms are ego syntonic and overvalued ideas tend to center on weight and shape; rituals usually include eating and misuse of food (e.g., cutting food into bits, excessive amounts of time spent on food preparation or exercise). In contrast, compulsive rituals of the obsessive (OCD or OCPD patients) are employed to reduce guilt or anxiety and have no manifest goal (i.e., are purposeless). However, the clinician must also carefully evaluate "OCD-like behaviors that appear not to be directly related to food or weight . . . a patient who repeatedly washes her hands before meals may be doing so to avoid having to eat rather than [through] fear of contamination" (Serpell et al., 2002, p. 654).

Some investigators believe that OCD and anorexia may be linked phenotypically because of underlying dysregulation of the serotonin system, and consequently both conditions may be alleviated to a greater or lesser extent by the SSRIs. With respect to issues of temperament, the clinician must be aware of the mounting evidence that anorexia is highly comorbid with other anxiety disorders and depression; the adolescent, whose genetic endowment predisposes them to rapid weight loss when they begin to diet, may initiate the behavior because of a terrible underlying *fear* of gaining weight. Premorbidly these adolescents avoid novelty, are driven to success in all they do, and are temperamentally quite brittle. After the onset of their anorexic symptoms, their preoccupation with weight loss may take on a delusional intensity while they otherwise appear indifferent to suffering and their body's growing emaciation. After recovery, inflexibility in thinking style may persist (Strober, 1980; Srinivasagam, Kaye, Plotnicov, et al., 1995).

Individuals who purge (anorexia nervosa, purging subtype or bulimia nervosa) have their own temperament characteristics that include anxiety, impulsivity and a potential for self-destructive behavior, and feelings of inadequacy and ineffectiveness (Bulik, Sullivan, Weltzin, & Kaye, 1995; Klump et al., 2000). In the future, temperament clusters will be parsed to further elucidate genetic linkages, pinpoint diagnosis, and guide treatment. At present many patients in the bulimic subtypes diagnostically appear to manifest (DSM-IV) cluster-B phenomenology. Their impulse control difficulties (cluster B) interdigitate with cluster A (paranoia) and cluster C (dependent) personality subtypes that predispose some patients to a difficult treatment course and poorer outcome. Other patients with bulimic symptoms appear to avoid these temperament issues altogether; their nascent ego strengths may predispose them to a more fortuitous prognosis (Zerbe, Yager, & Becker, 2002). In adolescents who are predisposed to feelings of self-destructiveness or ineffectiveness, the clinician may want to establish a firm contract (see Appendix A) that carves out the most dangerous or defeating actions for immediate intervention. When patients are able to make even the smallest steps to curtail their symptoms, praise, affirmation, and rewards (but not food) should follow in abundance (Russel, 2004; Yager, 1988, 1992).

Those patients predisposed to these temperament problems may have additional difficulties with self-soothing because the orbital prefrontal cortex is still maturing. Affective regulation and capacity to experience positive feelings may be enhanced by "prescribing" short periods of "alone time" or meditation (5 min to begin, increasing to 7, 10, 15, or more) while containing (see Chapters 1 and 2) the dissociated sense of hopelessness and optimism these adolescents also harbor. The agenic function of claiming positive affects will build on the ediface of improved self-soothing and executive capacity as the patient learns that she or he can modify innate temperament predispositions to achieve improved adaptive planning and decision making (i.e., not turn to the repetitive behavior of gorging or vomiting to reduce stress, feel effective or comfortable, achieve a sense of power, and only then self-soothe).

The Role of Infection

In some cases, infection with streptococcus may trigger an autoimmune-based anorexia nervosa (Sokol & Gray, 1997). Obsessive compulsive disorder and Tourette's syndrome can be brought on by infection with streptococcus bacillus and result in an autoimmune neuropsychiatric problem; Pediatric Autoimmune Neuropsychiatric Disorders may now include anorexia nervosa. Known by the acronym PANDAS AN, some anorexia nervosa patients actually improve when antibiotic treatment is given early in the course of their illness (Sokol, Steinberg, & Zerbe, 1998). The documentation of PANDAS AN includes prepubertal and acute onset, rapid exacerbation of the symptoms of infection before weight loss, evidence of an antecedent or concomitant streptococcal pharyngitis, positive throat culture, and positive serologic findings (e.g., antideoxyridonuclease B [anti-DNase B] and antistreptolysin O [ASO titers]).

Dena—A case of PANDAS AN?

A delightful, well-rounded, resourceful 16-year-old, Dena looked forward to her usual two weeks in summer equestrian camp. Her natural abilities for the sport and determination to succeed made it appear to her coaches and her supportive parents that her goal of becoming part of the Olympic equestrian team might be possible. Sadly for Dena, a sudden illness, heralded by rash, severe urinary tract infection, and heart palpitations, forced her to return home after only a few days.

The acute problems seemed to quickly recede under the care of the family physician. Dena returned to camp later in the summer, did well, but found herself losing a significant amount of weight. When she returned home for a second time, her parents sought additional medical consultation because "It's getting very difficult to feed our daughter. She used to eat everything we put in front of her. Suddenly she is very picky about food and we are so worried that she might be developing anorexia."

Dena's family and consulting physicians were alarmed and urged the parents to seek psychiatric consultation. Even though Dena did not admit to concern about her body image and said she actually felt hungry and wanted to eat, her menstrual periods had stopped and she found most food "uninteresting, nauseating, and bland." She only wanted to drink milk and to eat cheese, pretzels, and graham crackers. Every now and then she would try a salad or sample cooked carrots.

The consulting pediatrician, suspecting PANDAS AN, procured a series of laboratory findings (serum complement; ASO titer, etc) which were negative (Sokol & Gray, 1997). Everyone involved, including the parents, physician, and Dena, had the same question: Was this a bona fide or *forme fruste* eating disorder and should it be treated as such? Clearly, the DSM-IV criteria were not met. The family was further concerned about whether Dena should return to her equestrian pursuits. These parents were aware of the tendency of many anorexics to also have an activity disorder and develop the female athlete triad (i.e., disordered eating, amenorrhea, osteoporosis) or overtraining syndrome (see Powers & Thompson, 2007; Zerbe, 1993/1995a; Zerbe & Rosenberg, 2008).

In this case, the consulting psychiatrist and pediatrician chose to follow a conservative course and urged caution. Dena did not appear to have either the body image preoccupation or denial of weight loss typical of most anorexic patients. Her parents also wanted her to gain weight, and they did not appear overinvolved or enmeshed. From what one could deduce from a three-session consultation, the normative separation-individuation process of adolescence seemed to be occurring naturally (Anderson, 1995; Chodorow, 1978; Steiner-Adair, 1991a).

Knowing that in some adolescents weight loss may herald later symptoms of anorexia, the psychiatrist followed up quarterly with Dena and her family for two years. At the time of the initial consultation, the psychiatrist wondered if the weight loss and difficulties with taste and eating may have been a residual of the infectious process and would resolve naturally with time. In this fortuitous case, Dena was gradually able to reintroduce foods to her diet with the help and encouragement of her parents; anorexia never developed. However, a definitive reason for what caused the original problem was never found. In retrospect, Dena's "selective eating" (Bryant-Waugh, 2000; Lask and Bryant-Waugh, 2000) resolved uneventfully with the help of her appropriately involved, concerned parents who were "able to manage the child's extreme fussiness around food largely by making sure they had access to preferred foods" (Bryant-Waugh, 2000, p. 35) and gradually and patiently urging Dena to add new foods to her dietary regime (e.g., salmon, lean meat).

As so often occurs in medicine and psychiatry, clinicians can become frustrated when there is no final answer or definitive diagnosis. Situations like Dena's remind us to be aware of our limitations, keep an open mind about how symptoms may evolve or naturally be self limiting, and remain humble lest we be perceived as knowing more than we do at any point. Therapists are often left with more questions than answers about our patients, the actual etiology of an illness, and what prompted resolution after treatment is over. In Dena's case, watchful waiting by the health professionals involved with this family was useful because it (1) provided a supportive, containing environment for each member of the family; (2) continuously assessed the status of Dena's feelings about her body image and made preparations for interventions if these problems worsened; and (3) ensured that the parents and Dena were negotiating the normal individuation process of adolescence with "just the right" amount of struggle.

ADAPTING TREATMENT FOR THE DEVELOPMENTAL STAGE

Adolescents are transitioning through what psychoanalyst Peter Blos (1962, 1979) called the "adolescent passage." Drawing upon the earlier theory of Margaret Mahler, Blos noted the ambivalence all adolescents have toward attaining physical and psychosexual maturity; like the rapprochement child, the teen will need to move away from the parents (e.g., through arguments, different political causes, dress, and music) and then return to home base for refueling. Blos termed this transitional time "a second individuation" and noted how "body image is shaped by sensory perception in conjunction with environmental responses to the body" (1979, p. 429). He observed that excessive anxiety about physical maturation in adolescence will interrupt normal development and "exert a pathogenic influence in ego development" (1979, p. 466). His clinical work further showed how patients in this second individuation period move through the adolescent passage but can suffer "fixation" that will be "carried forward into the next developmental stage" (p. 497) unless corrected.

Although all adolescents are notoriously ambivalent about establishing and maintaining their autonomy, this is especially observed in eating disorder patients. On the one hand, these patients attempt to assert their independence by any and all means possible. However, they are not able to maintain this state and usually regress to more childlike behaviors. Even among the psychologically healthiest of adolescents, it is not uncommon for loved ones to be perplexed, frustrated, and sometimes driven to angry outbursts by the adolescent's mood swings, oscillations between infantile and more grown-up behaviors, and propensities to act out. Given the developmental issues present in the most grounded and resourceful teens during the "adolescent passage" (Blos, 1979), treatment must be adapted to include additional refueling, empathy, and skill building for those who struggle with particular interpersonal conflicts and severe emotional problems, such as eating disorders.

It is now generally conceded by researcher-clinicians that therapeutic techniques can be modified for the adolescent (Lock, 2005; Mufson, Dorta, Moreau, et al., 2004). In most situations, family involvement will be crucial. For example, cognitive-behavioral therapists suggest that parents be involved in helping the adolescent plan meals and monitor the high stress time after meals. The positive role of parents who educate and encourage the child about healthy eating patterns (such as eating breakfast) cannot be underestimated. In some families that may have inadvertently held high standards, particularly regarding appearance and weight, new messages will need to be conveyed. Parents may even have to swallow their pride and admit that they may have gone overboard with some of their admonitions. In particular, educating the adolescent about the media (i.e., the so-called media awareness process) can be an essential adjunct by parents who seek to help their child find healthier ways of looking at the body.

My colleague and coteacher, Nancy Winters, MD, associate professor and a child and adolescent psychiatrist at Oregon Health and Science University, has integrated psychodynamic and cognitive-behavioral techniques in the treatment of adolescents with eating disorders for a number of years (Winters, personal communication, 2006). She has observed that adolescents often feel micromanaged by parents, school counselors, and the team of professionals who seek to help them with their eating disorder. Taking into account the developmental needs of the adolescent to not only feel but to become more autonomous, Dr. Winters attempts to join her patient in her or his attempt to have more age appropriate psychological control. Rather than let the session devolve into complaints about those in the environment who seem to be making decisions and choices for them (e.g., "bossy parents"), she asks her patient, "What can you do today to make it better?" In this way, she attempts to collaborate with the adolescent. Dr. Winters avoids the pitfall of being seen as the expert by the patient who would just as soon reject another adult. She has found it useful to begin an intervention by saying, "I will help you negotiate this issue with your parents but you have to help me. We'll do the work together." The patient is thereby empowered and simultaneously given the message sub rosa that collaboration (i.e., healthy dependency) is a strength, not a weakness.

Given the cognitive limitations of the adolescent's developing brain, most of these patients will need more help than adults with problem solving. Motivational interviewing techniques can be employed to help adolescents to look at their symptoms, confront the cost of the symptoms, cope with how the symptoms may be holding them back, and understand a bit more about the psychological payoff in holding onto them. In this way, motivational interviewing also helps to get beneath the manifest symptoms of restriction, overeating, or purging by any method to enlarge the patients' scope of understanding about where the problem comes from.

Adolescents do need help with problem solving; cognitive-behavioral methods that assess symptoms, triggers, and life circumstances can be tailored to the developmental phase for just this purpose. For example, when employing a cognitive restructuring exercise, the clinician should illustrate what precisely is meant. Because the ability of adolescents to generalize is less than that of the adult, they benefit from hearing examples and stories from their therapist. Clinical experience also demonstrates that adolescents are less likely to do homework assignments (e.g., keeping food records; using affirmations or diverting themselves at high risk times; developing a relapse prevention plan) so therapists may need to spend some time in the session doing the homework assignment with the patient. However, doing the homework in the session can also be put to very good use because it helps patients begin to develop essential self-observational skills, such as assessing their emotional states (see Table 4.2).

TABLE 4.2 Keys to helping adolescents manage an eating disorder

- Family involvement is crucial. Studies show that meal planning and after-meal monitoring is essential to avoid relapse
- Make use of motivational interviewing techniques. Help the patient look at the cost of the symptom and what the payoff is
- Give additional support in problem solving. This includes "real life" concerns as well as triggers and symptom management of the eating disorder
- Spend additional time educating adolescents. Remember that cognitive shifts occurring at this time in the life cycle require more support and more exposure to a particular homework exercise or therapeutic technique. Be concrete and specific
- Be prepared to be more flexible in the sessions. Be prepared to do homework in the session (i.e., going over a food and weight record)
- Strengthen and support the ability to make choices. Help the patient learn to negotiate for self. Ask questions like, "What can you do to help your parents, etc., give you more control? What is something you can do today to improve the situation?"
- Give some examples/illustrations of what you mean. This helps the patient learn to problem solve
- Ask plenty of questions (e.g. "What were you feeling?" "What does it feel like to be you?"). This develops observational skills and makes the patient the expert on her or his experience in your presence
- Teach relapse prevention strategies. Remind patient that a setback does not mean total failure. Encourage family members to be aware of signs of relapse
- Remain flexible. The patient may not be able to delay gratification or focus on what the therapist wants to cover. When the individual has a hot issue, go with it. This builds the alliance for later work on the eating disorder

Perhaps most importantly, Dr. Winters has said that the therapist of adolescent patients must be ready and willing to "follow the patients' lead." These patients will often come to the session upset about some real world event and have a need to talk about it with the therapist. Should the therapist have the mistaken belief that they are not doing their job by "simply listening" and "being manipulated by getting off track" with respect to the eating disorder symptoms, expert opinion converges to help therapists with our inflated superegos. As James Lock (2005), a cognitive-behavioral therapist from Stanford University noted regarding the treatment of adolescents with eating disorders:

> Attention to the external context of the adolescent's life (i.e., family and school) is an important aspect of working with most teenagers. . . . Therapists working with adolescents, regardless of the specific focus of therapy, should expect to devote some attention to peers and school environments because these areas are important concerns for adolescents. (p. 279)

LOOK FOR WHAT IS HIDDEN IN PLAIN VIEW

In 1999, historians Jacqueline Tobin and Raymond Dobard published a scholarly study on how quilts were used as a means of conveying messages to the Africans who were escaping enslavement via the Underground Railroad before and during the American Civil War. The stitching, patterns, and designs on the quilts that hung in windows contained covert, secret messages that aided people in finding their way to freedom. The codes on the quilts were, of course, "hidden in plain view" to disguise the intent of escape from the slave masters.

In a similar way, adolescents use ingenious methods and codes, often in the form of their severe psychophysiological and persecutory symptoms, to tell their story covertly. Like all people who yearn to be "masters of their own destiny" (Tobin & Dobard, 1999, p. 67), our patients need the symbolic language and resources to make their way to emotional freedom. They must rely on us, their therapists, to help decode their story and to guide them on their own journey to freedom.

Sometimes the child or adolescent harbors a treasured family secret, and this deception keeps the patient from moving forward in her or his own life. The emotional impact of trying to squelch thoughts, of suppressing or otherwise keeping a memory or feeling out of mind, or simply holding back or keeping silent about something that we know to be a "forbidden" truth is often glossed over in contemporary life. Who among us has not had to bite our tongue lest a secret we've just been told almost "pops out" of our mouth? For the most part, keeping confidences and other "covert knowledge" is much less difficult when we are in our therapist role than when we are living our everyday lives.

In order to empathize with a child or adolescent who is placed in the position of keeping such information that may be hidden in plain view, try to imagine the last time you were entrusted with a piece of personal information about someone that you could not let slip, notice the energy it took not to tell, and then think about what that would be like for someone who had not yet matured to the full range of ego functions that you now have. Add to this, of course, the fact that whatever secret you held has much less emotional valence than something a youngster believes they must keep private, such as a fact about family life, because it means jeopardizing, letting down, or betraying someone they rely on for security. They may also harbor real fears about getting into serious trouble if they let their secret out.

Keeping a family's secret offers protection not only for members of the family but keeps the patient from knowing certain facts and truths about her- or himself. As the psychoanalyst and attachment theorist John Bowlby (1979) wrote in one of his most clinically insightful but rarely cited papers, "On Knowing What You Are Not Supposed to Know and Feeling What You Are Not Supposed to Feel," children frequently harbor knowledge "about events that parents wish that they had never observed" (1979, p. 405). This secret knowledge has a special role in troubled families where there are explicit and implicit messages for children to collude with a parent around a particularly troubling fact. Bowlby demonstrated that when children were implicitly given the message *not* to talk to the surviving parent after one parent suicided or was murdered, they complied. However, the secret keeping led to significant emotional and intellectual deficits in these children. Clinical experience demonstrates that similar dynamics contribute to the development of some eating disorders; secret knowledge may go "unnoticed" by children but causes nonpareil anguish.

I reported the case of Valerie, a 15-year-old girl with a four-year history of bulimia and anorexia who was admitted to a residential treatment center (Zerbe, 2001a). Outpatient treatment had failed with respect to controlling the eating disorder. Most troublesome on admission to the hospital was Valerie's chief complaint that she continually heard voices. The admitting team members worried that they were dealing with an incipient psychosis (e.g., schizophrenia, bipolar disorder), or wondered whether it was the untreated medical consequences of the eating disorder. Interestingly, Valerie's previous physicians knew about the voices and had attempted to medicate her with a variety of first and second generation antipsychotics, but to no avail. However, no one ever asked Valerie what the voices actually said to her.

The social worker who took a detailed family history found that Valerie was the product of in vitro fertilization; her parents tried unsuccessfully for many years to become pregnant and eventually made the decision to undergo expensive fertility treatment. A decision was made before Valerie was born to keep the biological father's identity a secret; her father had severe diabetes mellitus, had struggled with episodes of sexual impotence for years, but never wanted his daughter to think that he was "not a real man or her real dad." Valerie's parents decided to use her paternal uncle's sperm "because there is some genetic connection then."

When the consultant to the team asked Valerie to reveal what the voices actually said to her, the patient was most willing to tell. She reported that she heard a man's voice saying, "Don't speak it. Don't speak it." Despite efforts in the treatment to get Valerie to consider what the voice was asking her not to speak about, she refused to consider any possibilities. As in many cases where people within and outside the family nexus actually know the secret but the patient appears not to know, her two adopted siblings, aunts, uncles, and grand-parents, and every member of the hospital team, all had "secret" knowledge about the complicated circumstances that surrounded her birth.

Valerie's eating disorder came under better control only when psychother-apy and family therapy helped address the role of secrets in this family. In par-ticular, the family therapist gradually helped the parents to see that what they thought they concealed was actually known and discussed by many people and that it was likely that the patient knew about it too. The parents were told how the hallucinations served a protective function for *them*: The male voice instructing Valerie not to speak represented an internalization of the father's wishes not to have what he considered a shameful revelation consciously acknowledged by his daughter. By keeping truth concealed, something she "knew but was not supposed to know," Valerie paid a high psychological price. As the buried issues were unearthed in Valerie's individual psychotherapy, the patient made considerable headway with respect to better control over food intake. Eventually episodes of purging totally stopped.

Coming to grips with the actual secret in this family helped the patient face down her eating disorder and also pointed the way toward greater conscious access to a variety of affective states, allowing her to function better in school. As described by Bowlby (1979), Valerie was trying to be helpful to her parents, to shield them from their own feelings of failure and shame. Children will go to extraordinary lengths to protect a parent who has suffered a devastating nar-cissistic wound (e.g., loss of a job; marital infidelity) when they pick up on con-scious or unconscious messages that they are not supposed to speak about for fear of humiliating or undermining that parent or causing devastation to the family system, the child's source of security.[1]

When beginning psychotherapy with children or adolescents with an eating disorder, the therapist will gain considerable mileage by engaging the patient

---

[1] In the 2006 film *The Good Shepherd* (DeNiro & Roth, 2006), the lead character por-trayed subtly and brilliantly by Matt Damon, is a taciturn, seemingly emotionless CIA agent who is afflicted by a torturous family secret (i.e., his father's suicide when he was a youngster). The shame Damon's character feels, coupled with the understandably childlike desire to emulate the admirable qualities of his naval officer father and simul-taneously overcome family humiliation, is a powerful motivator for his eventual career in the CIA. As he moves up the career ladder, he becomes privy to many different kinds of secrets which embolden him to believe that he knows the morally correct stance for his country to take. This "good shepherd" is blinded to the toll his hidden life takes on his wife, son, and eventually himself until the end of the movie when he must unlock and confront the long concealed enigma to gain access, understanding, and eventual for-giveness for a life driven by powerful needs to avoid "knowing" and "feeling" the original, devastating loss and trauma that shaped his entire life.

in discussing a family secret that may be hidden, in plain view, such as an unmourned loss. Reiterate to the patient that therapy is a safe place where one is free to say anything one wishes but be sure to include that it can feel scary to talk. Most of the time families and patients will be more forthcoming and the covert issues more easily accessed than in the case of Valerie.

The case example which follows presents a more typical situation that makes use of this concept. Simply inquiring about recent or past losses within the family or learning the circumstances of the adolescent's birth helps her or him to find better ways of coping with the problem. The therapist will need to be patient in waiting for the secret to come out but just opening a channel by addressing "what is hidden in plain view" can be a head start. For example, reflecting "How do you understand your parents' divorce?" "How sad that your mother died." "Sometimes voices or intrusive thoughts have meaning. I wonder what you are not 'supposed to say?'" "It's interesting that you never mention that your folks seem to fight a lot even though they always seem to be bickering in the family sessions and when I come out to get you in the waiting area." Any of these simple statements or questions, derived from a basic historical perspective and clinical inference, may be all that is needed to help the patient go deeper and not keep issues or feelings to themselves. The therapist is there as a safe object to help them look—if the theoretical formulation is kept in mind.

Hilde Bruch underscored the need to listen in order to let the adolescent find and own her or his voice so that internal struggles and conflicts come into the open. Thus, the treatment process may serve as a parental process that has been heretofore unfulfilled or neglected. The therapist, like a "good enough" primary caretaker, is in the essential position of recognizing and allowing the adolescent to speak about any "unhappiness as valid, whereas the nonrecognizing reinforces the unhappiness, and the sharing of it helps to resolve it. But the child who never grows up never gets help on this point" (Bruch, 1988, p. 197). Adolescents with eating disorders stuff their feelings, obsessively ruminate, focus on seemingly "trivial, irrelevant events," and neglect their abilities, talents, and potential out of a sense of fear or danger of getting hurt or damaging a loved one no matter what they do. If they let it be known to themselves or the other person how upset and pained they feel by unspoken messages to keep silent, they might be faced with the greater danger of losing the love and care of the people on whom they must depend (Bruch, 1988, pp. 59, 68).

Clinical Example

Max was 15 years old, doing beautifully in school, and appropriately engaged in peer activities, when his mother, age 40, was diagnosed with acute lymphoblastic leukemia. Max's mother had been treated for Hodgkin's disease when he was 5; during his young life the family lived under the shadow of the possibility of the illness recurring or a new cancer developing. Still, his parents did all they could to shield Max from their concerns and nurtured him and his younger sister, Beth. They showered their children with love, attention, the advantages of private school, money for extracurricular activities, and regular family outings to the park and vacations.

The children seemed to be growing up with a sense of who they were and what they really wanted out of life (e.g., true self functions) when life played another cruel trick. Max's mother became acutely ill and died within weeks of her diagnosis, leaving the family little time to say good-bye. After the mother's death, Max's father became quite depressed. The family seemed to wither in the aftermath of this traumatic loss. Max's father tried hard to be strong and gave considerable emotional support to his children, but he was unable to help them mourn, understandably feeling the impact of his own deep grief.

Max's family had been stable, close knit, and grounding; this was undoubtedly a basis for some of the adolescent's psychological achievements to date. How unfair that life dealt such a devastating blow, especially when they had already confronted the Grim Reaper once before and temporarily won. Max reacted to his mother's death and to his father's emotional anguish by going on a hunger strike and attempting to contain his grief by overexercising. Within six weeks, Max lost significant weight (to 80% of his target BMI) and became preoccupied with his body image. "I want to be skinny and call the shots. Maybe then you'll leave me alone" were the opening salvos to the queries of his primary care physician. Once again, comprehensive, integrated treatment necessitated an in-depth appraisal of the individual and family's psychological needs in addition to treating the biological consequences of Max's anorexia.

Fortunately Max's father was able to accept the recommendation of the family doctor to begin his own psychotherapy process in order to address issues of loss and grief. The doctor said the father needed an adult relationship to help him strategize about additional supports he and his children needed in order to overcome the hurdle of living life without their mother and wife. The father's therapist recommended that each child have their own "safe place" to discuss their loss and that family therapy continue. In order to be respectful of their preferences, Max's father asked his children what they wanted to do, but made it clear that each family member needed support (i.e., he did not abdicate his parental, limit-setting role). Both Beth and Max agreed to the family sessions; Max decided to "try out" an individual therapist whom one of his peers also saw and liked. Beth opted for a support group for adolescents who had lost a parent to illness or suicide, which was sponsored by a community hospital.

In family sessions, Max, Beth, and the father looked straightforwardly at all of the "secret feelings" that they had about Max's mother, including times when they felt anger at her for leaving them. Herein the family therapy accomplished the task that Freud viewed as crucial in overcoming any significant loss: one must address the ambivalence one feels toward the object who is gone.

In Max's individual sessions, the eating disorder was conceptualized as a way Max identified with his mother's illness. Just as she had lost weight, Max was now doing so. Identifying with the lost object by becoming like him or her psychologically restores the object and is a frequently observed psychological concomitant to unresolved grief. Max's therapist pointed out that there would be healthier ways for Max to "take in" aspects of his mother over time.

Most importantly, however, is that within the therapy Max found a safe place where he could express the range of feelings that invariably accompany the grief process. In so doing, he was able to work through some of the major boulders that define grief and loss rather quickly. His eating disorder improved dramatically. In this case, making loss a speakable issue within the family of origin and refusing to designate the patient as the only person with an illness, helped to pave the way to adapting to the real loss every family member had suffered and needed to work through to reengage in life.

Max, now 22, occasionally writes his therapist to check in and let her know how he is doing. A secondary school teacher who writes poetry as a sideline, this brave young man confided in a card written to his therapist on Mother's Day:

> I'm glad you were there when I needed you. Don't get any ideas that you can replace my real mom, though. I do like to check in and let you know how its going. . . . Just the other day it was almost like I would feel my mom's presence. It made me tearful, like I was going through the loss again. I sat down and tried to write a poem but couldn't so I just got busy working on my lesson plans.

Max's note describes another essential facts about grief and loss. Much as we therapists help our patients work through trauma to a certain extent, the relationship that is lost is never completely mourned. A holiday, an odor, a dream, a thought triggered out of nowhere—these are just some of the everyday events that can bring the lost but never forgotten other back into our consciousness. When the person is able to withstand, discuss, or creatively work with their reminiscences, they are less likely to defensively retreat to their symptoms.

TAYLOR: A CASE OF MULTIGENERATIONAL EATING DISORDER?

When family members place a high value on physical perfection and attractiveness, children and adolescents are inevitably negatively affected. Grandparents' and parents' ideas about food and body image have an impact on the child's physical and psychological development (Winters, 2002). As children grow older, they are in particular need of adults to help them withstand cultural and media pressures regarding body image, but sometimes family pressures do just the opposite. It is important for therapists to consider that sometimes an older member is doing the best they can to be helpful. They may remember being teased themselves, and they want the child to have less trouble with peers then they did and to be considered successful and attractive. Clinicians must also keep in mind that the family is also immersed in the culture that is media driven (Rosenberger, 1999). Consideration of these two factors in addition to personality dynamics also helps the therapist to form an empathic connection with the family and eschew a blaming stance while also attending to narcissistic issues, misattunement, rigidities, and emotional neglect that may play a predominant role in the eating disorder.

Therapists must help parents and children sort out age appropriate interests in appearance from obsessive concern with the body that overshadows other talents and ability. The central psychological issues of adolescence—separation and individuation—are often conflictual for parents who experience the maturation of the child as a loss for themselves. The child is also ambivalent about growing up and losing the advantages of childhood. In some families, conflict over an overt behavior like dieting or eating "helps" the family avoid confronting the real issue: Separation and growing up are difficult for all concerned. In Table 4.3, I list some of the crucial questions that the clinician must focus on in treating an eating disorder in an adolescent; some of these queries will not be answered until well into the treatment, as earlier case examples in this chapter illustrate. The following case of Taylor, her mother, and her grandmother is another example of how some of the complexities of adolescent transition interdigitate when body and appearance present as the central foci of concern.

Taylor's preoccupation with dieting began when she was 12. Her disturbed eating patterns became quickly apparent as the individual psychotherapist and consulting psychiatrist posed a series of questions to the patient and her family (Table 4.3). Media messages, peer pressure, and a tendency toward obsessive nail biting and hair picking were only part of the symptomatic picture that perplexed Taylor's individual psychotherapist: By the time the designated patient was 18, she had already suffered with severe malnutrition, used laxatives, diet

---

TABLE 4.3 Questions to consider when treating the adolescent with an eating disorder

- Does a parent, grandparent, or primary caregiver struggle with letting the child grow up?
- What is the nature of normative ambivalence about giving up and maturing in the child or the family of origin? (Patients with ED may tend to have greater internal struggle than other adolescents about maintaining connections and separating from their family of origin)
- Does the patient harbor a family secret?
- Are there any unresolved issues of loss or grief in the family?
- Is there a history of eating disorder in parent or grandparent (i.e., multigenerational eating disorder)? Does a member of the family overvalue weight or shape?
- Could the patient be identifying with a peer or family member who has an eating disorder or who loses substantial amounts of weight for medical reasons? (Remember that adolescence is a time when identity is fluid and role models are often chosen willy-nilly or unconsciously)
- What family conflicts or developmental deficits impinge on the development of the true self?

pills, and diuretics and overexercised to the point of exhaustion in order to stay slender. Taylor said she would do anything "to be perfect in my family for my mother and grandmother." In the initial months of treatment the clinician attempted to tease out issues of temperament, cultural pressures, and dynamics while forming an enduring alliance.

In the individual sessions, Taylor described how a fascinating intergenerational pattern of emphasis on weight and body image had taken a huge toll on her development. Her grandmother, Peggy, teased Taylor's mother about her granddaughter's "baby fat" when she was still an infant.

It had always seemed to Taylor that her own mother spent too much time thinking about her own weight, size, and shape and trying to please the maternal grandmother. In fact, the entire family was tyrannized by grandmother's criticisms and tirades. Everyone jumped to her commands in an effort to please and avoid confronting a powerful presence who would sulk or avoid contact for weeks if she was challenged. The gift to grandmother of a mug with the inscription, "She Who Must be Obeyed" by Taylor's older brother, Dale, humorously but aptly captured how each family member felt held hostage by the grandmother's demands, moods, and angry outbursts when she didn't get her way.

Taylor and Dale exhibited the kind of premature psychological understanding of their parents that one often finds in families of eating disorder patients. They each independently told the family therapist how sorry they felt for their mother because, "grandmother just can't get off of her case, either." In actuality, Peggy's relentless preoccupation with weight and maintaining tight control of the thoughts, activities, and actions had an enormous effect on everyone in the family. Like others who signal a potential eating disorder out of preoccupation with weight, size, and shape to the exclusion of other interests and concerns about the child, Taylor's grandmother's problem further demonstrates how an eating disorder may actually be an intergenerational problem. All the females in this family were caught up with the addiction to maintain a certain weight and size regardless of the psychological costs. As Jane Fonda (2005) candidly revealed in her memoir, the eating problem in Taylor's family was "always there . . . hovering darkly. You carry the secret demon within you and it colors everything you do, at certain times more than others" (p. 404). In Taylor and Peggy's case, the individual and family therapists had to join the battle that had heretofore been relinquished out of fear.

In this case the family therapist asked Taylor's individual therapist and psychiatrist to attend a joint session with *all* members of the family. Given the longevity and severity of Taylor's problem, the entire treatment team communicated regularly but were concerned about the refractory nature of the problem. Each team member wondered independently if hospitalization would be the next step for Taylor! Because recent studies have indicated that siblings are negatively implicated when a brother or sister has an eating disorder, these team members worried about the overt and subtle effects on Dale's puberty.

Ideally, a joint meeting of this type signals to the family the gravity of the situation. It is the "full court press" routinely undertaken in residential and hospital units but occurs less frequently than it might in outpatient care due to time constraints and sometimes family resistance. Because the practitioners in this treatment all had offices near each other in a hospital complex and collaborated often, they were able to agree upon a time in their schedules to meet together, first without and then with the family. The initial planning meeting insured that all team members would be "on the same page" and say the same thing. Under circumstances where members are not able to meet in person with the family due to time constraints or practice preferences (e.g., the wish to keep the therapy relationship totally sacrosanct and confidential), I advise that all other treaters write out their concerns and give copies to family members, the patient, and other treaters to discuss in the full court press intervention (by the primary therapist or designated team leader) to minimize splitting and to impress on all concerned the teams stance and the serious nature of the disorder.

In Taylor's family, there was initial resistance to hearing the medical and psychological concerns (see Chapter 1). Because both parents wanted their children to grow and to become independent, they encouraged Taylor to make her own decisions but admitted to capitulating to Peggy's demands. Informed about this family pattern, the therapist decided to take the tack of drawing Taylor's true self into the open by strategic questions aimed at strengthening Taylor's capacity for self-reflection and decision making.

Taylor's individual therapist posed questions such as, "Taylor, what *do you* want for your life?" or "Why is it that everybody seems to try so hard to please Peggy? What's your idea about why this happens in you family? What function does it serve?" Of course the answers to these queries changed and evolved over Taylor's therapy. The gradual development of Taylor's capacity to answer them for herself and make different choices based on her own values paralleled control over her eating disorder. Without the use of psychotropic medication, she gained weight, overexercise stopped, and her tics and obsessionality diminished. The family and individual therapies gave the patient opportunities for change and honest self-discovery.

In this case example, I am fortunate to have some long-term follow-up. Taylor is now 32, married, and the mother of four children. No longer in therapy, she occasionally writes or calls to "provide updates and just check in." For Taylor, multidisciplinary, integrated therapy had many positive effects, even though she has weathered disappointing events in her career. Her husband, Duane, has helped her through those crises and she is pleased by her accomplishments. In a recent note she honestly portrayed the "ups and downs" of a mature relationship but also her genuine joy in "seeing the two older kids go to school" and "helping Duane deal with his own job." As an aside she added, "It has been interesting to watch my mother and grandmother fight about what *I* should feed my babies. I can tune them out pretty well these days. I love them dearly for who they are but I've had to accept that their 'eating issues' continue. I'm just too busy and involved with my real life to care about that anymore."

Taylor now exhibits the quality of a mature adult who can own the inter-generational family eating disorder but not let it affect her activities with her own children. She has been able to achieve autonomy and independence yet main-tain a connection with loved ones despite what she sees as flaws and the unre-solved issues of control and overinvestment in weight, eating, and body image. Taylor neither idealizes her mate nor devalues her mother and grandmother; she speaks ambivalently about everyone, including her therapist who "could not make everything perfect for me either" (see Chapter 3). Most importantly, Taylor also realizes the situations and external stressors under which she could relapse into disordered eating. Indeed, when this happened during her first two pregnancies (she lost significant weight by overexercising in the postpartum period), she briefly reentered individual therapy and a support group. She suc-cessfully traversed adolescence into full, functional adulthood. Family therapy also served a successful ballast for her brother, Dale, who is also doing well and with whom Taylor has a mutually supportive, adult relationship. The two speak weekly and e-mail each other, in no small way, I suspect, to keep forces joined against destructive and intractable dynamics in this otherwise loving and func-tional extended family system.

ADDITIONAL TREATMENT CONSIDERATIONS

Treatment of eating disorders must be adapted to the developmental stage of the patient even though virtually no research has assessed the interventions that improve outcomes in any age group. The therapist must keep in mind that the adolescent oscillates between the regressive attachment to childhood and the normative thrust toward adulthood; the task of the therapist remains to help the patient negotiate the steps in this "second individuation" in a healthy way. Body image and eating disturbances at this time reflect the struggle for iden-tity that all adolescents experience because they give the patient a sense that they can control their bodies, their feelings, their maturation, and sometimes even their loved ones (Steiner-Adair, 1991a, 1991b). While cultural, environ-mental, and biological factors no doubt play pivotal roles in individual devel-opment as well as the etiology of the eating problem, the clinician must address islands of maltreatment and deprivation, family dynamics, affect and tension tolerance, and individual conflicts and deficits that may interfere with the con-solidation of identity.

To tap the psyches of adolescents and young adults, psychoanalyst Heinz Kohut advised therapists who were working in a student health service to immerse themselves in the empathic understanding that derives only from "reverberations from our own early experiences" because it is only with "this recognition that one can understand another person psychologically, insofar as they are at least related experiences in ourselves" (cited in Elson, 1987, pp. 271–272). Kohut seemed to be saying, "put yourself in the shoes of your patient, remember what it was like to be that age yourself, feel *with* the patient, and don't fear getting lost in taking on the role because you won't."

Kohut's observation that we locate the adolescent within ourselves in order to identify with our patients' strivings remains stellar advice today. The personal qualities he also observed in this group of committed therapists he supervised included exquisitely tuning in to the adolescent developmental struggle that can also be parlayed into interventions that apply to those adolescences who have an eating disorder in your practice. They include (1) showing respect (p. 214); (2) maintaining warmth and feelings of kinship and understanding (i.e., your identification with the adolescent inside yourself) (p. 214); (3) raising self-esteem by simply liking the patient; (4) "respectful listening" (p. 214); (5) a nonjudgmental attitude (p. 187); and (6) accepting your patient's gratitude without interpreting it as bogus or defensive (p. 252).

Other therapeutic principles I have found useful in working with adolescent patients with anorexia and bulimia include:

1. Involve parents in treatment whenever possible. Therapists must always be alert to how pathogenic aspects of family life may impinge on the development of the child without necessarily taking a "blaming stance"; that does no one any good. Much remains to be learned about the influence of parents' body image preoccupations that can influence the psychological life of children.

2. Attempt to elicit the family secrets that remain hidden, yet are in plain view. They may play formidable roles in the developmental pathogenesis of some eating disorders. What can appear as an entrenched symptom may take on dramatic new meanings when understood within the context of the conscious and unconscious messages that have been given to the child to withhold information out of family loyalties.

3. Help the patient address cultural messages; teach the patient to critique media and advertising images and encourage the primary caretakers to do likewise. The distorted body image that occurs with an eating disorder exerts a pathogenic influence on ego development. Anorexia or bulimia can become ways that the individual tries to separate from the parent via an alliance with a group that has a respectable, culturally validated disease (Brumberg, 1988, 1997). Treatments of eating disorders in adolescence that address body image issues have an immediate and direct effect on ego functions, but they will not be successful unless peer group and social influences are understood and channeled into healthy outlets.

4. Keep in mind the cognitive style, intellectual endowment, and developmental limitations of adolescents. In psychotherapeutic work, both the therapist and the adolescent must attempt to address a range of difficult and unspoken emotions in order to help the patient grapple with the complex task of growing up and negotiating complicated symptoms. Therapeutic relationships offer a safe space for the adolescent in which thinking and integration of new ideas begin to take place. In particular, the processing that goes on in therapeutic relationship is the containing space the adolescent needs to have in order to remember and work through conflict, find new objects of identification, and begin to locate internal resources that enable the negotiation of the powerful transition of adolescence.

5. Find creative ways to engage adolescents who have difficulty telling their history. Adolescents with eating disorders may struggle with putting into words their stories, their feelings, and their goals because of neurobehavioral/cognitive limitations in the developing brain, any history of trauma or physical abuse, and personal dynamics that are unique to the individual. Treatment can sometimes be jump-started by asking the patient to see a film or read a story of interest and report back on it. Permitting and encouraging the patient to describe the experiences of the main characters or one character's emotional reactions may be all that is necessary to get the patient talking. This process may then gradually transition to discussions of the more salient therapeutic issues.

6. As in the treatment of other eating disorders, try not to "go at it alone" unless you must. A multidisciplinary team including a physician, nutritionist, family, or group psychotherapist, and an individual psychotherapist can support each other and be prepared for concerted action if the patient's symptoms worsen or if the family is resistant to doing their part. Sometimes hospital care will be essential if the symptoms become life threatening, and the entire team will be called upon to make the case to the family or insurance provider. Each of the treatment figures serves as a useful model for the adolescent to identify with, particularly crucial when such models have been lacking in the particular child's life (e.g., such as the case of abuse or maltreatment, loss of a parent).

7. Pose a question to the adolescent about her values and what she considers important in her life. Outcome studies of eating disorders in adolescence indicate that recovery is robust when the problem is diagnosed and treated early, when weight is stabilized and maintained, and when menses return and hormonal function normalizes. Patients also tend to do better when their treatment has been longer and more extensive in terms of services rendered (e.g., individual and family therapies). Tenacity, hopefulness, flexibility, openness to negotiation, provision of social support, and suggestions for better coping are other features of the therapist who successfully treats adolescents with eating disorders.

8. Remember that for treatment to be successful over the long run, the adolescent must learn to take responsibility for self while demonstrating concern for others. The adolescent's normative preoccupation with self-interest must give way to healthy self-esteem in adulthood and "a secure sense of self . . . to reach a level of maturity . . . [to] engage in relationships without vesting on others their own deprivation and suffering . . . [and enables] partnership and parenthood too in the future" (Rose, 1990, p. 179, 183).

CONCLUSION

Individual psychotherapy continues to be a mainstay in the treatment of adolescents with eating disorders. A growing number of studies now documents that psychological treatments are crucial in helping a significant percentage of individuals recover even though definitive data about the most effective kinds of treatment remain scant. It is essential to involve family members in the treatment, but recovery also necessitates that the adolescent negotiate the developmental challenge of establishing an identity of her or his own. Patients with eating disorders must, therefore, navigate the dual challenges of this developmental phase, sometimes called "the second individuation." This entails working through the myriad conflicts of maintaining separate while staying emotionally connected.

Cognitive-behavioral methods can be usefully employed to help adolescent patients learn new modes of coping, find ways of regulating strong feelings, and master problematic interpersonal and family situations. These methods must be titrated to the developmental needs of the adolescent. Moreover, an integrated approach will necessarily include psychodynamic principles that address family conflicts and deficits, trauma and attachment, and confront pathological defensive strategies. Psychodynamic methods permit a gradual unraveling of the incipient family and developmental deficits that impinge on the development of the sense of self.

In order for most patients to improve, they will need to mourn aspects of their parents that were less than perfect and come to accept each family member's strengths and weaknesses. Successful therapy ensures that the adolescent become more autonomous and have improved self-care while fostering age appropriate connections to family members and peers. Learning what healthy dependency is and how it can be achieved furthers this individuation process.

In order to consolidate an identity other than that of the eating disorder, patient education and group modalities may also be helpful. In each therapeutic modality, new objects of identification are available for the patient. Providing a base of security that implicitly encourages the goal of improved self-care, normalizes eating patterns, challenges the cultural bases undergirding the eating problems, and addresses core conflicts or family dysfunction are the central tasks of any therapeutic modality or technique at this developmental stage. All modes of treatment are also likely to converge on teaching important life skills that aid in affect regulation and provide greater understanding of what drives the eating disorder.

Though long-term outcome studies are needed to document the efficacy of these approaches, to date it appears that patients value the opportunity to learn about ways to master their problems and understand the meaning behind them. This increases a sense of personal autonomy and resiliency, both of which are deemed essential in overcoming the eating disorder; it also has the potential adjunctive benefit of improving self-esteem, self-worth, and a sense of authenticity that will be called upon repeatedly in the patient's adulthood. The emotionally accessible psychotherapist offers empathy, protection, containment, and understanding of the multifactorial nature of the patient's eating disorder and is thereby a model for competence and self-care the patient needs. These qualities are essential in assisting the patients in taking ownership of their bodies, facing problems in living, and mustering the strength to let go of their eating and body image problems.

CHAPTER 5

Adulthood

Gollum was defeated. He dared go no further. He had lost: lost his prey, and lost, too, the only thing he had ever cared for, his precious. . . . He wanted it because it was a ring of power. If you slipped that ring on your finger, you were invisible: Only in the full sunlight could you be seen, and then only by your shadow, and that would be shaky and faint.
—Tolkien (1977)

We cannot avoid
Using power,
Cannot escape the compulsion
To afflict the world,
So let us, cautious in diction
And mighty in contradiction,
Love powerfully.

—Martin Buber (cited in Friedman, 1993)

An emotionally healthy adult carries within the self a feeling of authentic power. This principle is manifested by an experience of mastery in work and a capacity to safely and securely engage in interpersonal relationships. Accruing this sense of healthy power is one of the central tasks of adult development, and those who successfully traverse this developmental period exhibit a satisfying engagement with the world by what they bring to life, including (but not exclusively), the capacity for maintaining intimate adult relationships, passionately enjoying one's work and hobbies, the raising of children, exhibiting generosity to the community in large and small ways, and being a good example to others by valuing our own self-care.

As theologian Martin Buber distinguishes in this stanza from his (1926) poem, "Power and Love," the attainment of authentic power requires embracing contradictions to define our truth and find meaning in life; the adult is required to think through and carefully consider those actions and deeds that will "Love, influence . . . impact . . . and make one's mark" (Buber, quoted in Friedman, 1993, p. 117). Most psychotherapists would concur with Buber's belief that communities are also transformed by those "heart-searching" (p. 42) individuals whose choices and intentions are propelled by "self-discovery and toward self-unfolding" (Buber, quoted in Friedman, p. 124). We adults cannot avoid using our inherent power because we are all called upon each day to sort through generative and destructive capacities within us. Will we follow the narrow path that permits us full expression of our unique selves in mutual dialogue with our fellows or will we take a detour, overtaken by avarice, greed, envy, or unhealthy competition with a dreaded, nameless other? Will our sense of purpose be put to good use or for ill, and who will benefit from or be damaged by our choices? Will we, like the character Gollum, seize and hold onto "the precious," false power that is inevitably self-destructive?

Gollum, as illustrated in Tolkien's original novels (and the cinematic version of *Lord of the Rings*), is an emaciated, hyperenergetic, avaricious goblin. His luminous, protruding eyes, reminiscent of our most malnourished patients, are at once frightening and pitiful. In his quest to fully possess the ring, he gradually extinguishes his real power, the true self, and in so doing he becomes unrecognizable. Only when the "precious," symbolic of one's desire for false power, is abandoned, is one free to discover and grapple with the essence of one's true, real source of power.

In their dichotomous style of black-and-white thinking, eating disorder patients avoid the ambiguities inherent in finding an authentic sense of power. Attaining the perfect body is the sought after "precious" that will finally provide self-validation, recognition, and especially affirmation from the world. This internal hunger for power and recognition prevents the adult's acquisition of those abilities that "are all necessary ingredients in authentic power" (Person, 2002, p. 342). In the obsessive search to gain false power by a focus on the body and beauty, individuals invariably fall victim to their own illusions about what is important in life. Tragically, our patients are not able to express their powerful love, and hence, they are never "seen" for the unique gifts they bring to the world.

In this chapter I discuss how a contemporary understanding of the adult development informs the treatment of individuals with eating disorders. Clinical examples illustrate how the central tasks of this developmental period are derailed by the eating disorder and will offer some guidance to the clinician who attempts to help the patient reengage with life and confront the eating disorder symptoms. I also review how cultural and biological issues may not only inform but be employed to enrich the treatment, primarily from an educational perspective. Strategies and interventions that specifically apply to the adult patient are also outlined.

I point out some of the deeper psychodynamic issues of eating disorder patients that impede full engagement at this point in the life cycle; they prevent the patient from the spontaneity, creativity, and dialogic possibilities to respond "with the whole of her or his being to the uniqueness of every situation that challenges him or her as an active person" (Friedman, 1993, pp. 247–248). By maintaining a focus on the potentials and pitfalls inherent in these adult developmental tasks, the clinician may more easily pinpoint at any moment in the treatment the work that must yet be done for the patient to have a full quality of life. While also offering some suggestions about how cognitive-behavioral (CBT) and interpersonal (ITP) interventions can be woven into the fabric of treatment for improved symptom control, I argue that the therapeutic process is incomplete and less than satisfactory until the patient is more able to fully embrace those adult developmental concerns that take into full consideration the impact of our culture, biology, individual psychology, and need for mutual relationships with others.

CULTURAL CONSIDERATIONS

The majority of clinicians and laypeople assume that our media driven, appearance obsessed, and perfectionistic and narcissistic society likely plays a formidable role in the development and maintenance of eating disorders. Some investigators who write extensively about dimensions of eating disorders as a culture-bound syndrome (Becker, 1995, 2003, 2004a, 2004b; Gordon, 2000) also describe how rapid social change and transforming gender roles exacerbate body concerns and dieting. Anorexia nervosa was described even in ancient medical texts, but this "template of the disease" in contemporary Western culture derives from extolling the virtues of dieting, exercise, the globalization of the fashion industry, and the heightened stigma of being overweight (Gordon, 2000; Vandereycken & Van Deth, 1994).

No doubt contemporary conflicts about the autonomous strivings of women and the ambivalence both sexes feel about female empowerment as social change occurs play contributing roles (Bernstein & Lenhart, 1993; Notman & Nadelson, 1991; Schuker & Levinson, 1991; Steiner-Adair, 1991a). Men and women may both turn to eating disorders if they are "unable to work out a satisfactory solution to the problem of identity" (Gordon, 2000, p. 109). Confusion about social roles, especially at times of marked cultural transition, such as our own, are temporarily assuaged by forging a personal identity in an eating disorder.

The role of cultural values and norms in the etiology and perpetuation of eating disorders must be pragmatically integrated into contemporary treatment. Utilizing books such as Richard Gordon's *Eating Disorders: Anatomy of a Social Epidemic* (2000) for more sophisticated patients will provide significant material for discussion in group and individual therapy. This comprehensive, standard reference about the influence of culture on eating disorder raises the consciousness of any adult on the pivotal roles just noted that are inherent in Western society's diet mentality. Gordon, who maintains an individual psychotherapy practice in addition to serving as a professor of psychology at Bard College, underscores throughout this book that discussion about the culture must not take away from focusing on individual dynamics, such as the conflicts inherent in achieving one's autonomy, a history of maltreatment or sexual abuse, and problems uncovered within the family of origin or in one's adult family or with one's peers.

In a truly integrated treatment, discussions of the role of culture will not replace a nuanced and detailed examination of any individual, family, and interpersonal issues that promote these illnesses. Taking up the topic of culture can actually be an impetus for elaboration of individual concerns. As Gordon further describes with respect to treatment, some therapists will be comfortable asking their patients to develop an "atrocity file" and then discuss in the session the toxic media images or advertisements the patient finds. Although there is limited clinical research follow-up to suggest that discussions of unrealistic standards promoted by the culture actually change unconscious attitudes, the therapist may take solace in the fact that he or she has attempted to help elucidate important cultural forces that may aid the patient to "potentially develop a more realistic body concept and an awareness of the distorted standards that she has internalized" (p. 134).

Other cultural factors that should be taken into consideration in the treatment include the globalization of eating disorders and the risks that transnational migration, modernization, urbanization, and the economic, social, and cultural changes that play roles in perpetuating anorexia and bulimia. In fact, the definition of what constitutes an eating disorder may change depending on the culture of the patient. Among Chinese women, "fat phobia" is often missing in persons who otherwise meet diagnostic criteria for the illness (Lee, 1996, 2004).

Ann Becker, a psychiatrist and anthropologist who practices at Harvard Medical School, has done some of the most respected and important original research on the rapidity with which attitudes about the body can change. She continues to explore how the introduction of television affected young women on the island of Fiji (see also Chapter 4) (Becker, 1995; Becker, Burwell, Navara, & Gilman, 2003; Becker, Fay, Gilman, Striegel-Moore, 2007). Among the 50 ethnic Fijian women who completed a self-report measure developed for studying dieting and attitudes toward body shape and change, Becker found that media and sweeping economic and social change influenced the development of binge eating disorder symptoms. Becker believes that it is premature to say whether the disordered eating she found actually parallels Western categories for eating disorders, but "television has certainly imported more than just images associating appearance with material success; it has arguably enhanced reflexivity about the possibility of reshaping one's body and life trajectory, and popularized the notion of competitive social positioning" (Becker, 2004a, p. 552).

Another study that simultaneously extends and challenges the meaning of Western beauty standards in fostering eating disorders is Pike and Borovoy's (2004) study of contemporary Japan. Noting the rise in the diagnoses of eating disorders in Japan, the researchers synthesize case examples, clinical and epidemiological studies, and their own extensive interview data of subjects to arrive at a pointed conclusion: Although eating disorders in Japan are linked to the social transformation of urbanization and industrialization, weight and shape concerns also reflect broader cultural and historical factors unique to Japan. Their 75 in-depth interviews of Japanese women provided "evidence of a rich and complex interplay of factors," (p. 513) about how

> the women struggled with finding a voice to constructively express their conflicts related to gender role expectations and ideals of thinness and appearance.... Their eating disorders arose within their individual experiences on a broader cultural stage, and served them in communicative and instrumental ways (p. 523).

Paralleling the observations of psychodynamically informed clinicians in Britain and the United States (Dare, 1995, 1997; Dare & Crowther, 1995; Farrell, 2000; Zerbe, 1993/1995a, 1993a, 1993b, 2001b), they conclude that the psychological distress, depression, and adult developmental challenges brought about by a pervasive "silencing of the self rooted in conflicts arising from broad gender role expectations" (p. 523) may contribute to the rise of eating disorders and other psychological vulnerabilities in women who grapple with a plethora of stressors, expectations, family conflicts, and adult responsibility.

Another cross-disciplinary investigation undertaken by Melanie Katzman and colleagues (Katzman, Hermans, Van Hoeken, & Hoek 2004) combined qualitative and quantitative data in examining subcultures in Curacao, a Caribbean island in economic transition. This investigation actually reversed an earlier opinion by the same groups of researchers that concluded that anorexia and culture are not related (Hoek, van Harten, van Haeken, & Susser, 1998). In the current study, Katzman, Hermans, and colleagues (2004) found that in any given population, there may be subpopulations more at risk than others. Their anthropological work led them to observe how, in Curacao, mixed race, mobile women who were educated and had lived overseas were more at risk than the majority black population who had not left the island. Noting the complex factors (e.g., temperament, frustration, anxiety, and other inherited neurochemical alterations) that contribute to eating disorders, they argue for more cross-cultural studies that pay attention "to potential subcultural 'surprises'," (p. 485) to inform, understand, assess, and intervene when appropriate across racial and ethnic backgrounds.

Their results also capture the importance of taking into consideration psychological vulnerabilities (e.g., perfectionism, conflict avoidance), peer relations, adaptive and protective factors, and the absence of eating disorders in subpopulations when studying cultures. One additional point from their study deserves emphasis for its daily *clinical* utility. As in some subpopulations of African Americans and Latinas in the United States, the black Curacao women found comfort in their bodies (despite their body's imperfections) and in their sexuality. In Curacao, "this comfort with curves is reinforced by local expressions, such as a woman looking *bon kome* or "well-eaten," a compliment meaning that she has a lot of meat to hold onto and is a "beautiful mama!" (p. 484). Although it is unlikely that any individual's mind will be significantly modified by educating about a particular culture or subculture's benevolent views, it does draw attention to the patient's rigid acceptance of particular societal norms and may initiate a process of *consciously* challenging excessive value of external standards.

Cultural research of this kind also demonstrates that understanding how the individual negotiates societal change, body image, and personal identity is a highly complex matter. Clinicians neglect this growing cross-cultural research at our peril. Cultural expectations play a pivotal role in how the individual feels about the self and deals with adult issues; this research reminds us of powerful forces of cultural norms, economics, and social vulnerability that can shape the view one has of oneself. Becker argues that young women who undergo social transition may turn to diet and changing their physical appearance to enhance "positioning oneself competitively through the informed use of cultural symbols" (2003, p. 553). Securing social advantage may play a greater role in the maintenance of eating disorder symptoms across cultures than clinicians heretofore understood because "vulnerable girls and women across diverse populations who feel marginalized from the locally dominant culture's sources of prestige and status may anchor their identities in widely recognized cultural symbols of prestige popularized by media-imported ideas, values and images" (Becker, 2004b, p. 555).

Clinical Example

Most importantly, clinicians must be prepared to hear about a given culture's impact as we listen to our patient's history every day. The importance of paying heed to cultural dimensions and learning from the patient was driven home again one afternoon when Dr. Ping-Ming, a Chinese immigrant and researcher in biochemistry living and working in the United States and being treated for an anxiety disorder, noticed a row of textbooks on my bookshelf related to eating disorders. Dr. Ping-Ming informed me that there is a Chinese expression that she grew up with, which is still in use to this day: "Whiteness covers any ugliness." I was shocked as she went on to tell me about the idealization she witnessed in her culture for those who were blond and blue-eyed. "You would be a knock-out over there Dr. Z.—any blond would be considered 'hot' to the guys! Even in middle-age!"

She went on to say that she would "never believe" in a purely genetic or biological etiology for eating disorders because of the fixation on appearance she continues to observe among her Asian compatriots who have moved to the United States. "I wish you could come to the lunchroom, Dr. Z., and hear us. Nobody's talking about our discoveries or research grants or even our kids. It's just diet, diet, diet. We Asian women go on and on about our short stature, single eye folds, and desire to get skinny. We don't like who we are." Because Dr. Ping-Ming was not overtly concerned with body image in her process, these observations were not central to our work, although they did educate me to a cultural dimension to potential self-esteem vulnerabilities and open a dialogue for her experiences with current peers, childhood "messages," and the implications of immigrating on any body image issues that might be exacerbated in a Western culture. I will also be grateful to Dr. Ping-Ming for teaching me something about Chinese culture that I would not otherwise have been aware of.

BIOLOGICAL CONSIDERATIONS

Much remains to be understood regarding the physiological changes that undergird and perpetuate eating disorders. To be sure, there is considerable evidence that neurophysiologic and endocrine alterations play primary roles in the etiology and maintenance of eating disorders, but as yet "there is considerable discrepancy between biological knowledge and its poor application in treatment of eating disorders" (Milos, 2003, p. 219). The pragmatics of clinical practice often lag behind our scientific understanding, but those maladaptive, core beliefs that patients maintain such as "my eating disorder won't hurt me" can be challenged by presenting this information. Clinical judgment will be necessary, of course, because some patients will have more interest in and intellectual capacity to absorb this information. Others will benefit from a cursory distillation of pertinent biological facts that emphasizes the longevity, pervasiveness, and life-threatening nature of their eating disorder.

Dieting lowers blood tryptophan levels in healthy women, likely resulting in decreased synthesis in the central nervous system (CNS) neurotransmitter serotonin and possibly contributing to an impaired satiety response and the high calorie binge episodes associated with bulimia. Dysfunction in the CNS serotonin system may play a role in the lack of response to antidepressant medications in some low weight patients. The persistence of serotonin, noradrenalin, and dopamine system disturbances after recovery from eating disorders suggests that dysregulation in one or more of these systems may contribute to the development of eating pathology (Brambilla & Monteleone, 2003; Kaye, Frank, & McConaha, 1999). At this time this question remains central but enigmatic for clinicians and researchers: Do these brain based changes arise from genetic influences or are they the results of starvation and disordered eating (Klump, 2003)?

Specific metabolic alterations, such as low lipid and proteins levels in blood and tissue, may induce modifications of the neuronal membrane composition, decreasing neurotransmitter function. Should impaired CNS efficiency result, medical and psychotherapeutic treatments may be made much more difficult (Kaye, 2003). That is, starvation induced metabolic alterations may alter neurotransmitter secretion and function to such an extent that a patient may not be able to respond to treatment.

Hypothetically, some patients who are acutely ill may require a higher fat intake during refeeding due to degradation of myelin sheaths. Emaciated patients and those who have exercise addiction have a higher proportion of resting energy expenditure than controls. Metabolic rate and dietary-induced thermogenesis also influence weight restoration. The therapeutic implication is that for at least some of our patients, a higher fat content may be beneficial in refeeding. Not surprisingly, high exercisers may also require significantly more dietary energy (see Treasure, 2003, for a concise review).

Brain abnormalities in serotonin, noradrenalin, dopamine, and endorphins that occur in eating disorder patients probably persist long after recovery. More research in this area will also broaden our understanding of eating disorders, because scientists in the 1990s learned through neuroimaging studies that total gray and white matter volumes are reduced in the brains of anorexics (Katzman, Lambe et al., 1996; Lambe, Katzman, Mikulis, Kennedy, & Zipursky, 1997). Functional neuroimaging also demonstrates reduction in brain activity, both global and regional; it is not yet clear whether these abnormalities are reversible. The time it takes for full organ recovery argues that the adult

> who is ill enough to require specialized inpatient or other high intensity care will need at least several weeks of this in a multidisciplinary medical psychiatry setting followed by a prolonged period of outpatient management often extended over several years. (J. Russell, 2003, p. 206)

Other studies used to corroborate this opinion show that the loss of gray matter in the brain persists after weight recovery and that lower weight patients actually perform poorly on cognitive tests (Castro, 2003).

Despite the extant and ongoing research studies on the endocrinological alterations involved in eating disorders, the precise influences or psychopathology remains unclear. At the current time there is considerable discrepancy between what is known biologically about these illnesses and application of that knowledge to treatment in clinical practice. Interestingly, patients with eating disorders who suffer from malnutrition have different medical and neurological complications from patients in developing countries who also suffer from malnutrition (i.e., marasmus, kwashiorkor) (Marcos, 2003). This fact alone points investigators toward the assumption that adaptation to the starvation state as well as activation of genes influencing the neuroendocrine system give rise to clinically observed phenomena of abnormal attitudes toward body shape, exaggeration of obsessional behavior, and poor insight and cognitive impairment.

Dysfunctions in the hypothalamus play an important role in regulating appetite; promising areas for further exploration and possible manipulations for treatment include corticotropine releasing factor (CRF), the peptides galanin, ghrelin, neuropeptide Y (NPY), and the satiety-inducing peptide cholecystokinin (CCK). The role played by cortisol and adrenocorticotropic hormone (ACTH) is also central. In anorexia nervosa, plasma cortisol adjusts only after normal weight has been regained; if hypercortisolemia turns out to be an intrinsic alteration of anorexia nervosa, it throws new light on why after recovery weight gain in anorexic patients seems to lead to fat distribution concentrated on the torso with less subcutaneous fat on the extremities (Baranowska, 2003; Brambilla & Monteleone, 2003; Stoving, Brixen, & Hagen, 2003).

Although most medical complications are alleviated once weight has been restored and normal eating habits resumed, menstrual problems do not always disappear after weight reaches a healthy range. Most clinicians tend to think of amenorrhea and dysmenorrhea as occurring only in anorexics, but normal-weight bulimic patients can be malnourished. Their dieting and purging leads to deficits in important micro–macro nutrients. Adult patients must be instructed that it will take *substantial time* to correct the micro–macro nutrient deficiency, independently of achieving a normal BMI. Although most psychopathological aspects of these disorders will likely disappear when the symptoms of manifest eating disorder are corrected, some patients will likely need a sustained period of eating rehabilitation (Brambilla & Monteleone, 2003) for full recovery. It is incumbent for clinician and patient alike to recognize that the medical complications, nutritional deficiencies, and psychological impairments that occur with eating disorders are likely much more complex than the original starvation and metabolic studies show (Keys, Brozek, Herschel, Mickelsen, & Taylor, 1950); considerable patience on the part of the patient and multidisciplinary team will be called upon because "tincture of time" after weight restoration is proving necessary for full recovery of biological processes.

Menstrual irregularities, such as oligomenorrhea and amenorrhea, occur in almost half of the women with bulimia nervosa and are a key diagnostic feature in anorexia nervosa. A number of patients seek out treatment at infertility clinics because of the dysfunction of the hypothalamic-pituitary-gonadal (HPG) axis leading to diminished secretion of sex steroid hormones such as estrogen, lutenizing hormone (LH), and follicular stimulating hormone (FSH). Because amenorrhea sometimes precedes weight loss but persists after recovery of normal body weight, loss of weight itself may not be the only determinant in the HPG axis dysfunction. Another likely culprit in anorexia, at least in some patients, is increased physical activity. Women athletes with amenorrhea or menstrual dysfunction have been found to have difficulties that correlate with intense physical exercise as opposed to numerical measures of body fat. Endogenous opioids may play a role in HPG axis dysfunction in anorexia and in this exercise associated amenorrhea.

In some patients with eating disorders, menstrual irregularities are correlated with anorexic behaviors as well as low BMI (Falk & Halmi, 1982). Patients with bulimia nervosa manifest HPG axis dysregulation in yet a different way: decreased levels of progesterone, decreased levels of 17-beta estradiol, and reduced circadian pulsatility of plasma gonadotropins are found (Baranowska, 1990, 2003; Brambilla & Monteleone, 2003; Naessen, 2006; Stoving, Brixen, & Hagen, 2003). These complex endocrinological aberrations that may lead to the physical consequence of amenorrhea demonstrate a fundamental question regarding the etiology and maintenance of eating disorder symptoms: To what extent can a physical change be specifically attributed to the disrupted eating and its consequences, or to what extent is an underlying endocrine disorder the primary cause of the illness? How these biological alterations affect the capacity of some patients to participate in treatment is another issue altogether that only future research will adequately answer (Naessen, 2006; Treasure, 2003).

More importantly, hypercorticosolema may be implicated in the impaired stress response and the affective shifts seen in some anorexic patients. Corticotropin releasing factor (CRF) can induce anorexia, decrease sexual behavior, and promote excessive physical activity in experimental animals. Endocrinal changes, although secondary to starvation, may play a role in the maintenance of certain symptoms and are important to remember. Not only do these biologic changes mean that the patient will not recover quickly and thoroughly but they may actually hinder the patient from responding to treatment.

Immunological impairments are less frequent and less severe among anorexic and bulimic patients; these patients rarely succumb to infectious disease. Patients with eating disorders do not show the same cytokine reactions, including fever, that occur in infection induced malnutrition. This has led some investigators to speculate that different nervous, endocrine and immune system feedback mechanisms are activated in eating disorders, contributing to weight loss, cachexia, and a unique type of secondary osteoporosis that differs from that seen in later life (Marcos, 2003).

The loss of bone mass that occurs in anorexia nervosa is likely to be irreversible. In part this occurs because bone is laid down in puberty; peak bone mass occurs around age 30. Poor nutrition at this time portends a lifetime of poor bone health. Anorexia sufferers are likely to be confronted with a lifelong insufficient bone structure and its consequences (Lucas, Melton, Crowson, & O'Fallon, 1999). The effect of amenorrhea in the pathogenesis of this osteopenia and osteoporosis remains controversial. Estrogen replacement has not been found helpful in the treatment of osteoporosis due to anorexia nervosa (i.e., so-called "secondary" osteoporosis). In anorexia nervosa, malnutrition, excessive cortisol secretions, insulinlike growth factor 1 (IGF1), and estrogen deficiency may all contribute to the development of osteoporosis in both men and women (Brambilla & Monteleone, 2003; Klibanski, Biller, Schoenfeld, Herzog, & Saxe, 1995; Rigotti, Nussbaum, Herzog, & Neer, 1984; Valla, Groenning, Syverson, & Hoeiseth, 2000). Bulimic patients who have a history of restriction are also prone to low bone density (Naessin, 2006). This subgroup of bulimic patients and all who suffer from anorexia should be considered at risk for developing osteoporosis and nontraumatic fractures later in life.

PUTTING ADULT DEVELOPMENTAL THEORY
INTO ACTION

Familiarity with the essential psychological tasks of normal adulthood helps the clinician formulate a treatment plan that encompasses the developmental shifts normally observed during this period in the life cycle. For those individuals who

TABLE 5.1 Summary of adult developmental tasks

- Establish a stable identity/sense-of-self continuity
- Develop the capacity for forming and sustaining intimate relationships; enjoyment of sexuality
- Commit to one's work/choice of career
- Establish friendships and an allegiance to them
- Continue to gain independence from one's family of origin while maintaining ties (so-called third individuation)
- Develop the capacity to adapt to inevitable change
- Gain a sense of accountability and responsibility to oneself and others
- Develop a sense of morality and purpose in life
- Cultivate spiritual values and practice
- Recognize the finiteness of time and one's eventual death

enter adulthood with an eating disorder or develop one in adulthood (age 20–35), typical goals of this "third individuation" (Colarusso, 1990) are not met. On the surface our patients may have attained some of the attributes of this period such as marriage or job, but they expend enormous psychological energy on maintaining their eating disorder symptoms despite the obvious risks to their physical health and psychological growth. The major emotional and developmental issues that characterize this period (see Table 5.1) are not what is first on the mind of the patient with a severe eating disorder, causing serious consequences in their experience of their quality of life as well. Patients with stalemates in their adult development are often left believing that they will never accomplish what they want to accomplish in their lives and are often not able to do so because psychopathology has forestalled realistic engagement and opportunity (Goin, 1990; Gottschalk, 1990; Nemiroff & Colarusso, 1990a, 1990b; Settlage, 1990).

Commonly the root problem begins in early development and results from the thwarting of normal separation and individuation processes—the so-called first individuation (Mahler, Pine, & Bergman, 1975). When this occurs, the patient does not have the ballast from which to build additional psychological structures in adulthood. Without the early internal structure in place, one enters adulthood with deficits that misuse of food may also buffer. Eating disorders in adulthood provide an excuse for the individual to avoid taking on the very tasks they are meant to fulfill at this time in their journey. Any illness can interrupt normal developmental processes and interfere with the individual taking on normative life tasks at a given point in the life cycle. In the case of eating disorders, clinicians observe the inability to deal with loss, repetition of destructive relationships, failures in the workplace, and problems in participating in meaningful adult relationships and activities as central issues brought about by failures to successfully negotiate and build upon earlier development.

In thinking through the initial treatment plan with the patient, the therapist gains ground by putting the symptom and its sequelae into an adult developmental context. Point out how the symptom is getting in the way of where the person should be in the life cycle. The patient then has the opportunity to see beyond just the physical consequences of the eating disorder and to begin to think about what getting better might mean.

Clinicians will often note anxiety on the patient's part when these developmental blocks are pointed out. Because patients who have had severe eating disorders have usually fulfilled at least some of the challenges of adult development, the therapist is able to build on what has already been achieved while emphasizing the possibility of continued growth over the rest of the life cycle. This intervention may help attenuate initial anxiety and the tendency for the patient to feel criticized or blamed (see Chapter 2). Even if the patient has had symptoms for many years, the alliance can grow when the therapist points out that development is a continuous, lifelong, and dynamic process. The therapist might share how each individual must continue to undergo positive change for as long as we live and few adults "arrive" with all tasks mastered.

The problem, of course, is that growth and development always mean that one must grow beyond and away from what one has been to embrace the self as one is and may become. As psychoanalyst and developmental theorist Margaret Mahler pointed out (cited in Winestine, 1973), "The growing away process is a lifelong separation-individuation process, since inherent in every step of independent functioning is a minimal threat of object loss" (p. 136). For the patient, the eating disorder may be felt as a potential loss that must be mourned to embrace adult life (Colarusso, 1979). Patients must grieve their eating disorder much as they must mourn all other real and perceived losses that accompany each of us as we move through the life cycle.

To achieve a sense of power as an adult, one must come to grips with the universal developmental task of deidealization. To live in one's adult body and take on adult roles, one must confront the absence of perfection and accept ambivalence in our relationships with others in ways that are not possible for the adolescent. Magic gives way to reality. The fantasy of finding a perfect mother, father, or partner is one of the leftover tasks from childhood that one comes to grips with in adulthood. Accepting flaws and imperfections in the self and others are requirements for finding one's power in oneself.

Power must be found inside the self, not externalized onto an idealized other or "precious." Because it is yet another essential developmental task, this is especially poignant and perplexing to the person with an eating disorder. When a block in confronting life's realities occurs, the transference situation is one fruitful arena in which to help the patient explore ambivalence and ambiguity inherent in all human relationships (see Chapter 8) and begin to embrace a sense of one's realistic, adult power (Fabricus, 1998; Hall, 1998; Zerbe, 1995, 2001a, 2001b).

Clinical Example

Genevieve is a 33-year-old multitalented executive who decided to take the plunge and join three colleagues in forming a start-up software company. Her penchant for fiscal detail and intuitive acumen in choosing capable, hard-working subordinates won her significant acclaim in her previous management position. Despite longstanding struggles with daily binge–purge episodes and assorted gastrointestinal complaints that waxed and waned depending on her level of stress, Genevieve managed to keep her eating disorder secret from her husband and her coworkers. Even though the ups and downs of her weight were symptoms hidden in plain view, her commanding presence and stylish attire led others to misjudge her. Superficially in command of her emotions, Genevieve would "stuff herself with health food" when she was annoyed or disappointed with a person who was never directly aware of her disapproval. Overwork was another way this patient managed her anger.

The decision to embark on a new career path brought the costs of Genevieve's eating disorder out into the open. In the company, she frequently had to absorb the criticisms of colleagues and contain anxiety about potential failure. She felt she was less effective than she had been in her previous position and, not surprisingly, her binge–purge episodes exacerbated. Genevieve risked becoming more vulnerable by asking for more therapy sessions. She finally also took the recommendation for psychotropic medication because she experienced herself as "spiraling out of control with my eating." Nonetheless, she was reluctant at first to pay much attention to the life cycle problem that had made its appearance as she took a step forward in the developmental life cycle.

Genevieve was grappling with a totally new experience of herself; her self-concept had not caught up with the shift in her new role. Moreover, Genevieve felt safe in her former position, and despite her newfound autonomy she wondered if she had the psychological wherewithal to be "the main boss" and stand alone. She missed her friends in her old position and the security of talking with her mentors. To add to the difficulty in her transition, at a moment that felt particularly unfair for her, her parents were killed in an automobile crash.

Genevieve's case is illustrative of some expectable crises of adult life, and the requirement to develop the capacity to mourn in order to move ahead. In essence, the task that faced this patient was "growing away" from the self she knew in the old job that was comfortable and secure. She had to grow into a new role. This process takes time and is buffeted by the real, supportive relationships in one's life including spouse, friends, and the therapist.

Psychotherapy, in particular, provided the haven for this patient to have a catharsis of feeling about her losses as well as the dangers she experienced in moving ahead. This patient also faced the universal developmental task of mourning the death of her parents; because their death occurred at a time of another significant transition, it compounded the psychological challenge before her. The temporary recrudescence of eating disorder symptoms ame-liorated only as the patient was able to take further steps into independent functioning. She learned that she could manage the plethora of affects that accompanied losses better than she thought she could as she reviewed her life and the feelings brought up by the expression of her narrative. The therapist frequently underscored how Genevieve was dealing with object loss on many levels—her parents, her former position, her former sense of self as she knew it, and a recognition that her own life was finite. This patient made particular use of the therapeutic opportunity to collaborate on the adult developmental tasks that lay ahead of her by redefining her self and object representations to arrive at a renewed sense of authentic power and capacity to love the life she was carving for herself.

LOCATING AND ACKNOWLEDGING THE "CHILD IN THE ADULT"

A basic tenet of psychodynamic developmental theory is that aspects of our childhood continue to reside in each of us. Empathizing with these child aspects in the adult is a psychotherapeutic task with enormous potential to solidify the alliance and promote growth. While always taking into account the constituents of the "third individuation" (Table 5.1) and championing all of those developmental tasks that are involved in helping the patient embrace full adulthood, the therapist must not be blindsided by seeing growth as only a linear process (Fitzpatrick & Friedman, 1983; Erikson, 1950, 1956, 1976; Wallerstein & Goldberger, 1998). Mature and adaptive functioning can be enhanced in therapy, but one must also honor and give voice to the child inside each of us. Most developmental theorists believe that "childhood assumptions continue to exert a powerful, shaping impact on adult development" (Fitzpatrick & Friedman, 1983, p. 403), and even though these assumptions will ultimately be transcended to assume phase appropriate functioning, they can be neither suppressed nor denied for psychological maturation to occur. Indeed, periodic regression is inevitable in even the most psychologically healthy adult (particularly at times of crisis, transition, or significant loss).

To hear this child, consider first the "regressions of everyday life" that are normal. For example, note the pleasure we find when cooing and using baby talk toward infant or pet, enjoying a hot fudge sundae with all the vigor of a 3-year-old, or laughing with such gusto that one's stomach hurts. It takes a savvy therapist to help a burdened, dependent adult begin to appreciate how the unspoken needs of the child remain latent within each of us. The patient must be permitted this expression to fully sense the true, full self and to thrive. Most patients have difficulty allowing themselves to get to know this "child self" in psychotherapy, out of shame, embarrassment, or false compliance. They mis-takenly believe that they know what the therapist wants and they try to give it. Patients go along with what they think we want because of important developmental antecedents and because they repeat in the present the pattern of an earlier period. As Russell and Mears (1997) observed:

> The parent consistently fails to recognize, or does not wish to recognize, certain feelings such as depression in the child. The consequence is that the child gradually finds herself unable to know whether her feelings are her own or merely given to her by others . . . The false self system becomes apparent in a variety of ways that include using psychological jargon, agreeing uncritically with whatever the therapist says, claiming changed attitudes and behavior despite evidence to the contrary, or acting in accordance with concern for the therapist's perceived need for gratification. At the same time, the patient appears to comply with treatment yet avoids emotionally connecting or giving up her secrets or her precious emaciation. (p. 692)

Clinical Examples

Returning to the case of Genevieve, engaging the child inside of the adult was as important a task in the therapy as was addressing the adult developmental task inherent in taking on her new job and enhancing her marriage. Genevieve's early years were rife with separations from her primary caretaker, and she grew up believing that it was her duty to "mother" her three siblings at the cost of her own needs to make her parents proud of her.

Genevieve hated disorder in her home. She had minimal furniture or art in order to avoid any hint that she was materialistic or spoiled. She also confided that making choices seemed like an "impossible chore" she would rather avoid than make a mistake. In actuality, her "lack of stuff" was a defensive maneuver that reflected a warded off sense of being needy, frightened, and hesitant to commit herself fully to certain choices. Unconscious derivatives of what held her back were evidenced in the therapist's office where she would from time-to-time spill her coffee or drink, comment on the furniture and paintings, and complain about her bowel rumblings, gastrointestinal aches, and episodes of urinary incontinence. Although medical workup of these problems yielded no organic pathology, her body seemed to be telling her and her therapist that much was stirring beneath the surface that yearned to be expressed.

Her therapist found herself pondering how a child who lacks caretaking early in life has less opportunity to make sense of her body's signals, let alone find recognition in the other person who might unconsciously signal or consciously demonstrate (i.e., "contain") that thoughts and choices are acceptable and worthwhile. The "emptiness" in Genevieve's apartment reflected an inner world devoid of the psychological anchor points we all need to learn to play and to grow. In her case a penchant for minimalism stemmed from the dearth of childhood love objects that failed to populate her inner world. Her eating symptoms were an unconscious attempt to rectify this problem.

To let Genevieve know that the therapist heard the child within her, she asked her how it felt to try to do so many grown-up things. When something would spill, the therapist commented in a playful way that "maybe a child in the office wanted to be messy." When the patient would risk becoming angry, the therapist would encourage the expression of her feelings but also wondered if the child within her was afraid that if she was too disappointed or upset with the therapist that she might be abandoned. Although the themes of these interventions could have been addressed in other ways, the idea I want to emphasize here is the crucial therapeutic maneuver of encouraging and permitting the unspoken, unsolicited "voice of the child" to come forth in the session.

The therapist might also take the position of the child in the family of origin when thinking through this kind of intervention. For example, well into the fourth year of her twice weekly process, Genevieve finally felt safe enough to elaborate on the paucity of nurturance she experienced from her primary caretakers. There were few memories of being touched or sharing family mealtimes, and she began to wonder if this had anything to do with her struggle with eating. The therapist interpreted, "You have to feel sorry for that little girl who hardly ever got a chance to eat with her parents and talk about her day." On another occasion the therapist hypothesized that "the little girl is pretty angry about a lot of things that happened when she was young, including not getting the kinds of feedings that she would have liked. I bet the same thing happens in here when I have only words, and not food, to give you."

This interpretive stance aims at empathically connecting with the original deprivation and linking it to the present day realistic disappointment in the treatment. The therapy makes expressible the long suppressed wishes of the child-self. As Genevieve could speak to these very early needs and desires, her true self-functions blossomed.

Sheena, age 33, decided to make another attempt at psychotherapy after two previous trials had gone sour. This recently widowed attorney and mother of two had struggled with significant overweight since high school. Now the sole support of her two children, ages 6 and 10, Sheena was more concerned than ever before about the health consequences of her overeating. She gave the new therapist at their first meeting some unsolicited reassurance, "At least I've never purged, used enemas, or taken any over-the-counter drugs to help me lose weight." The frequency and rapidity with which she ate clarified the formal DSM-IV diagnosis of binge eating disorder. The clinician entertained a tentative hypothesis that Sheena might be trying to soothe emotional pain, especially the acute grief of her recent loss, by overeating. Listening carefully to her story soon revealed that this was not the case and the initial formulation was revised.

The patient grew up in a conventional, middle-class household where stability and nurturance were conveyed by the "simplicity" of her traditional stay-at-home mother and the "routine of 6 a.m. to 3 p.m., 5-day-per-week, shifts" of her steel worker father. Sheena and her siblings were not privy to luxury, but her parents sacrificed for holiday presents and occasional outings to visit relatives in other states. When Sheena was 10, she remembers once again presenting her parents with a report card of straight As and remarking, "Someday I'm going to grow up, go to college, and become President." Her father, taken aback, said that her dream was "impossible" because "only boys can become President" and "college isn't for girls anyway." When Sheena blandly revealed this memory in the initial interview sessions, notably without prompting on the therapist's part, she appeared to indicate that she understood her situation as par for the course of any girl's life. Her therapist suspected otherwise; to be told early that one's dreams are foolish and unrealizable was not meant to be overtly mean but can be construed in some circumstances as a form of soul murder (Shengold, 1989). Clearly, Sheena understood that her father was also a victim of his age and circumstances and was doing the best he could (Sullivan, 1953; Blum, 1997). Yet, Sheena's revelation led the therapist to further suspect that the thwarting of dreams had powerful psychological consequences for the patient, even in the face of all of the positive attributes the patient disclosed about her family home life.

In the initial months of therapy, Sheena reacted with curiosity when the therapist gently probed the history of overeating, attempts to diet, and feelings about her body. At one point she admonished the therapist, "I don't know why you're looking into all of this. After all, Dr. X and Dr. Y (her previous therapists) both told me that I will always be fat. This is my 'set point.' I should just accept it and get on with life." At this moment of personal transition, Sheena reminded her therapist that she wanted to "focus on health," move through the grief brought on by her husband's death, and understand a bit more about why she was now losing interest in her career; she told the therapist that she had read several books about the experience of widowhood and wondered if she was "hung up" with "unconscious anger" at her husband that needed to be expressed to get through "reactions to feeling abandoned."

The therapist was impressed by Sheena's psychological mindedness and ability to speak her mind. Although the patient's forays into self-understanding and starting treatment again to address health concerns were positive, the therapist intuited that more seemed to lie beneath a façade of healthy denial (Druss, 1995, 2000). This case was about to take an unexpected turn that did not fit the typical picture of binge eating, years of struggle with being overweight, and the recent bereavement and temporary weight changes reflective of loss or depression.

As her story unfolded, Sheena shared stories of her youth. Family life centered around food and mealtime. Everyone would sit down together, swap stories, laugh, and leave feeling satiated both psychologically and physiologically. Confiding that she was "only slightly overweight" by age 12, Sheena recalled when her weight started to increase and become a family concern as "my brothers, sister, and father got on my case to lose." Meanwhile, the patient continued to excel in academics, seemingly untouched by her father's earlier comment.

Over the years, Sheena "packed on pounds" despite increasing family criticism and preoccupation with weight. In a separate corner of her life, the patient went on to win a scholarship to a prestigious Southern university, stayed on to finish law school, and met her husband-to-be. They went on to join a small law firm and settled down into the routine of married life. Both of their careers progressed quickly but Sheena felt tormented by her physical appearance. So accomplished and fulfilled in some areas, Sheena sought the help of physicians, weight management systems, psychotherapists, exercise physiologists and trainers, but none helped her achieve her goal of "getting down to a size 10 or 12 and looking as good as I feel inside." In her current therapy process, Sheena did not appear to have hope for any change on a conscious level, but her repeated storyline of weight-related concerns indicated that there was considerable meaning lying beneath the manifest sense of comfort she maintained with "my large, voluptuous body and enjoyment of cuisines, all kinds of them."

Meanwhile, Sheena's therapist was beginning to connect some of the dots. Silently, this therapist considered a tentative formulation that would parsimoniously explain some of the disparities in Sheena's life. Applying Winnicott's notion of the compliance that can lead to the false self, along with the notion that the true self is often buried beneath a veneer, the therapist considered the question: Where was Sheena's true self hiding? The process took still another turn when the patient was gently confronted with the notion that dieting and losing weight was not what therapy was about; however, the meaning of food in Sheena's life needed to be more fully understood. This made the patient very anxious, as the therapist noted, because Sheena had been on some form of diet for most of her life and she used her debating skills to argue with the clinician about the meaning of weight loss and definitions of health. The therapist acknowledged the defensive functioning of the bibliotherapy at this point, saying "Your appetite for reading is just as voracious as your appetite for food. We need to look deeper."

In the practice of therapy, wisdom from our training underscores how we must never take something away from the patient until we are ready to give something in return. In this case, Sheena's therapist offered a hypothesis that sparked the patient to consider other options. The therapist found herself thinking about what it was like for such a talented, gifted child to be told so early that her dreams were impossible. As described, the therapist "took the position of the child" and formulated to Sheena,

> It must have been very hard for the little girl to hear how her beloved, hard working father couldn't value her intelligence, her dreams, and longing for education. I wonder if your family's focus on food, your diets, and your weight was a way that all of you worked together to keep your real dreams silent. What became the "professional you" stayed under wraps. Young Sheena could go ahead and become a lawyer as long as nobody was noticing. The struggles with weight in your family became a way to survive and protect your creativity. It is impossible to imagine having a different body now and being a successful attorney at the same time.

As in the great majority of treatment processes where the true and false self become pivotal issues for discussion, Sheena was not magically transformed overnight. However, the tears and anger poured forth as more family stories and work with dreams also demonstrated how the therapist's interpretation had hit a deep chord.

Two years into the work, Sheena, now having lost 75 pounds and beginning to date again, poetically confirmed her therapist's interpretation of the true self that was insulated by the false self of adipose tissue. Sheena said,

> I feel like a character in a movie who has worn a fat suit all of my life. It's not exactly like there is this thin woman that is yearning to get out. It just feels more like the suit has been my mask. My weight was not my identity but to be my real self and achieve, the woman I yearned to be in my family, simply wasn't possible.

The therapeutic journey now proceeded along a path to help Sheena mourn significant losses, including those mirroring experiences that she did not receive in her childhood. She began to embrace her authentic self, a self much more at home with her body, her talents, her past, and the life that lay ahead.

A "GARDEN VARIETY" OF THERAPEUTIC TOOLS

I recommend that even if a therapist becomes proficient in one therapeutic modality, such as cognitive-behavioral, interpersonal, or psychodynamic psychotherapy, we can also greatly benefit from learning about and using a few interventions from a variety of schools. We must experiment to find what works for us in practice. Rather than becoming overwhelmed with how much one does not or can never know as a therapist, one has a ready-made, easy-to-return-to resource to draw on. In Tables 5.2 and 5.3, I outline some of the cognitive-behavioral and interpersonal techniques I routinely think about and employ when getting started with a new patient. This far from comprehensive list is meant to suggest how integrated treatment can weave modalities together so long as the therapist plans ahead and has a sense of what works for him or for her. I return frequently to classic texts and papers in between sessions to brush up or to add something new to this well-trod repertoire (Beck, 1995; Kleifield, Wagner, & Halmi, 1996; Kuechler & Hampton, 1998; Leahy, 2003; McMullin, 2000; Miller & Rollnick, 2002; Schuyler, 1991; Weissman, Markowitz, & Klerman, 2000; Yager, 1988, 1992, 2007a).

In adapting the treatment to the patient, I emphasize throughout this book the need for the clinician to take the patient's desires into account first and plan accordingly. Some people will want only symptomatic relief; others will want to explore further, particularly when other treatments have not been successful, if they have other psychological issues or comorbid problems, and when the eating disorder has sufficiently intruded into their quality of life. I borrow a metaphor from Kelli Holloway, M.D., an assistant clinical professor of psychiatry at Oregon Health and Science University (personal communication,

TABLE 5.2 Selected cognitive-behavioral strategies for adults

- Challenge idiosyncratic beliefs about food and weight
  - Remember that there are no "good" or "bad" foods
  - Self-monitor with a food journal
  - Work to identify basic misperceptions about food (e.g., "If I gain 5 pounds, I will get fat")
  - Link automatic thoughts to faulty ideas of weight, size, and sense of self (e.g., "If I gain 5 pounds, I am a fat person who is no good")
- Practice stimulus control
  - Eat three meals/day with two between-meal snacks
  - Identify triggers to bingeing or purging
  - Identify "high risk" times (e.g., being alone; preparing meals)
  - Ensure availability of safe foods
- Strengthen coping strategies
  - Use a journal or write a letter as a way to confront eating disorder, to develop capacity for reflection, to distract from thinking about food
  - Develop a list of friends you can call for support
  - Plan an activity or start a hobby and do it even when you don't want to do it
  - Give yourself a reward (but not food) if you carry out any of the above
  - When you do not accomplish your task, take away a privilege (i.e., self-determined contingency planning to increase motivation)
- Develop relapse prevention plan
  - Call a friend or family member at times of stress or when tempted to binge/purge
  - Structure time after meals
  - Practice meditation, prayer, deep breathing exercises at lease twice daily
  - Increase your daily, structured activities at times of risk of relapse, in particular

TABLE 5.3 Selected interpersonal therapy strategies for adults

- Help patient address interpersonal concerns that perpetuate illness (e.g., loneliness leads to bingeing; anger at spouse leads to "hunger strike")
- Minimize time spent talking about eating disorder; maximize time spent talking about major psychological issues (e.g., grief and loss)
- Shift focus from eating disorder to current life situation
- Address any interpersonal deficits, role transitions, unresolved losses, impasses, and conflicts in current relationships
- Help patient learn healthy ways of dealing with inevitable interpersonal conflicts by suggesting strategies to handle disputes. Use role playing as one tool
- Encourage patient to express feelings in important relationships and become adept at recognizing feelings that lead to misuse of food
- Encourage self-care. Point out ways that patient may practice setting appropriate boundaries, take time for rest or engage in pleasurable activities
- Emphasize how treatment is "an opportunity for change" (Fairburn, 1998)
- As patients make strides in these areas, judiciously acknowledge progress and give praise

2007), in introducing the blending of cognitive and psychodynamic therapy when I speak with a patient over the phone or during the first consultation hour:

> Getting started in therapy is a little like weeding a garden. Our work begins with pulling the weeds; we use some behavioral suggestions to get you more coping skills to feel better.
>
> As you are feeling better, it will likely be important to dig deeper and get to the root of the problem (i.e., the weeds). The origin of the problem has to be examined, understood, and "pulled out" over time. The weeds have less of a chance to grow back when the roots have been pulled.
>
> In therapy, as in gardening, some weeds are easy to pull out. Some will need a spade or trowel and take more time. That's why some issues will take more time and repeated effort. Patience will be necessary because the deeper work is unlikely to be done quickly.

Clinical Example

Dana was a 23-year-old former male model who began a 12-session therapy to achieve control over his thrice-weekly bingeing and purging. He stopped after he had achieved his goal of full symptom remission using the techniques listed in Table 5.2. He also derived benefit from fluoxetine, which his primary care physician prescribed.

Dana returned to therapy for more intensive treatment two years later. Now engaged, he was anxious about the additional responsibilities he faced as a husband and stepfather. Dana's eating disorder symptoms had "morphed" into restriction and overexercise, a pattern that came under significant control when the therapist worked on the meanings to Dana of his role transition. This therapy "chapter" lasted 16 sessions and used an interpersonal therapy focus (Table 5.3).

When Dana's wife became pregnant one year later, he entered therapy "before I ran into problems again." Thinking about becoming a father of his own biological child stirred anxiety and the likelihood of regressing to eating disorder symptoms. The therapist helped Dana to sort through some long buried issues with his own father, and his eating disorder did not return during the pregnancy or after the baby's birth. Nonetheless, reinforcement of some coping strategies Dana had used before (writing a daily journal, wood-working hobby) were also encouraged throughout this essentially psychodynamic process.

WORKING WITH SUBJECTIVE EXPERIENCE

In addition to incorporating more objective, scientifically validated therapies, the treatment of eating disordered adults necessitates that the therapist help patients embrace their subjective narrative. Patients who learn to value their inner voice, search for their own truth, and embrace themselves as the experts on their own experiences are better equipped to face down any severe symptom.

Treatment modalities derived from this approach place emphasis on data derived from content analysis of the patient's narrative and the synthesis of the data derived from unstructured interviews. Openness to finding the meaning and value in one's world increases awareness of an appreciation for that very world, leading to enhanced personal growth and a greater reckoning with the individual's place in the life cycle. In essence, the patients are encouraged to become their own "inner expert" (Belenky et al., 1986) to "talk back" to their eating disorder symptoms (Maisel, Epston, & Borden, 2004).

This emphasis on embracing and enhancing subjective knowledge derives from an amalgamation of psychodynamic and feminist theories, respectively (Mitchell, 1974; Young-Bruehl, 1993; Young-Bruehl & Cummings, 1993; Zerbe 1993/1995a, 1996a, 1996b, 2001a, 2001b, 2007a, 2007c). Many contemporary clinicians apply specific elements from these theories in practice without ever being aware of it. As psychoanalyst Nancy McWilliams (2004) wrote,

> most analytic practitioners work flexibly, shunning technical purity and basing their interventions on their intimate knowledge of each individual human being (or couple or group or family or organization) whom they try to serve. . . . (p. 14)
> Like most practicing therapists, I am grateful for any approach, whatever its theoretical origin, that increases my effectiveness or provides me with resources to offer to individuals who seek my help. (p. 23)

How are these different theories routinely put into use? In each model, prime importance is placed on the search for personal knowledge and the inestimable value of the individual's voice. This line of thought holds equal potential for male and female patients. When the adult does not have the capacity to express the story in words, treaters may begin with a three-pronged approach. These components of treatment with the adult include (1) structured patient education about the nature of eating disorders and the life histories of others who have struggled with similar afflictions (see Appendix B); (2) naming of feelings and linking them, when appropriate, to bodily sensations to bridge the gap between psyche and soma (e.g., the goal is to help put emotional pain into symbolic words); and (3) use of experiential therapies (e.g., art, psychodrama, music, dance) as still another mode of assisting the patient in translating the story from body into words.

In part, eating disorders in the adult may be formulated as difficulties in the expression of this personal narrative. The eating disorder is an effective bulwark in the silencing of the self. When the therapist emphasizes listening to the patient's narrative, attempts to help make sense of it, and values the courage it takes on the patient's part to take the risks incumbent in the telling, the finest aspects of the psychodynamic and feminist traditions are embraced (Zerbe, 1996a, 1996b, 2001b, 2007a, 2007b). Covert and overt permission is given to develop a sense of self, expand learning, and engage "in an individual search for an enlightened consciousness" (Paglia, 1992, p. 89). In this way, the individual sets forth on a course to value the self, interpersonal relationships, and new ways of enjoying the world, all essential developmental tasks of adulthood.

It is not surprising that quality-of-life studies (see Chapter 9) demonstrate that eating disorder symptoms diminish as the patient finds more overt ways of expressing concerns, psychological pain, and conflict. By emphasizing subjective knowledge of the self and personal experience, autonomous behavior is also encouraged. But during the adult life cycle, personal authority and a sense of healthy power must also be enhanced by helping the individual become comfortable with the concomitant dependency needs. Dialogue with the therapist does assert the restorative power of finding one's own voice while modeling the back-and-forth interaction inherent in a mature interpersonal relationship.

Patients in the later stages of therapy will often test out whether or not the therapist can practice what he or she preaches. Asking about areas of the therapist's personal life and showing curiosity speak to an enlargement in the patient's psychic space (see Chapters 2, 4, and 8). Note how groups, couples, and family therapy also make use of the conversational paradigm to promote the development of voice in a situation where the body has become a medium for communication (Fonagy & Moran, 1994; Orbach, 1994).

Conveying one's thoughts, one's personal, narrative truth, in letters, journals, poetry, and essays pays heed to the notion of solidifying identity and connections with others by defining who one is. Maisel, Epston, and Borden (2004) advised that therapists concretize their own assessment of the patient's dilemma by summarizing their own views in a letter and encouraging the patient to write back. They believe that this technique can "expose" and "challenge" the claims of the internal voice of the eating disorder, thereby "discerning and countering" and ultimately "unmasking and defying" that pathological voice to help patients establish an inner dialogue with the healthy part of themselves.

This highly pragmatic technique encourages the patient to relate her or his experience while staying in emotional contact with the therapist between hours (i.e., in Winnicott's sense, a transitional object/transitional phenomenon is employed by the technique suggested by Maisel, Epston, & Borden, 2004). Each therapist must apply techniques such as journaling or letter writing (Rabinor, 1991) in a way that fits personal circumstances; not everyone can or has the time or ability to write letters to patients or review journals outside of sessions. However, the time-honored principle of finding a voice of one's own by writing can be productively and creatively employed in these treatments and often gets at material that may not be revealed in any other forum.

Note how encouragement to write gives implicit permission to develop the self by thinking one's own thoughts. Nonetheless, this voice is inevitably intersubjective and rooted in relationships with others because the writer is inevitably speaking to another voice of the self or an implicit audience. For those who find writing a journal or letters burdensome, Holloway (personal communication, 2007) advises patients to jot down "bullet points" in between sessions as reminders of important topics or feelings that can be followed up later. Patients find this "shorthand technique" useful in remembering themes and "keeping track of what might have been forgotten," which Holloway further conceptualizes as a benign way of catapulting over natural resistance while empowering the individual to begin to value her or his observations, experience, and subjective voice.

Clinical Example

Joyce had been in individual psychotherapy for anorexia for over a year when she observed her therapist, Johanna, having dinner at a restaurant with Johanna's best friend. In the next session, Johanna asked Joyce to elaborate on how she felt about seeing her therapist in a restaurant, a context totally different from the therapy. Joyce obfuscated but said she would "think about it." Johanna encouraged Joyce to write about it in her journal and said that she would read it if the patient was too embarrassed to share her thoughts.

Johanna was struck by what the patient could say in her journal that she was not prepared to acknowledge directly in session. Joyce was "appalled" by Johanna's choice of food and "jealous" that she could go out with a friend. Joyce even took the risk in the journal of wondering if Johanna "might be having an affair" with the woman, even though she knew that Johanna was married and had a child. In this case, the journal revelations allowed the patient to give voice to dimensions of her experience with Johanna that likely would not have been revealed verbally at this point in the therapy because the patient had difficulty in "speaking truth to power."

Johanna was informed by reading Joyce's journal about certain key concerns with food that remained an issue (the patient's comment that she was "appalled" made the therapist wonder about hidden, self-hating aspects about eating that were being projected onto the therapist). The fact that Joyce could also entertain feelings of envy, competition, and erotic interest led Johanna to begin to bring these facets of subjective experience and adult developmental tasks (e.g., having a friend, going to a restaurant to talk) directly into the therapy.

THE DESIRE TO START A FAMILY

The desire to begin a family of one's own is a developmental achievement for the adult. Despite ongoing psychological issues, many eating disorder patients decide they want to have a baby. If their disorder has been undiagnosed or untreated, this desire may bring the patient to treatment for the first time. On other occasions, the patient who has been reluctant to become more involved in her recovery will make a decision to do more psychological work to overcome her difficulties.

The patient's relationship to her spouse or partner, ongoing conflicts within the family of origin, a history of earlier miscarriages or abortions, and conscious and unconscious competitive issues with one's mother, siblings, or friends are among a conglomeration of concerns that practicing clinicians have observed and written about that will need to be sorted out in the therapy (Vanderbroucke, Vandereycken, & Norre, 1997; Zerbe, 1993/1995a, 1996b,

1996c, 1999). Clinicians are also advised to take into account that despite conscious protestations to the contrary, no individual embarks on expanding her family without ambivalence. The parent-to-be must bid farewell to life as she knew it. Given the difficulties that most eating disorder patients have in mourning and taking into consideration the multifactorial nature of the eating disorder itself, the decision to have a child, while signaling increased hopefulness about one's life by the wish to bring new life into the world, will necessarily raise additional avenues for psychological work.

INFERTILITY

As previously noted, hormonal disturbances are quite common in eating disorder patients. Consequently, many women have difficulty becoming pregnant and researchers have found that these individuals will seek out the help of specialized fertility clinics (Norre, Vandereycken, & Gordts, 2001; Powers & Santana, 2002; Stewart, Robinson, Goldbloom, & Wright, 1990; Thommen, Vallach, & Kiencke, 1995). Sometimes expensive workups are undertaken before the gynecologist is made aware of the underlying eating disorder because the patient keeps the problem secret out of shame, guilt, or dissociation. Amenorrhea is a classic symptom of anorexia; a significant majority of bulimic women suffer from amenorrhea or oligomenorrhea and polycystic ovary syndrome. Patients with eating disorders may also exhibit sexual difficulties that lead to lack of sexual desire and infrequent sexual relations within the marital relationship (see Chapter 7).

Because infertility treatment can lead to multiple pregnancies, and given the psychological burdens that eating disorder patients face even without caring for a child, the American Psychiatric Association's "Practice Guidelines" (2006) discourage fertility treatment for patients with eating disorders. Indeed, most authorities recommend that these patients engage in psychological treatment for the eating disorder before beginning a family (Norre et al., 2001). Unfortunately, many patients deny their need for psychological help but continue to seek out fertility treatment. They may neither tell the therapist they are doing this nor consent to having the therapist discuss their difficulty with the gynecologist with whom they are consulting. Therapists who are aware of the patient's desire to start a family should encourage honest discussion with her medical team and urge realism about the capacity to parent. Confronting the patient may be uncomfortable and feel intrusive to the therapist but it may be necessary given the ego-syntonic and maladaptive core beliefs that affect these patients (Mountford & Waller, 2006).

Recognition of eating disorders remains a serious problem in medical specialties and the consulting gynecologist may not even suspect the patient has an eating disorder despite low body weight, amenorrhea or dysmenorrhea, or other medical comorbidities associated with anorexia or bulimia. Sometimes even spouses are shocked that the partner has had a serious problem bingeing, vomiting, or restricting. Once again, the problem may be hidden, but in plain view by the closest family members and medical personnel (Vandenbroucke, Vandereycken, & Norre, 1997; Zerbe, 2007a, 2007b; Zerbe & Rosenberg, 2008).

To become a successful parent, the patient must first engage in psychological treatment and understand the meaning of having a child and the role transition that becoming a parent necessitates. In media driven Western culture, there are numerous examples of poor mothering (e.g., celebrities with whom the patient may identify). The patient may also be unprepared for the demands and responsibilities of parenthood. Some authorities suggest that the patient and her partner write a future life story to help them realistically imagine what their life will be like after having a baby. This story then becomes a central and ongoing focus of the therapy (Norre et al., 2001).

The crucial responsibility of the partner must also be made explicit because after birth the partner's duty is to nurture the mother in order for the mother to nurture the baby (Rinsley, personal communication, 1978, 1982). Couples optimally need to assess whether or not they have the emotional, financial, and psychological resources available to do the work entailed in bringing new life into the world. These issues should be respectfully clarified in treatment planning.

PREGNANCY AND THE POSTPARTUM PERIOD

If the patient becomes pregnant, some research reports suggest that a spontaneous remission of food restriction, bingeing and purging, or preoccupation with body image may temporarily occur. In these cases, a desire to not harm the fetus may bring about a temporary remission of symptoms, and the patient may be motivated to tackle more of the fundamental issues associated with her eating disorder. Patients should be informed about risks to the fetus, including miscarriage, low birth weight, and birth defects, although once again the individualized treatment needs must be taken into account (see Table 5.4).

If an eating disorder begins *de novo* during pregnancy, the therapist and obstetrician must collaborate. The psychological treatment may need to be intensified. All clinicians on the multidisciplinary team should remind the patient that active symptoms of anorexia nervosa or bulimia nervosa are associated with higher risks of Caesarian section, infants with lower birth weight, small-for-gestational-age infants, and postpartum depression (see Table 5.4). This tack is taken to fully inform the patient and to increase motivation, not to frighten the patient.

After the birth, some patients will have a recurrence of their eating disorder symptoms, particularly if they become preoccupied with rapid loss of pregnancy-related weight gain. Some may even begin to exercise excessively for the first time to take off added inches. If a mother has conflicts with eating and feeding her baby, that infant may be at risk for not making normal developmental

TABLE 5.4 Impact of eating disorders on reproductive function

Infertility
- Hormonal disturbances (AN & BN)
- Polycystic Ovarian Syndrome (BN)
- Sexual dysfunction or lack of desire (AN especially)
- Ambivalence about having a child, starting a family (AN & BN)
- Costly workups for infertility if eating disorder is unknown to gynecologist (AN & BN)

Pregnancy
- Despite hormonal issues, many patients do become pregnant
- ED may exacerbate, stop, or start during pregnancy
- Higher rate of miscarriages
- Higher rate of birth defects
- Higher rate of low-weight newborns
- Higher rate of Caesarean section

Postpartum Period
- Higher rate of postpartum depression and anxiety
- Increased difficulty in feeding baby/conflictual feelings during mealtime
- Preoccupation with baby's physical appearance (i.e., "this baby is fat!")
- Conflicts with normal attachment and soothing infant
- Increased strain in marital relationship due to preexisting psychological issues, stressors associated with increasing size of family
- Potential exacerbation of conflicts within family of origin, including difficulty assuming role of parent due to competition or unresolved anger toward one's own parents

milestones (Winters, 2002). In fact, some pediatricians have referred mothers with current or past eating disorders to psychotherapists because they have been struck with the mother's concern about her "fat baby" and discovered emotional conflicts the patient has in feeding the child (Zerbe, 1996c). Patients with eating disorders will likely need more guidance and assistance from the treater regarding nutritional requirements for themselves and for their children; for example, some mothers actually know the difference in fat content of different baby foods, signaling their preoccupation with calories and body image.

Finally, the new responsibilities of motherhood put additional strains on individuals who already have significant psychological problems. As noted, pregnancy and birth inevitably awaken issues from the past, especially when one has had conflicts with one's own parents, if there has been a history of maltreatment or failure in attachment in the family of origin, and when there are any difficulties in the patient's partnership or marriage. When patients are motivated to do the best they can for their child, the period immediately following birth can be an excellent time to encourage the patient to enlist the additional support of group therapy, family therapy, couples' therapy, or a clinician-organized support group for new mothers with an eating disorder. Patients who are involved in treatment can also be reassured that limited research on mothers with eating disorders demonstrates that an exacerbation in eating disorder symptoms does not always occur. In fact, some patients find a renewed sense of meaning and purpose in life, enjoy the new role of parenting, and are able to avoid returning to eating disorder symptoms (Carter, McIntosh, Frampton, Joyce, & Bulik, 2003).

A WAR WITHIN ONE'S BODY

In contrast to eating disorder patients, healthy adults have the experience that their mind and body are integrated. In describing her own treatment process with D.W. Winnicott, psychoanalyst Margaret Little told how "D.W.," as she affectionately called him, always took her physical complaints seriously during her bouts of severe depression. For Winnicott, listening to the patient's bodily experience was an essential part of the psychotherapeutic experience because "body and spirit which deep down are interdependent aspects of the same reality" (van der Post, 1982, quoted in Little, 1990) reveal much about the patient's inner reality and emotional pain.

In her memoir, Little describes numerous physical illnesses, hospitalizations for severe anxiety and depression, and psychoanalytic sessions wherein she reexperienced feeling abandoned and annihilated as a child as a result of her parents' emotional disturbances. She was gradually able to put more of her experience into words, had fewer physical complaints and illnesses, and experienced subsequent significant emotional healing.

Just as Little describes, eating disorder patients also complain of psychosomatic problems. These physical complaints lead to a substantially high rate of referral to medical specialists for workups that are not related to the physical sequelae of the eating disorder and for which an objective illness is never found (Zerbe, 1992a). Even as these patients may take very poor care of their bodies, they paradoxically express concern for what is going on in their physical state. In contrast to other patients who willingly accept physical workups and the ministrations of doctors, eating disorder patients with psychophysiologic complaints may simultaneously reject help or become angry and accusatory when the clinician confronts their eating disorder symptoms. Out of a need to experience their body as truly their own, they paradoxically refuse care even while seeming to ask for more of it. This frequently observed phenomenon eventuates in the patient even berating the clinician for "taking over my body" (Zerbe, 1993a).

The patient is actually attempting a "self-cure" by focusing on the myriad of noneating disorder symptoms that occur within the body. In hopes of finding a physical abnormality in a particular body symptom, the patient with a psychosomatic issue is expressing a desire to be healed from underlying but unspoken emotional pain. In adults, an eating disorder serves as an expression of psychological pain and the body's quest for emotional, physical, and spiritual nourishment. What follows is one psychodynamic conceptualization of how an eating disorder may be understood in some individuals. A clinical example follows this formulation to demonstrate how such a conceptualization was put into practice in the treatment of an adult patient with a 20-year history of anorexia and bulimia.

1. The eating disorder patient experiences herself and her body as "distinct entities rather than as a psychosomatic unity" (Sacksteder, 1989, p. 367). Although most of us take for granted that we own our own bodies, meaning that we experience our bodies and minds as a unified whole, in the case of eating disorders the relationship between psyche and soma is fractured. An intense hatred of the body results, leading to poor physical care of the body and denial of the physical toll the symptoms take. This dynamic eventuates in the patient resisting medical advice, even when severely physically compromised. The individual feels misunderstood, anxious, ashamed, and enraged, and may even harbor the quasi-delusional belief that she can "starve the soma to death yet have the psyche survive" (p. 367). That is, the body is experienced as a persecutory object that is attempting to annihilate the self; the true self can survive only if the body dies.

2. Intense hatred of the body develops because of an early, highly pathological relationship with the primary caretaker. If the primary caretaker was not able to provide the child with the psychic space needed to grow, personal autonomy becomes stymied. In effect, mother and child never separate. The adult who becomes our patient carries the false belief that the only way to be able to separate is for the body, in effect, to die. This hatred of the body is also observed in patients who have been sexually or physically abused, where symptoms such as deliberate self-harm, eating disorders, and the addictions paradoxically attempt to soothe the human being in pain while also punishing it (Cross, 1993). The patient has, in effect, internalized the abusing other.

3. The eating disorder patient does not experience her body as her own because it was used unconsciously by the primary caretaker for that individual's psychic survival. The normal separation-individuation subphases (Mahler et al., 1975) were experienced by the primary caretaker as abandonments. Their child—our patient-to-be—was "addictively" used at the behest of the caretaker for unmet psychological needs (McDougall, 1980, 1995, 2001). Massive failures of attunement of the developmental needs leave the child unable to listen to internal body cues. The patient comes to believe that her primary caretakers will be destroyed if steps are taken to live her own life.

When the eating disorder patient does not develop the capacity to recognize internal signals that most of us take for granted, psychophysiological illness may result. The patients do not have the capacity to hear or listen to their bodies (Kramer & Aktar, 1992) The primary caretaker who used the child addictively was also unable to decode physiological and psychological stimuli. These patients, despite high intelligence and striking verbal ability, lack the capacity to put their feelings into words. When caretakers fail to recognize the adaptive needs of the child to grow, a kind of "soul murder" results that leaves the child with "a compulsion toward discharge into action" (Shengold, 1999, p. 258) of "unbearable intensity . . . that cannot be tolerated" (Shengold, 1989; 1999, p. 275). The caretaker is fulfilling her or his own needs for emotional self-regulation rather than helping the child acquire her or his own capacities to self regulate.

4. Nonetheless, the patients-to-be feel the ineluctable urge to grow and separate despite the caretaker's "addictive" need. This places them in a precarious position. When autonomous strides are made the patients wonder if there will be anyone to support them. They do not have some of the abilities of their peers who practiced gradual moves away from parents and were rewarded for doing so. My mentor, the late Donald B. Rinsley, MD, called this process "apersonification" or "depersonification" (Rinsley, 1980, 1982, 1989), meaning that the identity of the child is usurped to fulfill parental needs. If one does not experience oneself as a person in one's own right, it becomes impossible to ever experience the body as one's own, as in the case of severe eating disorders.

Steps taken away from the caretaker will awaken abandonment depression (Masterson, 1981, 1983, 1993, 1995; Masterson & Lieberman, 2004) in the child. Neither parent nor child understands how to let go of each other easily. This presents the patient-to-be with great difficulty in knowing if one can ever "let go" or how to do it, a dynamic that will be repeatedly tested out in therapy. One result of this skewed developmental pathway is a schism between psyche and soma. The body, identified with mother, continues to psychologically belong to her while the eating disorder is the noxious dynamic compromise that allows the psyche to have "my own space."

5. It is thus no surprise that many patients on the brink of dying from a severe eating disorder tell the clinician that they not only feel healthy but may feel better than they have in their lives. They falsely believe that they have finally wrested a degree of autonomy from the caretaker. The more they binge, starve, or punish the body, the more they feel freed from the internal persecutory relationship described above. Such a sadomasochistic relationship with the body serves two purposes. The internalized mother, who resides inside the adult patient, is punished, if not "killed off," by the neglect shown to the body. Simultaneously, the patient experiences a sense of self from her internalized caretaker the closer she actually gets to death. She believes she is actually "killing off" the abuser and separating from her. In effect, the patient cannot truly care for or love herself because she did not experience unconditional love as she made autonomous steps.

Clinical Example

Angela is the 35-year-old mother of 14-year-old twin daughters. For over two decades Angela has struggled with episodes of self-starvation, purging, delicate self-cutting, and self-inflicted burns. Now separated from her husband of 13 years, Angela sought out psychodynamic psychotherapy because "I'm having trouble letting my girls grow up." By her own admission, Angela let the therapist in on her secret overinvolvement with the twins: "I know I'm going to have trouble whenever they grow up. I am jealous that they are each other's 'best' friends even though that helps me with all I have to do for them! What will become of me when they go to college or have boyfriends? I'll be *so* lonely."

The psychotherapist listened carefully and gently pointed out the problems with the entangled mother–child relationships. Angela would, indeed, need to learn to withstand loneliness and needfulness as her daughters moved forward in life. The therapist went on to help the patient elaborate on how the investment with the daughters had interfered in her marriage and led to the withering of her body. In part, her enmeshed relationship was understood through the unmourned loss of an early tie to her own parents.

Angela did not even see how seriously emaciated she was. She castigated her therapist for being off the mark for advising her to gain. Angela exclaimed, "Just go ahead and call my primary care doctor! His staff will all tell you that I'm in there every six months for a check-up and that I'm doing great!"

The therapist did proceed with getting a release of information and calling the primary physician. In keeping with the philosophy of treating a person with an eating disorder with a multidisciplinary team, the individual psychotherapist told Angela that all people involved in her care would need to communicate. In actuality, the physician was very concerned about Angela's amenorrhea, osteopenia, and insistence that she was within her right to demand potassium supplements to keep her electrolytes normal (Eckert, Halmi, March, et al., 1995; Michel & Willard, 2003; Yager, Devlin, Halmi, et al., 2005).

Angela refused to hear that she was destroying her body. The primary care physician had urged her many times to seek psychotherapy and to see a nutritionist for additional support. Now at a body weight of less than 75% normal, the individual psychotherapist pointed out that the American Psychiatric Association's "Practice Guidelines" (2006) would recommend inpatient hospitalization for a refeeding process to begin. At the very least, a structured day program where meals were given, slow incremental weight gain was expected, and mandatory participation in group therapies and educational sessions would be necessary to halt the patient's downward spiral. Both the physician and the psychotherapist agreed to present the same message to the patient to help save her life and set up a united front against the sadomasochistic relationship she appeared to have with her body (e.g., confront attempts to split).

When these recommendations were presented to Angela by both therapist and physician, she became very angry and refused to accept more intensive intervention. Even when the team members gave her a summary of the "Practice Guidelines" and books to read about medical consequences to drive the message home, Angela became attacking and hostile. She screamed, "You're crazy! My BMI is within normal limits. I refuse to go into a hospital because I feel great." Her denial was of such intensity as to make the physician wonder if Angela was delusional, but this fixed idea is frequently observed in the most disturbed cases of anorexia nervosa (Andersen, 2006).

Angela's case demonstrates a malignant form of eating disorder that only long-term, intensive therapy after refeeding may unravel. Not surprisingly, the patient temporarily feels better (the "self-cure" aspects of the eating disorder) but, in actuality, she is walking very close to death. In all likelihood, she will be a chronic patient until she succumbs. For many chronic adult patients like Angela, the clinicians involved will have to be satisfied with helping her make small gains in weight and "become a bit more comfortable in life" (Strober, 2004, 2006; Yager, 2007b). But in this case the growth and development of two other human beings were also impacted. Her denial also perpetuates pathological enmeshment with her twins. Angela is not physically abusing them, but she is not permitting them to have age appropriate separation. In this way, Angela and her daughters stay psychologically fused, as if they live in one body, not three.

Gaining weight in an intensive treatment program is terrifying to Angela because it not only means that she will have to relinquish control and face down denial of her symptoms, but it will necessitate a total reordering of her psychological world. This is the reason many patients with an eating disorder fear gaining and then maintaining their weight or giving up any ancillary symptoms. They cannot imagine any way out of the hell of their eating disorder. Loss of the eating disorder entails mastering the loss of one's treasured object, the "precious" eating disorder, and allowing objects (in this case, the daughters) permission to grow. The patient's difficult therapeutic task is to learn to tolerate the strong affects that inevitably occur as one begins to psychologically individuate and to allow loved ones to do likewise.

ADDITIONAL TREATMENT CONSIDERATIONS

The features of eating disorders in adults are different from those in the adolescent. Although some of the same treatment guidelines apply (e.g., nutritional management; understanding intrapsychic, family, and interpersonal dynamics; the need for judicious pharmacotherapy; and, in severe cases, day hospital, residential, or inpatient hospitalization), a comprehensive, integrated treatment plan must include taking into account the developmental tasks of adulthood.

Psychoanalyst Clara Thompson, an early, prolific follower of the interpersonal theorist Harry Stack Sullivan, believed that in adulthood fulfilling these tasks can lead to "a constructive expansion of the self in the course of weakening the rigidity of the self system . . . undeveloped potentialities are discovered and encouraged, resulting in a fuller, more fruitful life" (Thompson, 1964, p. 40). Before one's adult power and capabilities can become apparent, "the patient must face and come to terms with the fact that one can never make up for the lost years. One can only hope to live from now on" (pp. 341–343). Most therapists of adults with eating disorders will thus hear at some point in the recovery words akin to, "I'm glad I'm doing this now, but I wish I had begun earlier. There's so much more to live for than I ever expected." As the "cramping circumstances of earlier life are removed" and grieved, the adult patient will more freely engage in the common but essential life tasks while knowing that "the feeling of having arrived is not a signal to stop growing" (p. 341) because the culture molds our broad outline but "each one has [our] own interpersonal experience which makes [us] different [from] everyone else, just as no two leaves on a tree are exactly alike, although they are more alike than different" (Thompson, 1964, p. 43).

1. Remember that biological, cultural, and familial factors are crucial in understanding the genesis and perpetuation of eating disorders in adults. The clinician must take into account the patient's adult family relationships (i.e., partner, children, extended family) in the treatment planning. Members of the adult patient's family can sometimes contribute to or perpetuate difficulties. On other occasions they may support or further the treatment. Integrated treatment of the adult patient with an eating disorder must include a good understanding of the core dynamics within (a) the family of origin and (b) the family of one's adulthood. (Garfinkel, 1996)

2. Keep in mind that adults must be empowered to take more control of their lives and develop a sense of personal responsibility. Sometimes this will include doing battle with third parties such as managed care and insurance companies to secure benefits (Zerbe, 1996a). The adult developmental tasks of achieving autonomy and embracing self-care can be furthered when the patient begins to advocate for his or her own needs, especially the needs for ongoing treatment.

3. Remind yourself that although all eating disorder patients harbor secrets and even a "secret self" (Bromberg, 1996, 2001; Sands, 1991) that must be elucidated in therapy, the narrative the clinician can expect from the adult patient is quite different from that of the adolescent. Marital conflicts, difficulties parenting, the impact of losses, maltreatment within the family of origin, and a paucity of adult friendships are some of the concerns frequently encountered in the treatment of adults. These adult development issues must also be explored, making connection with childhood dynamics whenever possible. As the self expands, the patient is able to depend upon essential others (Galatzer-Levy & Cohler, 1993) that aid in resolution of the false self-system.

4. Expect the unexpected revelation. Case reports have also identified that early parental mistreatment, extramarital affairs, rape, and long suppressed sexual abuse, etc. are uncovered in the course of treatment (Bromberg, 1996; Zerbe, 1993b, 2001b). These split-off aspects of the self account for significant intrapsychic disequilibrium and must be worked through to reorganize the psychic structure to attain a higher functional level.

5. Continue to review with the adult the desire to start a family and the risks to the child if the parent has an active eating disorder. Discuss problems

related to infertility, pregnancy, the early postpartum period, and the likely conflicts that occur with parenting and mealtimes should the patient decide to have a child. If at all possible, encourage the patient to successfully master the eating disorder before becoming pregnant.

6. Help the patient engage in the tasks of adulthood by facing the inevitability of time and the years left to live. A healthy adult accepts and anticipates events and consequences and the need to get on with what one wants to do in life. One defensive purpose of a severe symptom, such as an eating disorder, is the denial of the limits of time (Fabricus, 1998). For example, by attempting to maintain a more adolescentlike body, the adult eating disorder patient demonstrates an inability to accept the physical and emotional realities that are a part of growing older. In this way, too, adult patients must learn to embrace their adult body to achieve a real, authentic sense of power.

CONCLUSION

Understanding the tasks essential to adult development enables the clinician to plan treatment interventions based on those natural steps in the life cycle that have gone awry. Even when eating disorder patients have been ill for a number of years, research demonstrates that many patients can and do improve, reversing their downhill course and attaining the hallmarks of adult functioning (e.g., identity, responsibility, loyalty, ethicality, and an authentic sense of one's power). In part, this occurs because adulthood brings with it the opportunity to find new sources of identification and support. These resources include members of the interdisciplinary treatment team, adult friends, and members of the adult family of the patient, who must work together to provide extensive support for the patient.

Although clinicians cannot as yet define all of the ingredients of a successful treatment, empathic confrontation of the patient's self-destructive treatment of the body, along with providing new models for self-care, are two essential factors. Through successful internalization and identification with new objects including the therapist, the emerging adult self owns and integrates crucial regulatory and adaptive functions for a healthier life. Accountability, autonomy, and interdependence are those hallmarks of adult functioning that have not yet been achieved because of the structural deficits linked to eating and body image problems. These problems can be righted by faith in the individual's potential to develop over the life cycle and provision of therapeutic supports to develop psychic structure and consolidate therapeutic gains.

Treatment of the adult patient would be deficient without helping that patient address the sense of authentic power. Overinvestment in one's body must be shed to gain realistic satisfactions and appreciate one's own real achievements and those of others. As the patient improves, therapists will be witness to how envy and rivalry must be expressed in words and not destructively enacted in relationships, particularly with loved ones and within the therapy itself. Sublimation will also enable patients to express authentic power in their life, manifested by healthy ambitions and the capacity to appreciate different talents in others.

As symptoms diminish, these patients are also more able and willing to encourage others and have greater success in reining in and redirecting any narcissism, greed, or envy they harbor. One consequence of psychotherapeutic work is the development of integrity and strength of character that has a far-reaching effect on the individual's self reliance and relations with the outside world. This transformation of self is made manifest in a sense of greater hopefulness and trust in the world at large and in one's own goodness, leading to an enhanced capacity to cope with the ambiguities of life and to "love powerfully" because and in spite of them.

CHAPTER 6

Middle and Later Life

Caught in the middle
We're middle class, we're middle aged
We were wild in the old days, birth of rock 'n' roll days.

This girl of my childhood games has kids nearly grown and gone
Grown so fast like the turn of a page
We look like our mothers did now when we were those kids' age.

Nothing lasts for long, nothing lasts for long.
Time goes. Where does the time go?
I wonder where the time goes . . .

—Joni Mitchell (*Chinese Café/Unchained Melody*)*

We cannot live the afternoon of life according to the programme of life's morning; for what was great in the morning will be little at evening, and what in the morning was true will at evening have become a lie.

—Carl Jung (1933/1977)

Whether or not one has a bona fide eating disorder, middle age heralds physical and emotional changes for both sexes. Even the majority of us who satisfactorily make this transition can still attest to a moment in time, an unanticipated and unwanted epiphany of sorts, when we catch a glimpse of ourselves in the mirror and realize that we no longer look the same as we did in our 20s and 30s. "Where did the time go?" we ask ourselves. Is that person staring back in the mirror at me really me? In what might be thought of as the same curse as afflicted Dorian Grey, Oscar Wilde's fictional character who got his wish to stay young eternally as his portrait, his image, aged, we also may actually experience ourselves as younger than our chronological age. "I still feel and think like I'm 35 years old," we silently reflect, even though we may be 5, 10, or 15 or more years beyond that age. This discontinuity between aspects of ourselves is routinely and ferociously played out in the lives of patients with eating disorders, but even among the noneating disordered a disconnect can transpire between the real and the wished-for self, especially as we age.

It is not uncommon to be sitting with others "in the middle years"—that undefined period between ages 35 to 65—and hear them attest to their own resilience in sports, in the workplace, in the bedroom. "I'm on a whole new trajectory in my career and life," one 60-year-old colleague boasted, "my wife's pregnant again and I just got promoted to vice-president. With the huge raise, I can finally afford the SUV my wife's been nagging me about!" Several colleagues at the lunch table silently rolled their eyes and looked away. Was he fooling himself? Were we feeling envy? Is what he says real, or just some healthy denial that we all put to good use (Druss, 1995)? Those glances in the mirror should make us take stock of the fact that we do look different from the way we did in our younger years and should also bring about a moment of personal reckoning. They also give a clinician a taste of what a person with an eating disorder or body image lives with most of the time. Momentarily we find that our body image and sense of self are out of sync. We wonder about this stranger with more prominent jowls and conspicuous creases on the lateral sides of our eyes. We do not feel comfortably at home in our body, especially our aging body.

Most of us choose to ignore some of the normative changes that occur with aging such as stiff joints in the morning, greater effort in maintaining weight and exercise tolerance, a bit less energy for even the fun things of life, and the need for more sleep. We remember when we could and did pull all-nighters and could still get up and work hard the next day; with joy we saw the sun come up after some rowdy and rousing dusk-to-dawn parties. In our mind's eye we are still the "rock-and-rollers" full of vim and vigor and ready for more. Nothing puts the brakes on this kind of ubiquitous fantasy more than that first melancholy moment of recognizing the physical impermanence Joni Mitchell nails in her lyrics. We now look like our parents when we were their same age. No longer can we deny the passage of time and how "nothing lasts for long." Entering middle life means we must face the incontrovertible fact of our mortality and the passage of the baton to a younger generation. And following the advice of psychoanalyst Carl Jung, we must come to grips with the notion that to be psychologically healthy at this time in the life cycle, we must change. We must accept the fact that some of our goals need revision. A new version of "what constitutes who I am" must take root. Middle-life transition also requires learning to embrace one's middle-aged body.

AN EMERGING EPIDEMIC?

These normative struggles for every person, including the clinician, help us to understand and to empathize more fully with those who enter middle life with a body image or eating preoccupation. Those attributes that connote "healthy aging" (Valliant, 2002; Vaillant & Mukamal, 2001) are hard to achieve because they require transformation at the very core of one's being. For the middle and later years to be traversed successfully, one must begin to place less emphasis on the outward trappings of success and beauty than ever before and come to grips with the impermanence of the physical body, of life itself, and all one has striven to acquire and master, which will eventually need to be let go. The perpetuation or development for the first time of eating disorders in middle and later life are ways some people attempt to subvert and avoid these inevitable changes. As I will further describe, they take a significant and often unrecognized toll on the family members as well as the patient.

Until recently, the problem of eating disorders in middle and later life was largely overlooked in psychiatry in general and in the subspecialty of eating disorders, in particular. As the baby-boomer generation has aged, clinicians have been forced to face the fact that many people seek to defy aging by maintaining or developing a bona fide or subclinical form of an eating disorder. These clinical observations and case reports (Allaz, Bernstein, Rouget, Archinard, & Morabia, 1998; Gupta & Schork, 1993; Zerbe, 2002a, 2003; Zerbe & Domnitei, 2004a, 2004b) add to the small body of research that is already extant on the problems of eating disorders in middle life and is giving this growing problem the additional phenomenologic, sociocultural, and psychodynamic understanding that is warranted (Forman & Davis, 2005; Lewis & Cachelin, 2001; Tiggeman & Lynch, 2001).

Sometimes excessive dieting or exercise, episodes of purging, preoccupation with body image, significant weight loss, or use of appetite suppressants or drugs of abuse may be harbingers of an overt or subclinical eating disorder in middle-aged or elderly patients. Like younger women, these individuals often deny that they have a problem when asked directly by a well-meaning family member or their primary care physician. They rarely seek psychiatric help for this problem alone. Symptoms that can alert the clinician to the *possibility* of an eating disorder occurring in middle or later life are summarized in Table 6.1. How one goes about ruling the disorder "in" or "out" is expanded upon in the next sections of this chapter and the remainder of the chapter is devoted to treatment of a bona fide subclinical eating disorder in middle or later life. Particular attention is given to encouraging patient and clinician to "expand their dialogue" by asking those difficult but crucial questions that take into account potential medical issues, and the ways social and individual psychological factors may intertwine to either cause or perpetuate an eating disorder (see Table 6.2).

At the current time we do not know how many patients with an eating disorder develop this *de novo* in middle life as a way of coping with aging (Gupta, 1995; Lewis & Cachelin, 2001; Price, Babai, & Torem, 1986; Tiggeman, 1999), reaction to significant loss (Forman & Davis, 2005; Zerbe, 2002), or other psychological events. However, the majority of patients who present for evaluation or therapy have struggled with at least some of the presenting symptomatology for years (Forman, 2004; Gitlin & Zaphiropoulos, 2004). What is currently

TABLE 6.1 Symptoms of eating disorder of middle and late life

- Preoccupation with body image; difficulty mourning aging body and recognizing normal psychological changes
- Use of over-the-counter, prescribed, or illicit substances to lose weight
- Shame or embarrassment about normal signs of aging ("Just look at these wrinkles!")
- Exercise "addiction"
- Inability to make life transitions or to mourn significant losses
- Fear of aging; competition with younger generations ("I can't even look at a piece of cake anymore without gaining weight; when I was 20, I could have had three pieces and not put on an ounce")
- Unrealistic goals

known and understood about eating disorders in middle and later life comes largely from nonclinical case samples and clinical reports, but research on larger patient samples will likely expand as the baby-boomer generation makes its way through the middle and later years and seeks out residential treatment and psychotherapy with greater frequency (Forman, 2004; Forman & Davis, 2005; Grishkat, 2004; Novack, 2004).

CULTURAL CONSIDERATIONS

According to a 1997 *Psychology Today* poll, undertaken by the noted eating disorder researcher David Garner and esteemed clinician Ann Kearney-Cooke, one of the largest studies on body image and eating disorders to date (involving more than 3,400 women and 500 men from 13 to 90 years of age), gaining weight is at the top of the list for negative influences on body image in both men and women (Garner & Kearney-Cooke, 1997). This was true even though most of those polled were of normal weight. Two-thirds of the women and a third of the men in the study said that gaining weight produced the greatest detriment to their self-image. Nearly half of the women polled reported being preoccupied with weight and finding displeasure with their weight regardless of age. In contrast, the poll found that men of all ages were much less dissatisfied with their appearance than were women (women 30 to 39 and 50 to 59 years old were the most dissatisfied). Another large-scale survey, which includes women up to age 75, found that more than 70% of women ages 30 to 74 were dissatisfied with their weight even when they were of normal weight. This study suggests that as women age, body dissatisfaction increases because of fears of aging (Allaz et al., 1998).

In the *Psychology Today* poll, 89% of the women wanted to lose weight. The average woman in the study was 5 feet, 5 inches tall and weighed 140 pounds but would like to weigh 125 pounds, a desire that 15% of women said would be worth sacrificing more than five years of their lives to achieve! Another 24%

TABLE 6.2 Expanding the dialogue when you suspect the patient in middle or later life has or may have an eating disorder

Medical questions:	Has there been any change in your weight recently?
	Do you feel physically healthy?
	Do people tell you that you don't eat enough or seem overly concerned about your appearance?
	Do you feel "out of control" with eating or bingeing?
	Do you overexercise? Do you overuse laxatives?
	Do you worry excessively about age-related changes in your body?
	Have you had a "health scare" recently (arrhythmia, electrolyte imbalance, pancreatitis, fracture, etc.— all could suggest a hidden eating disorder)?
Cultural questions:	Do you feel that our society makes it hard for a woman/man to grow older?
	Have you suffered reversals at work or lost important relationships because of your age?
	Do you envy the "younger generation?" If so, why?
	Does it bother you that the media and our culture seem to place so much emphasis on maintaining a youthful appearance?
	What would you be willing to give up to be your "perfect weight" or have your "ideal body?"
	Do you find that you and your friends spend a lot of time discussing diets, weight, appearance, possible exercise routines, going to the gym, etc.?
Psychological questions:	Do you feel generally positive and optimistic about your future?
	Have you had any recent losses (i.e., death of spouse, change in career)?
	As you look back on your life, might there be some other losses you find it difficult to talk about (i.e., miscarriage; never giving birth; early death of parent, sibling, child)?
	Do you seem to worry about your body and aging more than your friends do? What do you do to hide these changes, if anything?
	How would you like to be remembered? (addresses issue of "ultimate concern")
	If you knew today that the remainder of life would be brief (e.g., five months), what would you do differently?
	What are your goals for the coming years? What is more important to you than achieving an "ideal body?"

of the women surveyed were willing to sacrifice three years of their lives to achieve their desired weight.

Mangweth-Mazek (2005; Mangweth-Mazek et al., 2006) at the University Medical Clinic, Innsbruck, Austria also found that these weight preoccupations do not fade with age. Among 1,000 randomly selected women between 60 and 70 years of age, half of the 475 individuals who responded to the questionnaires restricted their eating. To control weight, 80% used low fat or "light" products, or increased their physical activity to control weight. Nearly two-thirds reported dissatisfaction with weight and shape, and 6% used laxatives, diuretics, or vomiting in attempting to control weight. These kinds of studies are useful not only in alerting clinicians to recognize the scope of the problem but in suggesting to the patient that she or he is not alone in her struggle. They should be incorporated into an integrated treatment plan to demonstrate the formidable denial and rationalization that are pervasive among the eating disorders.

It is no surprise that the preoccupation with body image affects a woman's deeper sense of herself. The *Psychology Today* poll found that for more than 56% of women in the study, being a woman entailed preoccupation and dissatisfaction with overall appearance and body size. In the 1987 Harris Poll, 78% of women and 56% of men were dissatisfied with their weight, the majority pointing out the various degrees they would go to conceal signs of aging. Although it is not surprising that 62% of females 13 to 19 years old in the *Psychology Today* poll were dissatisfied with their weight, the startling fact is that this dissatisfaction with body weight rose to 67% in females over the age of 30. Not surprisingly, even residential programs noted for their treatment of adolescents and young adults with eating disorders find more patients seeking treatment at middle age than ever before and are adapting their programs to the special needs of this population (Forman & Davis, 2005).

Because middle age should be a time when men and women have already achieved identity and an authentic sense of power (see Chapter 5), one begins to wonder about the toll of this focus on body image in this age group. Body image dissatisfaction is not only higher than in past years, it has been accelerating—from 25% in 1972, to 38% in 1985, to 56% in 1997 according to the *Psychology Today* poll (Garner & Kearney-Cooke, 1997). These data raise the question about the use of ancillary methods such as liposuction or plastic surgery to improve appearance because diets often leave women dissatisfied with the results. In 2001, more than 93% of liposuction patients were women between the ages of 17 and 74 years old, but 98.7% were within 50 pounds of their ideal chart weight. Although the procedures have been improved and significant medical complications (e.g., bleeding, pulmonary emboli) have decreased, the success of liposuction does not address the increasingly negative body image of millions of women who believe that weight reduction or body fat removal will make them happier and healthier human beings (Bruner & de Jong, 2001; Haiken, 1997). No doubt additional factors such as discrimination in the work place based on age augment the anxieties of both sexes to do what they can to look younger, but here I stress what is known in a general way about the development and maintence of eating disorder symptoms.

Discussing alternatives to liposuction, although useful to some, addresses only part of the problem, namely the female desire in Western culture to come closer to the slender ideal. It fails to resolve the negative body image that fuels the self-defeating dieting that often precedes and follows such procedures and the existential issues incumbent in "aging well." Consideration of these facts makes clinicians wonder if women who seek reconstructive surgery at midlife should be screened for an eating disorder, a welcome trend now found in some enlightened women's health clinics and surgical centers. Patients are often startled when clinicians apprise them of these body image statistics and the ubiquity of the body image concerns in our culture. These clinicians are raising the essential questions. This intervention helps patients to be less self-incriminating, and more realistic, as they become aware of how their body image derives from both conscious and unconscious processes that are shaped over the years by life experiences. The patient can then better understand herself, her life, and the struggles that have shaped her into who she is today.

The patient is also in a better position to partner with her surgical team should she decide to undergo a procedure because expectations are closer to what can be realistically achieved. The procedure may, in fact, help her to look and to feel better, creating an improved self-image. Despite testimonial claims, it will not create "a whole, new you." Little wonder many reconstructive surgeons have a deep respect for exploratory psychotherapy; it helps them do their jobs well by assisting the patient to anticipate less than perfect outcomes and to confront what cannot be achieved without her undertaking thorough psychological work (Cook, 2004, personal communication).

Helping the Patient: The "Aging Self"

Studies of some non-Western cultures demonstrate that depression, loss, and status reversal in midlife are not ubiquitous. In Japan, narrative accounts demonstrate that there are numerous individual paths in midlife development; for women and men, maturity and growing older are welcomed (Lock, 1998). The physiological changes of female midlife are viewed differently as a whole by Japanese society. Women are expected to find meaningful activities and actually enjoy their sense of personal power, now having greater freedom in time and energy to cultivate one or more art forms. Social scientist Margaret Lock's (1986, 1998) research on Japanese culture suggests that in the future more emphasis will be given to women's subjective experiences—those essential narrative "accounts given by individual women about their encounters with aging" (p. 70). In Japan, an individual is considered to be at the acme of life in middle age because the culture values experience and "age denotes wisdom, authority, and a hard-won freedom to be flexible and creative" (1998, p. 58).

A similar trajectory is seen in the Hindu tradition in India (Kakar, 1998; Menon & Shweder, 1998). Among Oriya Hindu women, biological markers do not define "middle age" although there is a sense of the "normal and desirable" phases in a woman's life (Menon & Shweder, 1998). Growing older for Oriya Hindu women means finding meaning, purpose, and a sense of power in family life along with a sense that one is moving toward the last phase of life, the stage of completion. Although the impermanence of the world is stressed, and continual change is recognized as the only stable feature of life, mature adulthood is viewed as "the most satisfying period in a woman's life" (Menon & Shweder, p. 141). Women are expected to withdraw from family ties and family management to some extent. To address areas of "ultimate concern," men and women are required to embrace their existential loneliness, take stock of the role time plays in human affairs, and accept with equanimity the transitory nature of life (Kakar, 1998). Women in the West can benefit from the model of Hindu women who "think of themselves as intrinsically powerful," and, through identification with the goddess Kali, "share [the] power to create and destroy" (Menon & Shweder, 1998, pp. 182–183) that transforms itself over the life cycle.

Individuals who can be exposed to "alternative midlife narratives" such as these and reflect on how different cultures face the aging process may find a sense of liberation "from the most basic necessity of the ideology of aging" (Gullette, 1998). Perhaps this is one tool that can be used to begin to counter our prevailing culture's sense of decline in the middle years and take cues from our deepest sense of being rather than a preprogrammed script that views midlife as a crisis and the beginning of ultimate demise.

Western media and globalization may be implicated in the use of eating disorder behavior in some cultures (see Chapter 4) but in some subcultures there may be unanticipated protective factors (Anderson-Fye & Becker, 2004; Becker, 1995, 2004b; Pike & Borovoy, 2004). For example, in Belize, anthropologist Eileen Anderson-Fye (2004) demonstrated that young women were protected from eating disorder behavior because of a prevailing psychology of self-care and a culturally sanctioned belief that a woman must always care for her body. The young women used the phrase "Never Leave Yourself" as a guide to decision making in matters large and small, as if they were voicing an affirmation from "the true self."

Despite North American and European or Western media images, these girls maintained the viewpoint that beauty comes in all shapes and sizes, and there is within this diverse multicultural population "room for women to be all colors and ethnicities" (p. 568). Interestingly, weight control methods such as over-the-counter diet pills were observed among older women, reflecting weight-loss behaviors learned from Western media and changes in the economic structure. The questions that anthropological studies such as these are raising about the etiology and maintenance of eating disorder behaviors are numerous and complex but are suggestive about potential models for prevention. By building up a young woman's psychological strengths, and maintaining diverse national beauty ideals, a society may be better equipped to challenge eating disorder behavior, including at middle age.

In addition to having a discussion that educates a patient about these evolving anthropological studies, clinicians may draw upon contemporary cinema and biography to help the patient navigate change by finding new objects of identification. For example, the movie *Calendar Girls* (Cole, Firth, & Towhidi, 2003) starring Helen Mirren and Julie Walters tells the story of a group of Scottish women, well into their prime, who made history and raised millions for the treatment of cancer. The women got together and decided to pose nude to make a calendar to be sold by their women's group. What they thought might be of local interest proved to be an international phenomenon. Persons who see this funny and very moving film are poised to confront their own body shame and sense of narcissistic wounds in getting older. "What am I worried about? These women did it," one patient said after following the therapist's prescription to see the movie and journal about it before coming to her next session. A discussion then ensued about how these women faced aging that the patient could make her own.

A different kind of biographical example comes from the life of the magnificent opera singer Leontyne Price. When Ms. Price realized that her voice could no longer carry her through full operas, rather than ruminate on the changes in her body and become bitter, she burst into midlife generativity by modifying her career: she taught more master classes and gave recitals. Her counsel is sage advice to anyone weathering one of life's inevitable transitions: "You should always know when you're shifting gears in life. You should leave your era, it should never leave you" (quoted in Lanker, 1989, p. 44).

BIOLOGICAL CONSIDERATIONS

Physiologic aging has various effects on the human body that also alter body image, particularly in women (see Table 6.3). Until age 60, women tend to gain 5 to 10 pounds per decade of life. Body shape changes, skin loses its elasticity (i.e., crows' feet), and hair turns gray and thins. These normal life cycle changes are likely to be particularly problematic for women because body fat deposition tends to increase with each developmental milestone; for example, puberty, pregnancy, and menopause (Rodin, 1991, 1993; Rodin, Silberstein, & Striegel-Moore, 1985).

Body image can also be threatened by any medical problem, chronic illness, restriction in social activity, and change in relationships with family and friends (i.e., divorce, or becoming a grandparent). This gender-based finding likely contributes to the "normative discontent" (Byyny & Speroff, 1996; Rodin, Silberstein, & Striegel-Moore, 1985) women feel about their bodies, and may contribute to the initiation or maintenance of eating disorders and exercise addiction in middle life.

TABLE 6.3 Biological bedrocks of aging

- Until age 60, women tend to gain 5–10 lbs per decade (Rodin, Silberstein & Striegel-Moore, 1985)
- Fat deposits tend to increase with developmental milestones: puberty, pregnancy, menopause
- Women are also:
  - Born with more fat cells than men
  - Have slower metabolic rates than men
  - Hormonal influences (estrogen, progesterone) increase likelihood of weight gain over the life cycle

An integrated treatment approach educates patients about these biological facts. Specifically, women are: (1) born with more fat cells than males; (2) have slower metabolic rates than males; and (3) have different hormonal influences than males (i.e., estrogen, progesterone), which increase the likelihood of weight gain throughout the life cycle. They may be predisposed to feel worse about their bodies with age because these biological bedrocks make it harder to keep off the added pounds in a sedentary society where food is an abundant and easily available source of comfort for emotional issues.

Although all body systems change with age, it appears that women worry most about their weight and skin. For example, skin changes can be the most devastating for women because they are the most visible and also are the target of increasing media pressure for change. Women are bombarded with suggestions about defying their age and are urged to "lie about their age," leaving them with the impression that aging is bad and that they should not be satisfied with themselves when they develop "crows' feet" or other signs of aging. The overall message is that aging is a personal defeat, and that the only solution is to use products, reconstructive surgery, or virtually anything to achieve a younger, more ideal look.

Herein lies the difficult assessment that each man or woman must make about her- or himself in order to age successfully: Do we accept society's message that younger is better and strive for unattainable or unnatural ideals, or allow ourselves to become internally self-worthy and maintain a positive body image despite some noticeable and possibly inevitable physiological shifts?

As in other psychiatric disorders, the clinician must first rule out physical causes of weight loss, vomiting, or perceptual disturbances before assuming an eating disorder is the root of a person's problem (see Chapter 1). Clinical depression often presents with significant weight loss. Among the elderly, the refusal of food may be a symptom of depression or "hunger strike" where the patient is angry about aging and the loss of independence (Duggal & Lawrence, 2001; Giannini & Telew, 1987; Russell & Megen, 1992). In contrast, an older person with bona fide anorexia nervosa has body image distortion and idealizes thinness (see Table 6.4).

TABLE 6.4 Similarities and differences between depression and eating disorders in later life

Symptoms	Depression	Eating Disorders
Weight loss	+	+ (if anorexia)
Memory impairment	+	+
Concentration problem	+	+
Insomnia	+	−
Delusion about body	+	−
Body image preoccupation	Rare	+

Both depressed and anorexic patients complain of having low energy, anhedonia, poor concentration, memory difficulties, and other preoccupations. As a general rule, only the depressed patient will complain of the ancillary symptoms of insomnia or have a body image disturbance that reaches delusional proportions. These patients can usually be successfully treated with antidepressants, antipsychotics, or electroconvulsive therapy.

All eating disordered patients who present in middle or later life should have a comprehensive physical examination to rule out physiological problems associated with the eating disorder (e.g., electrolyte imbalance, vascular insufficiency, arrhythmias, pancreatitis). Malignancy, diabetes mellitus, inflammatory bowel disease, substance abuse, and infections must also be ruled out as a cause of the weight loss or appetite disturbance (see Tables 1.4, 1.6). Malnutrition is a significant problem in the elderly, affecting a third of institutionalized patients, and is considered a major etiology of anorexia tardive (geriatric, or late-onset anorexia) (Clarke, Wahlgrist, Rassias, & Strauss, 1999; Duggal & Lawrence, 2001; Gupta, 1995). The involvement of a skilled nutritionist to assess the dietary needs and make adjustments in calorie and nutrient requirements is an essential aspect of the treatment planning for these patients.

Clinical Example

One busy afternoon, Jack's 52-year-old daughter, Helen, called with an urgent issue. She and Jack's primary care physician were convinced that Jack, age 78, had developed late-onset anorexia (Russell & Megan, 1992). Helen had struggled with her own periods of food restriction and excuses for "just not wanting to eat" off and on since she was 18. Thus, the family history pointed toward a possible genetic factor; as Helen knew, recent research demonstrates that anorexia nervosa runs in some families (see Chapter 4). Jack had already lost 25 pounds and had no appetite, but he denied body image concerns and a complete medical workup was negative.

Hearing Jack tell his story led to an important clue. Although he was not particularly hungry, the main trouble with eating seemed to derive from "my mouth muscles are just not working. It's like they have no energy to do their job." Could Jack's soft voice and difficulty speaking also be an aspect of the problem?

A referral to a neurologist settled the issue with lamentable consequences. Jack actually had an unusual presentation of amyotrophic lateral sclerosis (i.e., Lou Gehrig's disease), the same disease that took the life of Dr. Morrie Schwartz, the central character in the best-seller *Tuesdays With Morrie* by Mitch Albom (1977). Unlike Morrie, whose demise took many months—long enough for him to impart much life wisdom to the narrator and student, Mitch—Jack was dead within six weeks of Helen's phone call.

The final chapter of Jack's life is instructive for all of us who work with eating disorders. In his case, denial of body image problems, a positive family history for anorexia (daughter), some manifest eating symptoms, and weight loss in the face of a full negative medical workup all pointed toward possible late-onset anorexia (i.e., anorexia tardive). One must "willingly suspend belief" and one's own tendency to draw a conclusion and keep turning over stones. In later life, an eating disorder is truly a diagnosis of exclusion, medical and neurological problems being much more likely culprits when fulminant weight loss and eating irregularities are the presenting problems (Berg & Andersen, 2007; Zerbe, 2003, 2007b).

DOES MY MOTHER HAVE A PROBLEM?

The following clinical examples demonstrate these dynamics and suggest that sometimes clinicians learn about an eating and body image problem not from the patient herself but from a concerned family member, adding to our clinical appreciation for the truly multigenerational nature of eating disorders.

Maura is an engaging 17-year-old college freshman making progress in her treatment for severe depression and a comorbid anxiety disorder. Like many young women, Maura has also struggled over the years with body image concerns and subclinical anorexia nervosa. Approximately seven months into her recovery from depression, she told her psychiatrist that she was angry but worried about her mother. When asked about what triggered these reactions, Maura replied,

> My mother has always been preoccupied with her figure and weight as well as mine. Since our family therapist told her to "get off my case" about those issues, she's stopped bugging me about how I look. But she still talks about her own weight and how she looks. She diets all the time. Last week, she came downstairs wearing some of the clothes I wore in high school that I can't fit into anymore. Those dresses are a size 3. I now wear a size 6. Do you think my mother has a problem?

The question Maura poses is impossible to answer without knowing more, but it is certainly suggestive of a complicated family and individual problem with eating disorders. Women in all age groups are urged by physicians to combat obesity by staying physically active, eating a diet rich in vegetables and low in fat, and maintaining an appropriate weight range derived from medical consensus. We do not know Maura's mother's ideal body weight or if she is making choices for herself based on her physician's recommendations.

On the other hand, Maura confides to us that her mother has always been concerned about physical appearance and "diets all the time." A clinician might also wonder how much of a struggle the mother is having in watching her daughter grow up and is unconsciously competing with her. What is the message suggested in wearing clothes that the daughter has long since discarded? Is Maura's mother signaling that she is struggling against, according to Erik Erikson, taking her rightful place in the "cycle of generations" and finding joy and fulfillment in enhancing the lives of others, such as participating in the growth and development of the younger generation (Erikson, 1976, 1981, 1982)? Following Jung, we might also ask ourselves if the mother is "living the afternoon of her life" as she tried to live the morning, and regarding her "earlier ideals only as something faded and worn out" (Jung, 1972, p. 19)?

A Mother Confides

To support Maura's growing autonomy, and age-appropriate separation and individuation from her mother, an intervention was made that encouraged Maura to bring her concerns directly to her mother Jesse's attention. First, Maura explained that she was alarmed about her mother's emphasis on dieting and that it was impacting her treatment for depression because she worried so much. To help Maura out of her position as a parentified child (Rinsley, 1980, 1982), knowing that this position is common among patients with overt or subclinical eating disorders (Zerbe, 1993/1995a, 1993a, 1993b, 1999, 2007a), the therapist compiled a list of potential referral sources that was given to Maura to give to Jesse. Boundaries that promoted the separation–individuation process were thereby maintained by keeping Maura's individual psychotherapy separate from that of her mother.

Fortunately in this example, Jesse did hear her daughter's concerns and sought psychotherapeutic consultation. (Sadly, clinical experience shows that the more common scenario for the parent is to be defensive or to deny the eating problem, just as in other eating disorders.) Part of Jesse's motivation was to help Maura; initially she "had no idea" how her remarks about weight, appearance, and getting older were impacting her daughter's well-being. Jesse confided to her therapist that she had become preoccupied with age-related body changes following her divorce 10 years earlier. Initially she had joined a local gym and exercised twice weekly at the recommendation of her primary care physician and to help her cope with her loss, but this healthy behavior had escalated in the past six months into excessive exercise patterns. Jesse admitted to going to the gym every day, always for at least two hours and often for up to four hours or more.

As she grew comfortable in her individual therapy process, Jesse also acknowledged that she purged twice weekly and took over-the-counter appetite suppressants to help her manage her weight (see Table 6.1). The initial period of therapy centered on helping Jesse address the feelings she stuffed following her divorce and increase her awareness of how her behaviors had unanticipated, negative consequences for her daughter, who had also been preoccupied with body image and thinness. By the middle phase of treatment, Jesse began to see how her behavior was unconsciously competitive and undermining of her daughter and took risks to help Maura be more open about how they saw life differently; Maura's autonomy was thereby promoted.

Jesse's individual therapist formulated the task as helping the patient come more to terms with the necessity of transitions of middle life (e.g., mourning her youthful body, adjusting to the notion that she would not accomplish all of her goals and dreams in her lifetime, and working through residual issues of loss and grief related to her divorce), which helped her embrace the possibilities of what could still be done. Her excessive eating and exercise patterns were curtailed as she participated in more age-appropriate and healthful activities (e.g., strength training and walking thrice weekly; yoga twice weekly). She came to understand that her preoccupation with her body was an attempt to control what was not fully under her control, such as the aging process and, eventually, her own death. Moreover, she had to grapple with the same issues that confront each generation as we grow older: unconscious envy and competition with the younger generation (Colarusso, 2000; Klein, 1957, 1963). By putting to rest the narcissistic preoccupation with her own body and working through her unconscious competition with her daughter, Jesse galvanized her daughter's own treatment process. Embracing where she was in the adult life cycle allowed Jesse to leave room for Maura to grow and to embrace where she was without feelings of guilt or harm to her mother for her own achievements or success.

A TIME OF TRANSITION FOR BODY AND SELF

In the 1970s, social commentator and essayist Susan Sontag quipped that there was a "double standard of aging" that faces the American woman. Whereas a man is usually perceived as more attractive and appealing to women as he ages and acquires gray hair, an expanding waistline, and even sagging skin, the same is not the case for women. Growing older for the male also means enhanced financial security and emotional stability and hence appeal to the woman who seeks, among other things, security. Women, on the other hand, tend to view ourselves and are viewed by society as a whole, as less attractive, desirable, employable, and marriageable as we age. It is not simply low self-esteem or unconscious fantasy that makes one take appearance seriously. A huge body of anthropological and cultural research attests to the fact that although what signifies attractiveness of men for women varies, marriageability, social standing, the availability of jobs, and the like are influenced by the dominant culture's view of desirability (Brumberg, 1988; Friday, 1996; Zerbe, 1995a). Beauty does matter. Although there have been some attempts to correct this pejorative view in the mainstream women's literature by emphasizing the wisdom and "inner beauty" one garners with each birthday, research demonstrates that a majority of the women studied express concerns of aging that center on body image and attractiveness and generally feel less desirable and worthy (Allaz et al., 1998; Mangweth-Matzek et al., 2006; Zerbe & Domnitei, 2004a, 2004b).

From a psychodynamic perspective, eating disorders in midlife and beyond can be understood as an attempt to solve, albeit inadequately, this cultural phenomenon and other dilemmas of adult life. Just as anorexia and bulimia nervosa in younger individuals have been demonstrated to serve multiple psychological needs and functions, so individuals in middle or later life may also make psychological use of eating problems to avoid addressing conflicts, rising above development difficulties, making crucial life transitions, and moving forward. Some clinicians have asked whether or not a "midlife crisis" is an essential developmental step for individuals (Jacques, 1965). Although most developmental theorists believe that the middle of life can be a time of enormous creativity and productivity, few clinicians would disagree that all adults struggle with new and perplexing issues that are not seen in younger individuals. Midlife may not always be a time of crisis but it is most certainly a crucible for change.

Development in adulthood is unique for all individuals and consequently defies easy formulas for the clinician who is accompanying the patient on her journey into what for her is a new world. However, the adult developmental literature does offer a map to assist patient and therapist to understand the essential stages of development that connote forward motion into uncharted territory. Enduring the death of one's parents, a sibling, or spouse, watching one's children leave home, becoming a grandparent, changing careers, making adjustments in one's marriage, or even divorce, are among the panoply of issues that heralds mid- and later life transitions. Add to this the notion that each of us carries unresolved issues and conflicts from earlier developmental periods to the next one, and even the most emotionally healthy among us recognize that there is always some "fertile soil" for symptom formation. Symptoms are manifestations of our attempt to cope with psychological deficit or conflict and like physical pain itself, they can be a "gift that nobody wants" (Brand & Yancey, 1993). If dealt with straightforwardly and psychologically they can increase a sense of security and personal transformation. If one's body has been the site where these conflicts were staged in the past, regression likely will occur in the same direction.

Clinicians must therefore be on the alert for eating problems and body image concerns to manifest themselves again at any time of life transition. For those people engaged in disordered eating in later life, adult developmental process is derailed. They are less able than they ideally would be to participate in life-affirming activities that constitute, to use Erik Erikson's term, *generativity*

(1950, 1976, 1981, 1982). Concomitantly, they do not mourn their youth, or their youthful body, and thereby remain narcissistically preoccupied with maintaining or attaining an idealized, stereotyped notion of what constitutes beauty. Preoccupied with external, not internal, markers of success and attractiveness, they lull themselves into a belief of invincibility and defensively deny life's inevitable changes by investing psychological energy on maintaining a youthful appearance. As our society has grown more competitive and champions perfection in all areas, so have the narcissistic disorders related to attainment of success increased demonstrably (Lasch, 1979). One area that may signal narcissistic preoccupation is an overinvolvement in the body at the expense of other activities and interests (Lieberman, 1995; Zerbe, 1993/1995a, 1996a, 1996b, 2002a) that truly engage the individual in what constitutes a "generative" life, counters "stagnation," and reflects the cycle of the generations (Erikson, 1976, 1981).

WHAT IS UNIQUE ABOUT TREATING A MIDDLE-AGED PATIENT?

The tasks of the clinicians working with individuals at mid- and later life who have an eating and body image problem are in many respects similar to working with these patients at other points in the developmental life cycle. The notable differences include addressing the essential developmental tasks of middle and later life that the patient may be avoiding. While the role culture plays in fostering the eating disorder interdigitates with the patient's personal concerns (e.g. career "burnout;" earlier choice to pursue career and not have a biological child; losing a spouse to a "trophy" wife), each individual must come to grips with essential psychological adaptations as we traverse mid- and later life. These include a stark realization that each of us confronts "a race against time" (Colarusso, 1979; Nemiroff & Colarusso, 1985); we must eventually relinquish power and position to a succeeding generation, and we will need to shed former stable and meaningful roles. Table 6.2 lists a series of questions the clinician can use to expand a dialogue if there are concerns that the patient may have an eating disorder, and the table makes some additional suggestions about deepening the conversation to understand what particular psychological issues or cultural biases may be affecting this particular patient.

An integrated treatment model may begin by incorporating education about the illness and the biological bedrocks of aging and teach how studies of diverse cultures are challenging our Western notion of aging. Media literacy may also be an important component. Finding new objects as role models for healthy aging may be essential for some patients. New coping strategies and other supportive life skills can be suggested, depending on the needs of the patient. The potential benefits of psychopharmacology must also be considered. Most times elements of these modalities can and should be employed conjointly for comprehensive care, but for every patient to find and maintain a sense of equanimity in middle and later life, they must make a "final renunciation of infantile omnipotence and grandiosity and the Faustian fantasies of youth" (p. 82), "accept the transitory nature of all relationships and emotional states" (p. 81), and "enter into a period of involvement with 'ultimate concerns' as the person prepares for the last stage of life" (Kahar, 1998, p. 79). Many of the interpersonal and cognitive-behavioral modalities described thus far will apply to the eating disorder patient in middle life, but clinicians will no doubt find themselves dealing with psychodynamic and existential issues as research in this population of patients has alerted us to do.

One crucial difference in working with patients in middle and later life is that the burgeoning reality of mortality and the time left in one's life can no longer be denied. This fact can help motivate a patient. In what sociologist and midlife researcher Bernice Neugarten (1968; Neugarten & Gutmann, 1968) called the "age 50 wake-up call," one's perspective dramatically shifts from the years since birth to the years left in one's life around this particular birthday. Middle-aged patients who have had a protracted eating disorder will necessarily have the additional task of mourning the "life they did not live" because the eating disorder disrupted the course their life might otherwise have taken (Lackman & James, 1999; Neugarten & Gutmann, 1968; Neugarten & Hagestad, 1976; Rosenberger, 1999). All individuals must work through losses and accept choices we make to live the fullest life possible at midlife and beyond (e.g., loss of parents, death of friends, children moving away from home). The following case examples illustrate some of the issues of midlife patients who have gained a more thorough understanding of the impact of eating problems and worked through them because they engaged in an expressive, psychodynamically oriented psychotherapy process.

Another task of the therapist who works psychodynamically is to help individuals begin to reflect and gain insight into the unconscious factors leading to the eating disorder. In contemporary parlance, these symptoms can be understood as unmentalized experiences (Mitrani, 1995); the work of analysis or psychodynamic therapy enables the patient to mentalize what was previously enacted by her pathological dieting, restrictive eating, overexercise, gorging, laxative abuse, and so forth (see Chapter 2).

The psychodynamic method and theory behind it divert sharply here from other modes of treatment, such as patient education, cognitive-behavioral strategies, and psychotropic medication, although these modalities may also be employed conjointly (Milton, 2001; Zerbe, 2001b, 2007a, 2007c). Indeed, other methods are sometimes experienced as "stuffing the patient" with concrete tools, or metaphorically, too much of the therapist's goodness. These treatment tools may at other moments be effective because, like analysis, they provide time and space for the patient to think about what she is doing and why (i.e., begin the process of mentalization) (Modell, 1976, 1993; Zerbe, 2007c). In addition, they strengthen adaptive defenses and facilitate new ego strengths.

If the therapist is charismatic or facilitates a positive therapeutic alliance, the patient may improve because self-cohesion has been promoted by an unobjectionable positive transference or identifitory object. These treatments may unwittingly foster the process of mentalization. On other occasions, these structured therapeutic strategies will paradoxically increase resistance, and non-dynamically trained clinicians routinely wonder why this occurs. In part, the patient already feels "filled to overflowing" with her mental contents. Giving her more plans, strategies, and information engenders a kind of mental claustrophobia wherein she experiences greater and greater entrapment in her body. Hence, the clinically observed phenomenon of eating disorder symptoms exacerbating when treatment begins as a way to unconsciously flee from inner experience or purge emotional pain. Psychological or biochemical techniques that do not give the patient a safe haven to process but, in contradistinction, force more into her, may dramatically increase her need to physically and psychologically evacuate. As one listens to the patient tell her story, it is best not to try "to feed" her with more than a few educative or cognitive-behavioral interventions at once. Give the patient an opportunity to metabolize what is provided and check back to see that she use it! Herein lies one implicit reason for the psychological rationale for reviewing homework assignments, journaling, and food diaries! The therapist is making sure that the patient can do the work and giving space for internal processing (see Chapters 1 and 2).

ENVY OF YOUTH AND THE YOUTHFUL BODY

Astrid is a 64-year-old, married mother of three who had successfully managed her household and a small number of women's retail stores since her 20s. She sought out thrice-weekly psychoanalytic psychotherapy in her late 30s for issues related to intimacy in her marriage and complicated bereavement following the death of her brother in an airline accident. Astrid found that four-year therapy process to be useful so when a family conflict arose she once again turned to a clinician with a psychodynamic perspective. The current consultation request occurred because her youngest daughter (age 33) developed a protracted course of anorexia that "everyone in my family is worried and talking about." Despite numerous trials of medication and cognitive-behavioral intervention, the daughter did not improve. Astrid wondered if residential treatment was in order because her daughter refused to gain weight on her own.

In the fourth hour of this process, Astrid shifted from the focus on her daughter to concerns about herself. She confided that for at least 40 years she used, "throwing up to manage my weight." These episodes had exacerbated in the past year, even though she realized it was not good for her health. Educational tools were discussed (e.g., vomiting does not help weight loss; the importance of keeping a food journal and charting emotions before and after overeating or vomiting; engaging in an activity immediately after a meal to divert attention from the usual purging).

The therapy moved forward as the patient told her life story. The purging stopped temporarily after the patient made her "confession" about the secret details of her life that she felt guilty about harboring. As she put it, "I wonder if I'll grow up in a different way now by sharing my worries." As she came to understand this dramatic shift with her therapist, the underlying reasons did appear to be less about practical tools to become healthy or even helping her daughter than finding a "new place to put how terrible I feel about myself for working all the time, cheating some customers, and expecting more from my daughter than was ever reasonable."

Like other patients in late midlife, Astrid expressed many concerns about life transition issues, and eventually her own death, that she felt unable to share with her friends or her husband. Again, the initial phase of psychodynamic psychotherapy served as a new and very different kind of "container" (Bion, 1967; Grinberg et al., 1993) for the patient. With time, this patient's material shifted as she did her own "life review," confiding a host of stories, memories, and thoughts about her colorful life. She did a portion of the work of mourning as we strategized about what she could still accomplish in her life and how she grieved that, "I don't have three more lifetimes to do all I want to do!"

Up to this point Astrid's therapy included psychodynamic, interpersonal, and cognitive-behavioral elements. After this initial phase of working through, an expectable regression occurred when more bulimic symptoms again emerged. Some therapists might have already concluded Astrid's process after 22 sessions because excellent symptom control had been achieved. Indeed, as previously noted, many treatments do end at this point because of patient preferences and third-party reimbursement. Astrid had the resources, and the will, to go further. She wondered why she was again doing damage to herself when both she and her therapist agreed that progress had been made.

In this case, the bulimic evacuations served as violent, vituperative explosions at the self for not having done more in her life; concomitantly, they represented angry, vengeful attacks on her life partner and envious attacks on "the younger generation," specifically her daughter. Astrid wondered why she had stayed in a largely unsatisfying marriage. She questioned herself about not finishing her master's degree. What had she sacrificed in her personal development because she was not ambitious in her young adulthood? Could she have been a better wife or mother? These questions were formed only as we spoke together, although she always had a sense "without words" that her purging was about anger and frustration within herself, a way to simultaneously punish and momentarily, albeit spuriously, curtail regret.

Astrid was like many of our patients who have greater psychological knowledge of themselves than they let themselves consciously know. Expressive psychotherapy helped her put words around some of these disappointments and questions and also normalized them as being part of what each person must come to grips with as we age. Two aspects of theory were pivotal in the therapist's mind as the work unfolded. First, the long-held tenet of making the unconscious conscious (Freud, 1900/1964b, 1912/1964d, 1913/1964e, 1925/1964f; Grotstein, 1999) and of putting personal history and the suppression of split-off mental contents into words through the naming affects makes what could not be spoken speakable. In essence, what appears seemingly unknowable becomes more known, and hence, psychologically manageable (Bion, 1967; Little, 1981).

The second theoretical guideline employed insights derived by the model of adult developmental stages. For maturity to unfold, the midlife transition necessitates mourning actual losses, recognizing the meaning of those losses to the self, and gaining a sense of equanimity about what one has been able to accomplish, albeit imperfectly and with some expectable regrets. Because eating disorders are diseases of the self, those aspects of the self that are unhealthy must still be mourned for one's life to move on and be full. As often happens, Astrid found unreceptive ears when she tried to talk about her failures and disappointments with friends. Therapy served as a safe place to review her life in detail and not have personal disappointments minimized.

What is more, giving up a cherished dream or a sense of "what someday might happen" or "if only" fantasies (Aktar, 1996) needs just as much or more working through than the loss of an actual beloved family member, friend, or mentor. In the latter case, the community helps us mourn. Our loss is seen and understood. The loss of a life-dream is more silent; it is difficult to bear because one experiences oneself as more alone and vulnerable. Individuals sense change in the self but have a hard time putting it into words.

What psychologist Christopher Bollas (1987) poetically grasped in the phrase the "unthought known" applies to patients like Astrid. These patients are aware of something deeply perplexing that is almost on the tip of the tongue, but nonetheless this "something" stays submerged in the mind. Psychodynamic therapy aims to alleviate this deep suffering and the manifest symptoms of disordered eating by provision of a safe place to become more familiar with what one intuitively knows about oneself but was unable to think through or express fully. This process is also coined by the contemporary term *mentalization* (Fonagy, 1991; Bateman & Fonagy, 2006).

One learns by listening to such patients that thought suppression comes at a high cost to personal development. Astrid's competition and envy of her daughter's appearance and the daughter's potential professional development posed other dynamic conflicts underlying Astrid's eating problem. As she put it in one stormy hour, "It kills me to go to a party and see all the younger women with their short skirts and cute figures. I can act charming when I'm talking to them, but if they *only* knew my rage at them for what they have that I *don't have* anymore!" In sessions Astrid frequently talked about herself as being "big" or "large" even though she was only slightly above the normal weight range for her age and height. Her distorted body image was part of an overall disordered sense of herself, an aspect of which revealed underlying shame as she made torturously unfavorable comparisons with others in her peer group.

Tracing deeper pre-Oedipal and Oedipal issues would surely enlarge the scope of her understanding of the multiple roots of her envy toward others, especially as they related to the body. But Astrid still had to face the adult developmental hurdle that she was no longer a young woman (Berke, 1990). Her envy of younger women signaled her resistance to entering into her maturity in a host of areas. She thereby was unable to partake of some of the real fruits of what might constitute the healthy adult life in maturity (Fitzpatrick & Friedman, 1983). In contrast, she remained "stagnant." Her concerns and strivings typically preoccupy middle age men and women and prohibited her from being as "generative" as she might have been (Erikson, 1950, 1976).

As described, cultural values must also be taken into consideration in the treatment of middle-aged patients (Rosenberger, 1999). Mainstream American society does not venerate older women as other culture groups may do, (e.g., American Indians). Western society values the stereotyped media images of a youth-dominated culture, so there appears to be little to envy or desire by growing older. Although some may argue that this observation may be slowly changing, few would quibble with the notion that the preponderance of media images idealizes youth. To face down the fantasy of youthful perfection, the individual must have significant ego strength to challenge prevailing cultural norms (Vailliant, 1993). The task of the clinician in this regard is to challenge the patient to look squarely at societal values and her unwitting acceptance of them. One must also help the patient to take stock and to make the most of the time and the possibilities one still has.

While maintaining neutrality, the therapist must help the patient wrestle with her unconscious collusion and self-denigration implicit in the idealization of youth and media-driven culture. The patient must start a new life in midlife much as the immigrants to a new country must grasp new inner and external realities brought about by enormous, and oftentimes unwanted, change. Moreover, the therapist must also maintain a high degree of vigilance for complicated countertransference reactions brought about by unconscious reactions to the culture and to our own aging processes.

To help the patient reflect on the necessity of making life transitions and some of the potential benefits in facing them squarely, Judith Viorst's *Necessary Losses* (1986) is regularly recommended. In this book, Viorst presents the case that all men and women, to make necessary life transitions through each stage of life, must give up a former self and former way of being to move forward into the next phase of life. In the treatment of patients like Astrid, one finds that there is often an overt resistance to dealing with losses. These include, but are not limited to, the loss of a youthful body and appearance, changes in the primary relationships to one's own parents, spouse, and children, and particular goals and career aspirations. Sometimes the loss is less overt and unconscious— such as the residual effects of miscarriage, abortion, failed early marriage, and the like. The therapist must be on the leading edge of the patient's associations, urging the patient to go as deeply as she can to fully grasp the multidetermined nature of her eating disorder and especially to recognize and to work through previously unacknowledged losses.

KEEP LOOKING FOR THE OBVIOUS

Sigmund Freud quipped in his autobiography that it was his fortune to discover the most explicit and apparent everyday phenomena, such as the sexuality of children (Freud, 1925/1964d). Scrutiny of the obvious continues to be the bread and butter of everyday psychotherapeutic work. Clinicians are no doubt repeatedly struck by the secrets people harbor and are too ashamed to verbalize. Once they do, remarkable shifts transpire. Thus far I have emphasized the crucial importance for clinicians to keep an eye out for those issues which are hidden, but in plain view, and this message is just as important for individuals who enter treatment during middle-age transitions. Pain and suffering diminish and the patient has more psychic energy with which to persevere. In this way, expressive psychotherapy can be truly life-transforming.

Clinical Example

Willa, a 48-year-old divorced mother of one had restricted her eating since adolescence. Although she never fulfilled the full diagnostic criteria of anorexia nervosa, she was always preoccupied with staying slender and would eat sparsely. After years of despondency, she finally entered therapy for her "depression." Willa's stooped posture, pale complexion, and hollow eyes put one in the mind of sitting with a person who lived much closer to death than life. She seemed so much older than she was.

In the first year of therapy, Willa's mother's lifelong battle with a chronic physical illness that left her unable to render much physical or emotional care to the patient was discussed. Brutally self-punishing, Willa blamed herself for her impoverished relationship with her mother. Gradually, she also came to tease apart her own internalized identification with this "bad object" (Fairbairn, 1943/1952; Grotstein & Rinsley, 1994). The mother had been unable to eat or to enjoy life because of her illness, so had the patient's subclinical anorexia become an unconscious way of self-abnegation that identified her with her mother? Especially after Willa's mother died at age 70, this patient's (who was then 40) restrictive eating and patterns of overwork and overexercise were exacerbated. The patient had so completely incorporated her mother into her psyche that she permitted herself only paltry personal gratifications. Pointing out this repetitive pattern led to the gradual diminishment of the self-abuse. Restricted eating subsided and dysphoria improved. Willa began to look less beleaguered and even seemed younger. Some days she would venture a joke or take note of something the therapist wore as she worked through the early attachment issues and eventual death of her mother.

Willa's capacity for deeper self-examination into what constituted her problematic eating led to significant personal development at midlife that included a redefinition of her career goals and staking new claims to autonomy by forming a relationship with a woman. Challenging the deep and unconscious identifitory patterns with the mother promoted healthier relationships to be internalized. Moreover, the lack of psychological availability in Willa's mother engendered times of "unmentalized" experiences (Mitrani, 1995). For example, the patient recalled pining for her mother's comfort alone in her room because she had no one to talk to. Skin-picking, compulsory masturbation, and occasional delicate self-mutilation (Cross, 1993) served a self-soothing function and was simultaneously an unconscious plea for her mother to "see" her pain.

In Willa's case, the work of therapy can be conceptualized as helping the patient become familiar and comfortable with what was previously enacted by her restrictive eating and self-injurious behaviors. Therapy provided her with a place for reflection, something she began to call her "midweek pause." Adjunctive cognitive techniques such as role-playing, giving her homework assignments such as writing a letter to her mother that spelled out what she missed but also received in her development, and analyzing the negative beliefs that she had caused the problem, facilitated her capacity to put things into words. For patients such as Willa who have had a dearth of parenting, cognitive therapy workbooks (Leahy, 2003) also provide structional analysis of the patient's difficulties and serve as a transitional function between sessions. The patient knows that the therapist is involved and cares when the homework assignments (e.g., tables, charts, etc.) are reviewed and the therapist takes the tasks seriously. For Willa, the therapist was "like a real, live, healthy mother I always wanted but never had before."

Dolores began therapy at age 59 because of longstanding marital discord and the physical invalidism of her only child, a daughter. Despite persistent negative transference, she continued to come to twice-weekly sessions and to work on expressing her feelings about her tragic situation. She felt "so little control" in her life that managing her food and weight became one reasonably successful arena for her to feel empowered.

In Dolores's third year of treatment, after her daughter died, her weight increased temporarily and she became frantic to take off the extra pounds. "I can't even control my weight," she screamed, "why can't you do something?" One of the "somethings" she wanted the therapist to unconsciously do, of course, was to magically restore her daughter to her, or at least (in the transference) be a better or more effective daughter to her. As the daughter in the transference, the female therapist was a safe target to rage against. Dolores could leave after every session instead of being left.

Links were made between the affects of hate, bitterness, and disappointment she felt toward the therapist for not being able to give her what she wanted and her disappointment about her child for dying. Ultimately, however, the therapist had to be content with the fact that whatever happened in the therapy with this patient was going to be wrong. Dolores needed to discharge the hate and aggression she felt for what she did not get from her daughter toward a safe target (e.g., the therapist). Her struggles with eating improved as she mourned the loss of her daughter, and as her feelings of loss of control in her life by the daughter's long illness and eventual death were more fully worked through. In effect, she learned to gain control by examining what she could never have controlled.

As Dolores's ego autonomy expanded, so did her focus on her body image become less a way to organize her feelings and sense of self. This particular example also demonstrates the value in expanding on, interpreting, and working through a seemingly intractable negative transference. Also essential is the therapist's general comfort with becoming "the bad enough object" (Fairbairn, 1943/1952; Rosen, 1993). Empathy with the patient's position was easier when one took into account her real loss and the frustration she bore over many years at witnessing her only child's physical decline. Dolores never experienced the realistic gratifications in watching her sacrifices and nurturing "pay off" by having a relationship with a mature, self-sufficient, capable adult. Her anger and need to defeat the treatment were projections of what she had experienced during her daughter's illness. As she had also experienced depletion at working so hard yet not being able to reverse her daughter's illness, so she unconsciously attempted to teach the therapist what her impotence had felt like throughout her long travail. Nothing that was said or pointed out ever seemed to help Dolores feel any better. A passive, receptive stance with the material and encouragement to speak to her disappointments in the therapist allowed her over time to find areas in her own life that were enjoyable and gratifying. The therapist's task was to absorb the patient's feelings of helplessness and loss of efficacy, and provide a model that even being insufficient could be endured.

Walter was 73 years old when his internist finally insisted he come for a thorough psychiatric evaluation. He had exhausted every specialist in his local community because of his never-ending list of physical complaints for which no bona fide illness could be found. Walter's weight loss began at age 63 when his second child, a son, died in a tragic car accident and he was laid off when his company downsized. This patient's anorexia tardive masqueraded as psychosomatic illness but was actually caused by two profound losses that could not be mourned. Physical illnesses were expressions of the inner anguish that Walter could not express verbally.

Most authorities in the assessment of bereavement concur that no loss is more devastating or harder to survive than the loss of a child. For the individual's life to proceed, one must find a way to cope. In each of these cases, the eating disorder was a "partial solution" to a grief that was truly the individual's "greatest" loss. Education about the grief process, in addition to helping the patient find new ways to directly express the loss, often leads to improvement in overall functioning and restoration of weight. Lessons learned from initial studies of and narrative report by centenarians demonstrate how, to adjust to the phases and changes of life, the older person must be able to mourn. If one is not able to mourn effectively, other less adaptive defensive strategies are called into play. Clinicians are advised to remember that behind an eating disorder or body image problem at any developmental period may lie a problem with unexpressed grief or mourning, but middle and later life herald particular issues of loss and grief that require support, knowledge, and working through (see Table 6.4).

ADDITIONAL TREATMENT CONSIDERATIONS

Eating disorders in middle and later life are becoming more common as the baby boomer generation ages, because striving for a "slimmer, better" body and pursuing unattainable goals and perfection do not necessarily diminish with age. These disorders may present much as they do in adolescence or early adulthood, and family, individual, and cultural risk factors must be taken into account in treatment. Traversing this phase of the life cycle *does* mean growing away from some of the pleasures, attitudes, satisfactions, and ambitions of youth.

As expressed by psychoanalyst Melanie Klein (1963), healthy maturity is defined by a sense of serenity wherein the individual is "able to watch without envy" and "admire another person's achievements" even when the gifts of others "outstrip our capacities" (pp. 16–18). From a psychological perspective, the person with body dissatisfaction or a severe eating disorder in middle age must confront her or his envy and rivalry of younger generations, experience gratitude for one's life and accomplishments, and let go of (i.e., mourn) the past in order to find a renewed source of "love and devotion. . . . [which leads] to enrichment of the personality and capacity to enjoy work, and open up a variety of sources of satisfaction" (Klein, 1963, p. 16).

1. An eating disorder in middle and later life is a diagnosis of exclusion. Spotting an eating disorder may be challenging in older people because appetite changes and weight loss can arise from many different medical illnesses. Overuse of laxatives is also common to this age group. Cull out medical mimics and psychiatric conditions that present with weight loss, gastrointestinal dysregulation, memory and concentration impairment, and severe body image distortion (see Tables 1.3, 1.6).

2. Encourage the patient to set healthy physical goals for herself but also to face the reality of the changes, and needs, of the middle-aged body. As in the treatment of eating disorders at other developmental periods, the quest for having an ideal body must be mourned and eventually given up for treatment to be considered successful.

3. Remind the patient that middle age may involve the negotiation of a series of developmental tasks, but every individual is unique. It is possible for life to change radically for the better after age 40, as many biographical studies, personal testimonials, and research studies on midlife development attest.

4. Remind the patient that one's perspective on time changes at midlife. The focus on "years left to live rather than the years since birth" (Neugarten, 1968) is often a powerful motivator to confront the eating problem. A "5-5-5" exercise

can aid the individual to find out what really matters in the time left. The therapist queries the patient to think about what one would do if one had only five years left to live? Five months? Five weeks? Even five minutes.

5. Encourage the patient to have empathy and to reach out to people both younger and older. The fact that people at midlife are now considered the "socialized not the socializers" (Neugarten, 1968) can be a powerful impetus for eating disordered patients to develop new coping skills by reaching out to others in their families and communities. Being a part of a community can be a sustaining force against the vicissitudes of aging and the pejorative views society still holds about growing older.

6. Help the patient mourn losses that have not been heretofore realized by bearing witness to the person's story. Awareness of unconscious conflict, deficit, and loss is the first step in the process of personal transformation. The goal of treatment is for the individual to appreciate her- or himself from within because in the "race against time" (Nemiroff & Colarusso, 1985), appearance can no longer be the center of one's life.

7. Encourage the cultivation of wisdom. Bibliotherapy can be a particular catalyst for excellent discussions about personal transformation and existential vicissitudes (Daniels, 2001; Fonda, 2005; L. Hall, 1993; Hall & Cohen, 1992; Hall & Ostroff, 1999; Reindl, 2001). The capacity to bear the sadness and loss that accompanies aging is a developmental achievement that facilitates "relationships, learning, and ultimately the capacity for happiness" (Zetzel, 1965/1970, p. 114).

8. Pay particular attention to transference–countertransference issues. The therapist is also a traveler on life's journey. The patient at midlife or later life with an eating disorder may be an unexpected, interesting companion. But, as in all treatments, the patient's difficulties must always take center stage. The therapist at midlife must wrestle with the temptation of identifying too much with what the middle-aged patient is experiencing or to collapse the protective therapeutic boundary by sharing too much of one's own life story.

CONCLUSION

Even though anorexia nervosa and bulimia nervosa are usually described in the adolescent and young adult populations, they are occurring with increasing frequency at middle life and beyond. Clinicians must inquire about weight management processes and concerns about body image as men and women make these longitudinal life transitions. Medical and other psychiatric conditions must be ruled out to make the diagnosis of an overt or subclinical eating disorder.

Assuming there is no organic cause for the malady, clinicians should turn their attention toward how the patient is coping with expectable life transitions. Particular issues that have been described to date that may impact the development of an eating problem include the need to control the aging process, competition with and envy of the younger generations, lack of resolution of losses, and coming to grips with one's mortality.

Those who have experienced an eating disorder for many years have yet another series of hurdles. They must come to terms with the psychological costs of their eating disorder. These include, but are not limited to, the inability to form and maintain mature relationships, infertility, lack of meeting career goals, and the place the eating disorder has held in one's psyche as a spurious solution to life's existential and spiritual dilemmas. The eating problem has robbed these individuals of much in every domain of life. For resiliency and generativity to occur in the middle years, these patients must learn, often for the first time, to embrace a geniality toward themselves and their appetites. One cannot sup at the table of life's delicacies while depriving oneself of physical sustenance or staying mired in the unreachable quest for perfection that is so prized in our society.

Finally, clinicians must also reckon with our own issues of life transition and aging when working with this population. All of us are mortal, time is limited, and the choices we make are important. "We must not forget that only a very few people are artists of life," wrote Carl Jung (1933/1977), "and the art of life is the most distinguished and rarest of all arts" (p. 19). Clinicians, no less than the patients we treat, must embrace the noble goal of becoming artists of our own lives.

PART III

SPECIAL ISSUES IN THE TREATMENT
OF EATING DISORDERS

CHAPTER 7

Sexuality

Being given food is the first expression of love which the child understands; it is his introduction to love. Hence, the symbolic value of being fed remains high throughout life. In the unconscious, Food = Love.

—Karl A. Menninger (1942)

The sound of the pans bumping against each other, the smell of the almonds browning in the griddle, the sound of Tita's melodious voice, singing as she cooked, had kindled his sexual feelings. Just as lovers know the time for intimate relations is approaching from the closeness and smell of the beloved, or from the caresses exchanged in previous love play, so Pedro knew from these sounds and smells, especially the smell of browning sesame seeds, that there was a real culinary pleasure to come.

—Laura Esquivel (1989)

Novels and their cinematic versions set the scene for a romantic encounter or seduction over dinner. Why do we commonly think of two adults who are attracted to each other going out for a date and having their first interactions over a meal? We might further ask ourselves about the 21st century phenomena of ever-expanding rows of cookbooks at bookstores, the blossoming of television shows featuring gourmet chefs, and the ballooning restaurant business, even as we witness the seemingly paradoxical decline in the sacredness of family mealtime? On the one hand, Western culture is mesmerized by food and its sublime value to engage our appetites. Osn the other hand, like our patients, we all have conflicted feelings about the role food should play in our families, and in our romantic lives.

As Karl Menninger (1942) astutely observed, "the sharing of food is an expression of love" (p. 273), probably because it harkens back to our earliest memories of our mothers nursing and feeding us. Whether we eat together or spend ample amounts of time thinking about food, are we not trying to recapture an early experience of that first meal from our mothers? This is the meal to which we can never fully return because we grow, are weaned, and individuate. Yet the elusive power of that first feeding remains a source of profound comfort and psychological nourishment throughout our lives, albeit usually unconsciously (Boverman, personal communication, 2002). The desire to recapture the ineffable nourishment of our babyhood works like a magnet in our minds to draw us back for a symbolical return, a psychological truth lovers have surreptitiously employed for centuries in courtship and marriage rituals that begin with a meal. Appetites for food and for sex are inexorably linked.

And, as writer Laura Esquivel eloquently demonstrated in her novel *Like Water for Chocolate* (1989), repressed sexuality can also find expression in obsessional thoughts about recipes and cooking for one's beloved. The main character, Tita, is even able to bring Pedro to orgasm with "turkey mole with almonds and sesame seeds," yet the ill-fated lovers are forbidden to express their actual love because Tita's mother lays claim to her life. According to the author, Tita's Mexican culture demands that the eldest daughter take the role of mother's caretaker. This novel portrays a culturally sanctioned but extreme version of a dynamic I have already described among many of our eating disorder patients. Conflicts around sexuality and eating go hand-in-hand in many people, but in those with eating disorders they can also be linked to early failures in attachment within the family of origin or demands on the adolescent or adult child to sacrifice her life—and her sexual being—out of filial loyalty to one or both of her parents (Crastnopol, 2001; Young-Bruehl, 1993; Young-Bruehl & Cummins, 1993; Zerbe, 1992b, 1993/1995a, 1995b, 1996a, 1996b, 2001b).

In this chapter I review the biological and psychological aspects of the problem, all the while urging the reader to stay emotionally resonant with the patient's inner experience. As in other chapters, I argue that the difference between our own and our patients' appetitive drives are relative—that is, when addressing the patient's interest and avoidance of food and/or sex—the clinician must be as fully versed as one can be in owning his or her own security needs, drives, and areas of discomfort (Barth, 2001; Petrucelli, 2001; Petrucelli & Stuart, 2001).

Clinical Examples

Consider also the common clinical scenario of the overweight binge eater who eschews sexuality in adulthood because of problems in a relationship. Isabella is a case in point. Acknowledging in the second year of twice weekly psychodynamic psychotherapy that she and her husband had not had sexual relations since the birth of their second child, a son, now age 18, she provocatively told her therapist, "that's why I took up eating!"

She complained about her celibate marriage but did nothing to change it. According to Isabella, her husband had never been particularly amorous, choosing to invest himself in a booming cardiology practice and in grueling, competitive doubles' tennis matches. She alleged that she finally gave up trying to lure him into the boudoir, transferring her desire for sex into a passion for cooking and food. "A woman has to have at least one vice," she quipped. "I told him it was either going to be substituting food or other men and he shot back 'food.' Therefore, I eat."

Isabella recognized that the layers of fat on her body had become a protection from her own sexual feelings and desires to find a suitable partner. In her case, her "addiction" to binge eating and the sequelae of obesity were a "perfect solution" for a relational problem. Filling herself with food anesthetized her sexual wishes and gaining weight made her feel unappealing and sexless, thereby keeping potential suitors at a distance.

In even more extreme circumstances, food appears to take the place of sex altogether.

Mark, age 47 at the time of consultation, has no friends and lives a schizoid existence. Still a virgin, he denies ever having any interest in having a sexual relationship with anyone. However, he describes his daily rituals of bingeing and purging as if he were preparing to go out on a date and make love.

> I am able to do all of my work at home before I get dressed and get ready to go out to lunch. There's an "all you can eat" buffet downtown that opens at 11:30. I go back to the table for at least three helpings of everything but I'm able to stay skinny because I 'get rid of it' in the afternoon. I can't wait to get in the door when the restaurant opens. My heart always pounds during the first round. It's a little bit less exciting by the third "tour." But I know a big black hole is coming when I go home and get rid of it all in the john.

For Mark, repetitive food rituals and normative sexual urges have become so fused and ego syntonic that he cannot imagine his life without them. Although Mark's eating disorder (anorexia, binge-eating/purging type) has roots in severe maltreatment in his childhood, his overinvolvement with food and eating rituals serves as a characteristic compromise formation that keeps him emotionally detached from the anxiety provoking experience of being with other people. Psychoanalyst Margaret Crastnopol (2001) described a case of a male patient with obesity whose overuse of food reflected his ongoing desire to remain mother's baby boy and her narcissistic extension:

> For many men, an overinvolvement with food results in the creation of an illusion of self-sufficiency and the partial recovery of whatever had been renounced in the maternal identification . . . eating activities may act as a sensory substitute for—but also a means of accessing—aspects of affective life that would otherwise be left unarticulated. (p. 159)

Not surprisingly, empirical studies now support the long held observation of practicing clinicians that patients with eating disorders are at heightened risk for having sexual problems (Eddy, Novotney, & Weston, 2004; Wiederman 1996). Sexual dysfunctions in an eating disorder patient can derive from either the physiological consequences or the psychological difficulties that underlie the eating disorder (Eddy et al., 2004; Wiederman, 1996).

Although numerous papers have been written about the range of sexual difficulties that affect eating disorder patients, particularly those with anorexia nervosa, less information is available to help the therapist make practical interventions to aid the patient with an eating disorder who experiences sexual difficulty. Clinicians tend to avoid bringing up these sexual concerns, possibly because of the life-threatening comorbidities and psychological deficits that take most of the clinician's time. However, less discussion about sex also occurs with eating disorder patients because of clinician discomfort, reluctance, and ignorance. As my colleague Jillian Romm, RN, LCSW, a sex therapist working at Oregon Health and Science University observed, the first and most important intervention a clinician can make is to be able to bring up sex as a discussable issue (Romm, 2005, personal communication). Introducing the topic of sexuality and becoming more "comfortable listening to sexual stories" (Levine, 2005) and sexual problems of the patient with an eating disorder might begin with some introductory questions (Table 7.1). Because sexual functioning must never be taken out of the context of other psychological and interpersonal concerns, the clinician will in all likelihood learn more about the patient's capacity for relatedness and autonomy when the subject is broached.

If the patient is at a point in the treatment where the topic of sexual preference, dysfunction, desire, and intimacy are discussable, the treatment can now be guided to address other psychological, biological, interpersonal, and cultural variables. Learning about what interferes with achieving "good enough" sexuality can generate additional hypotheses about the etiology and meaning of the eating disorder.

TABLE 7.1   Beginning and maintaining a dialogue about sex

- Do you have any concerns about your sexuality or sexual experiences?
- Are you generally satisfied with your intimate relationship? Has your partner complained or seemed dissatisfied with your responsiveness?
- Has your sexual difficulty been lifelong or has it come on recently? Do you believe the sexual concern is linked in any way to your eating disorder?
- Have you experienced any form of sexual trauma or physical abuse in the past? If so, do you think that it has interfered with your experience of sexual desire, arousal, or orgasm?
- Do you ever "go away" or dissociate when you are physically intimate?
- Have the medications you take (for eating disorder, depression, high blood pressure, etc.) seemed to interfere with your sexual desire or responsiveness?
- Was it easy or difficult to talk about sex in your family of origin?
- What haven't we covered that might be important for me to know about your sexuality? If you remember something after this session or down the road in our work together, I hope you feel that you can bring it up.

COMMON SEXUAL PROBLEMS THAT OCCUR IN THE PATIENT WITH AN EATING DISORDER

In one of the few actual case reports of sex therapy for female patients with anorexia and bulimia nervosa, Simpson and Ramberg (1992) described a conscious wish of five patients in committed relationships to undergo sex therapy. A reluctance to engage fully in the sex therapy emerged in the treatment despite early investment in the process. Simpson and Ramberg speculated that this reluctance to participate and to benefit resulted from failure in basic trust (i.e., failure in early attachment) and problems in communication within the couple.

For example, therapeutic attempts to engage the patients fully in the usual desensitization process of sex therapy (Kaplan, 1979) were foiled by the patient's inhibitions in touching their bodies and belief that their bodies were fat, ugly, and despicable. Interestingly, the partners colluded with the patients to support the couple's dysfunction. Yet both members of the couple consciously valued touch and nurturance. Simpson and Ramberg concluded that enmeshment in the family of origin kept the designated patient from more effective separation and individuation, leading to impaired sexual function.

A wide variety of sexual problems and interpersonal difficulties afflict patients with anorexia nervosa, bulimia nervosa, and binge-eating disorder. They pose special challenges for the practicing clinician and often go unaddressed. As indicated, they remain unspoken because therapeutic intervention usually centers on those problems that are more overtly life threatening, such as medical or psychological comorbidities (e.g., depression; sexual abuse). We clinicians are aware that patients with eating disorders have concomitant issues in their quality of life and lead particularly unhappy and unfulfilling sexual lives but may feel embarrassed or ill-equipped to ask clarifying questions. Limits on the time and money available for treatment and the wide array of individual and family problems no doubt also play a role. Clinicians wonder what we can do to more effectively help our patients address these often secret, crippling sexual issues that impede optimal functioning and enjoyment in life. Although I suggest some questions that therapists might use to begin to sustain a dialogue about sexuality in a person with an eating disorder (see Table 7.1), the therapist will also want to have at his or her fingertips some of the books and articles also referenced to become more proficient in working with sexual dysfunction in general.

A history of overt sexual or physical abuse in childhood, neglect and maltreatment, and abrogated boundaries in adolescence or in the formative adult years (e.g., rape) have been demonstrated to play a significant etiologic role in sexual disinterest and extreme body image distortion in some eating disordered patients (Brewerton, 2005; Johnson, Cohen, Kasen, & Brook, 2002; Mahon, Bradley, Harvey, Winston, & Palmer, 2001; Miller, 1993; Romans, Gendall, Martin, & Mullen, 2001; Rorty, Yager, & Rossotto, 1994; Wonderlich, Crosby, Mitchell, et al., 2001; Zerbe, 1993a, 1993b). Even without this particular intervening variable, large-scale research is confirming the long held clinical observation that people with anorexia nervosa are inhibited when expressing themselves sexually. These patients also tend to have less sexual experience with a partner than healthy controls or their bulimic or binge-eating counterparts (Eddy et al., 2004; Ghizzani & Montomoli, 2000). Anorexics demonstrate the personality variables of a restrictive, "prim and proper" attitude.

Patients with bulimia nervosa tend to be more sexually adventuresome and experienced, but can also have significant sexual dysfunction (Schneider, 1995; Schwartz, 1988; Wiederman, 1996; Yager, Landsverk, Edelstein, & Hyler, 1989). Evidence continues to accumulate suggesting that personality variables among the persons with eating disorders are quite broad and hence do not always fit neatly into the symptom picture described in the DSM-IV (American Psychiatric Association, 2000). These diverse personality variables are likely to account for more variance in sexual attitudes and behaviors than the eating disorder diagnoses or symptoms alone would suggest (Thompson-Brenner & Westen, 2005a; Westen & Harnden-Fischer, 2001; Yager et al., 1989).

According to this research (Eddy et al., 2004), actual adult sexual attitudes and behaviors in eating disorder patients show a continuity with childhood problems related to sexuality. Not surprisingly, early developmental experiences appear to be imperative. Most individuals who are emotionally constricted and overcontrolled tend to restrict their eating and to lack introspective awareness of hunger sensations. They also have a similar restrictive style in terms of sexual relations. Those individuals who are emotionally dysregulated and undercontrolled tended to "binge more, purge more, and gain weight more readily" (p. 204), manifesting the well-known bulimic personality profile of impulsivity, self-destructive sexuality, and affect dysregulation. For these patients, early developmental difficulties with parents, particularly fathers, and lack of stability appear to influence later patterns of destructive sexuality. In general, research on the sexual attitudes of eating disorder patients demonstrates lower levels of sexual satisfaction, greater performance anxiety during sex, and a sense of inadequate sexual functioning (e.g., sexual self-esteem).

Given the real needs and desires of patients to achieve enhanced sexual fulfillment in their interpersonal relationships and the multifactorial origin of the eating disorder, how might the concerned clinician begin to effectively intervene? The first step involves helping the patient understand that the sexual dysfunction, like the eating disorder, likely derives from multiple causes. By highlighting the multidimensional nature of the symptom itself, the patient, who feels guilty or ashamed of the difficulty, begins to reframe the problem and challenge it. Education about how the biology of an eating disorder influences sexual response introduces the subject in a forum that is less embarrassing to the patient while providing essential, state-of-the-art information. Summarizing this information in a user-friendly format also demonstrates that the clinician is willing to broach the arena of sexuality and make referral to a sex therapist when the patient is medically stable and emotionally prepared for this step (see Table 7.2).

TABLE 7.2 Educative interventions about biologic bedrocks of sexuality

- Make sexuality a speakable issue
- Review what happened to sexual drive of conscientious objectors who were voluntarily starved (Keys et al., 1950)
- Encourage patient to read memoirs of survivors of starvation who lost their sexual drive (e.g., Frankl, 1963, *Man's Search for Meaning*)
- Describe known effects of malnutrition on the endocrine system (Tuiten et al., 1993)
- Draw on evolving research on the importance of neurochemistry and neural pathways in attaining romance and maintaining adequate sexual responsiveness (Fisher, 1998, 2004; Leiblum & Rosen, 2000)

Clinicians do not always know whether the eating or sexual problem arose first or if one leads to the other. In some ways the question is moot. The patient's quality of life is seriously impacted by both problems, and, I argue, will not be considered sufficiently better until both difficulties are addressed if the patient is willing. Because the clinical eating disorder literature tends to focus on issues other than the assessment and treatment of sexual concerns in our patients, clinicians can be hoodwinked into believing that sexuality is not a paramount area of distress when it may likely be. Most importantly, emerging literature in the fields of sexual dysfunction, personality disorders, and eating disorders is beginning to reveal the complex role of early, dysfunctional attachment patterns that may yield novel strategies for intervention in the coming decades.

BIOLOGICAL FACTORS LEADING TO SEXUAL DYSFUNCTION

In the landmark study of conscientious objectors who volunteered to be starved (Keys et al., 1950), a sharp diminution in sexual drive was observed among the 36 original volunteers (see also Chapter 1). Their age-appropriate interest in sex shifted rapidly to an obsessiveness about food as they lost weight. In the classic text of existential therapy (i.e., logotherapy), *Man's Search for Meaning*, Victor Frankl (1963) commented on a similar phenomenon among men who craved food in the concentration camps. Initially talking about their families and alluding to sexual pleasure, Frankl observed that as the men went without food, their initial lively banter about women shifted to talking about eating. These personal observations corroborated what Keys found in his scientific study: "The starving live in their own little world with little interest in the larger areas of life" (cited by Guetzkow & Bowman, 1946, p. 72).

Interestingly, the description of women's lives in the concentration camps in *Schindler's List* (Keneally, 1982) makes a parallel point. These victims initially talked about their interpersonal relationships—husbands and children—but rapidly shifted their focus as the starvation process ensued. They became preoccupied by descriptions of foods and talked nonstop about recipes. These literary and research observations demonstrate the biological linkage between two of life's most enhancing activities. Without food, interest in sex and relationships dips sharply and quickly until only food remains the subject of rapt attention.

More recently, Tuiten and colleagues (1993) reviewed the etiology of impoverished sexuality among anorexics from the standpoint of endocrine changes. These researchers hypothesized that the sexual difficulties observed in anorexia result from an endocrine deficiency that is secondary to starving. They noted that a reduction of circulating levels of testosterone and ovarian steroids brought on by malnutrition may impact sexual function. Questionnaires administered to anorexics and matched controls confirmed that the premorbid sex life of anorexics was similar to the controls.

Although the importance of normal eating and healthy endocrine functioning may likely be the bottom line for any person who wishes to maintain a healthy sexual life, clinical practice suggests that the majority of eating-disordered patients with sexual dysfunction have more going on than just a medical or endocrine problem (Ghizzani & Montomoli, 2000; Morgan, Wiederman, & Pryor, 1995; Simpson & Ramberg, 1992; Zerbe, 1992b, 1993a, 1993b, 1995b, 1995c, 2002b). Bulimic patients, who are often normal weight or above normal weight, can have subclinical malnutrition due to their serious mismanagement of food (e.g., purging and laxative abuse leading to vitamin deficiencies; idiosyncratic preferences such as carbohydrates, and little protein). Bulimic behaviors may affect the hypothalamic-pituitary-gonadal axis and subsequently impinge on normative sexual response, leading to dysfunction. The primary hormones of desire are androgens, and deprivation by any medical cause contributes to sexual decline (Schover, 2000).

Since Tuiten and colleagues' work, neuroimaging studies and advances in neurochemistry are expanding our knowledge of the possible biological variables that influence sexual life and romantic love. According to the ongoing research of Helen Fisher (1998, 2004, 2005; Fisher & Thomson, 2006; Meloy & Fisher, 2005), neural correlates of intense romantic interest were observed using functional magnetic resonance imaging (fMRI) among healthy men and women volunteers. Activation in the ventral tegmental area (VTA), a central part of the brain's "reward system" associated with pleasure and arousal in the region of A10 dopamine cells, was found in volunteers who reported being intensely in love. The VTA sends projections to several important brain regions all involved with the experience of falling in love. Accumulated data support the hypothesis that human romantic love has a complicated biological substrate involving subcortical dopaminergic pathways that mediate reward; blocking the activity of those pathways diminishes sexual activity. When patients suffering from depression or a hypoactive sex drive take a medication that increases dopamine (e.g., bupropion) their libido improves.

Dopaminergic reward pathways have also been demonstrated to influence courtship patterns in animals. When dopamine antagonists are injected into the nucleus accumbens of animal subjects, attraction behaviors dramatically decline. Fisher (2004) summarized a wide array of emerging data that suggest that romantic attraction involves subcortical dopaminergic pathways that mediate reward and motivation. Might courtship and the experience of sex be influenced by brain-based changes and biological sequelae of starving and purging among our eating disorder patients, particularly as these changes affect the dopamine mediated reward pathways?

Central nervous system dopamine deficiency has been demonstrated in anorexics who also have ongoing struggles with mood, motivation, and pleasure, including sexual pleasure (Frank et al., 2005; Kaye, Frank & McCohana, 1999; Pothos, Creese, & Hoebel, 1995). These chemical changes in the dopaminergic system likely also influence the sex drive observed in eating disorder patients. It is crucial to remember that this research is still in its infancy. Still, patients should be reminded that there are hundreds of thousands of receptor sites and neural pathways in our brains that are likely affected by eating behaviors and that concomitantly influence desire for sex and romantic love. The appetitive drive is associated with the dopamine system and when this neurochemical is depleted, so is sexual arousal. In a general sense, desire dampens as dopamine declines. It is not yet clear if the low dopamine is present before weight loss (and hence genetically determined) or is a persistent effect of prolonged malnourishment. Even among weight restored anorexics, dopamine receptor binding is higher than in controls. For clinical purposes, the "chicken/egg" questions extend deeper into our biology!

In women, the sympathetic nervous system (SNS) has been found to play a principle role in sexual arousal (Basson, 2000, 2002). When the SNS is inhibited due to medication (and conceivably by any other factor such as starvation), sexual arousal is suppressed by direct inhibition of sympathetic outflow. As Meston (2000) notes in her review of female sexual arousal and sympathetic nervous system activity, anorgasmia in women may not be due to the common wisdom of "lack of sexual education, insufficient stimulation, or a variety of cognitive factors such as fear of loss of control, fear of pregnancy, religious concerns or religious factors" (pp. 32f–33f). On the contrary, a purely physiological component mediated by moderate levels of SNS activity is an essential ingredient for satisfactory sexual arousal and response. The eating disorder patient who desires to become sexual is likely facing a bedrock issue of diminished sexual responsiveness based on impaired neurochemistry, likely at the levels of the dopamine and sympathetic nervous systems. Patients may not be able to enjoy sex because their physical response is dampened due to an impaired, brain-based reward system (dopamine) or diminished SNS (sympathetic nervous system) activation influencing genital arousal. Inhibition in sexual arousal is complicated by, if not ultimately resulting from, physiologic changes brought about by the eating disorder.

SIDE EFFECTS OF MEDICATION

Side effects of medications may also play a role (see Table 7.3). As noted in Chapters 1 and 2, the serotonin reuptake inhibitors (SSRIs) are frequently used in weight-recovered patients with anorexia nervosa, and to decrease bingeing in patients with binge eating or bulimia nervosa. Sexual side effects are common, affecting as many as 70% of patients in some studies. The most common sexual side effects in this class of antidepressants include impairment in arousal, decreased libido, delayed orgasm, and anorgasmia (Gitlin, 1994; Kaplan, 2002; Powers & Cloak, 2007). Some SSRIs (e.g., fluvoxamine) have a higher rate of sexual side effects, which may be correlated with the degree of serotonergic inhibition. When psychotropic medication is thought to be the culprit, the treatment plan may be modified by adjusting the dosage or considering a change in antidepressants or using medications such as cyproheptadine, diphenhydramine, or yohimbine to curtail the side effects, or by suggesting a drug holiday. Clinical experience indicates that lowering the antidepressant dose rarely reverses the problem (Kaplan, 2002) and may lead to relapse in the eating disorder. Some patients whose eating disorder improves because of the addition of an SSRI will discontinue the medication because of the sexual side effects. For those patients, one of the phosphodiesterase inhibitors (e.g., sildenafil, tadalafil) may be an option, although they have been only variably effective in reversing sexual dysfunction in women.

The clinician is also in the difficult position of having to help the patient weigh her options, realizing that the source of the sexual problem may likely be deeper than the medication side effects (see Table 7.3). Only after significant recovery from the eating disorder and psychological work on intimate relationships can the clinician be certain that medication side effects alone cause the sexual dysfunction.

DEFINING "GOOD ENOUGH" SEXUALITY

Knowledge of what constitutes a mature sexual bond can further illuminate the commonly observed difficulties of eating disorder patients. What characteristics are implied in a mature, affirming sexual relationship? Among other qualities, a couple should be able to play with and to enjoy each other; it is common for couples who are still deeply in love to be able to describe the courtship phase of their relationship with much tenderness, even after many years (Wallerstein & Blakeslee, 1995). Sexual excitement may be heightened by sublimated aggression but should not be tainted with undue hostility (Blum, 1997; Stoller, 1979, 1985). Sexual interludes thrive when based on mutuality, balance, and love. Such a sexual encounter has the capacity to renew the bond between the couple and to help each individual recover from the disappointments and defeats of everyday life (Kaplan, 1979; Pines, 1993; Prozan, 1992; Scharff, 1982; Schnarch, 1997, 2000). Moreover, sexuality helps the individual prepare for

TABLE 7.3 Partial list of medications affecting sexual desire and response

Tricyclics	**Other antidepressants**
Desipramine	Trazodone (occasionally)
Clomipramine	
Imipramine	**Mood stabilizers**
	Lithium
Tetracyclics	Valproic acid
Amoxapine	
	Antipsychotics
Monoamine oxidase inhibitors	Chlorpromazine
Phenelzine	Fluphenazine
Tranylcypromine	Haloperidol
	Molindone
	Risperidone
SSRIs	Thioridazine
Fluoxetine	
Sertraline	**Benzodiazepines**
Paroxetine	Alprazolam
Fluvoxamine	
Citalopram	**Psychostimulants**
Escitalopram	Amphetamines
H2 Antagonists	**Antihypertensives**
Cimetidine	Quanethedine
	Bethanidine
	Nifedipine
	Diuretics
	Spironolactone
	Hydrochlorothiazide
	Chlorthalidone
	Antiadrenergic agents
	Methyldopa
	Reserpine
	Beta blockers
	Propranolol
	Labetalol

and endure separations, it enhances self-image, and it conveys forgiveness for inevitable relationship disappointments, as well as acceptance of the partner's basic humanness (Person, 1988).

Because eating-disorder patients rigidly cling to their symptoms as a way of dealing with life's vicissitudes, they have fewer internal resources to draw on in their relationships. No wonder that at least one study (Raboch & Faltus, 1991) has reported that 80% of anorectic patients lead impoverished sexual lives. Instead of using the eating disorder to assuage the pain of life and to fill their inner emptiness, these patients must learn to develop a sense of mature dependence on people rather than on inanimate objects such as food to regulate feelings (Schneider, 1995; Troop, Holbrey, Trowler, & Treasure, 1994; Vanderbroucke, Vandereycken, & Norre, 1997). The therapeutic relationship is often the first experience to challenge the eating disorder as the central organizer of the patient's life; other experiences are also gradually called on to arrest pain, fill emptiness, and lead to a fuller realization of the body's potential.

Before learning to feel alive and real in a sexual relationship, the individual must be able to develop the capacity to play, negotiate separations safely, and feel confident that aggression is not overwhelming. Developing "good enough" sexuality is predicated on transforming identity from that of an eating-disorder patient to that of a person willing to explore new, more mature modes of relating with others while concomitantly experiencing a vital, lively sense of self (see Table 7.4).

Before one can be a member of a pair, one must first be comfortable in one's own skin. Individuation, so long considered the key to successful treatment of an eating disorder (Bruch, 1973, 1974, 1978), is also essential for the establishment of intimacy. Sex therapist David Schnarch (1997, 2000) has operationalized this process of differentiation into four essential tasks: (1) maintaining a clear sense of self when one is with others; (2) regulating one's own anxiety; (3) not reacting to the other person's anxiety; and (4) tolerating discomfort as one grows emotionally. The therapist who undertakes the odyssey of helping eating disorder patients enlarge their world by expanding the give-and-take of human bonds, must first ensure that they have a sense of an individuated self. In the words of David Schnarch, becoming one's own best self

---

TABLE 7.4 Psychological issues influencing sexual responsiveness

- Disruption in early attachment to primary caretakers
- Poor role models in family of origin; witness to parental breakup, loveless marriages, ongoing bickering
- Childhood maltreatment; sexual and/or physical abuse; rape
- Lack of a sense of self; failed individuation
- Dissociation or fragmentation of self secondary to trauma
- Shame, particularly related to body issues or sense of personal failure
- Narcissistic investment in body image
- Inability to empathize with needs of other person
- Failure to resolve intrapsychic and interpersonal conflicts
- Punitive superego (severe inner self-critic)
- Spiritual malaise and sense of existential despair (e.g., "Nothing matters much anymore"; "I have no purpose in life")

---

is always "the most loving thing you can do" (1997, p. 73) because from that basis we are in the best position to love others, especially our chosen partner. Helping give birth to the self is ultimately the greatest act of love one can help to give our patients.

PSYCHOLOGICAL ISSUES THAT INTERFERE WITH SEXUAL RESPONSIVENESS: QUESTIONS THAT THE THERAPIST MUST CONSIDER

What Was the Patient's Experience of Her Parents' Marriage, Partnership, or Divorce?

Marriages that continue despite noxious bickering, argument, abuse, and derision are known to take their toll on children. Sequelae include the child's fear and inhibition in reaching out and finding mature relationships that sustain the self—for example, marriage (Blum, 2003; Coen, 1992; Fonagy, Gergely, Jurist, & Target, 2002; Scharff, 1982; Schnarch 1997, 2000). In one study of 114 women with a severe eating disorder, parental breakup was found to be a stable predictor of dropping out of treatment (Mahon et al., 2001).

Attachment theorists Mary Main and John Bowlby have developed a conceptualization and research methodology on the importance of early bonds to parents; applying it to the problem of eating disorder patients' sexual responsiveness, these authors speculated that problems in maintaining a trusting relationship with a treater is influenced by an insecure attachment style originating within the family. These research based findings support everyday clinical wisdom: Extra time may be needed in forming a therapeutic alliance in those patients who have experienced parental breakup. These attachment-based difficulties may likely also interfere in sexual relationships because these patients are insecure and lack a sense of basic trust (Bowlby, 1969; Main, 1995).

As already described throughout this book, eating disordered patients are commonly fascinated by the friendships and marriages of their therapists, and their capacity to be curious reflects their growing self-capacities and trust. While most patients will also demonstrate some curiosity, the persistence with which eating disorder patients ask questions about the treater's personal life may be a reflection of their early attachment based difficulties. Their voyeurism may be uncomfortable for the clinician who wishes to preserve firm therapist–patient boundaries. Personal questions are commonly discouraged and reframed by asking the patient why it is important for them to ask. These questions usually reflect the patient's desire to acquire another picture of the world of relationships but they can cause anxiety and disquiet in the therapist. Not being privy to a family where happiness, warmth, and complementarity were routinely experienced, the patient has little knowledge about what a healthy partnership entails. The result may be a psychological deficit with respect to forming and sustaining life-affirming connections that the patient attempts to correct by "research" into the therapist's life.

When asked direct personal questions, I have sometimes quipped to patients that if my life were as idealized or salacious as their fantasies about me, I would write romance novels instead of clinical papers! In broaching a heretofore forbidden topic, the patient is making a trusting leap into a new kind of object relationship which "is necessary for concurrent attenuation of conflict and psychic trauma" (Blum, 2003, p. 428). When psychic trauma and object loss have resulted in disrupted attachments, "benevolent relationships and identifications provide a foundation for reconstitution and psychotherapy" (p. 428).

With respect to treatment, ascertaining the patient's perception of the parental relationship and the relationships of parental surrogates (e.g., grandparents or other primary caretakers) is often a crucial first step in sorting out fears of intimacy. The therapist must then educate the patient that what transpired in the family of origin is not necessarily the only model for life. At the same time, the therapist must guard against idealizing marriage and family life (the "father and mother knows best" syndrome), because no family is ideal. Interestingly, the children of divorced parents often maintain a positive view of marriage or a committed partnership; perhaps they have been inoculated against negative messages by their parents' instruction, their own resiliency, or the benefits of growing up in the absence of verbal barrages.

Patients may have such unshakable beliefs in the misery of family life that they must find and form new models. Therapists can assign realistic books, movies, or television shows that appeal to the abilities and interests of the patient, and then work concretely with the patient on the lessons depicted in them. Patients will be attuned to the nuances of negative family interactions, and should be encouraged to share their reactions with the therapist by journaling or in dialogue. Their reactions give the therapist an opportunity to counter assumptions by pointing out the fun, playfulness, and growth inherent in many different kinds of relationships. The goal is to provide the patient with new models of identification and learning experiences.

Judiciously sharing the genuine pride the therapist takes in his or her own friendships or primary relationship can also prove instructive for many patients. Care must be taken to avoid arousing the patient's envy or overstimulating the patient by sharing too many details or stories. The goal is to help the patient enlarge her or his own capacity for mentalization, self-reflection, daydreams, and fantasy. Inevitably patients know more about us than we think they do, and sharing "just enough" often jumpstarts a stalled treatment (Brisman, 2001; Petrucelli, 2001; Petrucelli & Stuart, 2001). By underscoring these relationships' many positive and fulfilling moments, the therapist points the way to the patient's eventual acquisition of a robust and playful sexual life; it can begin with the sense of a more positive, beneficent view of adult dyadic relationships, especially nonsexual friendships, which tend to be less anxiety provoking as a starting point for intimate attachment.

Clinical Example

Margie was 21 and severely anorexic when she entered residential treatment. Functioning in the upper range of borderline psychopathology, she had been able to stave off the breakthrough of any sexual drive whatsoever out of loyalty to her mother. Her angry outbursts alienated her from staff members and most of the other patients. Margie's sexual repression and restriction of eating stemmed from the same source in psychodynamic terms. Her maternal grandmother and mother talked relentlessly about the patient's and their own weight to the exclusion of other satisfying activities. Marital conflict was pervasive in the family of origin. To please her mother, Margie turned off her sexual feelings only to lash out in vituperative at anyone within earshot. In this way, aggressive and libidinal energies became fused and were transformed into oral rage (Blum, 1997; Wilson, Hogan & Mintz, 1992).

Inroads were made in the treatment when the male family therapist confronted the parents about the impact of their anger and the message they gave that "Margie was promiscuous if she even had one sexual relationship." As Margie gained weight and participated in a range of group and therapeutic modalities, she was overheard talking to her peers about "some cute guys" who worked on the unit. Anger virtually melted away as her softer side and age appropriate interest in males was affirmed in the treatment. Margie's individual therapist repeatedly pointed out the messages she received from witnessing her parents' arguments and helped her explore how her fear of men and sex derived from many sources, *one* being the anger expressed that led her to feel unsafe and vulnerable.

Does the Patient Have a History of Trauma?

Trauma—particularly in the forms of childhood maltreatment and sexual and physical abuse—has been linked in numerous contemporary studies to the development of eating disorders, particularly bulimia nervosa (Brewerton, 2004; Connors & Morse, 1993; Dansky, Brewerton, Kilpatrick, & O'Neil, 1997; Feldman & Meyer, 2007b; Rorty & Yager, 1993; Rossotto, Rorty-Greenfield, & Yager 1996; Wonderlich et al., 2001). Recent reports also suggest that rape in adulthood may also be implicated in the etiology of some eating disorders. The majority of contemporary theorists believe that trauma leads to significant psychopathology, including depression, anxiety, posttraumatic stress disorder, and sexual dysfunction.

Although clinicians must never minimize the role of sexual trauma in the etiology of disordered eating or sexual experience, it is most critical to listen carefully to the patient's explanation of what happened and the perception of its impact. As Esman (1994) has noted, "It is wise, proper, and humane for us to hear what our patients tell us; it is unwise, improper, and hazardous for us to tell them what we want to hear" (p. 1102). Keep in mind that there are patients who have experienced the trauma of fellatio during rape and may gag or not be able to swallow. They may lose as much weight as an anorexic patient but they want to eat and express concern about the amount of weight they have lost. In both men and women sexual and eating problems may be connected to the original trauma and warrant nuanced and extended therapeutic support.

With respect to the experience of sensuality, many patients who have been abused lead full and satisfying sexual lives despite their belief that they cannot. In contrast, many men and women who have not been so tormented may struggle with a host of difficulties within relationships when they try to express themselves sexually (Allen, 2001, 1995/2005; Blum, 2003; Herman, 1992; Zerbe, 1999, 2002b, 2002c). Clinicians wishing to help their patients traverse a sexual impasse will thus be best guided by maintaining an open ear and an open heart to the patient's perceptions of the past, particularly as it relates to impingement in sexuality and relationship concerns.

An important lesson about one particular toll of abuse and loss is derived from the work of psychoanalysts Sandor Ferenczi (1949, 1955) and John Bowlby (1979). Ferenczi observed that childhood trauma is complicated by the multiple messages the family gives to the patient *not to talk about it.* As noted earlier in Chapters 2 and 4, Bowlby describes certain families in which a parent was murdered or committed suicide. The surviving parent gave frequent and pervasive messages to the child to never discuss the family trauma. These children suffered from a host of emotional difficulties, including learning and attention problems; on some occassions the child feels so unwelcomed into the world he wants to die. Central to this struggle is the sense that their own experience of loss was unspeakable and unknowable, which exacerbates a sense of shame and deviancy. Bowlby makes a strong case that the feeling of being all alone with such horrendous history equals or exceeds the pathogenic power of the original tragedy and further suggests that this kind of secret-keeping can lead to difficulties in adult life including sexuality (Bowlby, 1979, 1988; Ferenczi, 1955).

The therapist's sensitivity to the patient's personal story and painful reminiscences, coupled with appropriate support and education, is the first step in eradicating her or his sense of emotional abandonment. Regardless of the specific events or perceptions of the past, it is crucial to pace the work at a rate set by the patient. It cannot be hurried because the "unspeakable truths" have usually been buried for years. Open conversations with the therapist form the model for other open relationships where difficult, disquieting moments can be shared. Slowly and powerfully, the patient comes to realize that being with another person does not necessitate forsaking one's real thoughts, feelings, and memories. Most importantly, perhaps, the implicit aspects of therapy signal to the patient that the therapist has hope and a firm belief in the patient's capacity to live a full and vital life.

Clinical Example

Kim, age 30, was severely maltreated as a child but entered therapy following a brutal rape. Since adolescence she had struggled with feelings of disparagement toward her body, frequently putting herself on diets. She had periods where her weight would fluctuate to slightly above or below the normative range for her height and age. After the rape, Kim's eating disorder exacerbated. In particular, she binged on high calorie foods and gained about 30 pounds.

After about six months in therapy, which utilized relaxation methods, EMDR, and expression of the traumatic distant past as well as recollections of the rape, the therapist noted that Kim's weight was continuing to rise. Despite being asked out by several men, she preferred to go immediately home after her volunteer job at the local humane center. She rejected the therapist's formulation that the weight gain reflected difficulties in the therapy related to the transference situation. Kim denied anger or dissatisfaction with the therapist, and, in fact, the therapist enjoyed working with Kim.

The therapist took a step back and waited to hear the patient's own understanding of the predicament. She asked the patient to "theorize" the meaning of the weight gain. Kim reflected that the extra pounds actually made her feel safer. It was as if "the layers of fat form a protective wall around me." Kim went on to explain that she felt less attractive to men and less threatened around them at a higher weight. For this patient, sexuality was disavowed because it was too painful and this perspective was used to "maintain a state of mental and emotional equilibrium and thus . . . fend off the discomfort inherent in an acknowledgement of the unacceptable fact that one faces" (Goldberg, 1999, pg 75). In essence, feelings of shame and excitement were obliterated by overeating and the experience of sexual and romantic interest was disavowed because they were "too painful to contemplate" (p. 75).

Does the Patient "Disown," "Dissociate From", or "Shut Down" the Experience of Sexuality?

Because some eating disorder patients suffer from a lack of experience of a cohesive self, they rapidly, and often unpredictably, fragment in the context of stress, change, and intimacy. In these cases the eating disorder can be viewed as a defensive structure that covers up a defect in the self, leading to a loss of vigor, vitality, and resiliency. Dissociation of the "eating disorder self" may be another way to unconsciously promote survival of a secret self or be a reliable attempt to deal with painful affect, fantasies, memories, and experiences (Bromberg, 1996, 2001; Sands, 1991; Zerbe, 1993, 1993a, 1993b).

Conceptualized by the self-psychological schools as a state of self-enfeeblement, patients in our practices will frequently describe states of ennui, emptiness, depression, and lethargy. The split off, dissociated eating disorder self keeps them from experiencing enthusiasm or joie de vivre in their sexual lives. Even when normal weight is restored and the eating disorder is under better control, clinicians observe a persistent sense of self-enfeeblement or dissociation when sexuality is introduced as a subject in the therapy. For these patients, sex is not yet a consciously speakable issue.[1]

Validating the subjective experience of the patient (De Groot & Rodin, 1994; Goldberg, 1988, 1999; Kohut, 1971, 1984) promotes tolerance of the patient's feelings and "furthers the patients' cohesiveness and integration" (Zerbe, 1993b, p. 324). Understanding of this kind is required to maintain, restore, and consolidate the organization of self-experience, the first steps in helping the patient overcome sexual difficulties. In self-psychological terms, these patients may be understood as lacking the child's innate sense of vitality or perfection because others did not adequately mirror them in their youth. Thus, they are unable to safely say "Look at me" or "See me" because mirroring self-objects failed them. It is also common for such patients to avoid looking in a mirror or, in contrast, looking in it all the time. Both activities suggest the patient's underlying desire to be seen by the other but their inability to express it. They compulsively but inadequately attempt to overcome their lack of self-cohesion by this defensive posture.

Even the promiscuous sexual patterns of some bulimics are split-off self states, signs of the patient's sense of inadequacy or failure. These patients never actually experience themselves or their partners as individuals (Johnson, 1991; Schwartz, 1988). Yet the sexual act is a compelling comfort resulting in a sense of primitive fusion that temporarily extinguishes frightening anxieties. A trial intervention that addresses the concurrent self-destructive and self-healing aspects of the eating disorder and dissociated sexual acting out might be:

> When you have sex (or binge or restrict), a part of you feels alive. You feel in charge of your body. All the while, another part of you realizes you are hurting and are being self-destructive. You may hate that part but it feels like a vital

---

[1]In lectures I use Pablo Picasso's *Les Demoiselles d'Avignon* (1907), an iconic painting that ushered in the Cubist period to depict fragmentation or dissociation visually. The image of the woman/women in this work is distorted by depicting different angles, viewpoints, and perspectives of the face and torso. The mask that hides the face of one of the figures is likened to the split-off, dissociated eating disorder or sexual self while the other figures also kindle feelings of "five aspects of the ineffable self where the part may represent the whole," and "appear or feel alien. The painting reminds us that many parts of ourselves remain unknowable, or unfathomable, even as we are always attempting to pull together many perplexing, often contradictory, aspects of our personality" (Zerbe, 1993b, p. 319). Therapists, like the patients we treat, can have shifts in our experiences of self-continuity which help us empathize with the more disturbing or disorganizing experiences of our patient. Cubist works, particularly those of people, may resonate and be popular because they speak to that aspect of ourselves that displays different faces and attitudes depending on the situation. We can momentarily feel less than whole or have awakened a part of us we had heretofore not been privy to seeing or knowing.

aspect of who you are. In the fullness of time, we need to speak to each aspect of the self so that you will someday feel more whole as you get to 'know each part.'

Clinical Example

After years of searching to find her place in a satisfying career, Elena, age 41, achieved significant success as an architect. Her natural beauty assured her of having a choice of attractive partners. Yet after each sexual encounter she felt lonely and inadequate. Elena never really enjoyed sexual relations, telling the therapist after each encounter, "Oh, it was okay," and then going on to describe in detail why it was not. At other times the patient (who purged after each successful new professional contract or sexual conquest in bed), volunteered that she was "a slut, a whore, but a star in the boudoir." Some days she was in contact with an aspect of the self that was trying to "get rid of any good because I don't deserve it." By all appearances she had what it took to be a lively and engaging partner. Beneath the facade of success lay a grave sense of personal inadequacy and an unintegrated series of personality fragments.

Elena was aware of a deeply felt need to try and find a way to please a father figure. As she put it, "I'm always searching for 'his' approval [meaning her father] and I never find it because I never will." Indeed, the history of real and perceived abandonment by her narcissistically preoccupied father who refused to validate her, led her to a sense of inordinate need for external approval from others, particularly men. Her anorexia, purging subtype, was momentarily set aside by the physical presence of her partner but, without ongoing availability of the selfobject, she was unable to regulate psychic discomfort and maintain a sense of equilibrium (Goldberg, 1999).

Bulimic patients commonly seek out multiple partners promiscuously to avoid inner fragmentation and to find an omnipotent caretaker (Novick & Novick, 1991, 1996). When they are as physically attractive and charming as Elena, they are often able to find nurturing, undemanding partners who provide the necessary selfobject function. In their search for a childlike attunement (Ainsworth, Blehar, Waters, & Wall, 1978), they use sex as a form of gaining, and maintaining, the union that more closely approximates a mother–child relationship than an adult one. This is done to achieve some level of self-cohesion and relatedness without the perceived threat of overwhelming sensual stimulation that leads to fragmentation.

As is routinely observed in couples' therapy, the other half of the dyad unconsciously needs the partner to be "less than sensual." As noted in the series of cases of couples who requested sex therapy, Simpson and Ramberg (1992) described the husbands of several patients with an eating disorder as inordinately concerned about their wives' infidelity. Despite consciously saying they wanted to be sexual, in reality they did not push for a more active sexuality. Simpson and Ramberg concluded that the male partners may have had their own difficulties that led them to choose sexually unavailable women.

In essence, these men needed a mirroring selfobject, namely, the eating disorder spouse, who would in all likelihood not abandon them, but would also make few sexual demands on them. The couple formed a bond that on the surface looked like mature dependency where greater sexual responsiveness was the only problem that needed attention. When the sex therapy failed, and the eating disorder did not come easily into control with the usual cognitive and behavioral measures, deeper disturbances of the self were identified.

Does the Patient Experience Shame about Her Body?

Psychodynamic theory has made a belated but fortuitous shift toward giving equal weight to the etiological roles of guilt and shame in a variety of psychological illnesses (Broucek, 1991; Kohut, 1971, 1977; Lansky, 2005; Lansky & Morrison, 1997; Lewis, 1971; S. Miller, 1985; Morrison, 1987; Nathanson, 1992). Eating disorder patients usually minimize how often they binge or purge or engage in other inappropriate behavior such as stealing, having temper or crying outbursts, and neglecting to take prescribed medication, because they are *ashamed* of what they perceive as failure. It can also be quite humiliating for them to speak about the shame they feel toward their own or others' bodies.

Extended clinical experience reveals that body shame can usually be traced to earliest childhood, and our overt affirmation may be a counterphobic and subtly inhibiting expression of deeper fears, as suggested by many European and third-world commentators. In reality, American men and women receive a myriad of mixed messages from the culture that augment developmental and patriarchal attitudes promoting body shame (Benjamin, 1988; Dimen, 2003; Fallon, Katzmen, & Wooley, 1994; Gordon, 2000).

Patients will usually be straightforward when asked about how their parents dealt with nudity and sexuality in the home. Sometimes sensitive questioning alone may be therapeutic in attenuating prudishness, because the patient has never before been given permission to address such concerns and memories. Encouraging honest expression in a safe relationship conveys the message that it is possible to be decent and respectable while openly discussing physical and sexual matters. Treatment provides a unique "window of opportunity" for the therapist to unabashedly correct early misconceptions. The sympathetic clinician who can openly discuss competing familial and cultural messages about sexuality diminishes patients' tendencies to denigrate their bodies.

Clinical Example

Natasha, age 53, was despondent about controlling her binge eating disorder and losing weight. "I was always heavy," she complained. "I hated for either of my husbands to see me nude—ever. If I fail at this treatment, the world will see again that I can't do it. They'll also see that you failed me, too, and I'll never have the chance of finding love in my life."

Behind Natasha's body shame lay a host of other personal vulnerabilities that centered on humiliation. Her overall sense of being "vulnerable, weak, power-less, dependent . . . and valueless" (Lansky, 2005, p. 887)—the hallmarks of the sense of shame that erode one's sense of self as alive and effective—derived in part from her impaired body image. As Natasha alluded to the possible failure in the therapy, she captured a dynamic in the treatment relationship that often makes shame an unspeakable issue. Working with the sense of shame may stir the therapist's own sense of defeat and inadequacy, and "our own difficulty bear-ing shame, our helplessness, and our anxiety that we may prove defective and fail in our professional roles because we, in facing the patient's incipient expe-rience of shame, will be found to have nothing effective to offer" (Lansky, 2005, p. 887). Making the sense of shame speakable and interpreting how fearful Natasha was to see her own and her therapist's vulnerabilities, eventually led to an attenuation of shame and greater resiliency.

How Guilty Does the Patient Feel about Sexuality?

At other times a strict and archaic sense of internalized parental injunctions are the root of the sexual inhibitions. In other words, an overactive superego (e.g., severe inner critic, see Chapter 2) is the primary culprit inhibiting the patient from having a more lively, age-appropriate sense of her sexual self. Although traditional Freudian theory castigated women for having a "weaker superego" than men, contemporary psychoanalysts have suggested that females have some aspects of a stronger superego than males, leading to conflicts over aggression, sexuality, and feelings about the body (Dimen, 2003; E. Jacobson, 1976; Persons, 1988, 1992; Zerbe, 1988, 1996b, 2001a, 2001b). D. Bernstein (1983) pointed out how little girls worry more than little boys about dirtiness and social conformity. She demonstrated in a series of case reports how women have dif-ferent superego problems than do men and that these superego conflicts are actualized by massive repression in both the sexual and aggression spheres.

Female sexual inhibitions may be derived from the linkage of a host of early practices and experiences that are different for the genders, even when con-temporary culture is taken into consideration. Because the genital experience for the female is more diffuse than the male's, the woman is inclined to lump her experiences together (Chodorow, 1978, 1989). No wonder she equates sex-uality as if it were an anal, despicable function and thereby demonstrates devel-opmental impasse and conflict. For patients with superego conflicts, sex and eating are viewed as dirty, unpleasant, and unnecessary activities.

In anorexia, where there is a clear difficulty with the breakthrough of sex-ual and aggressive drives, a rigidified superego structure is routinely observed. If the patient becomes sexually expressive, the wrath of an archaic, punishing superego comes down on her. Guilt is intense. Clinicians must help the patient deconstruct the pivotal role of the superego by pointing out how punishing these patients can be to themselves.

An intervention that addresses this dynamic might be constructed along the lines of, "You are frightened by becoming sexual because when you do you feel so guilty. It is as if you fear becoming out of control and passionate (or aggressive/excited/stimulated) because if you do you will be punished." What becomes obvious as the patient recounts the history are the latent fantasies of self-criticism or punishment projected into the therapist before the patient ever says a word. It is not uncommon to watch the patient respond in silence, or say, "I just don't want to talk about sex," or accuse the therapist of having a dirty mind! The success of the intervention might be measured by hearing more tales of the person's early life that give the patient's history or fantasies a deeper meaning. Patients who courageously attempt to confront their eating disorders and sexual problems concomitantly find themselves between the Charybdis of intense self-criticism and the Scylla of self-fragmentation.

Early identification with each parent is crucial for superego development. Psychodynamic theory now postulates that the resolution of the Oedipus complex is no longer the primary developmental antecedent of superego formation; in fact, the superego begins to consolidate much earlier and development continues well into the post-Oedipal period. Strength and pervasiveness of superego conflicts derive from the fear of the omnipotent mother of the earliest years (Davies, 2003; Dimen, 2003; Horney, 1926, 1967; S. Mitchell, 2002; Schafer, 1960, 2003). Eating disorder patients often demonstrate this kind of early identification with such a punitive but idealized maternal figure. Their treatment necessitates a thorough deconstruction and working through of issues that derive from this early period.

Clinical Example

Lauren, age 40, has suffered from anorexia since age 12. A painful memory that required considerable attention in psychodynamic psychotherapy was her father's withdrawal from her at menarche, a time when she began to see her body become more womanly: "Get your clothes back on," her mother shouted, when Lauren came downstairs in shorts and halter top. This kind of dress had never been criticized before, but the parents' virulent recriminations took a large toll on this patient's psyche. "How can I ever have a relationship?" she asked in one poignant session, "because I always hear them telling me to 'cover up' and 'be good.'" These kinds of superego prohibitions that arise from early parental injunctions, are commonly heard in long term psychotherapy, and usually take years to work through because they are highly pathogenic and result in self-defeating behavior patterns, including but not exclusively, failed relationships and a belief that one's body must never be exposed.

How Does the Therapist Address Sexual Conflicts?

Intrapsychic and interpersonal conflict are major sources of sexual inhibitions in patients with eating disorders. The analysis and understanding of unconscious conflict and the role it plays in a patient's life has been the sine qua non of classic and contemporary psychodynamic theory (Brenner, 1982, 1994). Although some clinicians currently give short shrift to this seemingly outmoded way of hearing and working with clinical material, experience demonstrates that helping individuals bring to awareness aspects of themselves that they were not aware of has enormous practical value. In addition to identifying the issues that remain hidden under the umbrella affects of shame and guilt already described, dissecting interpersonal and intrapsychic conflicts ultimately frees the patient who is "continually attempting to avoid the pain of [self] ownership or the ownership of painful experience" imbedded in an eating disorder (Smith, 2005, p. 328).

Grasping the unconscious compromises imbedded in conflict, and formulating the understanding of the patient's struggle in terms of conflicts between love and hate, ultimately, finds value in improved object relations and less symptomatic behaviors (Kernberg, 2005). The range of conflicts that become apparent in the eating disorder patient's experience of sexuality include internalized relationships with each parent or siblings, views of the parents' relationship as it was witnessed or fantasized by the patient, and the "conflictual matrices" (Harris, 2005) one uncovers as one comes to know oneself in the presence of another human being (e.g., intersubjective conflict).

Clinical Example

An application of understanding the role of conflict occurred in the case of Jenny, a 15-year-old who was admitted to a medical ward for severe malnutrition secondary to anorexia nervosa. Prior to this admission, Jenny never voiced any interest in boys but, not surprisingly, as her eating disorder came under control and she gained weight, her interest in the world at large perked up. In art therapy, she began to draw cutouts of the latest pop stars and make collages of them, which she proudly plastered on her wall.

Jenny's parents were aghast at their daughter's new and age appropriate interest in boys. They promptly insisted that she be discharged from the hospital setting when she reached target weight even though the treatment team and the insurance carrier believed that significantly more treatment was indicated. For Jenny, growing up and becoming a sexual person was obviously quite threatening to both of the parents. One might reasonably wonder who in this family has the deepest conflict and what it is really all about.

From an interpersonal psychological point of view, the patient believed she would lose one or both of her parents if she began to emancipate herself by having an age appropriate relationship with a boy. From an intrapsychic perspective, if Jenny gave in to the id pressures of becoming sexual or eating, she faced the internal prohibition of a strict superego. By holding onto the self-defeating anorexia, she avoided the normative competition of a girl to equal, if not exceed, her mother (Chodorow 1978, 1989, 1994). The restriction of sexuality also kept her tied to both parents. This kind of conflict has many variations but is played out over and over in higher functioning patients with eating disorders.

The demands on the patient by the parents to stay in an enmeshed, infantile position notwithstanding, psychotherapy often uncovers a host of conflicts that are pitted against one another (Abend, 2005; Brenner, 1982, 1994; Busch 2005; Smith, 2005). Jenny was anxious and fantasized that any eruption of her anger would lead to retaliation. Initially, her compliant, false self hid an inner struggle to suppress unconscious, unspoken aggression, leading to a stifling of the patient's real, true self. As Jenny began to put her ideas into words in her journal and make use of the cognitive behavioral strategies for affect modulation and affirmations (e.g., she was not "a bad person" if she expressed dissatisfaction or anger), she became more conscious of her own wishes and how her eating disorder was an obstacle to their fulfillment. These latent conflicts were uncovered gradually but included struggles between love and hate for both of her parents and the wish to stay a child and yet move on to a more normative adolescence.

SPIRITUAL MALAISE

Because eating disorder patients focus almost exclusively on appearance and what goes into their bodies, precious little time is left for moral and spiritual development. In pursuit of physical perfection, these patients lose sight of the quest for higher ideals and the need to grapple with the existential concerns that face all human beings. So much emphasis is placed on how they look and outward signs of success that they neglect the vital significance of inner beauty and eternal values. Much time is wasted and many resources drained in attempting to be other than who they really are (see Zerbe, 1993/1995a for numerous case examples of this problem).

When the person whose life is organized around eating cannot reach out and fully enjoy the experience of giving to others, the deepest source of sharing in physical union is precluded (see Table 7.4 for a list of the psychological issues that affect sexual expression in eating disorder patients). Consider the patients already described who have regulated their feelings by sexual promiscuity and periods of bingeing and purging or excessive fasting. In these ego states, they find it impossible to seek higher spiritual fulfillment let alone interpersonal enrichment. To grow beyond the eating disorder, the patient must learn that there is a greater purpose in life than seeking only a physical ideal (Menninger, 1959, 1973). The therapist must repeatedly confront this external focus because it keeps the patient from finding more sustaining and reciprocal relationships and a sense of a higher purpose and meaning for one's life.

Values clarification exercises, urging the patient to meet with a chaplain or clergyman or attend religious services, and prescribed meditation periods can be valuable adjuncts early on in addressing spiritual and ethical development. On the whole, however, the patient will likely be unable to move forward in this realm until the other dynamic issues addressed above come under therapeutic scrutiny. Moral development and virtuous action ultimately derive from the establishment of a cohesive sense of oneself, where strengths and limitations can be straightforwardly acknowledged.

SEXUAL MINORITIES

For the most part, published research on gay and lesbian patients with eating disorders has focused on the question of prevalence of anorexia, bulimia, and eating disorders not otherwise specified, in order to see if there were protective or exacerbating factors within gay communities. Less attention has been paid to the sexual issues that sexual minorities with eating disorders experience that may be similar or different from those of heterosexuals.

Links between sexual orientation and eating disorders have been established in men. Among many male homosexuals, a thin, muscular appearance is preferred, thus increasing the man's tendency to shape his body in a manner that may predispose him to an eating disorder (Carlat, Camargo, & Herzog, 1997; Epel, Spanakos, Kasl-Godley, & Brownell, 1996; Feldman & Meyer, 2007; Russell & Keel; 2002; Yager, Kurtzman, Landsverk, & Wiesmeier, 1988). In contrast to heterosexual men, homosexual men report "greater body dissatisfaction and higher levels of bulimic and anorexic symptoms . . . [and] higher depression, lower self-esteem, and less comfort with sexual orientation" (Russell & Keel, 2002, p. 305). Gay and bisexual men may also be more at risk for an eating disorder because in order to "attract men they are subject to similar pressures and demands as heterosexual women [and] . . . are affected by social norms and values that guide cultural notions of beauty" (Feldman & Meyer, 2007a, p. 218). Recent research also links childhood sexual abuse to disordered eating as a way to cope with the effects of the abuse and ensuing sexual difficulties in some men (Feldman & Meyer, 2007b).

Some authorities have wondered if lesbians are less prone to developing an eating disorder than heterosexual women because of certain "protective" factors in same sex relationships. Feminist literature from the 1970s to early 1990s argued that eating disorders would be less likely among lesbians; a diversity among body shapes and sizes is encouraged and these individuals may be more comfortable with confronting social norms. That is, lesbians would be hypothetically at low risk for developing a disorder that is rooted in "identity concerns" because of the courage and personal strength required to "come out and stay out," affirm one's lifestyle to family members and in the workplace, and confront cultural stereotypes related to beauty (Feldman & Meyer, 2007a; Herzog, Newman, Yeh, & Warshaw, 1992; Lancelot, & Kaslow, 2005; Striegel-Moore, 1993). Could these factors, and others, act synergistically to be protective in some situations? This question has as yet no hard and fast answer; the practicing clinician certainly sees lesbians who develop eating disorders and have many of the same body image concerns as do heterosexual women.

Some research does point to how body dissatisfaction is generally associated with feminine attitudes and gender roles that influence eating pathology in male and female subjects (Murnen & Smoleck, 1997; Meyer, Blissett, & Oldfield, 2001). In particular, masculinity is correlated with relatively healthy eating attitudes and behaviors. Although more research is needed before broad conclusions can be made, traditional femininity may turn out to be a specific risk factor and masculinity a protective factor in the development of eating disorders. Homosexual and bisexual men who are uncomfortable with body image and manifest eating dysregulation tend to identify with more traditionally female attitudes. Their conflict seems to lie between role orientation and society's view of what a man should be (Andersen, 1992; Fast, 1990; Gilligan, 1982; Feldman & Meyer, 2007a, 2007b).

Whatever the roots of the body dissatisfaction, in the clinical situation, each patient is an individual with a unique personal history and her or his own view of the world. Working with sexual minorities challenges the therapist to take both sexual functioning and the eating disorder into account, once again listening for the impact that the eating disorder has on sexual functioning. Homosexual patients experience the same kinds of difficulties in expressing their sexual selves as do heterosexuals with eating disorders.

Clinicians must maintain an open attitude and a willingness to learn from the patient. Therapists must also be alert to any internalized homophobia on our part or the part of our patient. There are the same needs for the clinician to wrestle with the countertransference reactions that inevitably arise when working with someone who is different (see Chapter 8). As always, the therapist who has a conscious countertransference barrier for any reason is ethically bound to refer that person to another psychotherapist. As members of a marginalized minority group, homosexuals continue to face special pressures that impede their development and the true self, which can naturally exacerbate any underlying sexual anxieties or difficulties. As Ruth Striegel-Moore, one of the preeminent research scientists in the eating disorder field (1993) conceded, homosexuals may appear to accept themselves, yet "still struggle with a profoundly negative attitude about their own sexual orientation" (pg 4).

Particular clinical issues can arise in the treatment of the homosexual patient (Nichols, 2000; Striegel-Moore, 1993; Striegel-Moore, Tucker, & Hsu, 1990). Clinicians are advised to take an empathic view of the life and relationship concerns that arise with gays and lesbians and to refer them to sex therapists with experience in treating dysfunction in same sex couples. Margaret Nichols, a sex therapist who is noted for her work with gays and lesbian couples, advises validating the patient's lifestyle. She goes on to acknowledge the importance in heterosexuals, homosexuals, and bisexual persons that the therapist suspend "preconceived notions of gender and relationships as well as biases about sexual acts" (Nichols, 2000, p. 361). This kind of forthright, humble attitude encourages patients to teach the therapist about their relationships, their community, and their sexual concerns and ultimately broadens our knowledge. Yet it is easier to give this advice in the abstract than to put it into practice in an individual clinical encounter. We therapists must work diligently over the course of our professional lives to foster the kind of professional demeanor that allows us to "be taught" by our patients. As described throughout this text, patients are inevitably our best guides in helping us uncover our professional "blind" and "dumb" spots (Bernstein & Severino, 1986).

Even in the most open and accepting of therapeutic situations, the lesbian or gay man may find it difficult to override the (usually unconscious) personal sense of self-hatred (e.g., internalized homophobia; Downey & Friedman, 1995; Friedman & Downey, 1995). As with other secrets that the eating disorder patient harbors, the therapist may suspect but not know for a long period of time that the eating disordered patient is also a member of a sexual minority. Empathic resonance promotes acceptance and progress in treatment because these hidden struggles differ in degree rather than in kind from those of heterosexuals (Leiblum & Rosen, 2000). As Nichols (2000) insightfully advises clinicians who may have difficulty in initially working with someone who is seen as different from oneself, "Colorful and unusual differences in behavior and style may be prominent in minority clients; nevertheless, most therapeutic interventions will not vary that much from interventions used in the mainstream population" (p. 362).

It always pays for the therapist to be alert for the element of surprise. For example, after more that a year of a highly expressive individual psychotherapy, an extremely bright, professional man diagnosed with bipolar II and binge eating disorder, confided to me that he felt most sexually alive when he dressed as a woman prior to having sexual intercourse. Over many months, we came to understand this behavior as representing his desire to be accepted by people for his tender and feminine feelings. While I was initially startled by being caught off guard by his revelation, this patient had much to teach about his own internalized self-hatred and the reasons he kept his sexual likes and dislikes so secret (and, not surprisingly, his bingeing came under better control after he revealed his secret and his feelings about transvestite behavior).

His "confession" after many months was a test of my capacity to remain involved and interested (Weiss, Sampson, & the Mt. Zion Psychotherapy Group, 1986) after he revealed important aspects of the self. When I did not exhibit repugnance or reject him but rather encouraged him to continue, he was able to delve into sexual and relationship concerns that had felt "like an albatross around my neck for years," which obviously led to greater trust and depth in our therapeutic bond. Patients can amaze us as treaters by the secrets they hold dear. Such revelations require a shift in perspective, a revision in preconceived ideas, and assimilation of new information. In working with all patients, the therapist "must erase all preconceptions about 'normal' and 'abnormal' sex" (Nichols, 2000, p. 361) and welcome the new material as a significant sign of trust, intimacy, and deepening within the therapeutic bond.

ADDITIONAL TREATMENT CONSIDERATIONS

Erik Erikson once remarked that without the potential to see individuals as capable of growth, development, and ripening over the course of the entire cycle of life, psychotherapy retains a retrospective, traumatological perspective (Evans, 1967). In this chapter, I have attempted to delineate some of the issues facing the patient with an eating disorder who strives to become more sexually alive, whole, and true to themselves. An integrated treatment perspective necessitates that the clinician take into account the physiological repercussions of the eating disorder that likely impede sexuality (Basson, 2002; Schover, 2000; Tuiten et al., 1993); we must at the same time deepen our perspective by moving into the personal history of the patient. This often reveals a host of developmental deficits, interpersonal conflicts, and a sense of self-fragmentation that impinge on the sexual self. A fully integrated treatment plan must include addressing the patient's sexual life with the belief in that individual's potential for growth, for overcoming even the most insidious neglect and trauma, and for achieving a heightened sense of integration of sexuality within the personality (i.e., true self).

1. Make sex a speakable issue. Explain the role of malnutrition and any side effects from medication. Biology is bedrock when it comes to sexual functioning. One cannot feel or be sexual in a state of undernourishment. After providing the basic education, make some reasonable conjectures as to the multiple causes of this particular patient's problems (e.g., trauma, severe inner critic, etc.).

2. Assist the patient in becoming familiar with her or his intense feeling states, particularly anger. As noted, stymied aggression can underlie an eating disorder and be a contributant to the psychosexual dysfunction that accompanies it (Hitchcock, 1992; Young-Bruehl, 1993). Food refusal and body shaping symptoms go hand in hand, admixtures of powerful libidinal and aggressive elements. To have more access to the sexual self, the patient must get to know these disavowed (i.e. dissociated) aspects thoroughly. What is at first so frightening that a whole defensive structure is erected may become more manageable by the mere expression of that which is most feared. These include feelings of anger and the life stories that show the therapist why the patient has been unable to fully express her or his sexuality.

3. Suggest ways to manage affect appropriately. Sustained empathic enquiry (Stolorow, Brandchaft, & Atwood, 1987) helps patients to establish an attitude of interest in and find acceptance for their own unique emotional life. An initial phase of naming feelings may be protracted, but it builds affect tolerance. The cognitive-behavioral techniques that encourage exploration of feelings in journal writing and bibliotherapy may also facilitate affect integration and communication with the therapist. Learning to deal with strong feelings and positively identifying with others who have done so lays groundwork for later growth in the relational and sensual domains.

4. Model flexibility and a sense of humor. When appropriate, enjoy a good laugh with the patient. Taking life a bit less seriously is a good reminder of one's

humanness. This focus enables the patient to develop the necessary resiliency to enjoy romance and love and to survive life's inevitable disappointments and losses. The humanity of the therapist, including acknowledging her or his own errors and gaffes, also demonstrates to the patient that growth and development are capacities to be championed. A rigid, harsh superego is mollified over time by having healthier objects of identification.

5. Remind patients that one must be an individuated human being to partake of a sexually vibrant relationship (Schnarch, 1997, 2000). Differentiation of one's sense of self is the central, organizing task of psychotherapy with most eating disorder patients, but it is "crucial to emotionally committed relationships because they involve the intricate entwinement of these two basic human drives: attachment and the refusal to submit to tyranny" (Schnarch, 2000, p. 26). As a first step toward helping a patient build significant, differentiated relationships, encourage the formation and nurturing of friendship. Oftentimes our patients have experienced conspicuous parental absence or possessiveness and a concomitant paucity of age-appropriate relationships. Mature love will grow out of solid friendship, the formation of which teaches mutuality and helps establish the foundation for safe sexual expression.

6. Educate the patient that sexuality evolves over the life cycle. Even when one has had early developmental difficulties, love has the capacity to transform the self. In Ethel Specter Person's popular book *Dreams of Love and Fateful Encounters: The Power of Romantic Love* (1988), she explains how the deepest attachments evolve over time. As Person (1988) notes, "Love gives us one more chance" (p. 351) in life. Because patients with eating disorders derive significant emotional benefit from the therapist's validation of their worth (Beresin, Gordon, & Herzog, 1989), the treater is urged to acknowledge the patient's improved and newfound curiosity and applaud any steps taken to move out of a circumscribed orbit in life (i.e., eating disorder).

7. When appropriate, encourage the patient to take advantage of sex therapy or experiential therapies (Hornyak & Baker, 1989; Leiblum & Rosen, 2000; Leiblum & Sachs, 2002). The particular modality must be chosen according to the patient's needs, but for those individuals or couples who are open to more intensive treatment, attitudes can change and conflicts can be diminished by these effective tools. Comfort with one's body can grow by working in dance or movement therapy, practicing meditation or relaxation procedures, and even participating in psychodrama. For patients who have been sexually traumatized, referral to a reputable masseur or masseuse may be the patient's first experience of safe touch. It may also potentiate healing by its effect on neuropsychological integration as well as personal growth.

8. Help the patient to mourn. Whatever has constituted the real or perceived maltreatment and deprivation in the past, the patient must find new ways to move beyond it to have a full life. Accompany the patient to find new ways to put feelings into words, especially sad ones. Journaling, bibliotherapy, group and individual psychotherapies can be powerful tools in learning new modes

of affect regulation and finding safe spaces to share feelings. Remind the patient that to become more sexually alive, short-term goals include finding ways to draw an emotional boundary between past abuse and present circumstances and to develop life enhancing activities.

9. Whenever possible, include the partner. It is essential that the couple learn how to feel safe together. Encourage expressing affection outside of the bedroom and learning good communication skills. In the treatment of the patient with sexual dysfunction and an eating disorder, realistic goals must be assessed because the problem is multifactorial in origin and may derive from early deficits in attachment. Remind the patient (and yourself!) that success will rarely be achieved quickly, but each success will be a foundation on which to build others.

10. Above all else, maintain a sense of hopefulness (Menninger, 1959). Reassure the patient that although sexuality may have been painful or conflictual in the past, it need not be so for a lifetime. Underscore how the eating disorder and other psychological symptoms have not only taken their toll, but have been rigid ways of adapting to life. As more flexible coping strategies are instituted, and as the eating disorder no longer fills the emotional void or serves as a central organizer of the individual's life as it once did, other activities and relationships will naturally take its place. It is at this point that the eating disorder patient may be most able to tackle the arena of sexual responsiveness

CONCLUSION

Sexuality and sexual dysfunction are recognized as major areas of concern for eating disorder persons but their treatment has received scant attention in the professional literature. Urgent medical and psychological needs of the patient usually take precedent, but this must not prevent the clinician from inquiring into the sexual sphere of life. In any comprehensive treatment program that focuses on the quality of life of the individual, needs and conflicts related to sex and intimacy deserve more attention than they usually receive. Limits on treatment sessions by third parties and the persistence of intrapsychic and interpersonal difficulties in this population even after the manifest symptom is corrected interfere with restoration of the fullest sense of life for these patients.

Healthy sexual functioning is intricately tied to relationship issues and overall psychological functioning. The patient who has a history of sexual abuse or rape, or problems with attachment and bonding in childhood, lacks a consolidated sense of self, or experiences shame or internal criticism about the body will not be able to address sexual dysfunction before extensive groundwork is laid in these other arenas. The patient must be on the path toward psychological individuation before sexual and relationship needs can be fully attended to by treaters.

By serving as a resource and role model for the patient, the clinician conveys the message that growth throughout the life cycle is not only possible, but it is something to champion. The implicit value in such integrated treatment is our wish as clinicians to see our patients grow and to be able to experience for themselves more of life and love. This approach also fosters new understanding, optimism, solace, and love for others in their circle. Patients gain new meaning in their lives as they partake of the give and take of human bonds, including sexual ones.

As demonstrated by the two quotations at the beginning of this chapter, in the mind, food and sex are ineluctably and delightfully joined. It is unlikely that one can fully succeed in one sphere without being at peace with oneself in the other. Treatment outcomes for our patients should never be considered "good enough" unless symptom control also leads to full participation in all aspects of life. This knotty problem of what truly defines treatment success should include the eating disorder patient's entitlement to a life fueled by more love, intimacy, and sexual responsiveness as a goal. Among therapists, it is often facetiously said that the most important sex organ is the brain; to help eating disorder patients overcome disavow, repression, and denial of sexual needs, the therapist cannot afford to "lose one's own mind" by colluding with the patient to leave this complex but essential life issue go unspoken in the treatment.

CHAPTER 8

Managing Transference and Countertransference

A long life together is altogether wasted on most people, who quickly run out of enthusiasm or dreams and still have all those years ahead of them. Now, a fresh start, that would be something. Something rare. Unless, as people usually do, you manage to turn your new life into the old one.

—Susan Sontag (2000)

With progressive de-idealization of lost objects, meaningful living in the present becomes possible. . . . The past and future do not replace today; they enrich it.

—Salman Akhtar (1999)

In her final novel, the feminist essayist and social commentator Susan Sontag vividly portrays one woman's search for self-transformation and the ordeal inherent in letting go of one's past. In the brief passage quoted, the protagonist, Maryna, perceptively shares an existential issue faced by all human beings with her new lover, Bogdan. Maryna distinguishes between the ease with which human beings set out to remold our lives, only to retrospectively discover that we inexplicably and against our conscious will, repeat what we tried so hard to avoid.

This character has first-hand experience with the hardships inherent in personal metamorphosis; an actress by profession, she emigrates from her native Poland to America in search of opportunity, love, and security, and "a fresh start." Only as she self-analyzes and takes stock of her inscrutable quirks and penchant for change does she begin to confront the ease with which humans become inured to their past. Even the most strikingly new scenario can look and feel much like the old. Maryna observes this phenomenon in herself and begins to get curious about why this happens, even when one makes such a dramatic leap as immigrating to another country!

Indeed, cultivating a new life, and thereby establishing a new sense of one-self, is a more ambiguous and difficult proposition than it first appears. Most of us can deeply identify with the person who, like Maryna, is determined to embark on a new relationship, start all over in a new job or city, or simply avoid getting caught up in old patterns of behavior and thereby take a new lease on life. We discover that this task is exceedingly ambitious in psycholog-ical terms. In part, the problem of establishing a "new identity" occurs because it is hard to let go of what we know. The propensity to return to the past, to recapitulate and retread our old paths, even if they are harmful to us, finds expression in the often quoted folk wisdom: "The devil you know is better than the devil you don't." Despite the best of intentions, why is it that we humans somehow always manage to turn aspects of our "new life into the old one?"

Sigmund Freud observed early in his career how the tendency to repeat the past appears in all relationships and may be put to good use in therapeutic ones. His early case histories are full of details about how his patients foisted feelings from their past loves and hates onto him. With admirable modesty and a decidedly feminist bent, Freud observed that the passion that his female patients held for him was unwarranted by the manifest situation of his role as their doctor. Freud realized that he was neither as attractive nor as charismatic as his patients would have him believe when they confessed desire for him. In these early case histories, he eloquently described how his patients' idealized erotized transference feelings became a powerful factor that got in the way of their living in the present and moving forward. The repetition of old feelings in the new situation of therapy became a central vehicle for helping patient and therapist grapple with factors that were impeding the individual's ability to live fully in the present and embrace their dreams (Freud, 1912/1964f; 1913/1964g, 1913/1964h, 1913/1964i, 1913/1964j).

Most clinicians who treat eating disorders must bear in mind that for our patients to begin to thrive, we straddle the dual roles of being simultaneously a new object and a transference object. Patients must make peace with their past and let it go, and to a significant extent be able to transcend it, to be able to live in the present. As discussed throughout this book, they must also "immi-grate" from the land of eating disorders to a "new world" where they are more at ease with their body, and in so doing, their identity will also change.

As psychoanalyst Salman Akhtar (1999) observes in his seminal psychoana-lytic study of immigrants, many challenges must be faced when one attempts to establish and maintain an identity in a new country. Likewise, the eating disorder patient must be able to have an "ongoing psychic dialogue with the past. . . . for healthy psychic function" and be able "to give up many blissful fantasies and projections in order to do so" (p. 95). This new identity must encompass speaking the new language of feelings, coming to grips with the grim realities of impoverished past relationships, traumas, and lost time in liv-ing, while simultaneously making way for the risks and possibilities of a new life. On the therapeutic journey, the patient emigrates from the eating disorder world to the noneating disorder world. In the process, the therapist will feel pulls in the work that conjure up many unanticipated countertransference reactions. Like our patients, we are also anchored by our past, which gets replayed in the treatment.

As patients entrust us with their secrets, our empathy helps us share their burdens and their pain. This invariably happens at a cost to the therapist. As much as we make use of ourselves to understand, contain, and eventually help patients master their responses to the past, we get drawn into their dramas and may viscerally experience some of them. Psychodynamic theory, in particular, helps inform clinicians about the ubiquity of our personal responses and offers some strategies about how to make use of the roles the patients cast us in to move the treatment forward.

In some respects, our countertransference responses are another way we get a glimpse into our patients' past and can provide insight into how they might begin to untangle it, setting the stage for "meaningful living in the present." Working with transference and countertransference reactions is another avenue to unearth the self-vilifying internal criticism and personal vulnerability many patients with eating disorder experience. The goal of working through transference is to find greater hopefulness and discover a deeper understanding of the meaning of the eating disorder in the patient's life, leading to more opportunities to live life anew. In the most felicitous of scenarios, working with transference and countertransference reactions aids the patient in putting inner demons to rest.

Much as Sontag describes Maryna's transformation as "rejoining her destiny" and "beginning again" (p. 229), we therapists hope to give our patients a "fresh start" that is less determined by automatic feelings and reactions from the past. Interventions that take into account the immediacy of transference and countertransference paradigms enhance therapeutic collaboration and establish the patient's developmental potential by reclaiming the past, working it over, letting go of outmoded and destructive aspects of it, and pointing the way toward a future where new enthusiasms, meaning, and a deeper sense of vitality become possibilities.

CLINICAL RATIONALE INFORMED BY RESEARCH

In his first interview with his new psychiatrist, Nigel, a 44-year-old physician with episodic binge eating and periods of severe restriction, said, "What drew me to you was your voice on your answering machine. It was warm like my 1st girl friend's mother." Transference feelings were there from the start as revealed by his innocent remark about the quality of his therapist's voice. Nigel was conceding his need for warmth and a maternal presence to help him take the next steps in his journey.

Although it is generally conceded by clinicians of differing theoretical persuasions that transference is a ubiquitous phenomenon, controversy remains about whether or not working with transference is a sine qua non of treatment. In any psychotherapy process with an eating disorder patient that extends beyond more than a few sessions, it becomes incumbent on the therapist to at the very least recognize salient transference paradigms and develop a personal style in addressing the transferential themes that inevitably arise. Simply put, when we become whom the patient needs us to become, they have a new opportunity, grafted onto an old model, to rework and master what blocks them.

Many therapists make a deliberate decision to work outside of the transference (making so-called extratransferential interventions) and rarely address the therapeutic relationship per se. They prefer to deal with issues and events in the patient's life to drive home points related to destructive and constructive behaviors, family and relationship sabotage, emotional obfuscation, and cognitive restriction, providing a hefty amount of advice and confrontation to rectify pathology. The problem with this approach, of course, is that the relationship to the therapist always counts with the patient and will heavily influence the patient's acceptance or rejection of whatever treatment suggestions are offered.

Indeed, although Freud initially viewed the concept of transference as deriving from the patient's repressed memories that needed to be reconstructed and interpreted in the therapy, contemporary clinicians, informed by psychotherapy research, have also demonstrated how the transference is actually influenced by the behavior of the therapist in the session. Those clinicians who believe that it is important to work in the here-and-now (Gabbard, 2005) or "the present moment" (Stern, 2004) describe how helping patients bring their experience into the room has a unique and powerful impact that cannot be gotten at any other way in therapy.

Clinicians and researchers have always wondered about the specific, active ingredients in psychodynamic psychotherapy, and even in the early 21st century debate continues to rage about what these are. One dimension that emerges from contemporary research is the importance of forming a secure, stable attachment to the therapist, which activates old and stimulates development of new neural networks in the brain (Bradley, Heim, & Westen, 2005; Westen & Gabbard, 2002). The capacity to form a therapeutic alliance is one of the best predictors of treatment outcome in psychotherapy and reflects the brain's tendency "to map current onto past experiences and to craft responses that represent a combination of automatic activation of [cognitive] procedures and mental representations from the past" (Bradley et al., p. 348). Because attachment patterns are evoked in the "intimate, emotionally charged, asymmetrical, and typically nurturant relationship" (p. 346) of therapy, it provides a new opportunity for "examination of these patterns *in vivo*," which "can provide insight into some of the patient's central dynamics in close interpersonal relationships" and "generate changes in extra therapeutic relationships and their intrapsychic concomitants" (p. 346).

Working directly within the context of the therapeutic relationship, patients get a chance not only to develop insight into their past and current relationships,

TABLE 8.1   Common transference reactions

- Patient may place therapist in role of idealized parent, particularly early in treatment
- Patient may devalue or display unreasonable amounts of anger or frustration (e.g., so-called negative parental or "bad object" transference)
- Patient may test therapeutic boundaries and demand that the therapist disclose more than is comfortable or useful to the treatment
- Patient may experience and treat therapist as a peer (e.g., twinship transference)
- Patient may spoil or "vomit back" interventions to test perserverance or benevolence of therapist (i.e., projection of punitive superego onto therapist)
- Patient may withhold a family secret, either consciously or unconsciously, which gets played out in the therapy by shifting parental identifications and mental representations (e.g., the therapist may feel "confused," bewildered, or blindsided and suspect an important issue is being held back without any objective evidence for the feeling)

but learn to practice speaking directly to power about their most difficult feelings and experiences (see Table 8.1). For example, early in treatment it may be impossible for an individual who came from a home where expression of angry or sad feelings was inhibited to be able to state when they are upset, frustrated, or discouraged with the therapist. Over time and with practice and permission by the therapist to acknowledge intense, difficult feelings, patients' sense of self becomes strengthened. They become better equipped to speak their own truth, glean understanding of what they have suppressed, and develop new modes of working through that which had heretofore not been put into words.

One alternative to dealing directly with the transference is working with the interpersonal conflicts and problematic behavioral patterns in the patient's life. One rebuttal to this view now comes from psychotherapy research indicating that patients with poor object relations may benefit "more from therapy with transference interpretations than therapy with no transference interpretations" (Hoglend, Amlo, Marble, Bogwald, et al., 2006, p. 1736). This research demonstrates that for patients with a significant problem experiencing a stable sense of self or managing intense feelings and problematic interpersonal relationships, therapy actually goes better when transference interpretations are made directly to the patient (Gabbard, 2006a; Hoglend et al., 2006; Horwitz et al., 1996; Kernberg et al., 1972). Working with transference is likely to prove a significant boon for the treatment of eating disorder patients because their attachment-related problems are also more likely to be reworked and mastered when speaking to issues that arise in the interpersonal dyad of therapist and patient.

BIOLOGICAL CONSIDERATIONS

As cognitive neuroscience has documented the modifiability of neural networks, an understanding of the biological basis of transference is also beginning to unfold. It is now conceded that new representational capabilities and new synaptic connections are generated throughout a lifetime; in therapy, prefrontal circuitry can change and expand with accompanying changes in how the patient experiences crucial relationships. That is, neuroscientists now conclude that new interactions with the therapist may change the object relational experiences by alteration in actual neural circuitry. Different representations activate different neural networks; the clinical experience of witnessing multiple transferences to the therapist develop over time is corroborated in contemporary cognitive neuroscience. Gabbard (2006b) noted:

> A specific and unique pattern of neural connection is activated whenever the brain is exposed to a new person, a new idea, a new emotion, or even a new word. . . . When something evokes a neural pattern that is similar to the configuration representing a previous encounter of a person, event, or feeling state, recognition occurs, a process known as "pattern matching." (p. 284)

Procedural and declarative memory can also change in the course of treatment by conscious mastery of implicit and repetitive modes of relatedness and growing capacities of the individual to symbolize and to recognize problematic behaviors. The neural substrate of this psychotherapeutic change likely involves dorsal lateral prefrontal circuitry, the area of executive functioning one usually attributes to ego strengths (Viamontes & Beitman, 2006). Modifications in the cingulate gyrus-nucleus accumbens circuitry likely aid the individual in regulating overwhelming drives, impulsivity, social inappropriateness, lack of empathy, and poor judgment. According to recent imaging studies, psychotherapeutic interactions influence the orbitofrontal and amygdala circuits and modulate these problematic domains.

Changes in the neural networks lead to changes in the life narrative and the patient's experience of other people, including the therapist. From a contemporary neuroscience perspective, transference may be viewed as a series of pathological neural networks that can weaken over the course of therapy. As new memories are created and the individual has a more benign experience with the therapist, the historical narrative is reshaped, pathologic memories are recontexturalized and mastered, and new adaptations can be facilitated (Gabbard, 2006b; Pally, 2000, 2005; Viamontes & Beitman, 2006; Westen & Gabbard, 2002).

Finally, cognitive neuroscience sheds light on why particular transference paradigms are likely to be repeated; neural networks need cognitive "exercise" in order to change that may involve work both inside and outside of the therapy. Nonetheless, networks that have been activated together for years or even decades are capable of modification when tight linkages are weakened and new associations begin through the processes of silent reflection and mentalizaiton. As Gabbard (2006b) further summarized:

> Persistent change requires a relative deactivation of problematic links in activated networks and increased activation of new, more adaptive connections.

Analysis may also effect change by developing the patient's capacity for conscious self-reflection that will allow the patient to override unconscious dynamics once they are recognized and therefore "reset" some of the relevant connection weights. (p. 288)

CULTURAL CONSIDERATIONS

All of us have a variety of reactions to the cultural in which we grow up. Some of these feelings are quite conscious, such as when persons take pride in the resiliency of their heritage or become angry or ashamed when they hear someone disparage their ethnic background. These feelings become part of what I term "transference to the predominant culture" and they can be put to salient therapeutic use when the professional helps the patient "take the initiative to be culturally literate with a diversity of cultural groups" (Root, 1990, p. 53).

Eating disorder patients have their own realistic and unconsciously embedded thoughts about Western culture, the emphasis placed on shape and weight, and the diet mentality. Although many eating behaviors may be grounded in biology or the psychological makeup of the patient and family, so may patients use and misuse eating and dieting to express their feelings about the culture in which we live.

Our reaction to the cultural is also subject to change over the life cycle. A number of important sociocultural studies have demonstrated the rapidity with which feelings about the body, dieting, and physical appearance evolve when one moves from one culture to another one that emphasizes an ideal different from the indigenous one. For years I have used the classic study by Furnham and Alibhai (1983) in therapy sessions to illustrate how quickly thoughts can shift about one's body when one moves from one culture to another. In this study, subjects began to diet and assume the ideal body habitus of the new culture (London) within a few years after moving from Kenya. I ask the patient to help me understand their ideas of why these African women who had been previously satisfied with their bodies and full figures so quickly conformed to the desired stereotype of women in London.

The clinical implication of cultural transference is obvious but is often difficult to tease apart from other issues in the treatment. Some patients will easily talk about their feelings about the culture, only to have more deep seated issues make their appearance later in the treatment. Other patients will deny or blame their eating disorder exclusively on the culture. Even though transference manifestations are subject to change as the patient relinquishes defenses and gains more access to feelings, they must always be taken into account and explored. At these moments in the therapy, the patient is much more able to objectively examine how the culture has played a role in the maintenance of the eating disorder. They can be given the chance to "talk back" to the tyranny of dieting, the culture of narcissism, and the objectification of people by deemphasizing external requirements of success.

For example, discussing ways in which eating disorder symptoms manifested in previous eras can change "assumptions that hinder a comprehensive understanding of the causes and methods of healing from eating problems" (B. Thompson, 1994, p. 373). Historians argue that fasting behaviors have occurred for centuries, but the meaning of these behaviors varies tremendously (Bell, 1985; Brumberg, 1988; Bynum, 1987) depending on the culture in which the individual lives. What clinicians now observe as a "relentless quest for thinness" was also found in medieval Europe. Historian Rudolph Bell (1985, p. 985) refered to the condition as *anorexia mirabilis* and believed women pursued "holy fasts" to assert autonomy and reject patriarchy. Historian Caroline Bynum (1987) challenged this interpretation; in the fasting phenomenon she found evidence for "devotion, world-renunciation, *imitatio Christi*" (Lelwicia, 1999, p. 27); that is, spiritual pursuits as a way for women to choose to assert their "creative efforts to use the resources and roles most available to them—food, feeding, and their bodies—to shape their worlds and to achieve sanctity" (Lelwicia, 1999, p. 27).

Joan Jacobs Brumberg's comprehensive study of anorexia after the medieval period to the contemporary era provides significant perspective on the current secular meaning behind appetite control. For Brumberg, sexual desire, intellectual pursuits, and autonomous urges were threatening to male power structures that shaped the concept of a new disease that emerged (i.e., anorexia nervosa) in the 17th century and continue to the present era. These perspectives are important to reflect on given what they might say about the historical *relativity* of an eating disorder diagnosis. They also help demonstrate that the "shifting and competing meanings of female fasting in Euro-American history" (Lelwicia, 1999, p. 30) reflect the values, thoughts, and projections clinicians also bring to diagnosis based on our transference to the culture. As feminist theologian Michelle Lelwica further described:

> The meanings of cultural ideals and norms (such as female slenderness) are produced, circulated, and consumed by persons in different social positions. To illuminate this circuit of meaning production, we need a concept of "culture" not simply as shared webs of meaning that humans create to gain a sense of direction in life but also as webs of unstable relationships among a common repertoire of stories and symbols, diverse individual and group experiences, and the existing sociopolitical order. Culture is the *contested terrain* where persons in different social positions and with unequal resources engage in multifaceted struggles over meaning. (p. 33)

When the therapist helps the patient look at and begin to tease apart the "stories and symbols" that inform the "individual and group" experience inherent in living in a particular culture in a specific period of history, work with the patient's transference to the culture has begun. This enlarges the scope of the therapy by helping patients engage with, make conscious, and confront attitudes, feelings, and thoughts they have about this "contested terrain" as yet another way of finding meaning in their symptoms while challenging normative assumptions and values of our particular historical era and culture.

WORKING WITH COMMON TRANSFERENCE ISSUES

Attuning oneself to the most frequently occurring transference reactions that a clinician encounters when working with eating disorder patients (see Table 8.1) heightens the sense of immediacy and makes the treatment immeasurably more alive; it also is likely to enable the therapist to make some "high yield" interventions as the clinical examples will illustrate.

As psychoanalyst Harry Guntrip found through writing about his two psychotherapy processes with W. R. D. Fairbairn and D. W. Winnicott, respectively, the therapist's humanity and the personal relationship established between clinician and patient inevitably shape what happens that is mutative and transformative in therapy.

Guntrip concluded his autobiographical synopsis of his distinct therapeutic experiences with these two distinguished analysts with a statement that I find defines much of what we try to do every day in our work with the tools available to us at the moment, namely our own personality and the training we bring to bear on how we intervene. I share this quote from Guntrip (1975) here because I have never found a more succinct and explicit statement about the essence of psychotherapeutic treatment and the interplay of transference and the "real" relationship we have with each of our patients.

> To find a good parent at the start is the basis of psychic health. In its lack, to find a genuine "good object" in one's analyst is both a transference experience and a real life experience. In analysis as in real life, all relationships have a subtly dual nature. All through life we take into ourselves both good and bad figures who strengthen or disturb us, and it is the same in psychoanalytic therapy; it is the meeting and interacting of two real people in all its complex possibilities. (p. 155)

Love and Hate

The earliest vision that a healthy child has of the parent is of an omnipotent, omniscient caretaker. In normal development, one learns the human failings of one's parents over time and thereby integrates the "good" and "bad" aspects into one person. When one has not had the developmental experience of having an idealized parent in one's life, the longing never goes away until it is partially filled and then mourned. Establishing a positive transference is often key in forming a strong therapeutic alliance and may even influence the patient's self- and body image (Jacobs, 1991). An atmosphere that cultivates the expression and validation of loving feelings enables the patient to feel safe and secure, with the aim of developing basic trust and object constancy (Erikson, 1950; Rinsley, 1982).

Therapists of eating disorder patients commonly observe how positive, loving transference feelings can shift quickly to negative, hating ones as exemplified in a range of self-destructive behaviors and affectomotor storms (Blum,

1997; Gabbard & Wilkinson, 1994; Zerbe, 1988, 1992a, 1993/1995a, 1995b, 1996a, 1996b, 2001b, 2007a). A strong therapeutic alliance is cultivated when these transference feelings are experienced within the treatment and the patient grows in the capacity to speak directly about them. For the true self to emerge, the patient must experience the continuum of positive and negative feelings with the therapist. As feminist psychologist Susan Wooley (1991) wisely noted regarding the essential lessons of treatment, the individual "must learn to express the full range of human feelings, trusting the reparative force of truth. This is a sophisticated lesson—one that cannot be comprehended in a family in which feelings are concealed and in which conflict is avoided and never resolved" (p. 252).

By identifying with how the treater processes feelings and thoughts, the patient finds an essential role model he or she never had; one also discovers that even having "a good hate" can be contained and enjoyed to claim new aspects of affective awareness. One might intervene when strong affects of love or hate arise by saying to the patient, "Now you are trusting me with [love] or [hate]." Another intervention that encourages the discussion of uncomfortable affects that emerge in the transference might be, "You are starting to get familiar with [your love] or [your rage]."

Clinical Example

Helena, a 24-year-old administrative assistant who struggles with bulimia nervosa and kleptomania, exemplified a typical trajectory of transference feelings that psychologist René Spitz (1957) identified in young children. Spitz named this the "no before yes" phenomenon, noting the developmental achievement arrived at when the toddler revels in saying "no" for the first time. Just as most 2-year-olds seem to relish saying the word *no* and temporarily refuse the ministrations of the primary caretaker, the "no" is felt by most parents to be deflating of their own feelings of omnipotence, so Helena began the early months of her psychotherapy process by seeming to reject everything her therapist had to say.

Helena's therapist strategically planned to put developmental theory into practice. Taking a "one-down" approach, she capitalized on an early negative maternal transference that shifted quickly to a more positive one. She told Helena that the two of them had gotten off to a rocky start and she wondered if the patient would give her another chance at working together. The therapist was paying attention to the fact that she had to hear Helena's "no" before the patient would even begin to say "yes" to therapy.

Helena began to tell her therapist about her history of abuse and neglect: neither her eating disorder nor shoplifting resulted in her mother's paying attention to symptoms. Helena was, therefore, quite struck by the therapist's decision to take both her symptoms and her needs seriously. In particular, she seemed pleased that the therapist was not put off by her negativity. She said,

"No one has ever taken me at my word. Everyone has always talked down to me. I'm willing to give it another shot, too."

The initial recriminations shifted to an idealized maternal transference, and the patient began to do better with respect to her presenting symptoms and felt strengthened in many areas of her life. After receiving a significant raise at her job and making the decision to further her education by attending a local community college, Helena could enjoy the sincere gesture of congratulations her therapist gave. This therapist pointed out Helena's growth and decision to now engage in life positively. The patient began to weep and the therapist felt moved as well by the changes she saw in this one-time world-weary young adult. Helena went on to express her yearning for a mother's unconditional love and support. She pined, "I wish you could be my mother. You *always* give me great advice and seem to care. Why didn't my mother ever ask me questions?" Empathy by the therapist led to an idealized, loving maternal transference, which at this stage of the treatment facilitated the building of the therapeutic alliance.

Envy, Competition, and Devaluation

Other negative transference manifestations run the range from envy of the therapist's nurturant qualities, to competition with the therapist or the therapist's other patients, to attempts to negate the therapist's interventions or good intentions by devaluing them. The most insidious reactions that may actually threaten the treatment is the "devalued parent" transference. Through the defense mechanism of "identification with the aggressor" (A. Freud, 1936; Ganzarain & Buchele, 1988), these patients unconsciously take on the insensitive, attacking qualities of their caretaker and make the therapist feel as unworthy as they did as children.

Although most eating disorder patients will have a difficult time putting their feelings into words, some will act on their own feelings by attacking the treatment indirectly. Their self-destructive behaviors often escalate. They may not show up for sessions. They may not make use of or value the treatment that they are offered. Demanding that the therapist change his or her style or technique, they may need or request referral to another treater. They may appear to be doing well while they are actually thwarting the treatment, reflecting negative feelings they have about the therapist or themselves. In these cases, the self is inevitably perceived as a victim of the therapist who is experienced as the sadistic parent (Kernberg, 1995, 2005).

When the patient devalues the therapist, the therapist may point out that the patient is asserting autonomy by saying what is on her or his mind while rebelling against treatment. This masochistic dynamic is blatantly evidenced simultaneously when even a severely ill patient will forbid the therapist to intervene to save life and chide, "I don't want you taking over my body" (Zerbe, 1993a)! In these perilous situations, such patients would rather die than give in to what they perceive as the therapist's desire for control. They undermine and belittle what treaters attempt to do therapeutically because they maintain the fixed idea that the true self can survive only if the physical body dies.

Simultaneously, they envy the therapist's capacity to reach out to help, and they abhor any expression of warmth, humor, or tenderness. Their negative transference feelings can be understood as deriving from what was internalized within the original family nexus and must now be projected outward or displaced onto the therapist. The self is thereby rid of mental poisons. On these occasions it is the therapist's task to (1) contain the raw, angry, negative contents that are being projected, and (2) tolerate and interpret the concomitant separation and autonomous strivings the patient is also likely to be expressing.

Clinical Example

Michael, age 30, made significant progress in modifying binge eating in 24 sessions of manualized cognitive-behavioral therapy. Pleased that he had also finally "begun to get my act together," he decided to heed the psychiatrist's suggestion to do more work on family-of-origin issues. Over the next 18 months of individual and group psychotherapy, Michael's eating disorder stayed in remission as he made additional progress in interpersonal relationships and at work. For the first time in his adult life, he was able to set limits with a demanding, intrusive father and to curtail sexual acting out. He was developing his first, long-term serious relationship with another man when his individual psychotherapy process took a sudden, rocky downward dive.

The patient began to miss sessions, complain about the cost of therapy, and threatened to quit because the therapist was, "Just like my father—a jerk who thinks he knows all the answers and tells everybody what to do." Despite the therapist's insistence that Michael was feeling intense, important feelings and grappling with memories that needed further work, the patient suddenly broke off the therapy.

The therapist understood this action as Michael's need to curtail intimacy with a significant male and to try to launch himself in the separation-individuation process. Michael's transference devaluation, based on displacement of these feelings from his narcissistic father onto his male therapist, thwarted the momentum of his process until he returned to therapy six months later. Overcoming a sense of shame and defeat, Michael had regained some capacity to see that his therapist did not act like and was not his father. In essence, Michael took back his projections but in so doing came into contact with how he had felt repeatedly maligned by his father in his youth. His demeaning views of himself led him later to plead "to be taken back into therapy despite bad behavior," alerting the therapist that there was perhaps a new opportunity for Michael to gain access to tendencies for self-sabotage based on faulty internalization of good objects.

Peer, Friend, and the "Real" Object

As noted by Kohut (1971, 1977, 1984), patients will from time to time experience the therapist as a sibling, friend, or even mirror image of themselves.

This "twinship transference" is a common occurrence in patients who have eating disorders, particularly as they move away from masochistic traits and gain autonomy. In an effort to cultivate self-definition, early on patients will look to the therapist as an idealized parent imago but this view must shift for the therapy to move forward. Just as the developing child must make friends and cultivate peer relationships outside the home, so must the eating disorder patient test out in the therapy some newfound qualities of making and keeping friends and finding commonality with others.

Twinship needs are vital for development and indicate that the individual has found an "intense and pervasive sense of security as he feels himself to be a human among humans" (Kohut, 1984, p. 200). The phenomenon of, "I see some of you in me and some of me in you" often takes on a playful form. The sense that the patient is relating to the therapist as a peer or friend harkens improved object relations in the outside world and the beginning of a twinship transference. Although the therapist may perceive that the patient is engaging on a more realistic level with others outside of the treatment hours, transference feelings are very much alive within it.

Clinical Example

Sidney, a 34-year-old patient with a history of anorexia and severe depression was four years along in her recovery. She had begun to experience a range of pleasureful activities in her daily life. For example, some days she would come to her session and spontaneously review a new restaurant she had recently sampled. She would say, "There is plenty of good food in this town. You need to try out some of these places." On other occasions she would relate a new activity or interest and confide, "I even went to see a sexy movie." Sidney seemed to intuit that her therapist also had hobbies and outside interests and was pleased that they were likely not the same as her own.

Sidney rarely asked the therapist any personal questions but kept the focus of the sessions on her enlarging sphere of life. However, as the patient began to experience greater physical and emotional health, the therapist noted within herself a series of shifting countertransference feelings. Instead of being worried about Sidney's health, her dysphoria, or her future, she actually looked forward to the hours because Sidney seemed "so much more alive."

On one memorable day, Sidney burst into her session and pulled out three new sports bras from her backpack. Besotted with her boyfriend and preparing to go on a hiking excursion, she regaled the therapist with the attributes of each of the bras. She even advised the therapist about where she might buy some for herself. The therapist registered what must have been an aghast look at this "girl talk," as it seemed to come completely out of the blue from their earlier therapeutic work. Bemused that she had thrown the therapist temporarily off her mark, Sidney teased, "Doc, do they give you hazard pay for your work?"

In addition to reflecting a livelier sense of the self, Sidney exuded a twin-ship transference because she treated the therapist more like a peer and less as an authority in this instance. Sidney's teasing is a demonstration of self-awareness and an intensified sense of aliveness and joy in a simple human activity, elements that Kohut believed essential to growth. Note the pleasure the patient takes in catching the clinician off guard, not unlike a child who has gotten away with pulling a prank on an unsuspecting sister or brother. The humor and vitality in this therapeutic moment further demonstrate how the process is moving ahead based on commonality of experience and mutual recognition between patient and therapist where the patient locates "a security . . . a sense of belonging and participating . . . [and] confirmation of the feeling that one is a human being among other human beings" (Kohut, 1984, p. 2003).

Inanimate Objects

Transference is not simply a phenomenon that we have toward other human beings. Transference frequently occurs to our pets, our cars, and even other possessions. Naming one's car or pets is a manifestation of our transferential love for that object. Notice, also, how some people call their pets "my kids" and enjoy indulging them. By the same token, one sees corollary transferences to animals that are tragic; sociopaths, who frequently have been severely abused in childhood or witnessed ghastly trauma, torture animals as a way of displacing or depositing their hatred and destructiveness.

Sometimes persons with eating disorders have trouble making human connections. Their deepest connections appear to be with nonhumans in their environment (e.g., their pets or possessions). They may also signal establishing a deeper level of feeling toward the therapist by talking about the therapist's possessions (e.g., office furniture, books, works of art) or imitating a hobby or interest that the therapist has. Their "transference" becomes speakable only between the lines, as they tell the therapist about an object in their world that has gained special significance and, paradoxically, helps them feel more anchored and ready for human connectedness.

Clinical Example

For most of her adult life, Miriam, a 50-year-old stockbroker who had never married, struggled with episodic binge drinking, reveled in buying and selling high-risk bonds, and indulged in subclinical bingeing and purging followed by lengthy periods of self-starvation. Even though her symptoms were significant and caused her worry, she never sought therapy until she suffered significant financial reversals at her job, largely because of her high risk behaviors and poor judgment.

Miriam had no friends, had never had a serious romantic relationship, and her two-story townhouse was almost completely devoid of any material possessions.

She prided herself on being a "minimalist, tried and true" except when "I get an idea that a new market will explode and I buy all of it I can." Even after 2½ years of twice weekly psychotherapy, she continued to dismiss and seemingly devalue the therapist when the clinician brought up absences, the fee, or any other notable aspects of the interpersonal relationship between them. Indeed, when the therapist would probe Miriam's responses the patient would say, "We have no relationship. This is strictly professional. I pay you and you do your job." Miriam was letting the therapist know that her internal world was as empty as her townhouse and that it was difficult for her to allow anyone to matter.

Although the therapist at first understandably felt put off by Miriam's seemingly devaluing remarks, she came to understand their derivatives as she learned more about the patient's early family life. Not surprisingly, Miriam had been severely mistreated and neglected in the family of origin. She believed that no one could ever care about her because she was repeatedly told she was worthless and unlovable. She found it difficult to invest in herself, a pattern that was highlighted by the therapist when Miriam would attempt to stop the treatment because, "It just costs too much money." The therapist noted that Miriam's attempts to stop the treatment always followed an absence on the therapist's part; when she would attempt to help the patient elaborate on the importance of their attachment, Miriam would attempt to flee by saying their connection "doesn't matter because you come and go whenever you want."

One of the therapist's hobbies was collecting, learning about, and repairing watches. Again belying her attachment to the therapist, Miriam would comment frequently on the different watches the therapist would wear. Sometimes she would even ask her where she got them. It was difficult to engage this schizoid patient in normal everyday conversation and much of the time was spent in a supportive process, helping the patient to make simple observations, learn to keep a dialogue going with another human being, and otherwise begin to get to know the human world.

After several months of sprinkling questions about watches into the therapy, Miriam came into a session very excited one day. She told the therapist she "found my own dream watch." She proceeded to name the brand and asked many questions about it. She elaborated on the internal watch movement, the band, and other aspects of the watch she had been studying. She was particularly fond of the fact that the watch was 18 carat gold.

Although Miriam could not acknowledge that she cared for herself or valued the therapeutic relationship, the watch symbolized a bridge to a connection to the therapist and to the new self. Miriam could not talk about her feelings for the therapist directly but, in metaphor, she could acknowledge the beauty, specialness, and uniqueness of the watch. She wore it with great pride and, like a small child, particularly enjoyed showing it off to the therapist. The watch, an inanimate object, was a stand-in for the therapist and contained burgeoning elements of the positive transference and engagement with the human world.

MANAGING COMMON COUNTERTRANSFERENCE REACTIONS

Clinicians of all theoretical persuasions are challenged to become more self-aware of our internal reactions when working with eating disorder patients. Frequently, our interventions can and should be informed by our countertransference responses (see Zerbe, 1995c, for a case in point). Patients with eating disorders tend to engender a range of feelings in therapists; the task becomes one of utilizing these very feelings in a constructive way. To reconcile these intense and sometimes troubling countertransference feelings, the therapist must first become aware of them, particularly the strong desire to cure our patients. At such times the therapist may be tempted to offer more reassurance, more interpretation, and more education than is ultimately in the patient's best interest. By recognizing that a sense of uselessness stems from the patient's inner emptiness or need to defeat the treatment, the therapist is more likely to tolerate a more reflective approach and be less tempted to act on these difficulties by giving "too much of a good feed." Again, silent containment of the patient's affective storms remains the primary step in ego mastery and identity formation for these patients.

What follows is a systematic discussion of some of the most frequently encountered countertransference reactions that therapists need to manage to avoid feeling excessively burdened or defeated in the treatment (see Table 8.2).

TABLE 8.2 Common countertransference reactions

- Therapist may experience guilt, anxiety, anger (i.e., via projection identification with the patient's inner anguish)
- Therapist may experience exhaustion, despair, and psychophysiological complaints (i.e., via projection as patient seeks to rid herself of intolerable, intense feelings)
- Therapist may worry excessively about the medical consequences, suicidality, or potential for death, especially in the "chronic" or severely emaciated patient
- Therapist may become more self-conscious of her or his own body, weight, and body image
- Therapist may feel excessive sense of power, control, and grandiosity (e.g., the "seduction of idealization")
- Therapist may irrationally fear making mistakes or acknowledging human weakness (even though patient has developmental need for modeling, and seeing therapist as a "real" person, with imperfections)
- Therapist may feel tinges of excitement, including erotic excitement, particularly as patient improves
- If the patient has been the victim of sexual or physical trauma or is highly sadomasochistic, therapist may feel induced to abrogate the usual therapeutic boundaries
- Therapist may experience boredom due to patient's disavowed feelings, excessive focus on weight or somatic concerns, or repeatedly going over the same details of their history
- Therapist may feel induced to make patient feel special, unique, or valued

No amount of reading, however, can equal the importance of ongoing consultation or supervision to psychologically nourish the clinician and help master some of the powerful feelings that get stirred by a group of illnesses that are life threatening, and derive from early disturbances in attachment patterns, serious parental misattunement, overt physical and sexual trauma, and biological differences in temperament. Indeed, these developmental exigencies contribute to the difficulties many patients have in doing better. The persistence of a pattern of self-defeat is another of the most difficult countertransference feelings to manage and requires particular attention by the therapist who can easily be provoked to become "a bad object."

One of the most frequently asked questions concerns the sex of the therapist and the particular countertransference constellations likely to arise when a male or female treats the patient. Wooley (1991, 1994) observed that sometimes a male therapist may be more helpful than a female for the anorexic patient in the early stages of treatment. In this situation, the male's tendency to relate logically and to educate helps the patient establish a feeling of safety. Other patients will benefit from a more neutral and emotionally distant therapist. Wooley also noted that female therapists who are sensitive to the patient's need to avoid intense emotional involvement and intimacy may also foster solid collaboration.

In general, either gender may treat eating disorders as long as countertransference issues are managed appropriately. Patient preferences for working with a man or a woman should always be respected. Because boundaries are likely to be tested regardless of therapist gender, it is essential for the therapist to have a fulfilled life outside the office (Gabbard, 1989, 1996; Gabbard & Lester, 1996; Gabbard & Wilkinson, 1994). A therapist whose needs for intimacy are not being met may defensively seem aloof because of feeling devalued, worthless, and frustrated while the patient tries to foster closeness by demanding more and more "special" contact.

For those patients who came from homes lacking in psychological nurturance, particularly when there has been serious maltreatment or abuse, the therapist may pick up on significant neediness on the part of the individual. In these situations, the patient may ask the therapist to be more "real," demand physical contact or expressions of concern outside of the hours (such as daily phone calls or e-mail contact), or otherwise pull for a more "giving" or "parental response." Although some therapists now advocate direct expression of caring, including sharing one's feelings or giving hugs, on most occasions the therapist will want to avoid demonstrations of this kind; it is preferable instead to look deeply into oneself and what is elicited in the countertransference. That is, a prescription for a departure from a more neutral role and deviation from technical abstinence may reflect countertransference engendered by the illness—the wish to give to the patient that supersedes, compensates for, or repairs an original developmental failure that should only be processed, worked through, and eventually mourned.

In these situations, therapists must remember that extraordinary efforts to make up for earlier wounds may only exacerbate the patient's condition. Although the therapist may feel compelled to nurture the patient directly, the patient is best served by establishing a safe holding environment where all feelings and the residual effects of historical trauma can be explored with words. This ultimately nurtures the patient in the most appropriate therapeutic way by promoting a mature and boundaried relationship without provoking terror or excessive sexual arousal.

This is not to say that the therapist can never "step out" of the clinical role to be human. Although it is important to guard against overindulgence that may be fulfilling an unmet need of the therapist as much as it is consciously intended to help the patient, sometimes a small deviation (giving a gift; going to a graduation; telling a little bit about one's life) may be a necessary element that aids recovery. In these situations, it's best to seek consultation. Although eating disorder patients are very engaging and bright, the subspecialty has been plagued by boundary violations where, "implicit exploitation is inevitably countertherapeutic, if not frankly destructive" (Russell & Meares, 1997, p. 695).

CLINICAL RATIONALE INFORMED BY RESEARCH

Quantitative research demonstrates that countertransference phenomena can actually be measured clinically. This research further enables clinicians to recognize that there are common and predictable responses to certain groups of patients. Though individual clinicians may respond idiosyncratically to a particular patient, there are also some general responses that are expectable among groups. Thus, patients who tend to be overwhelming or stir a sense of helplessness in one therapist are more than likely to do this with other therapists as well.

Interestingly, this important countertransference research has also demonstrated that clinicians' countertransference reactions do not vary much because of a particular theoretical orientation. These data suggest that regardless of diagnosis, clinicians "of all theoretical persuasions should attend to and, where possible, make use of information provided in the context of the therapeutic relationship, including their own responses to the patient" (Betan, Kegley-Heim, Conklin, & Westen, 2005). Regardless of whether or not one practices primarily from a cognitive-behavioral, psychodynamic, multimodal or eclectic perspective, common countertransference scenarios are evoked that provide a "unique opportunity to understand the fears, defenses, and sometimes perverse satisfactions" that contribute to the clinical picture (Hughes, 1997, pp. 268–269).

In an important empirical study of 71 clinicians who were identified as specialists in the treatment of eating disorders, Franko and Rolfe (1996) found that anorexic patients evoked more anger, worry, and frustrations than patients with bulimia nervosa. Those therapists who had a greater number of eating disorder patients in their caseload felt more beleaguered and frustrated than those who treated fewer anorexics and bulimics, possibly because eating disorder patients "often demand more resources than other patient groups (more contact with other professionals and family members, as well as potential medical complications)" (p. 114). Franko and Rolfe also suggested that therapists take advantage of opportunities to "ventilate" and have peers or supervisors "validate" their responses "to ensure that they [therapists' feelings] are not acted on toward the patient" even though these understandable reactions will be difficult "to contend with under the best of circumstances" (p. 114).

The data summarized in this frequently cited study lend statistical validation to the wide range of affects that clinicians report they experience in supervisory sessions. Franko and Rolfe concluded, "As clinicians become aware of their feelings and learn appropriate ways to express and deal with their countertransference, both patients and therapists are likely to benefit" (p. 115). Research of this kind can only enhance treatment because of the implicit permission it gives the therapist to both acknowledge and get support for whatever is uncovered or stirred in the therapy; moreover, it lends credence to the range of overt and covert reactions the therapist encounters regardless of training, level of experience, choice of therapeutic technique or training and adaptations one makes when working in a pluralistic field. Applying Harry Stack Sullivan's famous remark, "We are all simply more human than otherwise," clinicians may also take solace in the fact that contemporary research also confirms that our countertransference feelings are also simply human and may wisely inform the therapeutic journey.

COUNTERTRANSFERENCE TO OUR CULTURE

In 1991, Dr. Catherine Steiner-Adair, an educator, clinician, and research scientist at Harvard University, described how therapists are as prone to being as affected by the culture and media stereotypes as are our patients. Steiner-Adair coined the term *cultural countertransference* for these reactions, which may catapult the therapist into making statements that unwittingly thwart recovery from an eating disorder (Steiner-Adair, 1991b). She observed that both dismissing the role of culture or introducing its destructive role in perpetuating eating disorders prematurely may interfere with therapeutic progress.

Steiner-Adair advised therapists to carefully and repeatedly examine their own reactions to cultural ideals, the diet mentality, and the desire for physical perfection, attitudes that undoubtedly will evolve over the course of our careers but can commonly be unconscious for even the most seasoned psychotherapist. Therapists who work with eating disorder patients are advised to be vigilant about the various countertransferences we have to the culture (Bloom et al., 1994; Farrell, 2000; Gutwill, 1994a) and to the role that dieting and body image plays in Western society (Gutwill, 1994b).

Sometimes discussing food and body image may be a resistance to deepening the therapeutic process, but at other times the patient needs "to identify and resist disabling cultural norms" (Steiner-Adair, 1991b, p. 239) by expressing thoughts about noxious elements of the culture to the therapist. The patient should not be confronted at these pivotal moments with the idea that they are resisting deeper work (Gutwill 1994a, 1994b; Steiner-Adair, 1991b) by focusing on their feelings about the media and the thin ideal. Clearly, clinical judgment is essential because at other times the therapist may inadvertently place too much emphasis on these cultural issues and contribute to the patient's reluctance to address family, individual, or medical issues.

As Susan Gutwill (1994a), a feminist psychoanalyst at the Women's Therapy Centre Institute in New York, further noted regarding therapists' work with cultural countertransference responses:

> Food and body obsessions both hide and give an opening to the deeper communications. . . . Although reference to the culture can, and indeed sometimes does, operate as a defense, the client still can and should be helped to know the deep grief, shame, and confusion spawned by her relationships to cultural symbols and institutions. (pp. 150–151)

Just as we therapists must help the patient become aware of how each person has transference feelings about the culture in which we live, and make those transference feelings to culture accessible and speakable in treatment, so must we also make use of ongoing self-scrutiny, reading, and consultation to rectify blind spots we have to the prevailing culture that may be impacting the treatment (e.g., our cultural countertransference).

BIOLOGICAL CONSIDERATIONS

Just as transference responses are based in biology, so do countertransference patterns ultimately reflect activation of the therapist's neural networks. These brain based mechanisms are another clinical implication of contemporary neuroscience that informs our work; the same patient's behavior is likely to elicit different reactions in different therapists because of neural network activation unique to each therapist (Solms & Turnbull, 2002; Westen & Gabbard, 2002). That is, when implicit declarative and procedural memories are evoked by a patient, automatic behaviors, defense mechanisms, and object relations patterns of the therapist are aroused that are fundamentally *biologically* based. As Gabbard (2006b) further described:

> Obviously, the patient also will stimulate particular networks lying in a potential state within the analyst. Hence, the patient's actual behavior may elicit reactions in the analyst that are desired unconsciously by the process of projective identification. . . . Some projected representations may be a better "fit" with a given analyst than others, both in the sense that they may be more concordant with the analyst's characteristics and that a given analyst may be more or less vulnerable to different kinds of countertransference. Analysts, like anyone else, differ in the extent to which their temperament and experience have laid down strong neural "tracks" that predispose them to take on particular roles. (pp. 284–286)

The therapist's implicit learning system (mediated by the ventromedial frontal cortex) enables us to make those intuitive, empathic responses that may "form the basis for the countertransference" (Solms & Turnbull, 2002). Judgments we make based on "intuition" are now believed to be finely honed neurobiological activities of the frontal lobes. In an era where neuroscience research is rapidly expanding, therapists can expect to learn more about how our countertransference reactions can be brought into conscious control while valuing how change also occurs nonconsciously based on diverse neural mechanisms that shape the coconstructed space between therapist and patient and result in implicit and explicit therapeutic actions (Pally, 2005).

MAKING USE OF THE THERAPIST'S COUNTERTRANSFERENCE REACTIONS

Based on her own experience as a patient and then psychoanalyst, Margaret Little explained that therapeutic success usually "depends upon how far we ourselves, despite our anxiety, can really accept and live by the very things we are trying to get our patients to accept" (1981, p. 152). The frequently quoted aphorism of our supervisors that "the patient can go only as far as the therapist" derives from the clinical wisdom of knowing oneself as fully as possible and bringing uncomfortable feelings that are inevitably stirred in the therapy into consciousness. In the sections that follow, I review some of the most disturbing countertransference responses encountered in working with eating disorder patients (see Table 8.2). Although uncovering and baring these feelings inevitably causes strain, growth and change are promoted when the therapist is "willing to feel, about his patient, with his patient, and sometimes even for his patient, in the sense of supplying feelings which the patient is unable to find in himself" (Little, 1981, p. 58).

Anxiety

The medical and psychological issues of bulimics and anorexics elicit significant anxiety in the therapist. Because the therapist will find her- or himself often anxious, we must become comfortable in posing a query about the nature of our patient's anxiety and need to make us worry (Hughes, 1997; Little, 1981, 1985; Zerbe, 1998, 1999, 2002b). This temporary, trial identification allows the therapist to gain some distance from the emotions that cause strain and are vexing; it promotes an opportunity to get to know our patient's inner world. Although it is difficult for the therapist to tolerate the anxiety, frustration, and the wish to rid the patient of these feelings, we must first understand and tolerate this distress (Zerbe, 1988, 1990, 1992a) so that the patient may ultimately know and master those emotions that disrupt their lives.

Clinical experience demonstrates how countertransference anxieties can run the gamut from fear of losing the patient through death to fear of loss of the patient's affection and positive regard, to worry that the patient will prematurely end the work or sabotage her progress. Those anxieties that seem to be about ultimate survival or annihilation derive from the patient's earliest infancy, and like all other issues must be understood, interpreted, and worked through for lasting relief. Psychological milestones on the patient's part can be said to be met when the therapist's countertransference anxiety is sparked less by the question of whether or not the patient will live or wants to live but more by how the patient will manage problems of living, including the inevitable fears of moving ahead, separating and mourning, and maintaining a sense of self-worth, even in times of stress, loss, and backsliding.

Clinical Example

For the first four years of treatment, Kit's life seemed on the brink of disaster. Requiring several periods of hospitalization for low weight, a sense that life was not worth living, and frustration that she would be "forever a failure" despite her obvious intellectual gifts and compassion for others, she stirred significant countertransference anxiety in her therapist. A consultant psychoanalyst made the observation that the therapist had successfully identified with Kit's annihilation anxiety and urged the therapeutic couple to continue their work until Kit was less despairing and more self-confident.

A shift in the nature of the countertransference anxiety alerted the therapist to how Kit's "journey from sickness to health" (Little, 1981) was coming about. Openly expressing anger, disappointment, and frustration with the psychodynamically oriented therapist, Kit was on the verge of making a notable foray into separation. For her part, the therapist felt she did nothing right as Kit complained and devalued the treatment, but she also did not worry about Kit's survival as she had in the past. This altered countertransference perception became accessible to verbal interpretation and a change in the treatment plan. The therapeutic couple mutually decided that it was time for Kit to transfer to another treater who would work on specific behaviors. The therapist was left to work through countertransference anxiety of separation and loss of self-esteem much as the parent of an adolescent must bear the pain of separation and growth even as the teen disavows angst at moving ahead.

Grappling with all of the feelings stirred by moving ahead or beyond the therapist is one of the most ubiquitous issues I have observed in supervisees and in myself that must be dealt with during termination (see Chapter 3). Like Kit, many patients leave without giving the therapist credit at the time of transition, and the feelings stirred must be contained and processed to avoid disrupting the patient's flourishing.

Feelings of Admiration and Love

As the patient makes progress in treatment, positive countertransference reactions naturally flourish. Although it is legitimate to feel a sense of pride and accomplishment for progress in the work, the therapist must avoid the tendency to want the patient to grow as a positive reflection on the therapist. Of course, this is an ideal that no therapist can ever achieve in absolute terms. After all, we have our needs to see our work have meaning and value, and none of us is without a quotient of narcissism about what we accomplish.

The patient's false self-system can be relinquished only as new paths are discovered, and movement can occur only at the patient's own behest, not ours. When the patient becomes more lively and expressive, the therapist may be importuned to make the patient feel special or recognized, especially if there were gaps in appropriate mirroring in the family of origin. Some patients put pressure on the treater to be more like a colleague or a friend. Patient and therapist are vulnerable at those moments when identity is consolidating, and the patient is moving through a normative separation-individuation process. The patient also pulls on the therapist's heart strings for a return of the affection. Both members of the dyad are better served by relinquishing the relationship and beginning the hard work of mourning.

As Rinsley (1980, 1982) observed regarding the needs of adolescents who move beyond their narcissistic, internalized parents who stymied growth, gratification on the therapist's part is permitted—but only to a point. The patient's natural urge to expand her universe and to separate in a healthy way must be fostered, even encouraged, even though this ultimately means saying goodbye to the therapist. The therapist who is aware of feelings of affection, admiration, and even love for a patient must use these positive feelings only in the service of the treatment, not as a ruse to receive personal, excessive gratification for him- or herself.

Clinical Example

Few people would suspect that Angus, age 40, periodically deprived himself of certain types of food that he enjoyed. He chose a diet of bland, flavorless staples, rarely allowing himself to eat rich meats, pastas, or sauces. Angus insisted he was not afraid of gaining weight and he was otherwise healthy and athletic. History confirmed that he "did not deserve" to have pleasure because he was deprived of mirroring and acceptance in the family of origin. Angus shared numerous examples of childhood maltreatment, and his therapist felt particularly tender and sad when he revealed how he had been forbidden to attend an important school event until he finished fixing the family stove. Angus reported that his father always said, "Do exactly what your mother tells you. Get the work done and then—maybe—you can play." This motif transformed in adulthood to a pervasive sense of worthlessness, workaholism, and avoidance of any kind of pleasure. Culinary treats were a particular anathema, perhaps because they represented the foreboding and forbidding maternal representation.

Shifts in Angus's internal world became manifest when he began to participate in pleasurable activities, including cooking. One day he brought a sample of his favorite new pasta dish for the therapist to try. Initially, he was self-effacing and shy, telling the therapist "you'll probably not like it much but it's a big deal for me to bring it to you." The therapist felt Angus's sense of pride and accomplishment as well as she enjoyed a delicious lunch. She also realized that by bringing the food, the patient was testing out whether or not she could be different from the original maternal object, and that this milestone in the work represented implicit affection between her and Angus, made symbolically explicit by the gift of food, and the joy he found in sharing his cooking talent. Angus was nourishing the therapist much as he had felt nourished and nurtured by her encouragement for him to become less self-punitive and take on more activities that affirmed a benevolent sense of self. Although termination was not yet around the corner, the therapist recognized in her feelings of admiration at his transformation that he would likely continue to test out his capacity to gain pleasure in activities unrelated to treatment and eventually be able to move on.

Aggression and Anger

When one feels angry or hateful toward the patient, containment and silent processing is the best therapeutic tact (Gabbard, 1989; Zerbe, 1992a, 1993b). This enables the patient to develop the capacity to self-soothe over a sufficient period of time and to have a sense of obect constancy. It also permits the therapist to take private space (Modell, 1976, 1993; Zerbe, 2007a, 1993b) to reflect on what is happening in the dyad on a deeper level.

Psychoanalyst M. Farrell (2000) called this therapeutic work "the silent and compassionate toleration" of difficult feelings and makes an important analogy to containing and tolerating "vomit within the sessions." Drawing on the work of Harold Boris (1984a, 1984b), Farrell believed that the therapist must "become what the child felt the mother could never be, a container and processor of her feelings, thoughts, and terrifying anxieties" (p. 78). In other words, the anger the therapist experiences may be "undigested material" that the patient may never have brought into the family of origin lest it be met with withdrawal or retaliation. For over a decade, I have shown a slide of Frida Kahlo's *Without Hope* (1945), in which Frida vomits up objects in her internal world to graphically make this point to audiences of therapists. Most of us relate to this image because we have on many occasions experienced being "vomited on" in treatment by having our interventions attacked and discarded.

By silently processing the countertransference aggression and anger, the therapist demonstrates that intense, negative feelings can be survived. One is able to help the patient move to new territory especially when the most difficult, noxious feelings are seen as important, meaningful, understandable, and, most essentially, part of the human condition. As noted previously (Chapters 2, 4, 5), patients may have had creative bursts or significant abilities that went unnoticed and unnurtured; the eating disorder serves as a defensive activity to hide their creativity in the family of origin. These patients may become angry as they improve and may simultaneously experience blocks in their work, their relationships, or even their recovery. They appear to be prisoners of their own success, held back by development of the true self. For these individuals, moving ahead in life "brings in its wake intense feelings of transgression, anguish, and guilt" (McDougall, 1999, p. 209). These powerful emotions must be psychologically worked through in the treatment "to heal the drive to destruction of oneself and/or others and thus overcome feelings of fragmentation and disorientation" (p. 211).

Clinical Example

Cybil, age 29, made dramatic gains in her first year of therapy. This overweight binge eater with comorbid bipolar disorder was grateful to her therapist for helping her stay out of the hospital, manage weight-related side effects of the medication used to treat bipolar disorder (e.g., carbamazapine and lithium), and significantly curtail her binge eating. Her relationship with her partner of five years also appeared to have stabilized, even though Cybil was pessimistic that they would ever "be sexual enough to suit me, given Marina's history of trauma and terrible relationship with her mother."

Perhaps these improvements were more difficult for Cybil to internalize than they at first appeared. Seemingly out of the blue she began blasting her therapist for "giving me hope that life can be better." For three months she spoke bitterly about "the bogus business of therapy where you can look at the past but not the present" and then decided to terminate precipitously. She demanded to see a psychopharmacologist and traveled several hundred miles to have a follow-up. It is important to note that this psychopharmacologist did not change the medication regimen, met only briefly at twice-monthly intervals, and urged Cybil to continue therapy at some point in the future. There was never a concern that either the binge eating or bipolar disorder were out of control.

This scenario of patient improvement followed by therapeutic impasse can stir a plethora of countertransference responses ranging from impotence to bitterness to "good riddance." In Cybil's case, the therapist primarily experienced anger and frustration, which were successfully contained and processed in a peer supervision group. Indeed, the therapist found a modicum of relief in hearing from others in the group that similar situations had happened to them. Nonetheless, the therapist's reaction persisted for some time. Although the therapist had a conscious understanding of why Cybil might be so attacking (i.e., the patient was quite ashamed of her illnesses and was sadistically and repeatedly demeaned by both parents in childhood), aggression of this type activates our internal critic (i.e., superego) as therapists, and we are also left fuming. The patient's inner rage and devaluation is projected into us and exacerbates any sadistic, attacking internal objects of our own.

The Therapist's Need to Change the Patient

The excessive need to change the patient or *furor therapeuticus* on the part of the therapist reflects underlying despair in the patient, and the projection onto the therapist of omnipotence. Given the developmental deficits that many of our patients have sustained and our own pull to try to reverse these gaps by "giving something good," therapists are prone to succumb to the temptation to give more and more. That is, instead of listening, containing, and processing with the patient, we become action oriented or attempt to reparent the patient. Giving too much advice or caving in to the patient's demands for more time or specialness are just two of the ways this frequent scenario occurs (see Hughes, 1997 for an excellent example of this reaction).

Via projective identification, these patients are inducing in us the tendency to become the parent they never had. This avoids the difficult task of helping them mourn the life they actually had, and moving forward. When the therapist is placed in the position of doing more and more for the patient, we must remember the maxim of Giovacchini (1980) who advised maintaining a neutral stance because mother's milk is never satisfying to an adult.

Clinical Example

Dr. W., a postdoctoral fellow in clinical psychology, was called by a psychiatrist faculty member to provide individual psychotherapy for a long term, chronic anorexia nervosa patient. Initially Dr. W. felt a sense of pride and accomplishment when this psychiatrist selected him out of a group of other psychology fellows because "you are up to the task of helping this engaging woman. I am impressed by your case formulations and therapeutic skills in the weekly seminar [I lead]."

Dr. W. saw the patient for three consultative visits that seemed to go well. Then the patient mysteriously cancelled further appointments without explanation, and attempts by Dr. W. to have her return failed. When Dr. W. explained the situation to the psychiatrist, the physician simply said, "She does that. Keep trying." Eventually the patient showed up and again kept several appointments and then stopped. This occurred about five times over the course of two years for a total of 17 psychotherapy sessions.

The point to emphasize in this vignette was Dr. W.'s feeling that it was a therapeutic duty to help the patient want to come to therapy and to change. In part, this countertransference anxiety was stimulated by the psychiatrist's statements that Dr. W. had special abilities and should indefinitely persist in trying to help. Dr. W. also liked this patient and sincerely hoped a path could be found to help her move from the stage of precontemplation to more active contemplation for change (Prochaska & DiClemente, 1986, 1992). After reviewing Michael Strober's (2004, 2006) seminal work on chronic anorexia, Dr. W. became more sober and realistic about this patient's capacity to make dramatic progress and embraced the idea of helping the patient to "become a bit more comfortable in life and manage her disease but not hope for a miracle" (see also Yager, 2007b).

The most important shift occurred within Dr. W. Through self-analysis and supervision, he came to realize that his excessive need to change the patient was a manifestation of the countertransference frequently encountered among psychotherapists of eating disorder patients. Although this reaction likely stems from a variety of personal dynamics unique to each therapist (e.g., the wish to cure one's parent or sibling), as a general rule we must all come to grips with our omnipotent desires to foster change and that doing "just a little" may not only be what *can* be done but is actually the intervention of *choice*, especially for our more chronic, difficult-to-treat patients.

Psychophysiological Reactions in the Therapist

As noted by Maltsberger and Buie (1974), the therapist's self-esteem is on the line when treating patients who are slow moving and exhibit negativity in the treatment. There is a tendency for treaters to turn against themselves and become self-punishing. As we strive to help our patients, we may also identify with any sadomasochistic tendencies they may have (Bromberg, 1996; Geltner, 2005; McDougall, 1980, 1985, 2001). These responses tend to accumulate over time and may find expression in an array of psychosomatic reactions within the therapist's body. These range from headaches, muscle soreness, and stomachache, to an actual fear of weight gain or preoccupation with one's physique (Zerbe, 1993a, 1995c). All speak to the perturbations in the therapist's capacity to hear and work through distressing narrative material and affective storms that the patient brings to the hour.

The high referral rate of eating disorder patients to other medical specialists reflects not only objective complications of the eating disorder but the patient's inability to put intense feelings into words (Zerbe, 1992a, 1993a, 1993b, 2001a). Like other patients who have a psychophysiologic illness, the patient with an eating disorder frequently has a paucity of words with which to describe feelings. This derives from traumatic events, maltreatment, and neglect in early life. Eating disorder patients use their bodies to communicate intense intrapsychic pain (McDougall, 1980, 1989, 1999, 2001), and the therapist becomes privy to some of these preverbal and projected experiences. In fact, verbal interventions may not be heard by eating disorder patients because they live within the world of an autistic capsule (Ogden, 1989; Tustin, 1986, 1990) until their preverbal experience has been tapped by experiential therapies (Hornyak & Baker, 1989) or other modes of treatment.

Therapists may be pushed to touch, hold, or otherwise engage in a physical manner with a patient because of her or his libidinal need for safe touch. The patient's protective shell may also encapsulate the rage and annihilation they feel for the psychological, and sometimes physical, trauma of early life. When helping the eating disorder patient to realize that their body "speaks" (Erskine

& Judd, 1994; Kearney-Cooke & Isaacs, 2004; Kramer & Aktar, 1992) through these psychophysiological reactions, the words spoken in verbal therapies and the ministration of experiential therapies help secure some succor and sense of attachment that were not perceived or actually provided in earliest infancy and throughout childhood.

It is easy for therapists to find these reactions perplexing, frustrating, and frightening. We must recognize that physiological reactions on our part are a form of communication by the patient. Our goal is to uncover what these communications tell us. Moreover, patients inevitably have questions about the therapist's body image, body integrity, and whether or not we ourselves have ever had an eating disorder. These communications are all part of the psychophysiological continuum that must be addressed for treatment to proceed. One additional goal in these situations is to help the patient name the formerly nameless dread (McDougall, 1995, p. 160) and thereby help the patient bear witness to what happened in their early life in order to move forward.

Although I do not recommend that the therapist feel obligated to tell the patient about past or current issues concerning body image or eating issues, it behooves us to make the patient's fantasies about us speakable. We are then in a better position to trace back where the problem stems from (e.g., working with the resistance to the transference), a veritable and essential ego building exercise for the patient. In particular, therapists who are recovering from an eating disorder must use caution and discretion in what is shared; what may feel like an honest, empathic, useful acknowledgment may be, in actuality, a burden for the patient to carry. The patient may experience the revelation as "just too much" and be given to worry, overidentification, or entitlement for more personal revelation. Better to be clear and scrupulously consistent about personal boundaries so the patient can have a healthy object of identification and a safe haven to address feelings and fantasies without fear of harming the treater.

Clinical Examples

Dr. S., an engaging and exceptionally perceptive psychiatry resident, attended a lecture on the treatment of anorexia and bulimia. In the Q and A session that followed, she asked the presenter, who had then worked with eating disorder patients for more than a decade, whether or not the clinician's body image was ever affected by her patients. The lecturer quickly responded that she had not experienced this and quickly moved on to another question.

On further reflection after the talk, the lecturer became aware of some irritation at the resident's question. She probed her feelings a little deeper and remembered how a series of her patients had recently commented that their goal was never "to get fat like you." The lecturer was actually at a healthy weight for her age and regularly exercised. Yet, she suddenly realized that she had recently increased the frequency of her workouts and had become more preoccupied than ever before with appearing fit and attractive. She wondered if she had actually taken in and unconsciously identified with her patients' comments more than she had heretofore realized. Was the behavioral change in her life outside the office merely a sign of wanting to maintain her health, as she originally alleged to herself, or was there more going on unconsciously that had prompted her actions?

Self-analysis of these queries helped the therapist to consider that the critical remarks were projections of her patients' body disparagement that she was simultaneously containing and internalizing (i.e., personal countertransference). Her patients had successfully stirred up a nascent, and ubiquitous, anxiety in this treater who then became more aware of her reaction to living in a culture preoccupied with rigid standards of aging and beauty (i.e., cultural countertransference). Therapists must be alert that working with a group of patients who focus attention on the body and construct their sense of self on external success, beauty, and maintaining an idealized body image is likely to stir up these kinds of concerns in the therapist.

Dr. H., another seasoned therapist, noticed that during one of her patient's therapy hours she routinely became ravenously hungry. What alerted the treater to the countertransferential nature of the phenomena was how it occurred *only* with this particular patient, who had struggled with anorexia for many years, and not others who also had an overt or subclinical eating disorder. Her growling stomach occurred regardless of the time of day the sessions were held. It was unlikely that the treater was simply hungry or ill but more reflective of some unconscious communication between patient and therapist.

Again, self-analysis held a clue to solving this mystery. The patient's mother had died of cancer when the patient was only 8. The mother was unable to eat or to feed the patient for months before she died. This patient successfully projected into the therapist her sense of "being starved for affection" as well as her desire to be fed by a loving mother. The therapist's "countertransference hunger" alerted her to an important therapeutic issue that was elaborated over a period of months, permitting the patient to come into contact with a particular aspect of her grief and sense of loss for the first time. Her eating disorder remitted as her pathological identification with the cachetic mother was recognized; she began the arduous but essential work of mourning the early, traumatic death. The therapist's stomach noises stopped as she worked through her countertransference identification with the patient's child-self.

Testing Treatment Boundaries

When the patient begins to get curious about the therapist's outside life, particularly relationships the therapist has with others, competition and jealousy are usually sparked and require compassionate probing and elaboration. These conflictual feelings have usually gone underground in the patient's past and are embarrassing for the patient to describe. Triadic object relations invariably accompany the growth and development of all persons from infancy onward and become apparent in therapy as the patient makes forays into the world. The patient may also express concern or hold back during these forward steps because achievements have not been mirrored. They fear that their progress will prove destructive to the therapist as they move ahead or that the therapist will envy them.

An eroticized transference can also be a sign of progress but sometimes the patient may implore the therapist to violate boundaries. Therapists who work with eating disorder patients must remain vigilant because these erotic transferences may be quite intense and yet are often reflective of significant developmental achievements on the patient's part. Erotic transference feelings occur in opposite and same sex patient–therapist dyads.

A bottom line therapeutic stance to take when these sensitive issues arise is to encourage open expression, address the patient's fears of competition, loss, envy by the therapist, and excitement about new possibilities, and make sure that the patient is not engaging in false self compliance to assuage any unmet needs of the therapist. The patient's expression of mastery and experience of a true self are fueled when the therapist encourages expression of the full range of feelings, including sexual ones, and does not abandon or retreat when moving ahead occurs.

Clinical Example

Olivia is a 42-year-old, overweight, twice married graphic designer with a long history of sexual abuse in her youth and a severe eating disorder since age 12. She was admitted for residential treatment because her periods of bingeing and purging had placed her in medical jeopardy yet again. Her primary care clinician and current therapist jointly concluded that outpatient, multidisciplinary work was insufficient to reverse her downward spiral.

Olivia told the staff about her prior relationships with two male therapists that eventuated in sexual boundary violations. She had been working on this issue in her current process and had begun to put together facts that made sense, but these feelings also aroused remorse and shame. Her current therapist hypothesized that she was turning against the self by her inability to let go of her eating disorder symptoms. Having identified with the aggressor of the original abuse (i.e., her father and brother), Olivia had taken her revenge out on her prior therapists by excessive neediness and demands to "demonstrate love and caring." These therapists fell into the trap of trying to overtly gratify the patient and became sexually involved with her. Failing to take heed of their personal vulnerability and erotic countertransference feelings, they did not seek consultation, supervision, or a treatment process of their own. These violations set Olivia back in her quest to have a healthier and safer erotic experience with a peer. Rather than helping Olivia work through and experience her desires by putting her feelings into words, much as goes on unconsciously in a healthy family where good boundaries are kept during pivotal developmental steps, these therapists had repeated and exacerbated the original trauma.

In the current therapy process, Olivia tested boundaries yet again but in a totally different way. She begged her therapist, "If you *really* wanted to help me, you would tell me more about your life. That will give me a better role model for living than just going over my food journals and talking to you about what happened with my brother and dad." She was curious about the therapist's professional life, her friendships, and her husband and her children. She became angry when the therapist told her that they were working to understand and clarify issues in Olivia's—not the therapist's—life. This therapist empathized with Olivia's needs but made the clinical judgment that in this particular treatment the boundaries needed to be firm, clear, and consistent to help the patient feel safe.

The current therapist frequently sought consultation to help her work on her countertransference anxiety and to master the sense that she was failing her patient whose eating problem seemed so refractory. The consultant was able to point out some subtle, incremental gains (Zerbe, 1988) that suggested how Olivia might be moving toward better functioning even though the manifest symptoms were not diminishing. For example, Olivia started to enjoy creative outlets and she became more forthcoming with staff on the residential unit.

The consultant suggested the therapist tell Olivia (1) she would never get enough information about the therapist to satisfy her, and (2) she was testing the therapist to see whether or not she would allow Olivia to have healthy self-interests. That is, the therapist was clarifying that self-interest was different from selfishness. The needs that the patient experienced, although real and understandable, could not be fully met in the transference situation. The therapist best served as a healthy role model for the patient with whom she could both successfully internalize and compete but where limits, limitations, and boundaries were also acknowledged and scrupulously enforced. Scrutiny of countertransference reactions enabled this therapist to gain access to what her patient yearned for and to meet it by verbal interpretation and empathy, not action.

ADDITIONAL TREATMENT CONSIDERATIONS

Working through commonly occurring transference and countertransference reactions furthers the growth and development of the patient with an eating disorder. Clinicians can expect to have strong feelings when they work with these patients because (1) the illnesses are life threatening; (2) patients frequently have a range of intense feelings toward their therapist but have had fewer opportunities than other people to express their unabashed, real emotions to an interested listener; (3) significant boundary violations or parental misattunement have been an aspect of the patient's childhood that will be played out in the process (e.g., identification with the aggressor); and (4) the patient has particular developmental needs to experience attachment, a sense of security, and mutual recognition that may push the therapist to treat her or him as special or to work extraordinarily hard in the treatment (e.g., trying too hard to be the better parent). Deficits in experience of the sense of self as a human among humans leaves many patients pining for a caretaker. The therapeutic needs to be "more real" by acknowledging mistakes, but sharing limited information about one's self must always be balanced with the treatment requirements of preserving consistent, clear, and appropriate therapeutic boundaries.

1. Encourage the patient to express negative feelings and do not become discouraged should a protracted negative transference reaction occur. The ability of the therapist to be placed in the role of and withstand becoming the "bad object" is likely to spark a move forward for the patient who has in the past needed to remain silent or falsely compliant within the family of origin.

2. Consider how one's own gender may be influencing the state of the transference and countertransference (Wooley, 1991; Zerbe, 1995b, 1996a, 1998, 2001b). Male and female therapists are likely to find that aspects of the maternal and paternal transference will be played out over time regardless of the gender of the therapist. It is always best to avoid gender role stereotypes; both sexes can work effectively with eating disorder patients as long as they can balance their nurturing and limit-setting capacities when called for in the moment. Indeed, clinical experience demonstrates that male therapists who work successfully with these patients are usually comfortable with both male and female aspects of themselves. Likewise, female therapists must find within themselves a degree of comfort with their own limit setting (e.g., traditionally considered paternal) capacities along with their nurturant, maternal qualities.

3. Pay particular attention to boundary issues. As the patient moves ahead, the therapist will invariably be tested to be more real. Capitulating to unreasonable demands for physical or sexual contact or acquiescing to internal pressure to gratify the patient's quest for extensive personal knowledge may place the therapist on the "slippery slope" of ultimately undermining the therapeutic alliance (Gabbard & Lester, 1995). Be aware that what appears to be a deviation from standard practice on the patient's behalf may be an attempt to fulfill an unmet personal need of the treater and an early indication of countertransference difficulties.

4. Be aware that working with eating disorder patients often stirs psychophysiological reactions in the therapist. Somatic reactions may reflect the patient's inability to put internal states into words. The therapist who is able to tolerate these states and to reflect on them demonstrates a capacity to enter the patient's preverbal world. Concomitantly, therapists are advised to take time to reflect on and to explore how feelings about their own body and body image is influenced in the treatment of patients whose own body image takes center stage during the therapeutic encounter.

5. Seek frequent supervision or consultation. These avenues of support are invaluable with respect to enhancing one's professional development, bolstering

the therapist's sense of professional efficacy, and maintaining appropriate therapeutic boundaries. If boundaries are repeatedly tested in a way that may undermine ultimate treatment goals, feel empowered to set limits or refer the patient to another treater. Frustration and gratification in balanced alternations are required for ordinary human development and for the therapeutic process to advance (Kris, 1988, 1996).

6. Remember that if the patient has a history of trauma, deprivation, or severe maltreatment in childhood (for example, the many forms that "soul murder" takes [Shengold, 1989, 1999]), he or she will bring feelings of abandonment, severe criticism, emptiness, and anguish into the treatment. The consequences of these historical antecedents will likely stir powerful transference reactions and countertransference responses that must be processed, at first silently, but eventually verbally, between therapist and patient. Therapists who can consistently point out why the patient may be self-depriving and self-punitive help that patient begin to face down internalized self-hatred. These patients then begin to affirm themselves more fully. Although the patient may attempt to externalize self-criticism by projecting it onto the therapist, try to begin to maneuver so as to help the patient see why it is that they may be depriving themselves of fulfillment as a repetition of the past.

CONCLUSION

Patients with eating disorders present the psychotherapist with extraordinary challenges in understanding and working with an array of transference and countertransference reactions. As the patient becomes more amenable to expressing feelings about the therapeutic relationship, the individual is usually on the path to becoming less reliant on the eating disorder symptoms for expression of psychological pain and avoidance of emotional contact with others. That is to say, understanding and exploration of transference reactions is a nonpareil means for therapists to enter into the patient's psychological world. Concomitantly, our patients can then experience themselves by becoming more human and real by sharing a range of feelings they have about us. The original crippling fears of eating, becoming fat or thin, and other reflections of the betrayal of one's body will also be played out in the intimate relationship between patient and therapist as the patient inevitably enacts conflicts and areas of deficit and deprivation with the therapist.

Countertransference reactions that arise are a function of the psychologies of both participants. Although working through these reactions fosters growth of both patient and clinician, they are likely to become intense, uncomfortable, and even disruptive at significant moments in the therapeutic dialogue. It is difficult to sit with a patient who looks like a concentration camp victim hour after hour, while she details incessant purging and otherwise regales us with the ways she intends to hurt her body. The effort to disentangle the powerful countertransference reactions these behaviors stir requires great perseverance on the part of the therapist. In becoming aware of how the eating disorder is a mode of relating that keeps others at a safe distance, the therapist experiences in vivo how original difficulties in the family of origin are inevitably played out over and over again in the therapeutic relationship.

For those eating disorder patients who have been severely maltreated, attempts will be made to reenact and master the original abuse by testing the therapist's professional boundaries. One may also note how the therapist is kept at an emotional distance by "vomiting" back treatment interventions. At these times the therapist may feel that nothing that has been said has been relevant or helpful and he or she may feel demoralized. However, over time the processing of these feelings with the patient leads to strengthening of the self and a capacity for improved relationships.

Empathic contact with the therapist is an essential treatment experience because it helps our patients grow in their capacity to take responsibility for their own self-preservation and personal development. However, this responsibility to self may have been perceived by the original caretakers or family members as an act of aggression. This paradigm will also be played out in the transference. Because the eating disorder may reflect a desperate attempt by the patient to control her- or himself and the other, reflective of a deeper sense of powerlessness that derives from early failure in development and in expression of healthy aggression, so the treatment must become a place for the patient to safely process powerful feelings of envy, rage, entitlement, disappointment, and affection for the therapist.

In our countertransference recognition of a desire to cure patients, we must deal with the concomitant needs of our patients to rebuff those very wishes. In so doing we avoid identification with the internalized parents who were perceived by the patient as wanting them to grow and develop only to enhance their own desires and ambitions (i.e., false self). It behooves therapists to continually ask the patient the ways in which they wish to change and to pose questions that demonstrate a genuine interest in the patient for true self-functioning to flourish. In this way, the patient learns that growth occurs at their own behest, and the therapist avoids the defeating countertransference trap of *furor therapeuticus*, which these patients easily sense and frequently defy.

In the treatment of eating disorders, there can be no substitute for tincture of time. The therapist must recognize that transference interventions will not be completely processed after the first attempt, and she or he will likely need to withstand a host of verbal barrages, tests of therapeutic resolve, intense negative countertransference reactions, and spoiling mechanisms. Even as patients sometimes "vomit back" or avoid "taking in" interventions, experience dictates that growth occurs when storms are weathered. Patients benefit from the therapist who attempts to withstand the need to defeat treatment even as the patient voraciously desires interpersonal contact. The therapist will also need to make good use of their realistic, countertransference hate by putting significant limits on an excessive demand for time, attention, and special treatment.

The therapeutic desire to be helpful, if not to actually "repair" our patient, may predispose clinicians to give more rather than interpret early deficits that the patient faced. Patients are usually reassured by the therapist's strategic limit setting and, unlike members of the patient's family of origin, the therapist is setting the example of being involved but not overly involved. This provides the patient with a mature identification object, showing the patient that the therapist is not afraid to establish and then support appropriate boundaries.

The disparity between the real potential for growth and involvement and the high cost of preoccupation with eating and body image in this patient group is most striking. By maintaining hope that even the most intractable eating disorder can be remedied over time, the therapist conveys a message that growth can occur, goals can be achieved, and the capacity to work and to love can flourish over the course of the lifetime. Such a hopeful attitude helps the patient and the therapist retain solid footing during many tumultuous storms that inevitably accompany forward steps of the treatment process as past and present are integrated.

CHAPTER 9

Assessing Outcome and Resiliency

The best definition I ever heard of our role in the therapeutic process came during a termination appraisal of her own therapy by a young woman . . . "What is it that he does?" she had been asking her self, "What is it that he does?" . . . Finally the evening before she had come up with an answer that had satisfied her, which she now tearfully related to me: "You help get people where they are going."

—Jacob Jacobson (1993)

Light dawns gradually over the whole.

—Ludwig Wittgenstein (1969)

How should therapists define or describe what constitutes outcome or recovery from an eating disorder? When do we know that what we and the patient have done together is "good enough?" Do we look at patient satisfaction surveys (Clinton, Bjorck, Sohlberg, & Norring, 2004) or study those factors that promote efficacy that are common to many schools of psychotherapy (Wampold, 2001)? Is it sufficient to only consider symptom control and what might be most efficient in terms of time and money, or are we best served when we are able to take into account the whole person and her or his lifelong personal development?

To some extent the answer to those questions depends on how we define our task as clinicians as much as the research instruments we use to assess treatment outcomes. Clinicians nowadays frequently debate constituents of "best evidence" of care. What objective measures of symptom control and which improved physiological variables are particularly important? What about the more subjective measures that rely on patient reports about their quality of life that are beginning to appear in the professional literature? In measuring our success as treaters, we must also take into account those patients who may spontaneously recover on their own and those who undergo setbacks because of "destructive" impact or "a serious error" (p. 114) experienced in the treatment (Beresin, Gordon, & Herzog,

1989). These elements have been largely ignored in treatment follow-up studies (Frank & Frank, 1991; Luborsky & Luborsky, 2006).

In helping patients arrive at a feeling that they have gotten to where they are going or aspire to go, clinicians no less than the patients we treat must never be content unless we first take into account the whole person and what that individual defines as "good enough outcome." As Beresin and colleagues (1989) wrote with respect to recovery from anorexia nervosa, the person with an eating disorder can move "from illness to health" only after they also experience "a cohesive sense of self (and) are known and loved by others for [themselves]" (p. 127), express the "ability to enjoy themselves and their relationships" (p. 110), and, despite what is often a "lengthy and slow process" (p. 125), find that they can "unravel . . . maladaptive, self destructive defenses . . . [in acquiring] a secure sense of themselves" (p. 127). As the quote by philosopher Wittgenstein indicates, we treaters can only be certain of the dawning light of recovery and ongoing resiliency when psychological, social, physiological, occupational, and symptomatic domains have received sufficient alteration in the treatment so that the patient is living a full life.

Moreover, as contemporary follow-up studies now also demonstrate, these criteria argue for "longer term treatment to obtain better results" (Richard, 2005, p. 178), in both anorexic and bulimic patients. Even when symptom control is easily acquired and maintained, it may not be enough for the individual. It appears that for the whole person (or true self) to be psychologically prepared to "get to where they are going," only "longer treatment may help in consolidating and maintaining change in behavior and attitudes and making early relapse less likely" (Richard, 2005, p. 178). Although objective measures of improvement statistically describe some important gains in symptom control that have bedeviled the patient, they are also not sufficient if either clinician or patient subjectively knows that the true self is not yet solidified. Patients will not be where they need to be in terms of life fulfillment if they still have poor social networks, feel badly about their self-image and personal well-being, lack a sense of belonging in their family of origin or in their adult family, or struggle with a lack of self-cohesion.

The reader might reasonably also wonder what "real life" specifics the patient was getting at in the quote at the beginning of this chapter from Jacobson's (1993) paper on the therapeutic relationship and the course of treatment. Although Jacobson does not describe the patient's treatment in depth in his example, he learned from her and other patients he references, using multiple models of the mind and avoiding the artificial dichotomies that are seemingly in abundance in our field. He found that we must work hard to tune in to what patients "are trying desperately to tell us." The patient must be made to feel "more important to us than our cherished theories" so clinicians remain "open to the unexpected, the unpredicted, and the freshly voided in their productions" (p. 546). Patient and clinician may creep toward a better outcome by ongoing empathetic immersion in the intensity of affects that can quietly recede from consciousness if the patient is threatened by progress or punishment and by vigilance about those "object losses occasioned by the incipient improvement and the forward movement it portends" (p. 546). When they mutually acknowledge goals that have been achieved and are witness to hard won skills, turning points in the life process, they are then eventually able to let go of each other.

I include in this chapter some of the long-term statistics about mortality and morbidity that can be arrived at only when one studies a large sample of patients. Contemporary researchers openly acknowledge that there are "serious deficiencies" in these data because sample size is "often insufficient to draw conclusions regarding efficacy across groups" (Bulik, Berkman, Brownley, Sedway, & Lohr, 2007, p. 311). The individual in the therapist's office is always an "n of 1" who is likely to derive minimal benefit from knowing the percentage of patients who die or develop a chronic medical condition from their eating disorder. Our patients are also prone to take any statistics we offer them and continue to deny the extent of their illness, extract data that appeals to them, or tell us why "these numbers" do not apply to them. In a sense, they may be especially reluctant to take our advice because:

> They do not feel real or understand the process of becoming a real, feeling person, but imagine it to be a mechanical activity and fear being hurt. . . . They do not experience being truly loved for themselves, and instead of withstanding the expectable bruises and failures in healthy intimate relationships, feel they must be beautiful, perfect, and compliant to be loved. (Beresin et al., 1989, p. 104)

None of us can know at the outset of treatment who will or will not improve or who will have an untoward side effect from a particular modality of treatment. For the patient who embarks on the journey of treatment in order to get where they want to go in life, the clinician is required to sensitively address the person as an individual and never lose sight of how human functioning and human flourishing must be looked at as a holistic process. In short, it is only when one focuses on the individual patient and what she or he decides is "good enough" and a satisfying life that we can begin to unravel the real questions, components of care, and definitions of full recovery that should matter the most.

Clinicians can take heart from some recent reviews that summarize and critique a significant number of outcome studies. Looking at outcome research performed in different countries from around the world and including reports of various designs (e.g., cohort studies, case series with and without comparison groups) yield an overall assessment that over two thirds of bulimic patients fully recover. As a group, anorexic patients appear to do less well (less than 20–25% achieve "full recovery") but those that begin treatment earlier and have a higher percentage of average body weight when treatment starts seem to function better over time. Even for anorexia nervosa, partial recovery is greater than 50% for both the binge/purge and restricting subtypes. Contemporary researchers are also quick to honestly point out that there are many gaps in the current evidence base, including lack of information on gender and demographics and premorbid personality traits that may persist after recovery and potentiate tendencies to relapse (Fairburn, Norman, Welch, O'Conner et al., 1995; McIntosh, Jordan, Carter, Luty, et al., 2005; Thompson-Brenner & Westen, 2005a; Westen, Novotny, & Thompson-Brenner, 2004). There is sorely little evidence that "provides definitive guidance for clinicians about factors that may facilitate (or hinder) therapeutic success" (Berkman, Lohr, & Bulik, 2007, p. 307).

In studies of anorexia and bulimia, attrition and drop-out rates are high (Bulik, Berkman, et al., 2007; Shapiro et al., 2007). Although this fact alone "compromises the integrity of outcome data" (Shapiro et al., p. 333), in even the most thorough reviews, clinical trials do show that medication is more effective for bulimia than anorexia, and that research monies must be allocated to identify new medications to potentiate weight gain in anorexia and "decrease the urge to purge (e.g., with antiemetics) or reduce the extent to which binge eating and purging are experienced as reinforcing" (Shapiro et al., 2007, p. 333). Quite a bit of evidence points toward the necessity of psychotherapeutic intervention in anorexia, bulimia, and binge eating disorder, but as yet no key factors have been teased out to address the core pathologies in these disorders that respond to one particular kind of therapy and therefore stand out in the studies (Fairburn, Jones, Peveler, Carr, et al., 1991; Fairburn, Jones, Pevelee, Hope, et al., 1993; Fairburn et al., 1995; Pope & Hudson, 2004; Wilson & Berkman 1996).

In part this reflects the observation that what is delivered in the community is not the same as what is delivered in a treatment protocol. Nevertheless, there is general agreement that patients with eating disorders require "behavioral interventions that target motivation to change and encourage retention in treatment" (Bulik et al., 2007, p. 318; Brownley et al., 2007, p. 346). Data derived from research follow-up of this kind will help clinicians fine tune our skills and adapt them to the various ages and life stages, sex, race, ethnicity, and cultural background of those we treat in coming decades. Synthetic research reports based on quantitative data of this kind (Berkman et al., 2007; Brownley et al., 2007; Bulik et al., 2007; Crow, 2007; Halvorsen, Andersen, & Heyerdahl, 2004; Kaplan & Garfinkle, 1999; Keel et al., 2003) also argue for the need to treat the patient as a whole because percentage reduction in symptomatic relief may "tell only half of the story" (Brownley et al., 2007, p. 346) because "a treatment that removes symptoms but does not restore functioning ultimately provides limited benefit" (Crow, 2007, p. 2; see also Keel, Mitchell, Davis, Fieselman & Crow, 2000).

As I see it, the clinician will only know what constitutes "good enough outcome" from listening to the narrative of her or his patient. Efficacy studies can guide us to some extent, particularly when drop-out rates and adverse events are included. Only then can we glean enhanced understanding of any "physical and psychological harms associated with interventions" (Bulik et al., 2007, p. 318); we will gain knowledge about tailoring interventions for those patients who no longer have a bona fide eating disorder but continue "to suffer for long periods of time with some forms of the conditions typically described as EDNOS" (Berkman et al., 2007, p. 306).

Because the eating disorder patient must always be considered as a human being first, not simply as a member of a diagnostic group, therapeutic outcome studies must also cut across the boundaries of objective, scientific inventories to include narrative and qualitative reports. We clinicians have much to learn from taking the patient's point of view into consideration. Qualitative data speak to the humanity of the individual, they immerse themselves in those characteristics that the patient will include in constructing a life well lived, and they concern themselves with those specific skills and strengths that enable the patient to love and to work as well as face down destructive symptoms. In the majority of qualitative studies of eating disorder patients, significantly diminished symptomatic behaviors as well as quality of life improvement are found.

Both clinician and patient must always eschew perfectionism; this characteristic of the eating disorder diagnosis is a rampant "symptom" of the prevailing "culture of narcissism" (Lasch, 1979). Both participants in the therapeutic dialogue may be afflicted with the notion of human perfectibility, whether it be in the domain of the body (and hence part of an eating disorder) or the domain of achievement and accomplishment (i.e., part of one's characterlogical style or character armour). Subjective reports by patients augur for a more reasonable measure of recovery. These qualitative analyses, based on extensive semistructured interviews and questionnaires, reveal that patients want a lasting sense of relief of psychic pain reflected by enhanced interpersonal relationships, a sense of belonging and finding purpose and meaning in life, and increased ability to communicate with others while enjoying work and play (Beresin et al., 1989; de la Rie, Noordenbos, Donker, van Furth, 2007; P.M. Miller, 1996).

We clinicians can only be assured of "good enough outcome" when our patients have the capacity to sense their life as a narrative whole. We must not be content unless the patient has a sense of and is more comfortable with her or his true self. Clinicians will also have a sense that they have come a significant distance on their therapeutic journey. Both clinician and patient will likely agree there is a new sense of mastery of the eating disorder symptoms; more importantly, perhaps, we will also witness together reengagement into the human life cycle, and a fresh capacity to triumph over encumbrances, personal and family limitations, and internal struggles that challenge all humans. Less likely to blame self or others for the hand life has dealt them, they tread closer to also letting go of us, their therapists and treatment team members.

MORTALITY RATES AND CAUSES OF DEATH: THE TIP OF AN ICEBERG?

Eating disorders are the most life threatening of all psychiatric disturbances (Andersen, 1992; Eckert et al., 1995; Garner, 1997; Halmi, 1992; Harris &

Barraclough, 1998; Sullivan, 1995; Theander, 1985, 1992). Anorexia nervosa, in particular, has a substantial risk of causing premature death from medical comorbidity (e.g., starvation; arrhythmia) and suicide (Herzog, Dorer, Keel et al., 1999; Latzer, 2005; Millar, Wardell, Vyvyan, Naji, et al., 2005). Patients with bulimia are prone to succumb to suicide or automobile accidents, although an elevated mortality rate compared to controls has not been found in most studies (Fichter & Quadflieg, 2004; Quadflieg & Fichter, 2003). However, predictors for mortality, such as comorbid psychiatric disorders or severity and length of illness, vary considerably depending upon the study design, statistical analyses used, and generalizability of subjects studied (Berkman et al., 2007; Bogh, Rokkedal, & Valbak, 2005; Fichter & Quadflieg, 2004; Keel, Dorer, et al., 2003).

The actual cause and mechanism of death for patients with eating disorders is often unknown. For example, in one case report, Derman and Szabo (2006) reviewed the postmortem findings in a 36-year-old woman with longstanding anorexia nervosa who lapsed into a coma. Neither clinical examination nor laboratory investigation revealed the cause of her neurological illness, but after she died an autopsy was performed. Pulmonary thromboemboli resulting from a silent bilateral calf vein thrombosis were discovered; the cause of death was due to the embolism that was likely brought about by circulatory problems and dehydration secondary to anorexia. The authors note that the cause of death in anorexia cannot always be established prior to death because the "pathology may not manifest with obvious clinical features" (p. 262). Because not all anorexia deaths are reported, these authors recommend a high level of vigilance on the part of clinicians who may encounter unexpected medical complications from eating disorders, and they suggest that postmortem examinations be obtained in "any AN death" because "this may lead to advances in knowledge and treatment practices" (p. 262).

In a review of all patients with a diagnosis of anorexia, Millar and colleagues (2005) found that myocardial infarction, diabetes, septic shock, infection, and suicide were causes of death likely linked to the diagnosis of anorexia. In the catchment area of Northern Scotland these researchers studied, they found that in only one third of death certificates was anorexia noted "but [AN] may well have played a part in the death in other cases" (p. 756). While the authors underscore that their findings confirm that anorexia is a serious medical illness in which long-term treatment plays a significant role in recovery, for many individuals the illness is chronic and death can occur after many years. It may never appear on the actual death certificate as the cause of death.

Patients who restrict, binge, or purge, regardless of a formal diagnosis of anorexia or bulimia, are particularly at risk for sudden death because of the propensity toward arrhythmia, cardiomyopathy, and gastrointestinal ruptures (Eckert et al., 1995; Herzog, Deter, Fiehn, & Petzold, 1997; Mehler & Andersen, 1999). Mortality may be greater than it appears for anorexia, bulimia, and eating disorders not otherwise specified because the patient denies or keeps the problem secret from health care providers. Only when diagnosis is confirmed in a known population can the death rate, actual causes of death, and pertinent demographics and clinical characteristics elucidate the full extent of an illness. For example, in the Millar and colleagues (2005) study, 524 cases of anorexia nervosa were identified in the catchment area studied. All patients were referred to the National Health Service for medical and psychiatric care. One may be reasonably sure that the serious medical complications and chronic nature of anorexia were identified accurately because the population was not only well-defined but the treatment resources were "readily accessible" by citizens, all of whom have coverage in the National Health Service (Millar et al., 2005). In the United States and other countries where access to care may be limited and population data may allow many cases to "slide through the cracks," many cases are likely not identified or treated, leading to an underestimate of mortality from anorexia and bulimia and underreporting of the precise medical problem that caused the death.

Consider also how since the mid-1970s, medical science has become more adept at making the diagnosis of osteoporosis and osteopenia, conditions more prevalent in Western society as people age and live longer. The sequelae of osteoporosis are a frequent cause of death in the over 65 population. For example, it has recently been reported that over half of women who sustain a fracture after age 70 will die of osteoporosis complications (e.g., pulmonary emboli when patient is immobilized).

In addition to the aging process, eating disorders cause loss of bone. As reported in the third revision of the American Psychiatric Association "Practice Guidelines" (2006), the treatment for osteoporosis due to eating disorders is neither estrogen nor biphosphonates. Young women who develop osteopenia and osteoporosis as a result of their eating disorder may have increased morbidity and mortality as they age due to the ramifications of this early bone loss and as yet there is no treatment other than refeeding and seeing if the loss of bone remits. In such a patient the root cause of premature demise may be chronic anorexia, but death will likely be registered as "complication of osteoporosis" or another medical cause (e.g., cardiac failure).

Crude mortality statistics for anorexia reported in our best research papers do not take into account these covert deaths. Thus, even the most ghastly statistics fail to fully reveal the potential lethality of eating disorders. The reader is urged to keep in mind the classic "case of Ellen West" who died after many years of self-imposed restriction. Long considered a failure of "existential analysis" wherein some of the finest clinicians of her time attempted to stymie her demise, Ms. West is today considered a "slow suicide" whose investment in dying could not be reversed (Jackson, Davidson, Russell, & Vandereycken, 1990). Ellen West's living legacy is the extraordinarily detailed and unique case history that Ludwig Binswanger (1944/1958) provided to the psychotherapeutic profession that demonstrates the "tomb-world" (p. 357) in which many 21st century patients with anorexia also reside and why clinicians who work with them are concerned with the high rate of suicide and "theme of death" that haunts many of their psychotherapy processes (see Jackson et al., 1990; Vandereycken & van Deth, 1994). Indeed, many practicing clinicians today believe that "attachment to life" by establishing a satisfying attachment to the therapist may be the best and most reliable predictor of successful recovery and prevention of overt and covert death from eating disorders (Latzer, 2005; Strober, 2004, 2006; Yager, 2007b; Zerbe, 1992a, 2007a).

MEDICAL AND PSYCHIATRIC MORBIDITIES: EVEN MORE DANGEROUS THAN WE KNOW?

In contrast to European studies (Theander, 1970, 1983a, 1983b, 1985, 1992) where an 18 to 30% mortality rate was observed over a 30-year course for anorexic patients, long-term studies in the United States have reported deaths at a frequency of about 5 to 10% (Eckert et al., 1995; Halmi, 1992; Halmi & Licinio, 1998). These mortality statistics may be low because, as noted above, a diagnosis of an eating disorder is not always known at the time of death or written on the death certificate. One must always wonder if the complication of a longstanding eating problem actually lay behind a manifest death due to arrhythmia or electrolyte imbalance.

The most frequent causes of known death from an eating disorder are listed in Table 9.1. In addition to keeping these consequences in the forefront of one's mind when treating a patient, the clinician must remind the patient (and family member involved in the treatment) from time to time of the lethal risks they are running with the disorder. In this way, all participants confront the human tendency to rationalize by maintaining the thought, "but it won't happen to me" (or them).

Many patients make a symptomatic recovery but the majority do not go on to flourish (Bemporad, Beresin, Ratey, O'Driscoll, Lindem, Herzog, 1992; Beresin et al., 1989; Deter & Herzog, 1994; Hsu, 1990; Keel & Mitchell, 1997; Pike, 1998; Steinhausen, 2002; Strober, Freeman, Morrell, 1997). While death from bulimia nervosa appears to be much less common than from anorexia, the disorder is still accompanied by significant psychological impairment and psychiatric comorbidities. Eating disorders consume significant medical resources because the medical complications that accompany the disorders necessitate

TABLE 9.1 Causes of death from eating disorders

- Effects of starvation (AN)
- Automobile accidents (BN)
- Suicide (AN & BN)
- Alcohol abuse (AN & BN)
- Acute myocardial infarction; arrhythmias; cardiac failure (AN & BN)
- Infection, septicemic shock (AN)
- Gastrointestinal rupture, pancreatitis (BN)
- Complications of osteoporosis (i.e., fracture causing temporary immobility leading to thrombemoli, etc.) (AN & BN)

---

frequent follow-up, diagnostic tests, medical workups, and sometimes hospitalization (Herzog, Greenwood, Dorer, Flores, et al., 2000; Keel & Mitchell, 1997; Thompson-Brenner & Westen, 2005a, 2005b). When compared to other groups of psychiatric patients, those with anorexia and bulimia have a higher rate of referral to medical subspecialists (Zerbe, 1992a). This reflects not simply the known medical complications but the polysomatizing nature of these patients. Among adolescent females, eating disorders are the third leading cause of chronic illness in the United States and other developed countries (Fisher et al., 1996).

In general, the psychiatric outcome literature demonstrates the unpredictability of the course of illness and, for a substantial minority of eating disorder patients, a poor prognosis (Herzog et al., 1999). In those who do recover, a lengthy time for recovery is typical (Finfgeld, 2002; Strober et al., 1997, 1999). Women with a history of anorexia tend to maintain a BMI that is markedly lower than most of the controls, indicating persistent cognitive restraint, perfectionism, and difficulties detaching from the identity of having an eating disorder (Bulik, Sullivan, Fear, & Pickering, 1997).

A recent authoritative review (Steinhausen, 2002) describes the substantial psychiatric impairment across categories found in over 200 studies of outcomes of eating disorder. In her 1998 study, Pike found problems of psychological adjustment in 50% or more of patients and suggested that the refractory psychosocial problems of anorexic and bulimic patients require more intervention for the comorbidities of separation disorder, anxiety, obsessive-compulsive disorder, substance abuse, and depression. Alcoholism, in particular, is associated with increased mortality rates among patients with anorexia nervosa (Keel, Dorer, Franko, Jackson, & Herzog, 2005). In Fichter and Quadflieg's (2004) 12-year, prospective, longitudinal study of 196 females with bulimia nervosa, 70% of patients showed substantial improvement at follow-up. Nonetheless, 23% of patients still carried either a diagnosis of bulimia nervosa–purging subtype or eating disorders not otherwise specified at 12-year follow-up. Even in recovered patients, body image disturbance and problems with socialization and impairment in sexual attitudes and adaptive functioning persisted.

Not all reports are as pessimistic as these. Basing their article on 208 residents in Rochester, Minnesota who were diagnosed with anorexia nervosa (193 women; 15 men over 63 years), Korndorfer and colleagues did not find reduced survival compared to other Minnesotans of comparable age (Korndorfer et al., 2003). Given the meticulous records the investigators used from the Mayo Clinic and its affiliated hospitals, these findings are impressive. The authors believe that their cohort had a benign prognosis because it unveiled "the mild clinical spectrum" of anorexia; nonetheless, there were still two suicides and six deaths from alcoholism. They are also quick to point out that "death certificates likely underestimate the frequency of anorexia as a course of death and as a contributing cause of suicide" (p. 281) and go on to underscore the potential medical complications of alcohol abuse in anorexia and bulimic patients.

They hasten to suggest how pneumonia and alcoholism may have been directly or indirectly related to an eating disorder diagnosis and argue for thorough history gathering and close follow-up given the potential medical and psychological consequences of these co-occurring conditions.

Based upon their work in residential and ambulatory settings, Johnson, Lund, and Yates (2003) found that "50% of anorexia nervosa patients remit within 1–3 years and never require an inpatient level of care" (p. 798). Taking into account their cohort analysis and clinical expertise, they believe "a 75%–90% rate of recovery is a more accurate estimate." These sanguine perspectives appear to be an important but minority view. Kordorfer et al. (2003) acknowledge that long-term consequences of comorbid medical conditions may prove eventually fatal but may not be known for decades. They go on to argue that "associated psychological issues also need to be addressed" and that clinicians must avoid "complacency in clinical practice because deaths do occur" (p. 283).

In 1992, I reported on the medical morbidity of a bulimic patient who kept her history of chronic pancreatitis secret from the hospital treatment team (Zerbe, 1992c). Pancreatitis is a well known and potentially life threatening complication of an eating disorder which, in this particular patient, presented as a fever of unknown origin. Because the patient was already hospitalized for bulimia, her eating problems were well known to the staff, but she had held back crucial medical data. Her case was instructive because her eating symptoms exacerbated after intravenous fluids and diagnostic procedures were administered, leaving her to want to reengage with formerly self-destructive behaviors such as restricting. Her case also demonstrated how clinicians may be aware of one facet of a person's illness and not another, particularly when denial, secret keeping, shame, and humiliation are also core features of the personality profile.

Clinicians are advised to keep reports such as these in mind during treatments that appear to be going well. Our patients are in substantial medical and psychological jeopardy because we are left in the dark about so much of their lives, and the full extent of the consequences of their eating disorder may never be known until a crisis brings it to medical attention. How many medical emergencies in any one year are caused by the electrolyte imbalance, arrhythmias, or infections that actually spring from an eating disorder? We are left to infer from single case reports like my own and others that many sequelae are actually never reported or even known; clinical experience of many in this subspecialty suggests that medical comorbidities and lethal effects are far greater in number than even the most sobering literature takes into account.

RANDOMIZED CONTROLLED TRIALS: BENEFITS
AND LIMITATIONS OF OBJECTIVE DATA

Most randomized controls of individual psychotherapy have a high drop-out rate (50–70%) which may inflate the positive results reported. For example, in an important paper that found that clinical management was superior to specialized therapy, 70% of patients did not complete the research or made small gains (McIntosh et al., 2005). Of the 56 women with anorexia nervosa who began the trial, only 35 completed the treatment protocols of cognitive-behavioral therapy, interpersonal therapy, or clinical measurements. While the authors of the study note that their findings support the notion that nonspecific supportive clinical management is better than formal psychotherapy based on the 9% of subjects who had "very good outcome" and 21% of subjects who "had improved considerably" (p. 745), in reality their conclusions are drawn from a small pool of patients.

Another example of multisite study of cognitive-behavioral therapy addressed relapse in 48 patients with bulimia nervosa (Halmi, Agras, Mitchell, Wilson, et al., 2002). This study found a 44% relapse rate after four months for those who had achieved symptom control. The authors report that their results are discouraging and suggested that "additional follow-up treatment is needed to consolidate improvement" (Halmi, 2002). While the majority of the patients (greater than 75%) reduced bingeing and purging, thereby supporting the role of cognitive-behavioral therapy in treatment of bulimia, the number of patients the conclusions are drawn from is still small. Moreover, other indicators of how well the patients flourished in other domains of life are lacking. These data are perhaps more readily procured from the in-depth qualitative reports and case studies that take into account the patient's satisfaction in work, interpersonal relationships, sense of meaning and fulfillment in life, as well as symptom control.

A number of investigators describe how many eating disorder patients can improve symptomatically with respect to their eating disorder but continue to suffer from various emotional problems, including depression, anxiety, psychosomatic complaints, substance abuse and characterlogical problems. In a particular patient, prognosis is impossible to predict unless the individual is highly motivated at the outset to engage in treatment or can be engaged early on to want to change (Geller & Drab, 1999; Treasure & Ward, 1997). In general, patients tend to do better when the disease is diagnosed early and treated with a repertoire of therapeutic interventions, and often for more than one year.

Quality of life is increasingly becoming recognized as an essential measurement of the outcome of treatment (Adair, Marcoux, Cram, Ewashen, et al., 2007); researchers are in the process of developing specific eating disorder outcome measurements to assess global functioning and the patient's experience of recovery, not simply reduction of eating symptoms and weight gain (Beresin et al., 1989; Lamoureux & Bottorff, 2005; de la Rie et al., 2007) as a more robust assessment of recovery. The small sample size of these reports (which varies from 9 to 146 patients) is one factor that limits the generalizability of the findings. Nonetheless, data garnered from these studies will be another step in helping clinicians formulate realistic treatment goals, determine the types of social and professional supports most useful depending on age, race, and comorbid psychological factors, and assess levels of adaptation and "individually chosen life domains" (de la Rie et al., 2007, p. 19) in defining full and partial recovery in our patients.

While most authorities concede that a significant percentage of eating disorders (about 30%) will become chronic, at the present time it is difficult to match particular patients to particular kinds of interventions (Kemp, Kirov, Everitt, Hayward & David, 1998; Treasure, 1989; Treasure & Schmidt, 1999). Yet, even the most optimistic reports reveal that between 40 and 60% of patients will have significant eating symptoms and other emotional difficulties even after treatment, and these reports all have limited follow-up (3 months to 2 years). Given the chronicity of many eating disorders symptoms, one is left to wonder what happens over the long term with respect to the patient's experience of her or his illness, especially because many patients are loath to report or remain lost to follow-up in these studies.

In Table 9.2, I list the common predictors of positive treatment outcome derived from reviewing these objective studies. Not only should they be used to remind the clinician of potential roadblocks in a given case, but the clinician might also consider including in the treatment record a statement that acknowledges specific prognostic variables that will likely make treatment more complex and risky (e.g., history of abuse, borderline personality disorder). These predictors may also be used in fostering the therapeutic alliance or working with third parties to secure benefits (Zerbe, 1996b). Knowledge is not only a powerful tool in general, but in the case of sharing outcome predictors, can be an impetus for some patients to "defy the odds."

INDIVIDUAL CASE REPORTS: WHAT MASTER CLINICIANS TELL US ABOUT RECOVERY

The majority of practicing clinicians also rely on the finely honed therapeutic wisdom found in case reports (see Werne, 1996, for a volume devoted to how practitioners from divergent theoretical backgrounds employ their skills in an individual case) to aid in treatment planning and assessing recovery. The benefit of these anecdotal reports is the emphasis placed on clinical technique; they also serve to help the practitioner expand her or his repertoire of interventions while making hypotheses about what worked—or didn't—under a particular set

TABLE 9.2 Predictors of positive treatment outcomes In eating disorders

- Increased length of treatment
- Younger age of onset
- Absence of alcohol and substance abuse
- Absence of severe character pathology (i.e., borderline personality disorder)
- Improvement in mood and anxiety symptoms during treatment
- No history of sexual abuse (BN)
- Supportive family relationships
- Lack of extreme drive to exercise, severe body distortion, substantial weight phobia
- Ability to initiate and maintain friendships

of circumstances. The readability of such reports makes them highly user friendly; when well done, the clinician feels as though she or he is immersed in a novel. Herein also lies the major criticism of these data: What may seem to work for an individual patient may not be replicable to a group, and the "gold standard" of the double-blind placebo controlled trial is clearly not met.

On the other hand, detailed clinical reports are more apt to describe particular interventions and formulate a case in a thoughtful manner. The practitioner often feels as though she or he is receiving a consultation gratis when the writer seems to "tune in" to an aspect of therapy one is struggling with and feeling "alone in the muck." Particularly when therapy seems to take a long time, is experienced as frustrating, or when one is stymied about "what to do next," there is nothing like reading and mulling over an individual case report to put some balm on the wounded healer's psyche.

With respect to describing beneficent clinical outcome in challenging cases, Hamburg (1996) described the case of Ms. Q., a patient whom Hamburg treated for over a decade. Hamburg felt "racked with boredom" and was "drawn to despair" by Ms. Q.'s recalcitrant anorexia. He questioned the wisdom of investing himself fully in one person's care given the limited time and energy each of us has, but ultimately he refused to give up. In this summary of his over 10 years of work with Ms. Q., Hamburg delves into the patient's use of metaphors in the middle phase of her treatment, the patient's gradual capacity to develop genuine empathy for others, and the working through of her symbiotic tie to her mother when she developed a romantic relationship. Hamburg concludes his case study with a brief formulation about what constitutes improvement and "good enough outcome." Hamburg's refreshing, reassuring tone is quoted at length because it provides yet another perspective on the constituents of improvement.

> In an era dominated by the economics of managed care and short-term, symptom focused treatments, Ms. Q's story should challenge our assumptions about psychotherapy for anorexia nervosa. When should the therapist despair? When do we stop investing optimism and energy into a patient's treatment? . . . From my labors as Ms. Q's therapist, I have learned something of inestimable value. In this current climate of therapeutic nihilism, we must remember that change is possible even when it least seems so. We cannot afford to discard individual lives because the road is so difficult and long. This work requires forbearance, extensive outside support, some inventiveness, and theoretical flexibility. (p. 99)

QUALITATIVE RESEARCH: WHAT PATIENTS TELL US ABOUT THEIR RECOVERY

The direct experience of patients and practitioners looks at the notion of recovery through an entirely different lens. A growing and significant body of work documents what the patient finds most useful in the healing process (Daniels, 2001; Reindl, 2001; Weaver, Wuest, & Ciliska, 2005). A current that runs throughout these autobiographical narratives is the new strength and resourcefulness the patient derives from the dialogic nature of individual therapy. Both interpretive and noninterpretive techniques prove essential in helping the person develop a sense of self (see Appendix B for an abbreviated list of autobiographical references).

As noted, since the mid-1990s, psychiatric outcome studies have also begun to focus more carefully on assessing the constituents of quality of life as important indicators of how patients are actually doing during their recovery. Qualitative research is labor intensive because extensive, open-ended patient interviews are used to glean perspective on the experience of recovery (Lamoureux & Bottorff, 2005). This type of research hones the patient's experience in real time and is employed in understanding recovery processes in *all* psychiatric disorders, not just eating disorders. It aims to assess disease-specific psychopathology and to monitor a wide range of personality, skill, and support variables that inevitably affect how the patient views her- or himself. This research has lent additional credence to the clinical observation that a patient may improve with respect to the manifest symptom only to be plagued by a host of other life difficulties such as sexual conflict or interpersonal strife (Fichter & Quadflieg, 2004).

In order to argue to third parties that treatment methods are cost effective, clinicians must demonstrate better outcomes, including better quality of life outcome. For the patient and their loved ones, these are often the areas of life that matter most. That is to say, clinical care must neither be based nor measured by symptom improvement alone. Better relationships, a greater capacity to meet the demands of the work place, and the experience of joy and hope may be some of the best indicators for recovery from any psychiatric illness. In the case of eating disorders, patients and clinicians must look not only at improved control over the eating disorder and body image symptoms as a measure of success but include parameters that gauge the capacity to engage more fully in life (de la Rie et al., 2007; Yager, 2007b; Zerbe, 2001a, 2001b).

An emerging body of scientific work actually demonstrates how much can be gained when improvement in eating disorders includes improvement in quality of life. In one case control design, Sullivan and colleagues (1998) found that therapeutic approaches that exclusively focus on weight but neglect detection and treatment of associated psychological variables are inadequate for patients to engage more fully in the cycle of life (Sullivan et al., 1998). Patients in this study needed more help than they received in their inpatient treatment program because outside of the hospital they continued to have problems with depression and anxiety, perfectionism, shape and body concerns, and alcohol dependence. In contrast, those patients who are able to enhance their coping skills, such as seeking out support, learning to tackle problems directly, and confronting avoidance, appear to be less vulnerable to relapse (Bloks, van Furth, Callewaert, & Hoek, 2004). Other outcome studies also highlight how recovery must be more broadly conceptualized because patients have different kinds of psychological concerns that affect their ability to engage fully and meaningfully in life (Herzog, Dorer, Keel, Selwyn, et al., 1999; Jager, Liedtke,

Kunsebeck, Lempa, et al., 1996; Keel & Mitchell, 1997; Mitchell, Hoberman, Peterson, Mussell, & Pyle, 1996; Wilson 1996).

Following the conclusions raised by Theander's seminal European follow-up investigation, Pike (1998) concludes her critique of extant outcome studies by challenging researchers that longer term and more systematic study of patients is necessary. Given the chronicity and morbidity of anorexia nervosa, clinicians must "derive more carefully and consistently the milestones of initial treatment response, relapse, remission, and recovery" (p. 473). While briefer, behaviorally based methods and pharmacological treatment definitely have their role in initiating and sustaining recovery of eating disorders, the long-term follow-up studies of Bemporad, Herzog, Theander, and Pike mentioned in this chapter all show how even the best treatment results are limited by the methods and parameters of how one defines recovery.

Writing from the vantage point of expertise in addictive disorders, Peter Miller (1996) argues that the criteria for overcoming an eating disorder have been viewed much too narrowly and simplistically by the mental health community. After reviewing more than 50 studies, he concludes that psychological health must be considered as important as physical health as defined by improvement in weight, decreased bingeing, or body image emphasis. He goes on to assert that in addition to medical health, eating habits, and exercise moderation, treaters must reckon with the fact that quality of life improvement develops slowly in the majority of patients. We must help them find solace in making "progress, but not being perfect" (p. 749). I would add that this point of view is as important for the clinician as the patient, even though our professional training, the predominant culture, and even scientific literature may covertly and overtly imply that anything less than a "total cure" is worth little.

Miller's remarks echo the qualitative data of the nine recovered anorexia patients interviewed by Marie Lamoureux and Joan Bottorff (2005). These researchers use the felicitous phrase of "inching away from anorexia" (p. 175) to synthesize the statement made by their interviewees whose recovery was "excruciatingly slow," full of "unpredictable setbacks," and other difficulties, but ultimately successful. These subjects were gradually able to change their anorexia mindset, attain a sense of self that was simultaneously real and "good enough," and develop a belief in their own power, competence, and identity that was not based on maintaining an emaciated body habitus (pp. 175–177).

Clinicians have much to gain from understanding more about how our patients assess what helps them and their experience of their recovery. While qualitative research of this kind is still in its infancy, data derived from these reports is summarized in Table 9.3 and can be used by the therapist "in the trenches" to assess where clinician and patient are in the journey to a fuller sense of recovery. Most of the points made by the patients are intuitively obvious to the therapist, but the sheer number of issues, adaptive skills, and interpersonal capacities listed attest to the complexity and difficulty of the task before us in any individual treatment process. They also argue for the slow, incremental process that only a long term perspective can provide.

TABLE 9.3 Eating disorder patients' experience of recovery

- Realistic appraisal of medical dangers
- Improvement in care of self (e.g., eating habits, use of leisure time)
- New ways to self-soothe, self-regulate
- Ability to access social support from family, friends, and fellow patients
- Enhanced problem solving skills
- Improved capacity to invest in and work on interpersonal relationship
- Gradual relinquishment of eating disorder identity and thoughts (e.g., "This food will make me fat"; "I'll feel better after I eat this package of cookies, etc.")
- Ability to take responsibility for self and eschew victim mentality
- Establishment of a sense of true self, "real me," or "knowing who I am"
- Capacity to formulate goals, tolerate setbacks, yet maintain positive motivation to get better
- Reclamation of a sense of one's personal power
- Decreased emphasis on perfectionism
- Firmer interpersonal boundaries; enhanced capacities to set appropriate boundaries
- Cultivation of sense of purpose, meaning in life

In essence, improvement for the person with an eating disorder must come to be seen as a "continuous process rather than definitive end product" (Miller, 1996, p. 752) that includes the important, classic variables of decreased mortality and fewer medical complications, suicides, and accidents, but does not end there. A broader perspective of what constitutes a life well lived and the patient's perception that their suffering has been ameliorated are perhaps just as important, if not more important, for a realistic assessment of what should be considered adequate and sustained improvement for an eating disorder.

The nine recovered patients in the Lamoreux and Bottorff study corroborated this view by saying that their development of self included finding a sense of meaning and purpose in life. Indeed, they emerged from their illness with a newfound responsibility for self; they eschewed blaming the culture, the media, and other people or family members for their past difficulties as they worked toward making positive contributions to others and learning over time to find and to accept unconditional support. By relinquishing the "blame game," they displayed maturity, a decreased tendency to use the splitting defense, and pari passu, improved and ambivalent interpersonal relations wherein good and bad object representations were synthesized.

RELATIONSHIPS BUILT ON TRUST AND BETTER BOUNDARIES: ANOTHER WAY TO SHOW IMPROVEMENT?

The majority of studies indicate that interpersonal factors are important in the recovery of eating disorders (Tozzi, Sullivan, Fear, McKenzie, & Bulik, 2003).

Patients who recover tend to have a greater sense of self-acceptance and better self-esteem than those who do not (Rossotto, Rorty-Greenfield, & Yager, 1996; Bulik et al., 1999). For example, the patients who respond rapidly and consistently to cognitive-behavioral therapy are more self-directed and accept responsibility for their own choices than nonresponders. Self-directedness includes the capacity to define one's own goals and have a sense of meaning and purpose in life. It includes the capacity to solve problems, accept the self, take personal responsibility, and be resourceful.

Interestingly, these factors describe aspects of the true self that define psychological health. These patients put less emphasis on weight and diet than they did previously and have improved self-care and self-acceptance. According to Rossotto et al. (1996), nonrecovered subjects continue to have a strong conviction that they benefit from their disorder in contrast to recovered patients who abandon "any perception that the eating disorder serves a positive purpose" (1996, p. 126). Those patients who are fortunate enough to have a supportive relationship, whether it be with a parent, partner, or therapist, are also found to have a better prognosis (Tozzi et al., 2003).

Unconditional, unwavering support emerges as a key ingredient in recovery because it promotes a sense of basic trust and helps build courage "to move cautiously from relying on anorexia to relying on trustworthy individuals" (Lamoreux & Bottorff, p. 176). Poor outcome has been associated with a history of childhood sexual abuse, family conflict, family preoccupation with weight and food, and low self-esteem. Not surprisingly, patients with better outcomes develop assorted coping and interpersonal skills in treatment that are actualized in greater comfort in setting boundaries. This task is essential for those persons who have had enmeshed, parentified, or other kinds of maltreatment in the family of origin.

ADDITIONAL TREATMENT CONSIDERATIONS

The constituents of "good enough" outcome are likely to be debated for years to come. As much as our assessment derives from our research methods, clinical consensus, and quantitative and qualitative analyses, the patient in the office will want the clinician to give some account of prognosis and answer the question "what do you think will help me?" Payors will demand the most effective treatment for the least cost. And our students and supervisees will continue to ask the hard questions about why we suggest an intervention and how we know it helps.

The late Peter Novotny (personal communication, 1981) once brought all these perspectives together by reminding clinicians that "the grateful patient can never pay enough; the patient who has not been helped will let you know they paid too much." Sidney, a patient I introduced in Chapter 8, and who has considerable mathematical abilities, once told me that the results of her psychotherapy are "absolutely unquantifiable." Like television and film censors over the past years who "know pornography when they see it" but couldn't define what it was precisely, we clinicians do have an intuitive sense when outcome seems to be felicitous. One way to get at it may be what Novotny hinted at— the patient's underlying gratitude when things go pretty well. Those who are able to be generous and generative will not be reliant on numbers or percentages as a measure of their own or our success, but they do know how to give and usually they will want to give something back to life.

Here are some other suggestions to help the practitioner think about and work with the inscrutable, unquantifiable, and still mysterious notions of outcome and resiliency while in your office.

1. Remain humble and stay vigilant. Mortality and medical morbidity statistics likely underestimate the medical risks of having a severe eating disorder. At the time that an illness is treated or a death reported, a physician who charts the diagnosis (such as on an insurance form or death certificate) may not realize that the eating disorder underlies the manifest problem. Therefore, clinicians must be cautious when reviewing the professional literature and drawing conclusions from even the most comprehensive outcome studies (e.g., Steinhausen, 2002).

2. Educate the patient throughout the entire treatment about the scope of the physical sequelae, including death, from eating disorders but do not expect this discussion to initially improve outcome. We must include these facts in our discussions with the patient and loved ones and underscore the notion that medical science is still learning about the physiological impact of these disorders.

3. Stay reasonably optimistic. Studies demonstrate that patients do tend to improve over the long run, and many recover even after a protracted illness. In particular, improved outcomes occur when patients keep working on their recovery and facing down denial. The potential for improvement from even a severe illness should be used as leverage with patients. Clinicians may "borrow" some optimism that helps us maintain a sense of purpose in the work from the recent qualitative research that asserts that human beings with anorexia "inch their way" to fuller, healthier lives.

4. Keep the "whole person" in mind at all times. Symptom control alone is likely an insufficient way to measure outcome. Qualitative research is also helping clinicians understand the importance of the patient's perspective in appreciating what constitutes good recovery. In addition to improvement in core eating disorders symptoms, the individual's quality of life must be taken into consideration before a patient is considered adequately improved.

5. Slow down the tempo of the process. Outcome studies suggest that clinicians who are empathic, emphasize the importance of making small gains that lead to big ones over time, and champion a belief that growth occurs over the entire life cycle appear to facilitate the recovery process. These studies also suggest that the majority of patients who improve symptomatically will also struggle with a number of psychosocial problems. Developing a sense of one's true self appears to be an essential component of facing down a severe eating disorder and attaining improved quality of life.

6. Scrub the old adage that "better is the enemy of the best." Clinicians and patients must strive for improvement, not just "cure" or an absence of eating disorder symptoms. Research now demonstrates that in most cases, recovery is actually a continuous process rather than a definitive end product (Crow, 2007; Kaplan, & Garfinkel, 1999; Miller, 1996; Yager, 2007b). Those patients who do better over time tend to have enhanced coping skills, improved interpersonal relations, and are content with being "less than perfect." They begin to embrace the notion that they are "good enough" and can be loved unconditionally for the unique human beings that they are.

7. Tune in to the patient's true self by looking into improved self-care and asking questions when you sense that they might be backsliding or a self-destructive action is in the offing. Because symptom control alone does not portend a sense of true self or the feeling of being "good enough," patients who recover symptomatically report that they must find their voice in treatment. Qualitative research is beginning to describe this process along with the crucial, affirming capacity to face down symptoms. To get a firmer grasp of the ways the patient may be improving or continuing to feel struck, occasionally ask the patient to elaborate on the question, "Tell me how your life is better now?" Qualitative research suggests that finding a sense of one's true self and facing down an eating disorder is operationalized by (a) improved self-care; (b) better problem solving abilities; (c) enhanced interpersonal relationships; and (d) more effective engagement in the life cycle.

8. Confront any tendency toward "the blame game." Patients who improve must relinquish the "victim mentality" to effectively engage in the life cycle. Neither patient nor therapist can avoid taking ultimate responsibility for her or his own life. Indeed, patients report that "a serious error in psychotherapy is to blame parents excessively" (Beresin et al., 1989, p. 114; see also Lamoureux & Bottorff, 2005). Learning to tolerate painful life experience and developing the capacity to grieve and to forgive are key components of recovery, which includes eschewing a tendency to go on a witch hunt to find any single culprit for one's problems, whether it be one's hereditary endowment, deficits and maltreatment within one's family of origin, or the unfortunate hand one has been dealt by the vicissitudes of life. In essence, maintain an open ear to the patient's past history and painful memories without dodging their aggression, both subtle and overt. It is the therapist's duty to hold both "states of mind" until the patient can fully integrate their loving and hating feelings.

CONCLUSION

Despite the large body of outcome studies that paint a sobering prognostic picture for the treatment of eating disorders, clinicians have reason to be hopeful. Quantitative and qualitative studies do show that over the long term many patients improve. Evolving studies seem to point toward the expectation that most of the time full recovery takes longer than anticipated and requires an array of therapeutic interventions.

Outcome studies that have been published to date do not yet tell clinicians enough about how patients get better or why they get better. Those patients who are able to "inch out" their eating disorder are important for researchers and clinicians to listen to and to learn from their experiences. These patients report a gradual taking on of responsibility for one's own self-care and an evolving understanding and appreciation for one's own self over a period of time. Although the clinician is in the honored position of witness to the development of a person right in front of our eyes, as in all development, this does not happen overnight. Contemporary research data clearly support this notion.

In order to feel encouraged during what is often a long and uncertain course of recovery, I have always taken some delight in the words of the late psychologist, Dr. Mary Cerney. From her experience as a nun and former elementary school teacher prior to becoming a therapist and psychoanalyst, she reminded mental health students and experienced clinicians alike that human growth is always an incremental process. "When you throw enough mud at something, some of it sticks!" she chided us (Cerney, personal communication, 1992). Some of those interventions will eventually adhere or take root, she seemed to be saying. I can almost hear the intervention: "You must stay the course, peel off those defenses one by one, keep listening, and let the Devil take the hindmost!" Her advice may also help the therapist avoid falling into the quicksand of countertransference discouragement in a treatment process that is likely to have much ebb and flow, and many backslides, ever in the face of gradual forward motion.

Our task remains to help our patients discover their own worldview and where they want to go, and why they may want to get there, and when they need to revise course or change direction. We must be prepared that the rewards of this process will dawn only gradually, require fortitude and patience, and repeatedly challenge the points of view of both participants. For the practicing clinician, there is no professional accomplishment more rewarding or gratifying than bearing witness to the birth of the true self and helping nurture its enfolding.

Epilogue

Alis volat propriis ("She flies with her own wings")

—Motto of the State of Oregon

The doctor crept into the tiny library to avoid disturbing the sleeping household. She pulled some books from the shelves to prepare for the morning lecture; after months of sorting, studying, scribbling, and working over some of the papers that were still strewn over the floor, she finally took a moment to put her feet up on the recliner and look over some of the writings and vignettes in the collection that mattered most to her. Even though it was not her spiritual tradition by birth, she always turned back to the Hasidic stories in the anthologies of Martin Buber and Elie Wiesel when she needed comfort or inspiration. This morning she once again read the rendition in Elie Wiesel's *Souls on Fire: Portraits and Legends of Hasidic Masters* of the Baal Shem Tov. It always seemed to her to imbue an essence of psychotherapy that she believed she might relate to the exhausted but eager interns she would meet with later in the day.

She would tell them that the story went something like this: The Rebbe Baal Shem Tov had many students and followers who revered him. One day he was observed by a couple of his students listening intently and respectfully to a fellow, who appeared, for all intents and purposes, quite inebriated. The disciples were shocked and wanted to protect their master; they also did not wish to be embarrassed by him. They told the Rebbe to cut it out and not waste his time on such a tawdry character. Better to spend his time teaching his truths to those that really counted and who would understand. The Baal Shem Tov compassionately explained to his followers, "When a man confesses himself, the way he chooses to do it doesn't matter. One must not turn away" (Wiesel, 1972, p. 21).

This is the message the doctor would try to get across to the interns today: to listen closely to their patients, whatever the circumstances, because their efforts might not be in vain. She would likewise try to remind herself throughout the day of the Baal Shem Tov's essential truth as she attended to her own patients in psychotherapy and psychoanalysis. The doctor knew she had a much easier task than the Rebbe, however, because for the most part her patients came to therapy very sober; in fact, her task was often to help them lighten up and feel better about themselves.

Thoughts about these patients continued to pass through her mind as she got ready for work. Her semiannual visit with her consultant once again yielded some productive insights. He had pointed out to her that sometimes an individual's ethical stance on an issue may be as repressed as any other problem they had because of the same kinds of family loyalties and conflicts that get in the way of a person's full flourishing in other areas. She wondered why she had not thought of this idea before and finally garnered the courage to ask him straight out how he got to be wise. He didn't answer at first, of course, because he understood that her question was as rhetorical as it was unanswerable by anyone other than the person themselves. Later in the 90-minute session, as the doctor continued to share her struggles, her interventions, and even some of her successes with him, the consultant offered the opinion that all clinicians get wise the same way. He told her, "The patient comes to own their story in their own way and at their own pace. By paying careful attention, we learn." There it was again, she thought, the importance of listening and keeping at it, especially at those crucial times when our patients might not be overtly receptive but will still want and need to release their burden.

Some noise from the lower level interrupted her associations; the doctor could hear that the menagerie had finished breakfast and were ready for their morning constitutional. She placed her late father's classic Rolex Oyster Datejust watch over her wrist; as she fastened the jubilee style bracelet she bought for it, she smiled to herself that the new look of either sex wearing larger timepieces meant that she could laugh off any sardonic quips or interpretations about the deeper meanings of sporting such a sizable piece of jewelry that had belonged for years to her father. How much her profession had changed, she mused, because those kinds of antiquated and canned meanings weren't very much in vogue anymore in the mental health field; she was free to wear this or any other family heirloom whenever she chose as yet another way of keeping those she loved and remembered always close to her heart.

The doctor then stumbled over another association to the 21st century fashion phenomenon of wearing larger watches: As the dials grew bigger and more complicated, seemingly telling us that time matters so much that we must see it clearly and distinctly, were we also paradoxically depriving ourselves of those precious moments that we can never return to once they are gone? She also considered that perhaps the variety of bezel shapes and sizes in these stylish timepieces might also reflect openness to honoring the different body types, sizes, and shapes that typify the human race. Could this trend in watches signal a turning point that might be taking root in the culture? She had her doubts but also her hopes that this could be the case.

As she quickly descended the staircase, the doctor took note of the George Rodrigues' print of Blue Dog titled *Dawn of New Love*. She and her beloved had purchased it on a trip to New Orleans and hung it prominently so as not to miss its essential message whenever they went up or down the stairs. As she took in Blue Dog's quizzical grin, she wondered what kinds of manifestations of love, and retreats from it, she would find in her practice on this new day. She would try to fly just below the radar of her patients' associations, and try to teach her students to do likewise, to help deepen the material but not push too far or too fast. She noted how her usual metaphor of "treatment as a journey" was shifting today to aerial motifs; perhaps this was because she had just come home from a plane trip and had once again been mesmerized by the variegated landscape of the country.

Suddenly the doctor caught herself thinking again about some of her patients and students, this time floating, as if they were characters from an oil, watercolor, or gouache of Marc Chagall. It occurred to her that the artist's fanciful figures are fully at peace with their bodies, free to soar above the mundane and stultifying, in part because they know how to take themselves lightly. Just as Chagall's multicolored and vivid images of flowers, animals, and people rise, swerve, sway, and play, as in a dream world, the doctor wished that her patients would be able to access their dreams and true self through mastery of their own unique internal landscapes. She hoped especially that they, and others she held dear, might someday experience the kind of creative partnership that Chagall had cultivated with his wife, Bella, in Vitevsk and which he depicted surrealistically but lovingly in *La Promenade* (1917–19) and other works.

Then, "a voice from another country," as her maternal grandmother might have said, announced itself. Melodiously, the doctor was being summoned. "We've got to get going, honey, because we can't be late for our first patients, and I know you'll want me to stop on the way so you can buy a mocha." The doctor, still working on her punctuality despite the treasured timepiece, took a few more moments to gather together her briefcase, her rain jacket, receipts, and recyclable hangers for the dry cleaners, and some magazines for the new office; she even quickly changed her handbag to match her outfit, something that would have pleased her mother and would especially tickle a couple of her patients who knew she could be fussy about such things. "Hop in, because we have really got to fly now." Yes, the doctor thought as she smiled to herself, that's so true. We must fly.

APPENDIX A

Sample Therapeutic Handout

1. Learn about the wide range of physical problems caused by eating disorders and the impact they have on psychological well-being.
   a. Be aware that eating disorders are real illnesses. Face down denial.
   b. Remember that eating disorders have the highest mortality rate of any psychiatric illness. Although this striking fact can lead to discouragement, most people who are able to return to normal eating patterns also show substantial psychological improvement.
   c. Find and keep appointments with a primary care clinician who knows about and treats the physical consequences of having an eating disorder (such as heart palpitations, electrolyte imbalance, malnutrition, and osteoporosis). A medical professional should be a principal player on your multidisciplinary treatment team that may also include an individual, group, family or couple's therapist; a nutritionist; a psychiatrist or nurse practitioner who prescribes psychotropic medication. Because your team members will want to communicate about your care, please sign a medical release of information which allows you to be sure of what will and will not be shared to protect your confidentiality.
   d. Remind yourself of the physiological consequences of your eating disorder behaviors when you are tempted to relapse. This suggestion may help you face any tendency to deny your problem and to refrain from engaging in self-destructive patterns.
2. Educate yourself about healthy nutrition and exercise and their effect on psychological resiliency.
   a. Recognize that contradictory cultural messages place you in a dilemma about weight and eating. Research shows that dieting and Western society's emphasis on beauty and physical perfection are contributors to eating disorders in many people.

b. Work toward placing less emphasis on external appearance and outward success. Discover what you do well and be true to your real self. Psychoanalyst Karen Horney (1950) captured the qualities of a psychologically healthy person when she observed, "The less self-conscious, the less intimidated, the less a person tries to comply with expectations of others, the less the need to be right or perfect, the better to express whatever gifts one has." (p. 328)

c. Stay away from fad diets as a first step to feeling better; learn how to eat wisely and well. Healthy eating patterns must be individualized so discussion with a nutritionist who has experience working with eating disorder patients can be particularly useful.

d. Try to be open and honest about any rituals or misuse of food (hoarding food, only eating a few kinds of food, etc.) with all members of your treatment team.

e. If you have anorexia, increase your caloric intake under skilled medical supervision to achieve a healthy weight range (i.e., at least 95% of low-average body weight).

f. If you have bulimia, stop using over-the-counter and prescribed diuretics, laxatives, syrup of ipecac, or other purgatives. Although purging may help you feel better temporarily after a binge or may serve as a strategy for coping with feelings of stress, these activities can actually be life-threatening. Because these behaviors can lead to sudden death, it is essential that you are honest about them with your team, especially your primary care provider and psychiatrist.

g. Do not diet. Most women begin their eating disorder behaviors by going on a stringent diet. Evidence demonstrates yo-yo dieting may sometimes lead to weight gain.

h. If you need to lose weight, seek out consultation from a nutritionist who is knowledgeable about eating disorders and follow the tried and true plan of going slowly under the care of a primary care clinician. For some individuals, joining a group that offers support and helps plan meals is useful.

i. Confront any tendency to use exercise in an unhealthy manner (e.g., only as a way to keep your weight low; to avoid or escape feelings or important life issues).

j. If you cannot avoid the tendency to get on the scale or look in the mirror multiple times everyday and criticize yourself, throw the scale away and cover your mirror.

3. Develop a relapse prevention program.

a. Figure out those times when you are most likely to engage in your eating disorder. Work with those on your treatment team to help you define those high-risk times when you are likely to restrict, binge, or purge.

    b. Find ways to feel more assertive and empowered in life. Work on developing a sense of self-worth so that the reactions of others are not so important.

    c. Remember that structure is your friend and a key to recovery. Have a list of activities and diversions for when you are tempted to binge or purge.

    d. Identify, admit, and express your feelings. It is essential for recovery to recognize the range of emotions that can trigger your tendency to binge, purge, or to use other destructive coping strategies. Find new ways of handling your feelings, such as journaling, playing music, dancing, meditating, or talking with a friend.

4. Learn new coping skills.

    a. Develop and maintain a sense of humor. Poke fun at your own foibles. Psychologists who have studied optimism and coping have learned that one of the best ways to reduce stress or to cope with illness is to watch a funny movie or TV show or to actually learn something new.

    b. Develop a support system of people you can call when under stress. Sometimes the 12-step fellowships (i.e., Overeaters Anonymous or even Alcoholics Anonymous or Narcotics Anonymous) or other support groups can help you with your eating disorder. They are usually free. No support group can meet all your needs and some people are tempted to not take advantage of what is offered because others' issues are "different from mine." Take the good things the group members offer and disregard what does not fit for you.

    c. Challenge and think through your tendency to "catastrophize" situations. At times we all tend to overestimate the likelihood of negative situations or terrible consequences (e.g., "I will get fat if I eat that brownie"; "My husband will leave me if I gain more weight").

    d. Look carefully at each situation that you fear and discuss it with your therapist and other members of your team. Develop a dialogue with yourself about how to cope more effectively with your problems. Cognitive-behavior therapists call this technique "cultivating self-talk," and it is a most effective tool in overriding eating disorder behavior.

    e. Try to be less rigid. People with eating problems tend to see things in a "black-and-white, either/or" mode. Confront your tendency to think in absolutes.

    f. Don't expect perfection when dealing with high-risk occasions. Eating disorders are likely to be an ongoing vulnerability, particularly at times of stress or transition, and holidays and parties when food is abundant.

    g. Read some of the many excellent self-help books, articles, and testimonials by other people who have had an eating disorder. They are available at your local library or bookstore. These life stories can be inspirational and suggest some new and useful coping methods.

h. Beware friends, groups, Internet chat rooms, and websites that encourage eating disorder behavior (e.g., "proanorexia" or "probulimia" websites).

5. Master some of the psychological issues that may lie behind your eating disorder.

   a. Disavow the commonly held notion of attaining perfection. Hilde Bruch, a pioneer in the study and treatment of eating disorders, once remarked that goals for recovery from an eating disorder include healthy living and the discovery that one is unique and has substance and worth. The individual can be said to be "in recovery" when one no longer needs the strain and stress of trying to attain "artificial perfection."

   b. Develop the courage to allow yourself to become a person who is at peace with yourself, even if you are not at your ideal weight. Recognize the value of finding one's own strength in adversity.

   c. Develop patience to confront the particular emotional issues that underlie your eating disorder. Remain committed to recovery even during inevitable setbacks and times of loss. Reversals and disappointments are unavoidable aspects of everyone's life.

   d. Maintain trust in yourself as the one who will find your unique path to recovery. Sometimes writing in a journal or simply jotting down some thoughts will help you define aspects of yourself and your goals that will jump start you on the road to feeling "less stuck." Maintain forward movement on your journey by celebrating small and large goals that you achieve.

   e. Cultivate a sense of meaning or purpose in life by addressing spiritual needs.

   f. Try not to "go it alone." Instead, seek out an experienced, trusted psychotherapist who, most importantly and fundamentally, will listen to you and help you to listen to yourself, your body, and your feelings.

   g. Try to be less self-critical and more forgiving of your own flaws and those of others.

6. Confront family issues.

   a. Be sure to tell your doctor about any family patterns of excessive dieting, obesity, or overexercise, because new research indicates that eating disorders tend to run in families (i.e., are at least in part genetic in many individuals).

   b. Consider how family emotional patterns may also play a role in your eating disorder. These multigenerational patterns include overemphasizing achievement, being slender, staying loyal at all costs to what parents or grandparents want you to do or be, and can lead to the tendency to develop and maintain eating disorder behavior.

    c. Educate partners and family members about your eating disorder and ask for their support in your recovery. Strive to be open about this issue.

    d. Engage in a family therapy process if others are willing to attend and to look at their roles in any dysfunctional patterns. When family members are not willing to grapple with their own mistakes or foibles, as often happens, you will need to work through (e.g., mourn) what these flaws mean to you over a period of time in your own therapy.

7. If you are a parent, be aware of how your eating disorder affects your children.

    a. Avoid placing your baby or child "on a diet" without medical consultation. Although obesity in children has become a national health concern and is certainly to be discouraged, a parent with an eating disorder or body image problem may be excessively focused on their infant's or child's weight and unwittingly potentiate problems in offspring.

    b. Recognize that even very young children are now receiving messages from the media about weight and appearance. Try to address some of these at home by making unrealistic standards of any kind a discussable issue.

    c. Reinvent family mealtime. It is hard with today's family structure to eat together, but this is a time when children and teens not only learn to eat wisely but also develop social skills. Eating with your children will help you notice any early tendency she or he might have toward restriction of food intake, overeating, or using the bathroom after a meal to purge.

    d. Recognize that certain occupations or activities increase the risk for eating disorders. Gymnasts, dancers, runners, wrestlers, models, actresses, and girls who attend boarding school have a higher incidence of eating disorders.

    e. Avoid telling your child that she or he "looks fat," needs to lose (or maintain) weight, or needs to "take off a few inches" for a sport or activity. Such comments can lead to eating disorder behaviors.

    f. Underscore the positive attributes your child has and give unconditional love. This obvious advice is actually a cornerstone of psychological nurturance that helps build healthy self-image and resiliency.

    g. Listen and provide support when your child discusses weight concerns. Model healthy eating patterns and regular physical exercise.

    h. Be aware of websites and Internet chat rooms that promote eating disorder behaviors in children and teens. Visitors to these sites get tips on how to purge and how to eat the bare minimum.

    i. If you suspect your child has difficulty with eating issues, even if not to the extent of a full-blown eating disorder, seek out professional advice. Keep the lines of communication open.

APPENDIX B

Annotated Bibliography

SELF-HELP BOOKS FOR ANOREXIA NERVOSA

Crisp, A.J., Joughin, N., Halek, C., & Bowyer, C. (1996). *Anorexia nervosa: The wish to change* (2nd ed.) New York: Brunner-Routledge. This simple manual is divided into 30 "steps for change" and addresses important subjects such as gaining weight, family relationships, and living at a normal weight. Patients will benefit from the straightforward format that focuses on nutrition issues but does not neglect suggestions for how to cope with the disorder over the long term.

Hall, L., & Ostroff, M. (1999). *Anorexia nervosa: A guide to recovery.* Carlsbad, CA: Gurze Books. This best-selling paperback is written by two people who acknowledge that they battled with anorexia for years. In addition to sharing their personal stories, they address the "questions most often asked about anorexia nervosa" and "where to start" and how to "get support" in the struggle to recover. The final section of the book provides some psychological strategies based on cognitive-behavioral therapy that aim to increase self-esteem, improve body image, help the individual find ways to relax, and challenge cultural influences.

Johnston, A. (1996/2000). *Eating in the light of the moon: How women can transform their relationships with food through myths, metaphors, and storytelling.* Carlsbad, CA: Gurze Books. This highly popular book of stories addresses self-help through the practical experience and insight that can be derived from reading. Topics included in the 20 chapters are the importance of self-nurturance, cultivation of one's intuition and reclamation the body's inherent wisdom, dealing with addictions and sexuality, and accepting one's flaws and "shadow self." Therapists who believe that the patient can glean strength from reading about myths, fairy tales, and metaphors can use this text at any point in the treatment when bibliotherapy might catalyze discussion or help cement some ideas that are worked on during the treatment.

Treasure, J. (1997). *Anorexia nervosa: A survival guide for families, friends, and sufferers.* Hove, UK: Psychology Press. This superb resource contains a wealth of suggestions about how to understand and problem solve on practically every major issue that a person with anorexia is likely to encounter. The author is an expert in the field, and she includes case examples from her practice that demonstrate how each person must develop her or his own unique solutions for recovery. Sections for family members, spouses, and even teachers and family physicians round out the topics, which include medical risks, self-understanding, improving relationships, and steps to take regarding long-term weight management after a target weight is achieved.

SELF-HELP BOOKS FOR BULIMIA NERVOSA

Hall, L., & Cohn, L. (1992). *Bulimia: A guide to recovery* (2nd ed.). Carlsbad, CA: Gurze Books. This book addresses the most frequently asked questions that people have about bulimia and then provides an extensive list of strategies and self-help exercises to aid in overcoming the problem. The senior author writes her own "true story of the binge-purge syndrome" to let the reader know from the beginning that there is hope when one can truly engage in the treatment process. Examples about techniques that have worked for many sufferers such as journal-writing, planning safe amounts of physical exercise, establishing family support, and engaging in body image work are excellent additions to any comprehensive treatment program. The text also offers a two-week program to stop bingeing, advice for loved ones and family members, and a set of guidelines for those who form or participate in a support group.

Reindl, S.M. (2001). *Sensing the self: Women's recovery from bulimia.* Cambridge, MA: Harvard University Press. Dr. Reindl bases her book on her own in-depth research and clinical work, and she succeeds brilliantly in conveying how the complex components of recovery derive from the patient's desire to get to know her or his suppressed needs and feelings. This sophisticated analysis is written for a professional audience but contains patient histories of healing. Patients will benefit from the case examples of how others gradually learned to embrace their self-experiences and profited from the attuned responses of others. The author has much to say about how deficits in self-structure and self-regulation were overcome in her cohort of patients by attentive listening on the part of both patient and therapist.

Schmidt, U., & Treasure, J. (1993). *Getting better bit(e) by bit(e): A survival kit for sufferers of bulimia nervosa and binge-eating disorder.* New York: Brunner-Routledge. Packed with coping strategies and tools for overcoming the major concerns of patients with bulimia, this text also walks the patient through steps to learn more about oneself, the body, and how it functions. Classic strategies such as keeping a personal therapeutic food diary, with actual examples on how to begin to chart it out, accompany other hints for preventing relapse. Because so many patients with this disorder are victims of sexual or physical abuse, additional chapters are devoted to the wounds of childhood, patterns of self-destructiveness, and tips for taking better care of oneself by putting appropriate assertive behaviors into practice. In essence, this book provides excellent psychotherapeutic support as well as state-of-the-art information about the physiological problems that accompany restrictive dieting, overeating, and methods of purging.

GENERAL RESOURCES FOR FAMILIES AND PATIENTS

Michel, D., & Willard, S. (2003). *When dieting becomes dangerous: A guide to understanding and treating anorexia and bulimia*. New Haven, CT: Yale University Press. Authoritatively and compassionately written by a psychologist and social worker with considerable experience in the continuum of care for eating disorders (i.e., inpatient, partial hospital, and outpatient treatment), this succinct book addresses all of the major worries family members are likely to have about their loved ones. One chapter is devoted to the special needs of male patients. Suggestions are made for how family members can help each other to understand and support their loved one to get and to stay well.

Strober, M., & Schneider, M. (2005). *Just a little too thin: How to pull your child back from the brink of an eating disorder*. Cambridge, MA: Da Capo Press. This accessible book for parents is chock full of advice about "what you can do" to help a child avoid an eating disorder. Based on Dr. Strober's 30 years of clinical research and treatment with patients at the UCLA Eating Disorders Program, the numerous case examples demonstrate what can go wrong inside a family system and responses parents can make so things go much better at home. While anyone who lives or works with an adolescent can benefit from the matter of fact advice about "what to say" or "what not to say" to the teen, particular suggestions about how to introduce the subject of seeing a nutritionist or entering therapy will be particularly welcome for family members who have a child with an eating disorder who is reluctant to begin treatment.

Walsh, B.T. & Cameron, V.L. (2005). *If your adolescent has an eating disorder: An essential resource for parents*. New York: Oxford University Press. This informative guide combines the latest scientific findings with practical advice for parents. The brief, easily readable sections cover just about anything parents will want or need to know, helping them to begin to communicate with their child about starting treatment and stay in it long enough for recovery to occur. A special feature highlights how parents can find treatment if it is needed and help prevent the eating disorder from returning. Sections on brain chemistry, genetics, males, comorbidity, and the dangers of "doing nothing" are just a few of the subsections that are interwoven with case histories that will leave parents feeling more empowered about what to do to help their child.

Zerbe, K.J. (1993). *The body betrayed: Women, eating disorders and treatment.* Washington, DC: American Psychiatric Press. (paperback edition: Carlsbad, CA: Gurze Books, 1995) Considered a landmark textbook that addresses all aspects of diagnosis, medical management, and psychiatric treatment of eating disorders, this crossover book was written for patients, parents, significant others, and eventually "crossed over" to professionals who desire a deeper understanding of what brings eating disorders about and the psychotherapeutic strategies that aid in their recovery. Eating disorders are looked at across the life span, from childhood to old age. Numerous case examples of women in certain "at-risk" groups such as athletes, the pregnant patient, the sexually abused patient, and the older patient are also addressed.

FIRST PERSON ACCOUNTS

There are numerous first person accounts written by patients who have struggled valiantly, although at first reluctantly, to overcome an eating disorder. These six authors are inspiring to read for clinicians as well as patients. They eloquently speak to the wide range of psychological issues that individuals have, and how a variety of counseling techniques, including CBT, interpersonal, and psychodynamic psychotherapy, and even psychoanalysis, have been useful for individuals who must find new coping strategies and overcome core conflicts, abuse, parental neglect, and developmental deficit to develop a true, resilient sense of self.

Chernin, K. (1986). *The hungry self: Women, eating disorders and identity.* New York: Times Books. Kim Chernin has written passionately and extensively about her recovery from a complex eating disorder in a thoughtful and psychologically sophisticated way, touching the lives of millions worldwide who have suffered with the problem. In addition to this chronicle wherein Chernin applies psychodynamic theory to her life (especially the perspective of Melanie Klein), patients are encouraged to read her sensitive and revealing memoir, *The obsession: Reflections on the tyranny of slenderness* (New York: Perennial, 1981). Chernin demonstrates that there are often many false starts when one undertakes therapy, but that persistence and honest self-assessment pay off over time.

Daniels, L. (2001). *With a woman's voice: A writer's struggle for emotional freedom.* Lanham, MD: Madison Books. Dr. Lucy Daniels is a clinical psychologist and professional writer born to a family of wealth and privilege. Behind a veneer of success and health lay neglect by well-intentioned parents; they failed to recognize and to intervene as their daughter lost significant amounts of weight and experienced the anguish of internalized hatred and despair. After years of travail and multiple attempts to engage in treatment and get well, the author finally finds a portion of relief and begins the journey of self-discovery in psychoanalysis. Patients will recognize aspects of themselves in her memoir while finding encouragement and a sustaining presence as they embark on their own journey.

Hall, L. (Ed.). (1993). *Full lives: Women who have freed themselves from food and weight obsession.* Carlsbad, CA: Gurze Books. This series of autobiographical accounts of women who have had, and subsequently recovered from, a serious eating disorder is a straightforward, fast-paced, and compelling read. The authors are from different walks of life and reveal in their extraordinary stories divergent pathways that propelled each of them to misuse food. Struggles with anorexia, bulimia, binge eating, and obesity are covered. Practical suggestions and strategies for recovery are offered to help the patient come to terms with the role of eating in one's own life and follow an individual path to recovery.

Knapp, C. (2003). *Appetites: Why women want.* New York: Counterpoint. Carolyn Knapp is best known for her riveting memoir, *Drinking, A love story,* (New York: Counterpoint, 1996). In *Appetites,* she tells the gripping tale of her other addiction—restricting her eating to become dangerously thin. While acknowledging the role of culture in the development of her anorexia nervosa, Knapp is direct in explaining how her family dynamics, unaddressed personal losses, suppressed feelings, and emotional abandonment induced by deficits within her family of origin led to her eating disorder. Before her untimely death from lung cancer in 2002, Knapp found significant solace and self-understanding through intensive psychotherapy, the benefits of which she hints at throughout this searing memoir.

Liu, A. (2007). *Gaining: The truth about life after eating disorders.* New York: Warner. Amy Liu is a former professional model who combines first person accounts of others with an eating disorder history and interviews with numerous experts in the field to help her readers become more "self-aware and self-confident enough to avoid psychological traps such as eating disorders" (p. 260). She mentions her own struggle with anorexia and covers a wide array of family and personal dynamics. The particular strength of this book is its emphasis on how experts are beginning to unravel the ways in which neurobiology, temperament, and genetics come into play in some cases.

Schaefer, J., & Rutledge, T. (2004). *Life without ED: How one woman declared independence form her eating disorder and how you can do it too!* New York: McGraw-Hill. This humorous, vivid, first person account describes how one woman found a way to face down her severe eating disorder. The author names her problem "ED" and addresses him as if she were confronting a destructive relationship with a boyfriend named Ed. Commentary by her psychotherapist (Thom Rutledge) strengthens the recommendations the primary author makes about sticking to a food plan, developing relapse prevention methods, and defining recovery. A wide range of patients will be impressed by how Jenny Schaefer frees herself from her dependence on and pathological relationship to "ED." The concept of describing a life with and without ED illuminates how many patients experience their eating disorder as a compelling, albeit destructive, intimate relationship which must be given up to fully live one's own life.

RESOURCES FOR ADDRESSING BODY IMAGE CONCERNS

Cash, T.F. (1997). *The body image workbook: An eight-step program for learning to like your looks.* Oakland, CA: New Harbinger Workbooks. Written by an eminent researcher and pioneer in the field of body image, this practical manual delves into the psychology of personal appearance and the reasons why men and women can be so critical of our bodies. To counter self-defeating behaviors and internal criticism, Cash provides a list of "help sheets" that guide the reader through eight steps to improved body image. These documents are geared to improve life by countering a negative body image. They also suggest relaxation exercises, positive affirmations, physical fitness techniques, and "self-talk" dialogues to correct negative feelings about one's body. A final chapter addresses the often neglected topic of aging.

Freedman, R. (1989). *Bodylove: Learning to like our looks—and ourselves.* New York: Harper & Row. This well-known text on developing a positive body image is filled with advice and easy exercises to help anyone learn to feel better about her or his body. The case examples, therapeutic exercises, and succinct review of society's role in helping shape body image invite the reader to become less self-critical and feel more physically attractive by "making over body image from within."

Hutchinson, M.G. (1985). *Transforming body image: Learning to love the body you have.* Freedom, CA: Crossing Press. Another excellent and accessible guide to transforming negative body image, Hutchinson's book challenges readers to go beneath surface concerns and to confront how we may be sabotaging ourselves repeatedly but unwittingly by worrying too much about appearance. Exercises and guided visualizations are provided along with tools to help the individual process the feelings and thoughts that the exercises arouse. The goal is transforming the myth of physical perfection and forming a positive, realistic identity.

Kearney-Cooke, A., with Isaacs, F. (2004). *Change your mind: change your body: Feeling good about body and self after 40.* New York: Atria Books. While written specifically for women entering midlife who struggle with the problems of aging and body image, virtually anyone can benefit from Kearney-Cooke's exercises and strategies for enhancing self-care, self-esteem, and personal power. The author brings years of clinical experience with patients in individual and group therapy where she developed and put into practice the suggested strategies she recommends for treating eating and body image problems. A tone of empathy and compassion pervades this superb resource.

RESOURCES FOR BINGE EATING AND SUCCESSFUL
LONG-TERM WEIGHT MANAGEMENT

Hirschmann, J.R., & Munter, C. H. (1988). *Overcoming overeating.* New York: Ballantine Books. This standard reference for the compulsive overeater who must learn to forego dieting and begin to recognize signals of satiety while embracing self-acceptance is an excellent adjunct to pharmacotherapy and psychotherapy for binge eating. A widely available guide to breaking free of an addiction to eating, it includes the authors' three-phased plan to address the problems of living in a world where food is ubiquitous, to learn how to feed oneself appropriately, and to develop the self after "the circuit of excessive eating" is broken.

Nelson, M.E., & Wernick, F. (1997). *Strong women stay young.* New York: Bantam Books. Drawing on seminal research from the Friedman School of Nutrition, Science, and Policy at Tufts, this book outlines a program of thrice-weekly strengthening exercises shows women how they can attain more energy, improve balance and physique, have greater body tone and flexibility, and live longer. For persons with an eating disorder, tips on how to "bone up the skeleton" are particularly important for reversing osteopenia. Aerobic and strength training exercises based on the research of the Tufts group can help women at any age feel stronger and better. (The authoritative bimonthly *Tufts Health and Nutrition Newsletter* also provides reliable, sensible, and evidence-based information on nutrition, exercise, fad diets, vitamin supplements, etc. to a lay and professional audience).Tips for regular workouts will help overweight patients tone and lose weight; persons with anorexia or bulimia nervosa will be guided by the sensible dietary advice and scientifically tested exercise recommendations.

Oliver-Pyatt, W. (2003). *Fed Up! The breakthrough ten-step, no-diet fitness plan.* New York: Contemporary Books. Written by a psychiatrist, this book again addresses the myth of dieting, the cultural epidemic of eating disorders, and the desire to have an ideal body. Oliver-Pyatt's extensive knowledge of biology and psychology is geared to teach the general reader why weight loss without exercise is almost impossible. She makes reasonable but simple recommendations about how to increase physical activity that are as realistic as they are affirmative for achieving a healthier lifestyle. Other sections of the book delve into the psychological and existential aspects of food and body preoccupation, aiding the individual in her or his understanding of the guilt, shame, and narcissism that drive the problem. A final, crucially important chapter for parents addresses prevention of eating disorders and obesity in children.

Tribole, E., & Resch, E. (1995). *Intuitive eating: A revolutionary program that works.* New York: St. Martin's Paperbacks. Most patients with eating disorder problems have read copiously about nutrition and dieting. Much of what they learn is either misinterpreted or incorrect. This book, written by two seasoned, successful nutritionists, sets the record straight. Although clinicians will usually recommend that a patient see her or his own nutritionist who can collaborate in the multidisciplinary, integrated treatment, sometimes that resource is not available. This excellent guide provides straightforward information about eating wisely and the pitfalls of having a "diet mentality." Advice for healthy living and principles to follow to normalize the relationship with food lend support to the person who struggles to learn her or his body's hunger signals.

References

Abend, S. (2005). Analyzing intrapsychic conflict: Compromise formation as an organizing principle. *Psychoanalytic Quarterly, 74,* 5–26.

Adair, C., Marcoux, G.C., Cram, B.S., Ewashen, C.J., Chafe, J., Cassin, S.E. et al. (2007). Development and multi-site validation of a new condition-specific quality of life measure for eating disorders. *Health and Quality of Life Outcomes, 5,* 23.

Agras, W.S., Dorian, B., Kirkley, B.G., Arnow, B., & Bachman, J. (1987). Imipramine in the treatment of bulimia: a double-blind controlled study. *International Journal of Eating Disorders, 6*(1), 29–38.

Ainsworth, M.D.S., Blehar, M.C., Waters, E., & Wall, S. (1978). *Patterns of attachment: A psychological study of the Strange Situation.* Northvale, NJ: Aronson.

Akhtar, S. (1992). *Broken structures: Severe personality disorders and their treatment.* Northvale, NJ: Aronson.

Akhtar, S. (1995). *Quest for answers: A primer of understanding and treating severe personality disorders.* Northvale, NJ: Aronson.

Akhtar, S. (1996). "Someday" and "If only" fantasies: Pathological optimism and inordinate nostalgia as related forms of idealization. *Journal of the American Psychoanalytic Association, 44,* 723–725.

Akhtar, S. (1999). *Immigration and identity: Turmoil, treatment, and transformation.* Northvale, NJ: Aronson.

Albom, M. (1997). *Tuesdays with Morrie: An old man, a young man, and life's greatest lesson.* New York: Doubleday.

Alexander, F. (1956). *Psychoanalysis and psychotherapy.* New York: W.W. Norton.

Alexander, F., & French, T.J. (1946). *Psychoanalytic therapy principles and application.* New York: W.W. Norton.

Allaz, A.F., Bernstein, M., Rouget, P., Archinard, M., & Morabia, A. (1998). Body weight preoccupation in middle aged and ageing women: A general population survey. *International Journal of Eating Disorders, 23*(3), 287–294.

Allen, J. G. (2001). *Traumatic relationships and serious mental disorders.* Hoboken, NJ: Wiley.

Allen, J.G. (2005). *Coping with trauma: Hope through understanding.* Washington, DC: American Psychiatric Publishing. (Original work published 1995)

Alpert, J., & Spencer, J.B. (1986). *Morality, gender, and analysis.* In J.L. Alpert (Ed.), *psychoanalysis and women: Contemporary reappraisals* (pp. 83–112). New York: Analytic Press.

Alvarez, A. (1992). *Live company: Psychoanalytic psychotherapy with autistic, border-line, deprived, and abused children.* New York: Routledge.

American Psychiatric Association. (2000). *Diagnostic and statistical manual of mental disorders* (4th ed. rev.). Washington, DC: Author.

American Psychiatric Association. (2006). Practice guideline for the treatment of patients with eating disorders (3rd ed.). *American Journal of Psychiatry, 163,* 6–54.

Amundsen, G. (1999). Therapists' identifications with common social values as obstacles to increased socio-cultural sensitivity. *Psychoanalysis and Psychotherapy, 16,* 189–210.

Andersen, A. (Ed.). (1990). *Males with eating disorders.* Philadelphia: Brunner-Mazel.

Andersen, A.E. (1992). Analysis of treatment experience and outcome from The Johns Hopkins Eating Disorders Program: 1975–1990. In K.A. Halmi (Ed.), *Psychobiology and treatment of anorexia nervosa and bulimia nervosa* (pp. 93–124). Washington, DC: American Psychiatric Press.

Andersen, A.E. (1994). Stories I tell my patients: The door and the carpenter's plane. *Eating Disorders: The Journal of Treatment and Prevention, 2*(3), 273–275.

Andersen, A. (2006). Revising the diagnosis of anorexia nervosa will improve patient care. *Eating Disorders Review, 17*(2), 1–3.

Anderson-Fye, E.P. (2004). A "Coca-cola" shape: Cultural change, body image, and eating disorders in San Andres, Belize. *Culture, Medicine, and Psychiatry, 28,* 561–594.

Anderson-Fye, E.P., & Becker, A.E. (2003). Cross-cultural aspects of eating disorders. In J. Kevin Thompson (Ed.), *The handbook of eating disorders and obesity* (pp. 565–589). Hoboken, NJ: Wiley.

Anderson, M. (1995). Mother-daughter connection: The healing force in the treatment of eating disorders. *Journal of Feminist Family Therapy, 6,* 3–20.

Anonymous. (1995). "My secret." *Journal of the American Medical Association* 274(7), 1395.

Appolinario, J.C., & McElroy, S.L. (2004). Pharmacological approaches in the treat-ment of binge eating disorder. *Current Drug Targets, 5*(3), 301–307.

Armstrong, K. (1993). *A history of God: The 4,000-year quest of Judaism, Christianity, and Islam.* New York: Knopf.

Armstrong, P.S. (2000). *Opening gambits.* Northvale, NJ: Aronson.

Aronson, J.K. (1993). *Insights in the dynamic psychotherapy of anorexia as bulimia: An introduction to the literature.* Northvale, NJ: Aronson.

Aronson, J.K. (1996). The use of the telephone as a transitional space in the treatment of a severely masochistic anorexic patient. In J. Edward & J.B. Sanville (Eds.), *Fostering healing and growth: A psychoanalytic social work approach* (pp. 163–178). Northvale, NJ: Aronson.

Bacaltchuk, J., & Hay, P., (2003). Antidepressants versus placebo for people with bulimia nervosa. *Cochrane Database System Review 4,* CD003391.

Badman, M.K., & Flier, J.S. (2005). The gut and energy balance: Visceral allies in obesity wars. *Science, 307*(5717), 1909–1914.

Balint, M. (1987). *Thrills and regressions.* New York: International Universities Press. (Original work published 1959)

Baranowska, B. (1990). Are disturbances in opiod and adrenergic systems involved in the hormonal dysfunction of anorexia nervosa? *Psychoneuroendocrinology, 5,* 371–379.

Baranowska, B. (2003). Anorexia nervosa and bulimia nervosa-neuroendocrine dis-turbances. In M. Maj, K. Halmi, J.J. Lopez-Ibor, & N. Sartorius (Eds.), *Eating Disorders* (pp. 212–214). London: Wiley.

Barbarich, N.C., McConaha, C.W., Gaskill, J., La, V.M., Frank, G.K., Achenbach, S., Plotnicov, K.H., & Kaye, W.H. (2004). An open trial of olanzapine in anorexia nervosa. *Journal of Clinical Psychiatry*, 65, 1480–1482.

Barlow, J., Blouin, A., & Perez, E. (1988). Treatment of bulimia with desipramine: A double-blind crossover study. *Canadian Journal of Psychiatry*, 33, 129–133.

Barth, D. (2001). Thinking, talking, and feeling in psychotherapy with eating-disordered individuals. In J. Petrucelli & C. Stuart (Eds.), *Hungers and compulsions: The psychodynamic treatment of eating disorders and addictions* (pp. 41–52). Northvale, NJ: Aronson.

Basson, R. (2000). The female sexual response—A different model. *Journal of Sex and Marital Therapy*, 26, 1–65.

Basson, R. (2002), A model of women's sexual arousal. *Journal of Sex and Marital Therapy*, 28, 1–10.

Bateman, A., & Fonagy, P. (2006). *Mentalization-based treatment for borderline personality disoder: A practical guide.* Oxford: Oxford University Press.

Battegay, R. (1991). *The hunger diseases.* Lewiston, NY: Hogrefe & Huber.

Beck, A. (1993). *Cognitive therapy and the emotional disorders.* New York: American Library Trade.

Beck, J.S. (1995). *Cognitive therapy: Basics and beyond.* New York: Guilford.

Becker, A.E. (1995). *Body, self, and society: The view from Fiji.* Philadelphia: University of Pennsylvania Press.

Becker, A.E. (2003). Eating disorders and social transition. *Primary Psychiatry*, 10(6), 75–79.

Becker, A.E. (2004a). Editorial: New global perspectives on eating disorders. *Culture, Medicine and psychiatry*, 28, 433–437.

Becker, A.E. (2004b). Television, disordered eating, and young women in Fiji: Negotiating body image and identity during rapid social change. *Culture, Medicine and Psychiatry*, 28, 533–559.

Becker, A.E., Burwell, R.A., Gilman, S.E., Herzog, D.B., & Hamburg, P. (2002). Eating behaviors and attitudes following prolonged exposure to television among ethnic Fijian adolescent girls. *British Journal of Psychiatry*, 180, 509–514.

Becker, A.E., Burwell, R.A., Narvara, K., Gilman, S.E. (2003). Binge eating and binge eating disorder in a small scale indigenous society: The view from Fiji. *International Journal of Eating Disorders* 34, 423–431.

Becker, A.E., Fay, K., Gilman, S.E., & Striegel-Moore, R. (2007). Facets of acculturation and their diverse relations to body shape concerns in Fiji. *International Journal of Eating Disorders* 40(1), 42–50.

Becker, A.E., Grinspoon, S.K., Klibanski, A., & Herzog, D.B. (1999). Eating disorders. *New England Journal of Medicine*, 340, 1092–1098.

Belenky, M.F., Clinchy, B.M., Goldberger, N.R., & Tarule, J. (1986). *Women's ways of knowing: The development of self, voice and mind.* New York: Basic Books.

Bell, R. (1985), *Holy anorexia.* Chicago: University of Chicago Press.

Bemporad, J.R., Beresin, E., Ratey, J.J., O'Driscoll, G., Lindem, K., & Herzog, D.B. (1992) A psychoanalytic study of eating disorders I. A developmental profile of 67 index cases. *Journal of the American Academy of Psychoanalysis*, 20, 509–532.

Bemporad, J.R., O'Driscoll, G., Beresin, E., Ratey, J.J., Lindem, K., & Herzog, D.B. (1992). A psychoanalytic study of eating disorders II. Intergroup and intragroup comparisons. *Journal of the American Academy of Psychoanalysis*, 20, 533–542.

Benjamin, J. (1988). *The bonds of love: Psychoanalysis, feminism, and the problem of domination.* New York: Pantheon.

Beresin, E.V., Gordon, C., & Herzog, D.B. (1989). The process of recovering from anorexia nervosa. *The Journal of the American Academy of Psychoanalysis*, 17(1), 103–130.

Berg, S.L., & Andersen, A.E. (2007). Eating disorders in special populations: Medical comorbidities and complicating or unusual conditions. In J. Yager & P. Powers (Eds.), *Clinical Manual of Eating Disorders* (pp. 335–356). Washington, DC: American Psychiatric Press.

Berke, J. H. (1990). *The tyranny of malice: Exploring the dark side of character and culture.* New York: Summit.

Berkman, N.D., Lohr, K.N., & Bulik, C.M. (2007). Outcomes of eating disorders: A systematic review of the literature. *International Journal of Eating Disorders, 40*(4), 293–309.

Bernstein, A.E., & Lenhart, S.A. (1993). *The psychodynamic treatment of women.* Washington, DC: American Psychiatric Press.

Bernstein, A.E., & Severino, S. (1986). The "dumb spot": A special problem in countertransference. *Journal of the American Academy of Psychoanalysis, 14,* 85–94.

Bernstein, D. (1983). The female superego: A different perspective. *International Journal of Psychoanalysis, 64,* 187–201.

Betan, E., Kegley-Heim, A., Conklin, C. & Westen, D. (2005). Countertransference phenomena and personality pathology in clinical practice: An empirical investigation. *American Journal of Psychiatry, 162,* 890–898.

Binswanger, L. (1958). The case of Ellen West. In R. May, E. Angel, & H. Ellenberger (Eds.), *Existence: A new dimension in psychiatry and psychology* (pp. 237–364). New York: Basic Books (Original work published 1944, 1945).

Bion, W.R. (1965). *Transformations.* London: Heinemann.

Bion, W. (1967). *Second thoughts: Selected papers on psychoanalysis.* London: Heinemann.

Bion, W.R. (1974). *Brazilian lectures,* (Vol. 2, pp. 1–105), Rio de Janeiro: Image Editora.

Bion, W.R. (1977). Learning from experience. In *Seven servants: Four works by Wilfred R. Bion.* New York: Aronson.

Blatt, S.J., & Shahar, G. (2004). Psychoanalysis with whom, for what, and how? Comparisons with psychotherapy. *Journal of the American Psychoanalytic Association, 52*(2), 393–447.

Blatt, S.J., & Shichman, S. (1983). Two primary configurations of psychopathology. *Psychoanalysis and Contemporary Thought, 6,* 187–254.

Bloks, H., van Furth, E., Callewaert, I., & Hoek, H. (2004). Coping with strategies and recovery in patients with a severe eating disorder. *Eating Disorders: The Journal of Treatment and Prevention, 12*(2), 157–170.

Bloom, C., Gitter, A., Gutwill, S., Kogel, L., & Zaphiropoulos, L. (1994). *Eating problems: A feminist psychoanalytic treatment model.* New York: Basic Books.

Bloom, C. & Kogel, L. (1994a). Tracing development: The feeding experience and the body. In C. Bloom, A. Gitter, S. Gutwill, L. Kogel, & L. Zaphiropoulos (Eds.), *Eating problems: A feminist psychoanalytic treatment model* (pp. 40–56). New York: Basic Books.

Bloom, C. & Kogel, L. (1994b). Symbolic meanings of food and body. In C. Bloom, A. Gitter, S. Gutwill, L. Kogel, & L. Zaphiropoulos (Eds.), *Eating problems: A feminist psychoanalytic treatment model* (pp. 57–66). New York: Basic Books.

Bloom, C., Kogel, L., & Zaphiropoulos, L. (1994). Learning to feed oneself: A psychodynamic model. In C. Bloom, A. Gitter, S. Gutwill, L. Kogel, & L. Zaphiropoulos (Eds.), *Eating problems: A feminist psychoanalytic treatment model* (pp. 83–115). New York: Basic Books.

Bloom, H. (1994). *The western canon: The books and schools of the ages.* New York: Riverhead Books.

Bloom, H. (2000). *How to read and why.* New York: Simon & Schuster.

Blos, P. (1962). *On adolescence: A psychoanalytic interpretation.* New York: Free Press.

Blos, P. (1979). *The adolescent passage: Developmental issues.* New York: International Universities Press.

Blum, H. (1997). Clinical and developmental dimensions of hate. *Journal of the American Psychoanalytic Association, 45*(2), 359–376.

Blum, H. (2003). Psychic trauma and traumatic object loss. *Journal of the American Psychoanalytic Association, 51*(2), 415–431.

Boachie, A. Goldfield, G., & Spettigue, W. (2003). Olanzapine use as an adjunctive treatment for hospitalized children with anorexia nervosa: Case reports. *International Journal of Eating Disorders, 33*(1), 98–103.

Bogh, E.H., Rokkedal, K., & Valbak, K. (2005). A 4-year follow-up on bulimia nervosa. *European Eating Disorders Review, 13*, 48–53.

Bollas, C. (1987). *The shadow of the object: Psychoanalysis of the unthought known.* New York: Columbia University Press.

Boris, H.N. (1984a). The problem of anorexia nervosa. *International Journal of Psycho-Analysis, 65*, 315–322.

Boris, H.N. (1984b). On the treatment of anorexia nervosa. *International Journal of Psycho-Analysis, 65*, 435–442.

Bowlby, J. (1969). *Attachment and loss: Vol. 1. Attachment.* London: Hogarth Press and Institute for Psychoanalysis.

Bowlby, J. (1979). On knowing what you are not supposed to know and feeling what you are not supposed to feel. *Canadian Journal of Psychiatry, 241*, 403–408.

Bowlby, J. (1988). *A secure base: Clinical applications of attachment theory.* London: Routledge.

Bradley, R., Heim, A.K., & Westen, D. (2005). Transference patterns in the psychotherapy of personality disorders. *British Journal of Psychiatry, 186*, 342–349.

Brambilla, J., & Monteleone, P. (2003). Physical complications and physiological aberrations in eating disorders: A review. In M. Maj, K. Halmi, J.J. Lopez-Ibor, & N. Sartorius (Eds.). *Eating Disorders* (pp. 139–192). London: Wiley.

Brand, P., & Yancey, P. (1993). *Pain: The gift nobody wants.* New York: Harper-Collins/Zonderoan.

Braun, D., Sunday, S.R., Fornari, V., & Halmi, K. (1999). Bright light therapy decreases winter binge frequency in women with bulimia nervosa: A double-blind, placebo-controlled study. *Comprehensive Psychiatry, 6*, 442–448.

Brazelton, T.B., Tronick, E., & Adamson, L., Als, H., & Wise, S. (1975). Early mother-infant reciprocity. In *Parent-infant interaction* (pp. 137–154). Ciba Foundation Symposium 33. Amsterdam: Elsevier.

Brenner, C. (1982). *The mind in conflict.* New York: International Universities Press.

Brenner, C. (1994). The mind as conflict and compromise formation. *Journal of Clinical Psychoanalysis 3*, 473–488.

Brewerton, T.D. (Ed.). (2004). *Clinical handbook of eating disorders.* New York: Dekker.

Brewerton, T.D. (2005). Psychological trauma and eating disorders. In S. Wonderlich, J. Mitchell, M. De Zwann, & H. Steiger (Eds.). *AED Review of eating disorders, part I* (pp. 137–154). Oxford: Radcliff.

Brisman, J. (2001). The instigation of dare: Broadening therapeutic horizons. In J. Petrucelli & C. Stuart (Eds.), *Hungers and compulsions: The psychodynamic treatment of eating disorders and addictions* (pp. 53–64). Northvale, NJ: Aronson.

Brody, S. (2002). *The development of anorexia nervosa: The hunger artists.* Madison, CT: International Universities Press.

Bromberg, P. (1996). *Standing in the spaces: Essays on clinical process, trauma, and dissociation.* Hillsdale, NJ: Analytic Press.

Bromberg, P. (2001). Out of body, out of mind, out of danger: Some reflections on shame, dissociation, and eating disorders. In J. Petrucelli & C. Stuart (Eds.), *Hungers and compulsions: The psychodynamic treatment of eating disorders* (pp. 65–80). Northvale NJ: Aronson.

Broucek, F.J. (1991). *Shame and the self.* New York: Guilford.

Brownley, K.A., Berkman, N.D., Sedway, J.A., Lohr, K.N., & Bulik, C.M. (2007). Binge eating disorder treatment: A systematic review of randomized controlled trials. *International Journal of Eating Disorders, 40*(4), 337–348.

Bruch, H. (1973). *Eating disorders: Obesity, anorexia nervosa, and the person within.* New York: Basic Books.

Bruch, H. (1974). *Eating disorders.* London: Routledge & Kegan Paul.

Bruch, H. (1978). *The golden cage: The enigma of anorexia nervosa.* Cambridge, MA: Harvard University Press.

Bruch, H. (1988). *Conversations with anorexics.* D. Czyzewski & M. Suhr (Eds.). New York: Basic Books.

Brumberg, J.J. (1988). *Fasting girls: The history of anorexia nervosa.* New York: Penguin.

Brumberg, J.J. (1997). *The body project.* New York: Vintage Books.

Bruner, J.G. & deJong, R.H. (2001). Lipoplasty claims experience of U.S. Insurance Companies. *Plastic and Reconstructive Surgery, 107*(5), 1292–1293.

Bryant-Waugh, R. (2000). Overview of eating disorders. In B. Lask & R. Bryant-Waugh (Eds.), *Anorexia nervosa and related disorders in childhood and adolescence* (2nd ed.) (pp. 27–38). New York: Brunner-Routledge.

Bulik, C.M., Berkman, N.D., Brownley, K.A., Sedway, J.A., & Lohr, K.N. (2007). Anorexia nervosa treatment: A systematic review of randomized controlled trials. *International Journal of Eating Disorders, 40*(4), 310–320.

Bulik, C.M., Sullivan, P.F., Carter, F. A., McIntosh, V.V., & Joyce, P.R. (1999). Predictors of rapid and sustained response to cognitive-behavioral therapy for bulimia nervosa. *International Journal of Eating Disorders, 26*(2), 137–144.

Bulik, C.M., Sullivan, P.F., Fear, J., & Pickering, A. (1997). Predictors of the development of bulimia nervosa in women with anorexia nervosa. *The Journal of Nervous and Mental Disorders, 185,* 704–707.

Bulik, C.M., Sullivan, P.F., Fear, J.L., & Pickering, A. (2000). Outcome of anorexia nervosa: Eating attitudes, personality, and parental bonding. *International Journal of Eating Disorders, 28*(2), 139–147.

Bulik, C.M., Sullivan, P.F., Weltzin, T.E., & Kaye, W.H. (1995). Temperament in eating disorders. *International Journal of Eating Disorders, 17*(3), 251–261.

Burack, C. (1994). *The problem of the passions: Feminism, psychoanalysis, and social theory.* New York: New York University Press.

Busch, F. (2005). Conflict theory/trauma theory. *Psychoanalytic Quarterly, 74*(1), 27–46.

Bynum, C.W. (1987). *Holy feast and holy fast: The religious significance of food for medieval women.* Berkeley: University of California Press.

Byrne, S.M., & McLean, N.J. (2002). The cognitive behavioral model of bulimia nervosa: A direct evaluation. *International Journal of Eating Disorders, 31*(1), 17–31.

Byyny, R.L., & Speroff, L. (1996). *A clinical guide for the care of older women: Primary and preventive care.* Philadelphia: Lippincott, Williams & Wilkins.

Callahan, M.L. (1989). Psychodrama and the treatment of bulimia. In L.M. Hornyak & E.K. Baker (Eds.), *Experiential therapies for eating disorders* (pp. 101–120). New York: Guilford.

Candelori, C. & Ciocca, A. (1998). Attachment and eating disorders. In P. Bria, A. Ciocca, & S. DeRisio (Eds.), *Psychotherapeutic issues on eating disorders: Models, methods, and results* (pp. 139–154). Rome: Societa Editrice Universo.

Carlat, D.J., Camargo, C.A., & Herzog, D.B. (1997). Eating disorders in males. A report on 135 patients. *American Journal of Psychiatry, 154,* 1127–1132.

Carter, F.A., McIntosh, V.W., Frampton, C.M., Joyce, P.R., & Bulik, C.M., (2003). Predictors of childbirth following treatment of bulimia nervosa. *International Journal of Eating Disorders, 34*(3), 337–342.

Carter, W.P., Hudson, J.I., Lalonde, J.K., Pindyck, L., McElroy, S.L., & Pope Jr, H.G. (2003). Pharmacologic treatment of binge eating disorder. *International Journal of Eating Disorders*, (S1), S74–S88.

Casement, P. (1985). *On learning from the patient*. London: Tavistock.

Casement, P. (2002). *Learning from our mistakes: Beyond dogma in psychoanalysis and psychotherapy*. New York: Guilford.

Cash, T.F. (1997). *The body image workbook: An eight-step program for learning to like your looks*. Oakland, CA: New Harbinger Workbooks.

Cash, T.F., & Pruzinsky, T. (Eds.). (2002). *Body image: A handbook of theory, research, and clinical practice*. New York: Guilford.

Casper, R., Hedeker, D., & McClough, J. (1992). Personality dimensions in eating disorders and their relevance for subtyping. *Journal of the American Academy of Child and Adolescent Psychiatry*, 31(5), 830–840.

Caspi, A., Moffitt, T. (2006). Gene-environment interactions in psychiatry; joining forces with neuroscience. *Nature Reviews Neuroscience*, 7, 583–590.

Castelnuovo-Tedesco, P. (1989). The fear of change and its consequences in analysis and psychotherapy. *Psychoanalytic Inquiry*, 9, 101–118.

Castro, J. (2003). Biological abnormalities in eating disorders. In M. Maj, K. Halmi, J.J. Lopez-Ibor, & N. Sartorius (Eds.), *Eating disorders* (pp. 216–217). Hove, UK: Wiley.

Cerney, M.S. (1989) Use of imagery in grief therapy. In J.E. Shorr, P. Robin, J.A. Connella, & M. Wolpin (Eds.), *Imagery* (pp. 105–119). New York: Plenum.

Cerney, M.S., & Buskirk, J. (1991). Anger: the hidden part of grief. *Bulletin of the Menninger Clinic*, 55(2), 228–237.

Chatam, P.M. (1985). *Treatment of the borderline personality*. Northvale, NJ: Aronson.

Chernin, K. (1986). *The hungry self: Women, eating disorders and identity*. New York: Times Books.

Chodorow, N.F. (1978). *The reproduction of mothering: Psychoanalysis and the sociology of gender*. Berkeley: University of California Press.

Chodorow, N.J. (1989). *Feminism and psychoanalytic theory*. New Haven, CT: Yale University Press.

Chodorow, N.J. (1994). *Femininities, masculinities, sexualities: Freud and beyond*. Lexington: University of Kentucky Press.

Clarke, D.M., Wahlgrist, M.D., Rassias, C.R., & Strauss, B.J. (1999). Psychological factors in nutritional disorders of the elderly: Part of the spectrum of eating disorders. *International Journal of Eating Disorders*, 25(3), 345–348.

Clinton, D., Bjorck, C., Sohlberg, S., & Norring, C. (2004). Patient satisfaction with treatment in eating disorders: Cause for complacency or concern. *European Eating Disorders Review*, 12, 240–246.

Coen, S.J., (1992). *The misuse of persons: Analyzing pathological dependency*. Hillsdale, NJ: Analytic Press.

Colarusso, C.A. (1979). The development of a sense of time: From birth to object constancy. *International Journal of Psycho-Analysis*, 60, 243–251.

Colarusso, C.A. (1990). The third individuation: The effect of biological parenthood on separation-individuation processes in adulthood. *Psychoanalytic Study of the Child*, 45, 170–194.

Colarusso, C.A. (2000). Separation-individuation phenomena in adulthood: General concepts and the fifth individuation. *Journal of the American Psychoanalytic Association*, 48(4), 1467–1490.

Cole, N. (Director), Firth, T. (Writer), & Towhidi, J. (Writer) (2003). *Calendar girls* [Motion picture]. United States: Harbour Pictures.

Connors, M.E., & Morse, W. (1993). Sexual abuse and eating disorders: A review. *International Journal of Eating Disorders*, 13(1), 1–11.

Cooper, D. (1997). *God is a verb: Kabbalah and the practice of mystical Judaism.* New York: Riverhead Books.

Cooper, S. (2000). *Objects of hope: Exploring possibility and limit in psychoanalysis.* Hillsdale, NJ: Analytic Press.

Crastnopol, M. (2001). The male experience of food as symbol and sustenance. In J. Petrucelli & C. Stuart (Eds.), *Hungers and compulsions: The psychodynamic treatment of eating disorders and addictions* (pp. 147–160). Northvale, NJ: Aronson.

Crisp, A.H. (1995). *Anorexia nervosa: Let me be.* London: Psychology Press.

Crisp, A.H., Joughin, N., Halek, C., & Bowyer, C. (1996). *Anorexia nervosa: The wish to change* (2nd ed.). New York: Brunner-Routledge.

Cross, L. (1993). Body and self in feminine development. Implications for eating disorders and delicate self-mutilation. *Bulletin of the Menninger Clinic, 57*(1), 41–68.

Crow, S. (2006). Fluoxetine treatment of anorexia nervosa: important and disappointing results. *Journal of the American Medical Association, 295*(22), 2659–2660.

Crow, S. (2007). Recovery from eating disorders. *Renfrew Perspective,* Winter 1–3.

Dalai Lama XIV. (2002). *Advice on dying and living a better life* (J. Hopkins, Trans.). New York: Atria Books.

Daniels, L. (2001). *With a woman's voice: A writer's struggle for emotional freedom.* Lanham, MD: Madison Books.

Dansky, B.S., Brewerton, T.D., Kilpatrick, D.G., & O'Neil, P.M. (1997). The National Women's Study: Relationship of victimization and posttraumatic stress disorder to bulimia nervosa, *International Journal of Eating Disorders, 21*(3), 213–228.

Dare, C. (1995). Eating disorders: Psychoanalytic psychotherapy. In G. Gabbard (Ed.), *Treatments of Psychiatric Disorders* (Vol. 2, pp. 2130–2151). Washington, DC: American Psychiatric Press.

Dare, C. (1997). Chronic eating disorders in therapy: Clinical stories using family systems and psychoanalytic approaches. *Journal of Family Therapy, 19,* 319–351.

Dare, C., & Crowther, C. (1995). Living dangerously: Psychoanalytic psychotherapy of anorexia nervosa. In G. Szmukler, C. Dare, & T. Treasure (Eds.), *Handbook of eating disorders: Theory, treatment, and research* (pp. 293–308). New York: Wiley.

Dare, C., Eisler, I., Russell, G., Treasure, J., & Dodge, L. (2001). Psychological therapies with adults with anorexia nervosa: Randomized controlled trial of outpatient treatments. *British Journal of Psychiatry, 178,* 216–221.

Davies, J.M. (2003). Falling in love with love: Oedipal and postoedipal manifestations of idealization, mourning and erotic masochism. *Psychoanalytic Dialogues, 13,* 1–27.

Davies, J.M. (2004). Whose bad objects are we anyway? Repetition and our elusive love affair with evil. *Psychoanalytic Dialogues, 14*(6), 711–732.

De Groot, J., & Rodin, G. (1994). Eating disorders, female psychology, and the self. *Journal of the American Academy of Psychoanalysis, 22*(2), 299–317.

de la Rie, S., Noordenbos, G., Donker, M., & van Furth, E. (2007). The patient's view on quality of life and eating disorders. *International Journal of Eating Disorders, 40*(1), 13–20.

DeNiro, R. (Director), & Roth, E. (Writer) (2006). *The good shepherd* [Motion picture]. United States: Universal Pictures.

Derman, T., & Szabo, C.P., (2006). Why do individuals with anorexia die? A case of sudden death. *International Journal of Eating Disorders, 39*(3), 260–262.

Deter, H.C. & Herzog, W. (1994). Anorexia nervosa in a long-term perspective: Results of the Heidelberg-Mannhein study. *Psychosomatic Medicine, 56,* 20–27.

Dimen, M. (2003). *Sexuality, intimacy, power.* Hillsdale, NJ: Analytic Press.

Downey, J., & Friedman, R.C., (1995). Internalized homophobia in lesbian relationships. *Journal of the American Academy of Psychoanalysis, 23,* 435–447.

Druss, R. (1995) *The psychology of illness in sickness and in health.* Washington, DC: American Psychiatric Press.

Druss, R. (2000). *Listening to patients: Relearning the art of healing in psychotherapy.* New York: Oxford.

Duggal, A., Lawrence, R.M. (2001). Aspects of food refusal in the elderly: The "hunger strike." *International Journal of Eating Disorders, 30*(2), 213–216.

Eckert, E.D., Halmi, K.A., March, P., Grove, W., & Crosby, R. (1995). Ten- year follow-up of anorexia nervosa: Clinical course and outcome. *Psychological Medicine, 25*, 143–156.

Eddy, K.T., Novotny, C.M., & Westen, D. (2004).Sexuality, personality, and eating disorders. *Eating Disorders: The Journal of Treatment and Prevention, 12*, 191–208.

Edelman, G. (1992). *Bright air, brilliant fire.* New York: Basic Books.

Elson, M. (Ed). (1987). *The Kohut seminars on self psychology and psychotherapy with adolescents and young adults.* New York: W.W. Norton.

Emde, R.N. (1983). The prerepresentational self and its affective core. *Psychoanalytic Study of the Child, 38*, 165–192.

Engle, G.L. (1977). The need for a new medical model. *Science, 196*, 129–136.

Epel, E.S., Spanakos, A., Kasl-Godley, J., & Brownell, K.D. (1996). Body shape ideals across gender, sexual orientation, socioeconomic status, race, and age in personal advertisements. *International Journal of Eating Disorders, 19*(3), 265–273.

Epstein, L., & Feiner, A.H. (Eds.). (1979). *Countertransference.* New York: Aronson.

Erikson, E.H. (1950). *Childhood and society.* New York: WW Norton.

Erikson, E.H. (1956). The dream specimen in psychoanalysis. *Journal of the American Psychoanalytic Association, 2*, 2–56.

Erikson, E.H. (1976). Reflections on Dr. Borg's life cycle. *Daedalus, 105*(2), 1–31.

Erikson, E.H. (1981). On generativity and identity. *Harvard Educational Review, 51*, 249–269.

Erikson, E.H. (1982). *The life cycle completed.* New York: W.W. Norton.

Erskine, A., & Judd, D. (Eds.). (1994). *The imaginative body.* London: Whurr.

Esman, A.H. (1994). "Sexual abuse," pathogenesis, and enlightened skepticism (editorial). *American Journal of Psychiatry, 11*, 1101–1103.

Esquivel, L. (1989). *Like water for chocolate: A novel in monthly installments with recipes, romances, and home remedies.* New York: Doubleday.

Evans, R.I. (1967). *Dialogue with Erik Erikson.* New York: Harper & Row.

Fabricus, J. (1998). Refusal of autonomy: The use of words by a young adult in analysis. *Journal of the American Psychoanalytic Association, 46*(1), 105–120.

Fairbairn, W.R.D. (1952). The repression and return of bad objects (with special reference to the war neuroses). In *Psychoanalytic studies of the personality.* London: Routledge & Kegan Paul (pp. 59–81). (Original work published 1943)

Fairburn, C.G. (1998). Interpersonal psychotherapy for bulimia nervosa. In J.C. Markowitz (Ed.), *Interpersonal psychotherapy: Review of Psychiatry* (Vol. 17, pp. 99–128). Washington, DC: American Psychiatric Press.

Fairburn, C.G., & Cooper, A. (2003). Relapse in bulima nervosa (letter to the editor) *Archives of General Psychiaty, 60*, 850.

Fairburn, C.G., Jones, R., Peveler, R.C., Carr, S.J., Solomon, R.J., & O'Connor, M.E., Burton, J., & Hope, R.A. (1991). Three psychological treatments for bulimia nervosa: A comparative trial. *Archives of General Psychiatry, 48*, 463–469.

Fairburn, C.G., Jones, R., Peveler, R.C., Hope, R.A., & O'Connor, M.E. (1993). Psychotherapy and bulimia nervosa: Longer-term effects of interpersonal psychotherapy, behavior therapy, and cognitive-behavior therapy. *Archives of General Psychiatry, 50*, 419–428.

Fairburn, C.G., Norman, P.A., Welch, S.L., O'Conner, M.E., Doll, H.A., & Peveler, R.C. (1995). A prospective study of outcome in bulimia nervosa and the long-term effects of three psychological treatments. *Archives of General Psychiatry, 52*, 304–312.

Falk, J.R., Halmi, R.A., (1982). Amenorrhea in anorexia nervosa: Examination of the critical body weight hypothesis. *Biological Psychiatry, 17,* 799–806.

Fallon, P., Katzman, M.A., & Wooley, S.C. (Eds.). (1994). *Feminist perspectives on eating disorders.* New York: Guilford.

Faris, P.L., Kim, S.W., Meller, W.H., Goodale, R.L., Oakman, S.A., Hokbauer, R.D. et al. (2000). Effect of decreasing afferent vagal activity with ondansetron on symptoms of bulimia nervosa: a randomized, double-blind trial. *Lancet, 355,* 792–797.

Farrell, M.M. (2000). *Lost for words: The psychoanalysis of anorexia and bulimia.* New York: Other Press. (Original work published 1995)

Fassino, S., Abbate-Daga, G.A., Boggio, S., Garzaro, L., & Piero, A. (2004). Use of reboxetine in bulimia nervosa: A pilot study. *Journal of Psychopharmacology, 18*(3), 423–426.

Fast, I. (1990). Aspects of early gender development: Toward a reformulation. *Psychoanalytic Psychology, 7,* 105–117.

Feldman, M.B., & Meyer, I. H. (2007a). Eating disorders in diverse lesbian, gay, and bisexual populations. *International Journal of Eating Disorders, 40*(3), 218–226.

Feldman, M.B., & Meyer, I.H. (2007b). Childhood abuse and eating disorders in gay and bisexual men. *International Journal of Eating Disorders, 40*(5), 418–423.

Ferenczi, S. (1949). Confusion of tongues between the adult and the child. *International Journal of Psychoanalysis, 30,* 225–230.

Ferenczi, S. (1955). The unwelcome child and his death instinct. In *Final contributions to the problems and methods of psychoanalysis* (pp. 102–107). London: Hogarth Press.

Ferro, A. (2002). *In the analyst's consulting room.* Hove, UK: Brunner/Routledge.

Fichter, M.F., & Quadflieg, N. (2004). Twelve-year course and outcome of bulimia nervosa. *Psychological Medicine, 34,* 1395–1406.

Finfgeld, D.L. (2002). Anorexia nervosa: analysis of long-term outcomes and clinical implications. *Archives of Psychiatric Nursing, 16*(4), 176–186.

Firestein, S.K. (1978). *Termination in psychoanalysis.* New York: International Universities Press.

Fisher, H. (1998). Lust, attraction, and attachment in mammalian reproduction. *Human Nature, 9,* 23–52.

Fisher, H. (2004). *Why we love: The nature and chemistry of romantic love.* New York: Henry Holt

Fisher, H. (2005, October 28). *The drive to love.* Paper presented to the International Study of Women's Sexual Health, Las Vegas, NV.

Fisher, H., & Thomson, J.A. (2006). Lust, attraction, attachment: The neural mechanisms of mate choice and how antidepressants jeopardize romantic love, attachment, and one's genetic future. In S.M. Platek, J.P. Keenan, & T.K. Shakelford (Eds.), *Evolutionary cognitive neuroscience* (pp. 245–283). Cambridge, MA: MIT Press.

Fisher, M., Golden, N.H., Katzman, D.K., Kriepe, R.E., Rees, J., Schebendach, J. et al. (1996). Eating disorders in adolescents: A background paper. *Journal of Adolescent Health, 16,* 420–437.

Fisman, M.D., Steele, M., Short, J., Byrne, T., La Vallee, C. (1996). Case study: Anorexia nervosa and autistic disorder in an adolescent girl. *Journal of American Academy of Child & Adolescent Psychopharmacology, 35*(7), 937–940.

Fitzpatrick, J.J., & Friedman, L.J. (1983). Adult development theories and Erik Erikson's life-cycle model. *Bulletin of the Menninger Clinic, 47*(5), 401–416.

Fonagy, P. (2001). *Attachment theory and psychoanalysis.* New York: Other Press.

Fonagy, P., Gergely, G., Jurist, E., & Target, M. (2002). *Affect regulation, mentalization, and the development of the self.* New York: Other Press.

Fonagy, P., & Moran, G. (1994). Psychoanalytic formulation and treatment: chronic metabolic disturbance in insulin-dependent diabetes mellitus. In A. Erskine, & D. Judd (Eds.), *The imaginative body* (pp. 60–86). London: Whurr.

Fonagy, P.Y., & Target, M. (1996). Predictors of outcome in child psychoanalysis: A retrospective of 763 cases at the Anna Freud Centre. *Journal of the American Psychoanalytic Association, 44*, 27–78.

Fonagy, P.Y., & Target, M. (1997). The problem of outcome in child analysis: contributions from the Anna Freud Center. *Psychoanalytic Inquiry, 17S*, 58–73.

Fonda, J. (2005). *My life so far.* New York: Random House.

Forman, M.E. (2004). A descriptive overview of middle-aged women with eating disorders. *Renfrew Perspective,* Summer 1–4.

Forman, M.E., & Davis, W. N. (2005). Characteristics of middle-aged women in inpatient treatment of eating disorders. *Eating Disorders: The Journal of Treatment and Prevention, 13*(3), 231–243.

Frank, G.K., Bailer, U.F., Henry, S.E., Drevets, W., Meltzer, C.C., Price, J.C. et al. (2005). Increased Dopamine D2/D3 receptor binding after recovery from anorexia nervosa measured by positron emission tomography and [(11)] raclopride. *Biological Psychiatry June 28.*

Frank, G.K., Kaye, W.H., & Marcus, M.D. (2001). Sertraline in underweight binge eating/purging-type eating disorders: Five case reports. *International Journal of Eating Disorders, 29*(4), 495–498.

Frank, J.D., & Frank, J.B. (1991). *Persuasion & healing: A comparative study of psychotherapy.* (3rd ed.). Baltimore, MD: Johns Hopkins Press.

Frankl, V. (1963). *Man's search for meaning: An introduction to logotherapy.* New York: Washington Square Press.

Franko, D.L., & Rolfe, S. (1996). Countertransference in the treatment of patients with eating disorders. *Psychiatry, 59,* 108–116.

Freedman, R. (1989). *Bodylove: Learning to like our looks—and ourselves.* New York: Harper & Row.

Freud, A. (1936). *The ego and the mechanisms of defence.* London: Hogarth Press.

Freud, S. (1964a). Analysis terminable and interminable. In J. Strachey (Ed. & Trans.), *The standard edition of the complete works of Sigmund Freud.* (Vol. 23, pp. 209–254). London: Hogarth Press. (Original works published 1937)

Freud, S. (1964b). *The interpretation of dreams.* In J. Strachey (Ed. & Trans). *The standard edition of the complete psychological works of Sigmund Freud,* Vols. IV& V. London: Hogarth Press. (Original work published 1900)

Freud, S. (1964c). Notes upon a case of obsessional neuroses. In J. Strachey (Ed. & Trans.) *The standard edition of the complete psychological works of Sigmund Freud. 20,* (pp. 153–318). London: Hogarth Press. (Original work published 1909)

Freud, S. (1964d). An autobiographical study. *The standard edition of the complete works of Sigmund Freud:* (Vol. 20, pp. 7–61). London: Hogarth Press. (Original work published 1925)

Freud, S. (1964e). Extracts from the Fliess papers. In J. Strachey (Ed. &Trans.) *The standard edition of the complete psychological works of Sigmund Freud, Vol. I* (pp. 175–280), London: Hogarth Press. (Original work published 1889)

Freud, S. (1964f). Recommendations to physicians practicing psychoanalysis. In, J. Strachey (Eds. & Trans.). *The standard edition of the complete psychological works of Sigmund Freud.* (Vol. 12, pp. 111–120). London, Hogarth Press. (Original work published 1912)

Freud, S. (1964g). On beginning the treatment. In J. Strachey (Eds & Trans). *The standard edition of the complete psychological works of Sigmund Freud.* (Vol. 12, pp. 123–144). London, Hogarth Press. (Original work published 1913)

Freud, S. (1964h). Remembering repeating, and working through: Further recommendations on the techniques of psychoanalysis. In J. Strachey (Ed & Trans). *The standard edition of the complete works of Sigmund Freud.* (Vol. 12, pp. 147–156). London, Hogarth Press. (Original work published 1913)

Freud, S. (1964i). The dynamics of transference. In J. Strachey (Ed & Trans) *The standard edition of the complete works of Sigmund Freud.* (Vol. 12, pp. 99–108). London: Hogarth Press. (Original work published 1913)

Freud, S. (1964j). Observation on transference love: Further recommendations on the technique of psychoanalysis. *The standard edition of the complete works of Sigmund Freud.* (Vol. 12, pp. 159–171). London, Hogarth Press. (Original work published 1913)

Friday, N. (1996). *The power of beauty.* New York: HarperCollins.

Friedman, L. (1978). Trends in psychoanalytic theory of treatment. *Psychoanalytic Quarterly, 47* pp. 524–567.

Friedman, L. (2004). What is psychoanalysis? 39th Freud Anniversary Lecture. *The Psychoanalytic Association of New York Bulletin, 42*(3), 5.

Friedman, L. (2006). What is psychoanalysis? *Psychoanalytic Quarterly, 75,* 689–714.

Friedman, M. (1993). *Encounters on the narrow ridge: A life of Martin Buber.* New York: Paragon House.

Friedman, R.C., & Downey, J. (1995). Internalized homophobia and the negative therapeutic reaction. *Journal of the American Academy of Psychoanalysis, 23,* 99–113.

Fung, S.M., & Ferrill, M.J. (2001). Treatment of bulimia nervosa with ordansetron. *Annals of Pharmacotherapy, 35*(10), 1270–1273.

Furnham, A, & Alibhai, N. (1983). Cross-cultural differences in the perception of female body shapes. *Psychological Medicine, 13,* 829–837.

Gabbard, G.O. (1982). The exit line: Heightened transference-countertransference manifestations at the end of the hour. *Journal of the American Psychoanalytic Association, 30,* 579–598.

Gabbard, G.O. (Ed.) (1989). *Sexual exploitation in professional relationships.* Washington, DC: American Psychiatric Press.

Gabbard, G.O. (1996). *Love and hate in the analytic setting.* Northvale, NJ: Aronson.

Gabbard, G.O. (2005). *Psychodynamic psychiatry in clinical practice* (4th ed.) Arlington, VA: American Psychiatric Association Press.

Gabbard, G.O. (2006a). When is transference work useful in dynamic psychotherapy? (Editorial). *American Journal of Psychiatry, 163*(10), 1667–1669.

Gabbard, G.O. (2006b). A neuroscience perspective on transference. *Psychiatric Annals, 36*(4), 283–288.

Gabbard, G.O., & Lester, E.P. (1995). *Boundaries and boundary violations in psychoanalysis.* New York: Basic Books.

Gabbard, G.O. & Wilkinson, S.M. (1994). *Management of countertransference with borderline patients.* Washington, DC: American Psychiatric Press.

Galatzer-Levy, R.M., Cohler, B.J. (1993). *The essential other: A developmental psychology of the self.* New York: Basic Books.

Ganzarain, R.C., & Buchele, B.J. (1988). *Fugitives of incest: A perspective from psychoanalysis and groups.* Madison, CT: International Universities Press.

Garfinkel, P.E. (1996). Multimodal therapies for anorexia nervosa. In J. Werne (Ed.), *Treating eating disorders* (pp. 313–334). San Francisco: Jossey-Bass.

Garfinkel, P.E., & Garner, D.M. (1982). *Anorexia nervosa: A multidimensional perspective.* New York: Brunner/Mazel.

Garner, D.M. (1997). Psycho-educational principles in treatment. In D. Garner & P.E. Garfunkel (Eds.). *Handbook of treatment for eating disorders* (pp. 145–177). New York: Guilford.

Garner, D.M., Kearney-Cooke, A. (1997). Special reports: The Psychology Today 1997 body image survey results. *Psychology Today, 30*(1), 30–82.

Geller, J. (2002). Estimating readiness for change in anorexia nervosa: Comparing clients, clinicians, and research assessors. *International Journal of Eating Disorders, 31*(3), 215–260.

Geller, J., & Drab, D. (1999). The readiness and motivation interview: A symptom-specific measure of readiness for change in the eating disorders. *European Eating Disorders Review, 7,* 259–278.

Geller, J, Brown, K., Zaitsoff, S., Goodrich, S., & Hastings, F. (2003). Collaborative versus directive interventions in the treatment of eating disorders: Implications for care providers. *Professional Psychology: Research and Practice, 34*(4), 406–413.

Geller, J., Cockell, S., Drab, O. (2001). Assessing readiness for change in the eating disorders: The psychometric properties of the readiness and motivation interview. *Psychological Assessment, 13*(2), 189–198.

Geltner, P. (2005). Countertransference in projective identification and sado-masochistic states. *Modern Psychoanalysis, 30*(1), 73–91.

Ghizzani, A., & Montomoli, M. (2000). Anorexia nervosa and sexuality in women: A review. *Journal of Sex Education and Therapy, 25*(1), 80–88.

Giannini A.J., & Telew, N. (1987). Anorexia nervosa in geriatric patients. *Geriatric Psychiatry, 6,* 75–78.

Gilligan, C. (1982). *In a different voice: Psychological theory and women's development.* Cambridge, MA: Harvard University Press.

Giovacchini, P.L. (1980). The psychoanalytic treatment of the alienated patient. In J.F. Masterson (Ed.), *New perspectives on psychotherapy of the borderline adult* (pp. 20–40). New York: Brunner Mazel.

Gitlin, B., & Zaphiropoulos, L. (2004). Gaining perspective: Transference and countertransference, eating problems in middle age. *Renfrew Perspective,* Summer 4–6.

Gitlin, M.J. (1994). Psychotropic medications and their effects on sexual function: Diagnosis, biology, and treatment approaches. *Journal of Clinical Psychiatry, 55,* 406–413.

Goin, M.K. (1990). Emotional survival and the aging body. In R.A. Nemiroff & C.A. Colarusso (Eds.), *New dimensions in adult development* (pp. 518–528). New York: Basic Books.

Goldberg, A. (1988). Self psychology and external reality. In A *Fresh look at psychoanalysis* (pp. 61–73). Hillsdale, NJ: Analytic Press.

Goldberg, A. (1999). *Being of two minds: The vertical split in psychoanalysis and psychotherapy.* Hillsdale, NJ: Analytic Press.

Golden, N.H. (2003). Osteopenia and osteoporosis in anorexia nervosa. *Adolescent medicine 14,* 97–108.

Goldstein, D.J., Wilson, M.G., Ascroft, R.C., & Al-Banna, M. (1999). Effectiveness of fluoxetine therapy in bulimia nervosa regardless of comorbid depression. *International Journal of Eating Disorders, 25*(1), 19–27.

Goleman, D. (1995). *Emotional intelligence.* New York, Bantam Books.

Gordon, R. (2000). *Eating disorders: Anatomy of a social epidemic* (2nd ed.), Oxford: Blackwell (original edition published 1990).

Gottschalk, L.A. (1990). Origins and evolution of narcissism through the life cycle. In R.A. Nemiroff & C.A. Colarusso (Eds.). *New dimensions in adult development* (pp. 73–90). New York: Basic Books.

Greenfield, L. (2002). *Girl culture.* San Francisco, Chronicle Books LLC.

Grinberg, L., Sor, D., & de Blanchedi, E.T. (1993). *Introduction to the work of Bion.* (rev. ed.). Northvale, NJ: Aronson.

Grishkat, H. (2004). Thirty something and beyond: Residential treatment programming for midlife eating disorders. *Renfrew Perspective,* Summer 7–8.

Grosh, W., & Olsen, D.C. (1994). *When helping starts to hurt: A new look at burnout among psychotherapists.* New York: W.W. Norton.

Grotstein, J.S. (1999). The fate of the unconscious in the future of psychotherapy. *American Journal of Psychotherapy, 53*(1), 52–59.

Grotstein, J.S., & Rinsley, D.B. (Eds.). (1994). *Fairbairn and the origins of object relations.* New York: Guilford.

Guetzkow, H.S. & Bowman, P.H. (1946). *Men and hunger: A psychological manual for relief workers.* Elgin, IL: Brethren.

Gullette, M.M. (1998). Midlife discourses in the twentieth century United States: An essay on sexuality, ideology, and politics. In R. Schweder (Ed.), *Welcome to middle age (and other cultural fictions)* (pp. 3–44). Chicago: University of Chicago Press.

Gunderson, J.G., (1984). *Borderline personality disorder.* Washington, DC: American Psychiatric Press,

Gunsberg L., Tylim, I. (1995). Ownership of the body and mind: Developmental considerations for the adult psychoanalytic treatment. *Psychoanalytic Review, 82,* 257–266.

Gupta, M.A., (1995). Concerns about aging and a drive for thinness: A factor in the biopsychosocial model of eating disorders? *International Journal of Eating Disorders, 18*(4), 351–357.

Gupta, M.A., & Schork, N.J. (1993). Aging-related concerns and body image: Possible future implications for eating disorders. *International Journal of Eating Disorders, 14*(4), 481–486.

Guntrip, H. (1975). My experience of analysis with Fairbairn and Winnicott. *International Review of Psycho-Analysis, 2,* 145–156.

Gutwill, S. (1994a). Transference and countertransference issues: The impact of social pressures on body image and consciousness. In C. Bloom, A. Gitter, S. Gutwill, L. Kogel, & L. Zaphiropoulous (Eds.), *Eating problems: A feminist psychoanalytic treatment model* (pp. 144–171). New York: Basic Books.

Gutwill, S. (1994b). Transference and countertransference issues: The diet mentality versus attuned eating. In C. Bloom, A. Gitter, S. Gutwill, L. Kogel, & L. Zaphiropoulous (Eds.), *Eating problems: A feminist psychoanalytic treatment model* (pp. 172–183). New York: Basic Books.

Haiken, E. (1997). *Venus envy: A history of cosmetic surgery.* Baltimore: Johns Hopkins University Press.

Hall, J. (1998). *Deepening the treatment.* New York: Aronson.

Hall, L. (1993). *Full lives: women who have freed themselves from food and weight obsession.* Carlsbad, CA: Gurze Books.

Hall, L., & Cohn, L. (1992). *Bulimia: A guide to recovery* (2nd ed.). Carlsbad, CA: Gurze Books.

Hall, L., & Ostroff, M. (1999). *Anorexia nervosa: A guide to recovery.* Carlsbad, CA: Gurze Books.

Halmi, K.A. (Ed.). (1992). *Psychobiology and treatment of anorexia nervosa and bulimia nervosa.* Washington, DC: American Psychiatric Press.

Halmi, K., Agras, W.S., Mitchell, J., Wilson, T., Crow, S., Bryson, S. et al. (2002). Relapse predictors of patients with bulimia nervosa who achieved abstinence through cognitive behavioral therapy. *Archives of General Psychiatry, 59*(12), 1105–1109.

Halmi, K., & Licinio, E. (1998). A 24-year-old woman with anorexia nervosa. *Journal of the American Medical Association, 279*(24), 1992–1998.

Halvorsen, I., Andersen, A., & Heyerdahl, S. (2004). Good outcome of adolescent onset anorexia nervosa after systematic treatment: Intermediate to long-term follow-up pf a representative county sample. *European Child and Adolescent Psychiatry, 13,* 295–306.

Hamburg, P. (1996). How long is long-term therapy for anorexia nervosa? In J. Werne (Ed.), *Treating eating disorders* (pp. 71–100). San Francisco: Jossey-Bass.

Hamburg, P., Herzog, D.B., & Brotman, A. (1996). Treatment resistance in eating disorders: Psychodynamic and pharmacologic perspectives. In M.H. Pollack, M.W. Otto, & J.F. Rosenbaum (Eds.), *Challenges in clinical practice: Pharmacologic and psychosocial strategies* (pp. 263–275). New York: Guilford.

Harris, A. (2005). Conflict in relational treatments. *Psychoanalytic Quarterly, 54*(1), 267–294.

Harris, E.C., & Barraclough, B. (1998). Excess mortality of mental disorder. *British Journal of Psychiatry, 173,* 11–53.

Herman, C.P., & Polivy, J. (1980). Restrained eating. In A. Stunkard (Ed.), *Obesity* (pp. 208–225). Philadelphia: Saunders.

Herman, C.P., & Polivy, J. (1998). Studies of eating in normal dieters. In B.T. Walsh (Ed.), *Eating behaviors in eating disorders* (pp. 95–112). Washington, DC: American Psychiatric Press.

Herman, J.S. (1992). *Trauma and recovery.* New York: Basic Books.

Herzog, W., Deter, H.C., Fiehn, W., & Petzold, E. (1997). Medical findings and predictions of long-term physical outcome in anorexia nervosa: A prospective, 12 year follow-up study. *Psychological Medicine, 27,* 269–279.

Herzog, D.B., Dorer, D.J., Keel, P.K., Selwyn, S., Ekeblad, E., Flores, A. et al. (1999). Recovery and relapse in anorexia and bulimia nervosa: a 7.5-year follow-up study. *Journal of the American Academy of Child and Adolescent Psychiatry, 39*(7), 829–837.

Herzog, D.B., & Eddy, K.T. (2007). Diagnosis, epidemiology, & clinical course of eating disorders. In J. Yager & P. Powers (Eds.), *Clinical manual of eating disorders* (pp. 1–30). Washington, DC: American Psychiatric Press.

Herzog, D.B., Greenwood, D.N., Dorer, D.J., Flores, A.T., Ekeblad, E., Richards, A. et al. (2000). Mortality in eating disorders: A descriptive study. *International Journal of Eating Disorders, 28*(1), 20–26.

Herzog, D.B., Newman, K.L., Yeh, C.J., & Warshaw, M. (1992). Body image satisfaction in homosexual and heterosexual women. *International Journal of Eating Disorders, 11*(4), 391–396.

Hirschmann, J.R., & Munter, C.H. (1988). *Overcoming overeating.* New York: Ballantine.

Hitchcock, J. (1992). The importance of aggression in the early development of children with eating disorders. In C. Wilson, C.C. Hogan, & I.L. Mintz (Eds.), *Psychodynamic technique in treatment of the eating disorders* (pp. 223–236). Northvale, NJ: Aronson.

Hoek, H.W., van Harten, P.N., van Hoeken, D., & Susser, E. (1998). Lack of relation between culture and anorexia nervosa—Results of an incidence study on Curacao. *New England Journal of Medicine, 338*(17), 1231–1232.

Hoek, H.W., van Hoeken, D., & Katzman, M. (2003). Epidemiology and cultural aspects of eating disorders: A review. In M. Maj, K. Halmi, J.J. Lopez-Ibor, & N. Sartorius (Eds.), *Eating Disorders* (pp. 75–103). London: Wiley.

Hoglend, P., Amlo, S., Marble, A., Bogwald, K-P., Sorbye, O., Sjaastad, M. et al. (2006), Analysis of the patient-therapist relationship in dynamic psychotherapy: An experimental study of transference interpretations. *American Journal of Psychiatry, 163,* 1739–1746.

Hoopes, S.P., Reimherr, F.W., Hedges, D.W., Rosenthal, N.R., Kamin, M., Karim, R. et al. (2003). Treatment of bulimia nervosa with topiramate in a randomized, double-blind, placebo-controlled trial, part 1: Improvement in binge and purge measures. *Journal of Clinical Psychiatry, 64,* 1335–1341.

Horne, R.L, Ferguson J.M., Pope, H.G. Jr., Hudson, J.I., Lineberry C.G., Ascher, J. et al. (1988) Treatment of bulimia with bupropion: A multicenter controlled trial. *Journal of Clinical Psychiatry, 49,* 262–266.

Horney, K. (1926). The flight from womanhood: The masculinity-complex in women, as viewed by men and women. *International Journal of Psycho-analysis, 7,* 324–339.

Horney, K. (1950). *Neurosis and human growth: The struggle toward self-realization.* New York: W.W. Norton.

Horney, K. (1967). *Feminine psychology.* New York: W.W. Norton.

Horney, K. (1970). The tyranny of the should. In *Neurosis and human growth: The struggle toward self-realization* (pp. 64–85). New York: W.W. Norton.

Hornyak, L.M., & Baker, E.K. (Eds.) (1989). *Experiential therapies for eating disorders.* New York: Guilford.

Horwitz, L., Gabbard, G.O., Allen, J.G., Frieswyk, S.H., Colson, D.B., Newsom, G.E. et al. (1996). *Borderline personality disorder: Tailoring the psychotherapy to the patient.* Washington, DC: American Psychiatric Press.

Hsu, G. (1990). *Eating disorders.* New York: Guilford.

Hughes, P. (1997). The use of countertransference in the therapy of patients with anorexia nervosa. *European Eating Disorders Review, 5*(4), 258–269.

Hutchinson, M.G. (1985). *Transforming body image: Learning to love the body you have.* Freedom, CA: Crossing Press.

Jackson, C., Davidson, G., Russell, J., & Vandereycken, W. (1990). Ellen West revisited: The theme of death in eating disorders. *International Journal of Eating Disorders, 9*(5), 526–536.

Jacobs, T.J. (1991). *The use of the self: Countertransference and communication in the analytic situation.* Madison, CT: International Universities Press.

Jacobson, E. (1976). Ways of female superego formation and the female castration conflict. *Psychoanalytic Quarterly, 45*(4) 525–538.

Jacobson, J.G. (1993). Developmental observation, multiple models of the mind, and the therapeutic relationship in psychoanalysis. *Psychoanalytic Quarterly, 62,* 523–552.

Jacques, E. (1965). Death and the mid-life crisis. *International Journal of Psychoanalysis, 46,* 502–514.

Jager, B. Liedtke, R., Kunsebeck, H.W., Lempa, W., Kersting, A., Seide, L. et al. (1996) Psychotherapy and bulimia nervosa: Evaluation and long-term follow-up of two conflict-oriented treatment conditions. *Acta Psychiatrica Scandinavica, 93,* 268–278.

Jarman, M., & Walsh, S. (1999). Evaluating recovery from anorexia nervosa and bulimia nervosa: Integrating lessons learned from research and clinical practice. *Clinical Psychology Review, 129*(7), 773–788.

Jewison, N. (Director) & Shanley, J.P. (Writer) (1987). *Moonstruck* [Motion Picture]. United States: MGM Studios.

Jimerson, D.C., Wolfe, B.E., Brotman, A.E., & Metzger, E.D. (1996). Medications in the treatment of eating disorders. *Psychiatric Clinics of North America, 19*(4), 739–754.

Johnson, C.L. (Ed.) (1991). *Psychodynamic treatment of anorexia nervosa and bulimia.* New York: Guilford.

Johnson, C.L., Lund, B., & Yates, W.R. (2003). Recovery rates for anorexia nervosa (Letter to the editor). *American Journal of Psychiatry, 160*(4), 798–799.

Johnson, J.G., Cohen, P., Kasen, S., & Brook, J.S. (2002). Childhood adversities associated with risk for eating disorders during adolescence or early adulthood. *American Journal of Psychiatry, 159,* 394–400.

Joiner, T. (1999). Self-verification and bulimic symptoms: Do bulimic women play a role in perpetuating their own dissatisfaction and symptoms? *International Journal of Eating Disorders, 26*(2), 145–151.

Jordan, J.V., Kaplan, A.G., Miller, J.B., Stiver, I.P., Surrey, J.L. (1991). *Women's growth in connection: Writings from the Stone Center.* New York: Guilford.

Jung, C.G., (1977). The stages of life. In J. Campbell (Ed.), *The portable Jung*. New York: Penguin. (Original work published 1933).

Kahar, S. (1998). The search for middle age in India. In R.A. Shweder (Ed.), *Welcome to middle age!* (and other cultural fictions.) (pp. 75–100). Chicago: University of Chicago Press.

Kaplan, A.S., & Garfinkel, P.E. (1999). Difficulties in treating patients with eating disorders: A review of patient and clinician variables. *Canadian Journal of Psychiatry*, *11*(7), 665–670.

Kaplan, H.S., (1979). *Disorders of sexual desire and other new concepts and techniques in sex therapy*. New York: Brunner/Mazel.

Kaplan, M.J. (2002). Approaching sexual issues in primary care. In K.J. Zerbe (Ed.), *Primary care: Women's mental health* (pp. 113–124). Philadelphia: W.B. Saunders.

Katzman, D.K., Lambe, E.K., Mikulis, D.J., Ridgley, J.N., Goldbloom, D.S., & Zipursky, R.B., (1996). Cerebral gray matter and white matter volume deficits in adolescent girls with anorexia nervosa. *Journal of Pediatrics*, *129*, 794–803.

Katzman, D.K., Zipursky, R.B., Lambe, E.K., & Mikulis, D.J., (1997). A congitudinal magnetic resonance imaging study of brain changes in adolescent with anorexia nervosa. *Archives of Pediatrics and Adolescent Medicine*, *51*, 793–797.

Katzman, M., Hermans, K.M.E., VanHoeken, D., & Hoek, H.N., (2004). Not your "typical island women": Anorexia is reported only in subcultures on Curacao. *Culture, Medicine, and Psychiatry*, *28*(4), 463–492.

Kaye, W.H., (1999). The new biology of anorexia and bulimia: Implications for advances in treatment. *European Eating Disorders Review*, *7*, 157–161.

Kaye, W.H. (2003). Eating disorders: Minimizing medical complications and preventing deaths. In M. Maj, K. Halmi, J.J. Lopez-Ibor, & N. Sartorius (Eds.), *Eating disorders* (pp. 199–201). Hove, UK: Wiley.

Kaye, W.H., Gwirtsman, H.E., Obarzanek, E., & George, D.T. (1988). Relative importance of calorie intake needed to gain weight and level of physical activity in anorexia nervosa. *American Journal of Clinical Nutrition*, *47*, 989–994.

Kaye, W.H., Frank, G.K., & McConaha, C. (1999). Altered dopamine activity after recovery from restricting-type anorexia nervosa. *Neuropsychopharmacology*, *21*(4), 503–506.

Kaye, W.H., Nagata, T., Weltzin, T.E., Hsu, L.K., Sokol, M.S., McConaha, C. et al. (2001). Double-blind placebo-controlled administration of fluoxetine in restricting and restricting-purging type anorexia nervosa. *Biological Psychiatry*, *49*(7), 644–652.

Kearney-Cooke, A. (1991). The role of the therapist in the treatment of eating disorders: A feminist psychodynamic approach. In C.L. Johnson (Ed.), *Psychodynamic treatment of anorexia nervosa and bulimia* (pp. 295–318). New York: Guilford.

Kearney-Cooke, A., & Ackard, D.M. (2000). The effects of sexual abuse on body image self-image, and sexual activity of women. *Journal of Gender-Specific Medicine*, *3*(6), 54–60.

Kearney-Cooke, A., with Isaacs, F. (2004). *Change your mind: Change your body: Feeling good about body and self after 40*. New York: Atria Books.

Keel, P.K., Dorer, D.J., Eddy, K., Franko, D., Charatan, D.L., & Herzog, D., (2003). Predictors of mortality in eating disorders. *Archives of General Psychiatry*, *60*, 179–183.

Keel, P.K., Dorer, D., Franko, D., Jackson, S.C., & Herzog, D. (2005). Postremission predictors of relapse in women with eating disorders. *American Journal of Psychiatry*, *162*(12), 2263–2268.

Keel, P.K., Klump, K.L. (2003). Are eating disorders culture-bound syndromes? Implications for conceptualizing their etiology. *Psychological Bulletin*, *129*(5), 747–769.

Keel, P.K., Mitchell, J.E. (1997). Outcome of bulimia nervosa. *American Journal of Psychiatry*, *154*(3), 313–321.

Keel, P.K., Mitchell, J.E., Davis, T.L., & Crow, S.J. (2002). Long-term impact of treatment in women diagnosed with bulimia nervosa. *International Journal of Eating Disorders*, *31*(2), 151–158.

Keel, P.K., Mitchell, J., Davis, T., Fieselman, S., & Crow, J. (2000). Impact of definitions on the description and predicleor of bulimia nervosa outcome. *International Journal of Eating Disorders, 28*(4), 377–386.

Kemp, R, Kirov, G., Everitt, B., Hayward, P., David, A. (1998). Randomised controlled trial of compliance therapy: 18 month follow-up. *British Journal of Psychiatry, 172*, 413–419.

Keneally, S. (1982). *Schindler's list*. New York: Simon & Schuster.

Kernberg, O. (1995). Technical approach to eating disorders in patients with borderline personality organization. *Annual of Psychoanalysis, 23*, 33–48.

Kernberg, O. (2005). Unconscious conflict in the light of contemporary psychoanalytic findings. *Psychoanalytic Quarterly, 74*(1), 65–82.

Kernberg, O.F., Burstein, E.D., Coyne, L., Appelbaum, A., Horwitz, L., & Voth, H. (1972). Psychotherapy and psychoanalysis: Final report of the Menninger Foundation's Psychotherapy Research Project. *Bulletin of the Menniinger Clinic, 36*(1/2), 3–268.

Keys, A., Brozek, J., Herschel, A., Mickelsen, O., & Taylor, H. (1950). *The biology of human starvation*. Minneapolis: University of Minnesota Press.

Kierkegaard, S. (1962). *The present age*. New York: Harper & Row. (Original work published 1940)

Kinoy, B.P. (Ed.) (2001). *Eating disorders: New direction in treatment and recovery*. (2nd ed.). New York: Columbia University Press.

Kleifield, E.I., Wagner, S., & Halmi, K.A. (1996). Cognitive behavioral treatment of anorexia nervosa. *Psychiatric Clinics of North America, 19*(4), 715–738.

Klein, M. (1957). Envy and gratitude. In *The writings of Melanie Klein* (Vol. 3, pp. 176–235). London: Hogarth.

Klein, M. (1963). *Our adult world and other essays*. London: Heinemann.

Klibanski, A., Biller, B.M., Schoenfeld, D.A., Herzog, D.B., & Saxe, V.C., (1995). The effects of estrogen administration on trabecular bone loss in young women with anorexia nervosa. *Journal of Clinical Endocrinology and Metabolism, 80*, 898–904.

Klump, K.L. (2003). Physiological aberrations: Cause and consequence? In M. Maj, K. Halmi, J.J. Lopez-Ibor, & N. Sartorius (Eds.), *Eating disorders* (pp. 209–211). Hove, UK: Wiley.

Klump, K.L., Bulik, C., Pollice, C., Halmi, K., Fichter, M., Berrettini, W.H. et al. (2000). Temperament and character in women with anorexia nervosa. *Journal of Nervous and Mental Diseases, 188*(9), 559–567.

Klump, K.L., & Gobrogge, K.L. (2005). A review and primer of molecular genetic studies of anorexia nervosa. *International Journal of Eating Disorders, 37*(S1), 543–548.

Klump, K.L., Gobrogge, K.L., Perkins, P.S., Thorne, D., Sisk, C., & Breedlove, S.M. (2006). Preliminary evidence that gonadal hormones organize and activate disordered eating. *Psychological Medicine, 36*(4), 539–546.

Klump, K.L., McGue, M., & Iacono, W.G. (2002). Genetic relationships between personality and disordered eating. *Journal of Abnormal Psychology, 111*(2), 380–389.

Klump, K.L., McGue, M., & Iacono, W.G. (2003). Differential heritability of eating pathology in pre-pubertal versus pubertal twins. *International Journal of Eating Disorders, 33*(3), 287–292.

Klump, K.L., Wonderlich, S., Lehoux, P., Lilenfeld, L.R.R., & Bulik, C.M. (2002). Does environment matter? A review of non-shared environment and eating disorders. *International Journal of Eating Disorders, 31*(2), 118–135.

Knapp, C. (2003). *Appetites: Why women want*. New York: Counterpoint.

Kohut, H. (1971). *The analysis of the self: A systematic approach to the psychoanalytic treatment of narcissistic personality disorders*. New York: International Universities Press.

Kohut, H. (1977). *The restoration of the self*. New York: International Universities Press.

Kohut, H. (1984). *How does analysis cure?* Chicago: University of Chicago Press.

Korndorfer, S., Lucas, A.R., Suman, V.J., Crowson, C.S., Krahn, L.E., & Melton, L.J. (2003). Long-term survival of patients with anorexia nervosa: A population-based study in Rochester, Minn. *Mayo Clinic Proceedings, 78,* 278–284.

Kramer, S., Aktar, S. (Eds.). (1992). *When the body speaks: Psychological meanings in kinetic clues.* Northvale, NJ: Aronson.

Kris, A.O. (1988). Some clinical applications of the distinction between divergent and covergent conflicts. *International Journal of Psycho-Analysis, 69,* 431–441.

Kris, A.O. (1996). *Free association: Method and process* (rev. ed.). London: Karnac Books.

Kuechler, J., & Hampton, R. (1998). Learning and behavioral approaches to the treatment of anorexia nervosa and bulimia. In B.J. Blinder, B.F. Chaitin, & R.S. Goldstein (Eds.), *The eating disorders: Medical and psychological bases of diagnosis and treatment* (pp. 423–432) . New York: PMA.

Kupers, T.A. (1988). *Ending therapy: The meaning of termination.* New York: New York University Press.

Lackman, M., & James, J.B. (1999). Charting the course of middle life development: An overview. In M.E. Lachman & J.B. James (Eds.), *Multiple paths of midlife development* (pp. 1–13). Chicago: University of Chicago Press.

Lam, R.W., Goldner, E.M., Solyom L., & Remick, R.A. (1994). A controlled study of light therapy for bulimia nervosa. *American Journal of Psychiatry, 151,* 744–750.

Lambe, E.K., Katzman, D.K., Mikulis, D.J., Kennedy, S.H., & Zipursky, R.B. (1997). Cerebral gray matter volume deficits after weight recovery from anorexia nervosa. *Archives of General Psychiatry, 54,* 537–542.

Lamoureux, M.M.H. & Bottorff, J.L. (2005). "Becoming the real me:" Recovery from anorexia nervosa. *Health Care for Women International, 26,* 170–188.

Lancelot, C., & Kaslow, N.J. (1994). Sex role orientation and disordered eating in women: A review. *Clinical Psychology Review, 14,* 139–157.

Lanker, B. (1989). *I dream a world.* New York: Stewart, Tabori, Chang.

Lansky, M. (2005). Hidden shame. *Journal of the American Psychoanalytic Association, 53*(3), 865–890.

Lansky, M., & Morrison, A. (1997). Shame in Freud's writings. In M. Lansky & A. Morrison (Eds.), *The widening scope of shame* (pp. 3–4). Hillsdale, NJ: Analytic Press.

Lasch, C. (1979). *The culture of narcissism: American life in an age of diminishing expectations.* New York: W.W. Norton.

Lask, B., & Bryant-Waugh, R. (Eds.). (2000). *Anorexia nervosa and related eating disorders in childhood and adolescence.* (2nd ed.). New York: Brunner- Routledge.

Lask, B. (2000). Overview of management. In B. Lask, & R. Bryant-Waugh (Eds.), *Anorexia nervosa and related disorders in childhood and adolescence* (2nd ed., pp. 167–187). New York: Brunner-Routledge.

Latzer, Y. (2005). Attachment to life in anorexia nervosa. *Eating Disorders Review, 16*(4), 1–3.

Lazerson, J. (1984). Voices of bulimia: Experiences in integrated psychotherapy. *Psychotherapy, 21*(4), 500–509.

Leahy, R.L. (2003). *Cognitive therapy techniques: A practitioner's guide.* New York: Guilford.

Lee, S. (1996). Reconsidering the status of anorexia as a western culture-bound syndrome. *Social Science and Medicine, 42,* 21–34.

Lee, S. (2004). Editorial: Engaging cultures: An overdue task for eating disorders research. *Culture, Medicine, and Psychiatry, 28,* 617–621.

Leiblum, S. & Rosen, R. (Eds.). (2000). *Principles and practices of sex therapy* (3rd ed.). New York: Guilford.

Leiblum, S., & Sachs, J. (2002). *Getting the sex you want.* New York: Crown.

Lelwicia, M.M. (1999). *Starving for salvation: The spiritual dimensions of eating problems among American girls and women*. New York: Oxford University Press.

Leombruni, P., Amianto, F., Delsedime, N., Gramaglia, C., Abbate-Daga, G., & Fassino, S. (2006). Citalopram versus fluoxetine for the treatment of patients with bulimia nervosa: a single blind randomized controlled trial. *Advances in Therapy, 23*(3), 481–494.

Lerner, H.D. (1993). Self-representation in eating disorders: A psychodynamic perspective. In Z.V. Segal & S.J. Blatt (Eds.), *The self in emotional distress* (pp. 267–287). New York: Guilford.

Levine, S.B. (2005). A reintroduction to clinical sexuality. *Focus: The Journal of Lifelong Learning in Psychiatry, 3*(4), 526–531.

Levy, S.T., Seelig, B.J., & Inderbitzen, L.B. (1995). On those wrecked by success: A clinical inquiry. *Psychoanalytic Quarterly, 64*, 639–665.

Lewis, D.M., Cachelin, F.M. (2001). Body images, body dissatisfaction, and eating attitudes in midlife and elderly women. *Eating Disorders: The Journal of Treatment and Prevention, 9*, 29–40.

Lewis, H.B. (1971). *Shame and guilt in neurosis*. New York: International Universities Press.

Lichtenberg, J. (1988). A discussion. In A. Rothstein (Ed.), *How does treatment help? On the modes of therapeutic action of psychoanalytic psychotherapy* (pp. 181–188). Madison, CT: International Universities Press.

Lichtenberg, J., Lachmann, F., & Fosshage, J. (1992). *Self and motivational systems: A theory of psychoanalytic technique*. Hillsdale, NJ: Analytic Press.

Lichtenberg, J., Lachmann, F., & Fosshage, J. (2002). *A spirit of inquiry: Communication in psychoanalysis*. Hillsdale, NJ: Analytic Press.

Lieberman, A., Padron, E., VanHorn, P., & Harris, W.H. (2005). Angels in the nursery. The intergenerational transmission of benevolent parental influences. *Infant Mental Health Journal, 26*(6), 504–520.

Lieberman, S. (1995). Anorexia nervosa: The tyranny of appearances. *Journal of Family Therapy, 17*, 133–138.

Little, M.A. (1981). *Transference neurosis and transference psychosis*. New York: Jason Aronson.

Little, M.A. (1990), *Psychotic anxieties and containment: A personal record of an analysis with Winnicott*. Northvale, NJ: Aronson.

Lock, J.D. (2005). Adjusting cognitive-behavioral therapy for adolescent bulimia nervosa: Results of a case series. *American Journal of Psychotherapy, 59*, 267–281.

Lock, J.D., & le Grange, D. (2007). Family treatment of eating disorders. In J. Yager, & P. Powers (Eds.), *Clinical manual of eating disorders* (pp. 149–170). Washington, DC: American Psychiatric Press.

Lock, J., le Grange, D., Agras, W., Dare, C. (2001). *Treatment manual for anorexia nervosa: A family-based approach*. New York: Guilford Press.

Lock, M. (1986). Ambiguities of aging: Japanese experience and perceptions of menopause. *Culture, Medicine and Psychiatry, 10*, 23–46.

Lock, M. (1998). Deconstructing the change: Female maturation in Japan and North America. In R.A. Shweder (Ed.), *Welcome to middle age! (and other cultural fictions)* (pp. 45–74). Chicago: University of Chicago Press.

Luborsky, L., Singer, B., & Luborsky, L. (1975). Comparative studies of psychotherapies: Is it true that "Everyone has won and all must have prizes?" *Archives of General Psychiatry, 32*, 995–1008.

Luborsky, L. & Luborsky, E. (2006). *Research and psychotherapy: The vital link*. Lanham, MD: Rowman & Littlefield.

Lucas, A.R., Melton, J., Crowson, & C.S., O'Fallon, M. (1999). Long-term fracture risk among women with anorexia nervosa: A population-based cohort study. *Mayo Clinic Proceedings, 74,* 972–977.

Mahler, M.S., Pine, F., & Bergman, A., (1975). *The psychological birth of the human infant.* New York: Basic Books.

Mahon, J., Bradley, S.N., Harvey, P.K., Winston, A.P., & Palmer, R.L. (2001). Childhood trauma has dose-effect relationship with dropping out from psychotherapeutic treatment for bulimia nervosa: A replication. *International Journal of Eating Disorders, 30*(2), 138–148.

Main, M. (1995). Recent studies in attachment: Overview with selected implications for clinical work. In S. Goldberg, R. Muir, & J. Kerr (Eds.), *Attachment theory: Social, developmental, and clinical perspectives* (pp. 407–474). Hillsdale, NJ: Analytic Press.

Maisel, R., Epston, D., & Borden, A. (2004). *Biting the hand that starves you: Inspiring resistance to anorexia/bulimia.* New York: W.W. Norton.

Maj, M., Halmi, K., Lopez-Ibor, J.J., & Sartorius, N. (Eds.). (2003). *Eating disorders.* Hove, UK: Wiley.

Malan, D., & Della Selva, P. (2006). *Lives transformed: A revolutionary method of dynamic psychotherapy.* London: Karmac.

Maltsberger, J., Buie, D.H. (1974). Countertransference hate in the treatment of suicidal patients. *Archives of General Psychiatry, 30,* 625–633.

Mangweth-Matzek, B., (2005). *Body image and attitudes in late middle age.* Paper presented at the Eating Disorders Research Society Annual Meeting, Amsterdam.

Mangweth-Matzek, B., Rupp, C.I., Hausmann, A., Assmayr, K., Mariacher, E., Klemmler, G., Whitworth, A.B., & Biebl, W., (2006). Never too old for eating disorders or body dissatisfaction. A community sample of elderly women. *International Journal of Eating Disorders, 39*(7), 583–586.

Marcos, A., (2003). A special situation of malnutrition triggering organism adaptive changes. In M. Maj, K. Halmi, J.J. Lopez-Ibor, & N. Sartorius (Eds.), *Eating disorders* (pp. 220–222). Hove, UK: Wiley.

Marcus, G. (2004). *The birth of the mind. How a tiny number of genes creates the complexities of human thought.* New York, Basic Books.

Marrazzi, M.A., Markham, K.M., Kinzie, J., & Luby, E.D. (1995). Binge eating disorder: Response to naltrexone. *International Journal of Obesity and Related Metabolic Disorders, 19*(2), 143–145.

Marrazzi, M.A., Wroblewski, J.M., Kinzie, J., & Luby, E.D. (1997). High dose naltrexone in eating disorders—liver function data. *American Journal of Addiction, 6,* 621–629.

Marx, R. (1992). *It's not your fault: Overcoming anorexia and bulimia through biopsychiatry.* New York: Penguin. (Original work published 1991)

Masterson, J.F. (1981). *Narcissistic and borderline disorders.* New York: Brunner/Mazel.

Masterson, J.F. (1983). *Countertransference and psychotherapeutic technique.* New York: Brunner/Mazel.

Masterson J.F. (1993). *The emerging self—A developmental, self, and object relations approach to the treatment of closet narcissistic disorders of the self.* New York: Brunner/Mazel.

Masterson, J.F. (1995). Paradise lost—Bulimia, a closet narcissistic personality disorder: A developmental, self, and object relations approach. In R.C. Marohn & S.C. Feinstein (Eds.), *Adolescent psychiatry: Developmental and clinical studies* (Vol. 19, pp. 253–266). Chicago: University of Illinois Press.

Masterson, J.F. (2005). Integrating attachment and object relations theories and the neurobiologic development of the self. In J.F. Masterson (Ed.), *The personality disorders through the lens of attachment theory and the neurobiologic development of the self: A clinical investigation* (pp. 1–18). Phoenix, AZ: Zeig, Tucker, & Theisen.

Masterson, J.F., & Lieberman, A.R. (Eds.). (2004). *A therapist's guide to the personality disorders: the Masterson approach.* Phoenix, Arizona: Zeig, Tucker, Theisen.

McDougall, J. (1980). *Plea for a measure of abnormality.* New York: International Universities Press.

McDougall, J. (1989). *Theaters of the body: A psychoanalytic approach to psychosomatic illness.* New York: W.W. Norton.

McDougall, J. (1995). *The many faces of Eros: A psychoanalytic exploration of human sexuality.* New York: W.W. Norton.

McDougall, J. (1999). Violence and creativity. *Scandinavian Psychoanalytic Review,* 22, 207–217.

McDougall, J. (2001). The psychic economy of addiction. In J. Petrucelli, & C. Stuart (Eds.), *Hungers and compulsions: The psychodynamic treatment of eating disorders and addictions* (pp. 3–26). Northvale, NJ: Aronson.

McElroy, S. (2003). *Topiramate for binge-eating.* Paper presented at the American Psychiatric Association Annual Meeting, San Francisco, CA.

McElroy, S.L., Arnold, L.M., Shapira, N.A., Keck Jr, P.E., Rosenthal, N.R., Karim, M.R. et al. (2003). Topiramate in the treatment of binge eating disorder associated with obesity: a randomized, placebo-controlled trial. *American Journal of Psychiatry,* 160(2), 255–261.

McIntosh, V.V.W., Jordan, J., Carter, F.A., Luty, S.E., McKenzie, J.M., Bulik, C.M. et al. (2005). Three psychotherapies for anorexia nervosa: A controlled trial. *American Journal of Psychiatry,* 163, 741–747.

McMullin, R.E. (2000). *The new handbook of cognitive therapy techniques.* New York: W.W. Norton.

McWilliams, N. (1994). *Psychoanalytic diagnosis: Understanding personality structure in the clinical process.* New York: Guilford.

McWilliams, N. (1999). *Psychoanalytic case formulation.* New York: Guilford.

McWilliams, N. (2004). *Psychoanalytic psychotherapy: A practitioner's guide.* New York: Guilford.

Mehler, C, Wewetzer, C., Schulze, U, Warnke, A., Theisen, F., & Dittmann, R.W. (2001). Olanzapine in children and adolescents with chronic anorexia nervosa: a study of five cases. *European Child and Adolescent Psychiatry,* 10(2), 151–157.

Mehler, P.S., & Andersen, A.E. (Eds.) (1999). *Eating disorders: A guide to medical care and complications.* Baltimore, MD: Johns Hopkins Univ Press.

Meisel, R., Epston, D., Borden, A. (2004). *Biting the hand that starves you: Inspiring resistance to anorexia and bulimia.* New York: W.W. Norton.

Meloy, J.R. & Fisher, H.E. (2005). Some thoughts on the neurobiology of stalking. *Journal of Forensic Sciences,* 50(6), 1472–1480.

Menninger, K. (1942). *Love against hate.* New York: Harcourt, Brace, & World.

Menninger, K. (1959, April). *Hope.* Academic lecture given at the 115th Annual Meeting of the American Psychiatric Association, Philadelphia.

Menninger, K. (1973). *Sparks* (L. Freeman, Ed.). New York: Crowell.

Menninger, K.A., & Holzman, P.S. (1973). *Theory of psychoanalytic techniques.* New York: Basic Books.

Menninger, K.A., Mayman, M., & Pruyser, P. (1963). *The vital balance: The life process in mental health and illness.* New York: Viking Press.

Menninger, W. (1967). Functional disorders of the gastrointestinal tract: The "gastrointestinal neuroses." In *A psychiatrist for a troubled world* (pp. 227–239). New York: Viking Press. (Original work published 1937)

Menninger,W. (1967). Psychological factors in disease. In *A psychiatrist for a troubled world* (pp. 126–150). New York: Viking Press. (Original work published 1938)

Menninger, W. (1967). Living in a troubled world. In W.C. Menninger, *A psychiatrist for a troubled world: Selected papers of William Menninger.* New York: Viking Press. (Original work published 1964)

Menon, U., & Shweder, R.A. (1998). The return of the "White Man's Burden": The moral discourse of anthropology and the domestic life of Hindu women. In R. Shweder (Ed.), *Welcome to middle age and other cultural fictions* (pp. 139–188). Chicago: University of Chicago Press.

Meston, C.M. (2000). Sympathetic nervous system activity and female sexual arousal. *American Journal of Cardiology* 86(Suppl.), 30F–34F.

Meyer, C., Blissett, J., & Oldfield, C. (2001). Sexual orientation and eating psychopathology: The role of masculinity and femininity. *International Journal of Eating Disorders*, 29(3), 314–318.

Michel, D., & Willard, S. (2003). *When dieting becomes dangerous: A guide to understanding and treating anorexia and bulimia.* New Haven, CT: Yale University Press.

Millar, H.R., Wardell, F., Vyvyan, J.P., Naji, S.A., Prescott, G.J., & Eagles, J. (2005). Anorexia nervosa mortality in Northeast Scotland, 1965–1999. *American Journal of Psychiatry*, 162, 753–757.

Miller, A. (1981). *Prisoners of childhood: The drama of the gifted child and the search for the true self.* New York: Basic Books.

Miller, B. (Director) & Fullerton, D. (Writer) (2005). *Capote* [Motion Picture]. United States: United Artists and Sony Pictures.

Miller, K.J. (1993). Prevalence and process of disclosure of childhood sexual abuse among eating-disordered women. *Eating Disorders: The Journal of Treatment and Prevention*, 1, 211–225.

Miller, P.M. (1996). Redefining success in eating disorders. *Addictive Behavior*, 21(6), 745–754.

Miller, S. (1985). *The shame experience.* Hillsdale, NJ: Analytic Press.

Miller, W.R., Rollnick, S. (2002). *Motivational interviewing: Preparing for change* (2nd ed.). New York: Guilford.

Milos, G., (2003) Towards an understanding of the biological causes and consequences of eating disoders. In M. Maj, K. Halmi, J.J. Lopez-Ibor, & N. Sartorius (Eds.), *Eating Disorders* (pp. 218–220). London: Wiley.

Milos, G., Spindler, A., Schnyder, U., & Fairburn, C. (2005). Instability of eating disorder diagnoses: Prospective study. *British Journal of Psychiatry*, 187, 573–578.

Milton, J. (2001). Psychoanalysis and cognitive behaviour therapy—Rival paradigms or common ground? *International Journal of Psycho-Analysis* 82, 431–447.

Mitchell, J. (1974). *Psychoanalysis and feminism.* New York: Pantheon.

Mitchell, J.E., & Selders, A. (2005). Recent treatment research in bulimia nervosa. *Eating Disorders Review*, 15, 1–4.

Mitchell, J.E., Hoberman, H.N. Peterson, C., Mussell, M., & Pyle, R.L. (1996). Research on the psychotherapy of bulimia nervosa: half empty of half full? *International Journal of Eating Disorders*, 20(3), 219–229.

Mitchell, S. (2002). *Can love last? The fate of romance over time.* London: W.W. Norton.

Mitrani, J.L. (1995), Toward an understanding of unmentalized experience. *Psychoanalytic Quarterly*, 64, 68–111.

Mitrani, J.L. (2001). "Talking the transference": Some technical implications in three papers by Bion. *International Journal of Psycho-Analysis*, 82, 1085–1104.

Modell, A.N. (1976). "The holding environment" and the therapeutic action of psychoanalysis. *Journal of the American Psychoanalytic Association*, 24, 285–308.

Modell, A.H. (1993). *The private self.* Cambridge, MA: Harvard University Press.

Morgan, C.D., Wiederman, M.W., & Pryor, T. (1995). Sexual functioning and attitudes of eating-disordered women: a follow-up study. *Journal of Sex and Marital Therapy*, 21(2), 67–77.

Morrison, A. (1987). *Shame: The underside of narcissism.* Hillsdale, NJ: Analytic Press.

Mountford, V., & Waller, G. (2006). Using imaging in cognitive-behavioral treatment for eating disorders. *International Journal of Eating Disorders*, 39(7), 533–543.

Mufson, L., Dorta, K.P., Moreau, D., & Weissman, M.M. (2004). *Interpersonal psychotherapy for depressed adolescents* (2nd ed.). New York: Guilford.

Murnen, S.K., & Smolak, L. (1997). Feminity, masculinity, disordered and eating disorder: A meta-analytic review. *International Journal of Eating Disorders*, 22(3), 231–242.

Naessen, S., (2006). *Endocrine and metabolic disorders in bulimic women and effects of antiandrogenic treatment*. Stockholm: Karolinska Institutet.

Nathanson, D. L. (1992). *Shame and pride: Affect, sex, and the birth of self*. New York: W.W. Norton.

Nelson, M.E., & Wernick, F. (1997). *Strong women stay young*. New York: Bantam.

Nemiroff, R.A., & Colarusso, C.A. (Eds) (1985). *The race against time: Psychotherapy and psychoanalysis in the second half of life*. New York: Plenum.

Nemiroff, R.A., & Colarusso, C.A. (1990a). *New dimensions in adult development*. New York: Basic Books.

Nemiroff, R.A., & Colarusso, C.A. (1990b). Frontiers in adult development in theory and practice. In R.A. Nemiroff & C.A. Colarusso (Eds.), *New dimensions in adult development* (pp. 97–124). New York: Basic Books.

Neugarten, B.L. (1968). The awareness of middle age. In B.L. Neugarten (Ed.), *Middle age and aging* (pp. 93–98). Chicago: University of Chicago Press.

Neugarten, B.L., & Gutmann, D.L. (1968). Age-sex roles and personality in middle age: A thematic apperception study. In B.L. Neugarten (Ed.), *Middle age and aging* (pp. 58–76). Chicago: University of Chicago Press.

Neugarten, B.L., & Hagestad, G.O. (1976). Age and the life course. In B.H. Binstock & E. Shanas (Eds.), *Handbook on aging and the social sciences* (pp. 35–55) New York: Van Nostrand Reinhold.

Newman-Toker, J., (2000). Risperidone in anorexia nervosa. *Journal of American Academy of Child & Adolescent Psychiatry*, 39(8), 941–942.

Nichols, M. (2000). Therapy with sexual minorities. In S. R. Leiblum & R.C. Rosen (Eds.), *Principles and practices of sex therapy* (3rd ed., pp. 335–367). New York: Guilford.

Norcross, J.C. (1996). The lifetime lessons of six psychologists: An introduction. *Psychotherapy*, 33(1), 129–151.

Norre, J., Vandereycken, W., & Gordts, S. (2001). The management of eating disorders in a fertility clinic: Clinical guidelines. *Journal of Psychosomatic Obstetrics and Gynecology*, 22, 77–81.

Notman, M.T., & Nadelson, C.C. (Eds.) (1991). *Women and men: New perspectives on gender differences*. Washington, DC: American Psychiatric Press.

Novack, D. (2004). A case illustration of bulimia nervosa in midlife. *Renfrew Perspective*, Summer, 16–18.

Novick, J., & Novick, K. (1991). Some comments on masochism and the delusion of omnipotence from a developmental perspective. *Journal of the American Psychoanalytic Association*, 39, 307–331.

Novick, J., & Novick, K. (1996). *Fearful Symmetry: The development and treatment of sadomasochism*. Northvale, NJ: Aronson.

Novick, K., & Novick, J. (1998). An application of the concept of the therapeutic alliance to sadomasochistic pathology. *Journal of the American Psychoanalytic Association*, 46(3), 813–846.

Odvina, C.V., Zerwekh, J.E., Rao, D.S., Maalouf, N., Gottschalk, F.A. & Pak, C.Y. (2005). Severely suppressed bone turnover; A potential complication of alendronate therapy. *Journal of Clinical Endocrinology and Metabolism*, 90, 1294–1301.

Ogden, T.H. (1979). On projective identification. *International Journal of Psycho-Analysis*. 60, 357–373.

Ogden, T.H. (1982). *Projective identification and psychotherapeutic technique*. New York: Aronson.

Ogden, T.H. (1986). *The matrix of the mind: Object relations and the psychoanalytic dialogue.* Northvale, NJ: Aronson.

Ogden, T.H. (1989). *The primitive edge of experience.* Northvale, NJ: Aronson.

Oliver-Pyatt, W. (2003). *Fed up! The breakthrough ten-step, no-diet fitness plan.* New York: Contemporary.

Orbach, S. (1978). *Fat is a feminist issue: The anti-diet guide to permanent weight loss.* New York: Paddington.

Orbach, S. (1994). Working with the false body. In A. Erskine, & D. Judd (Eds.), *The imaginative body* (pp. 166–179). London: Whurr.

Pagels, E. (1979). *The Gnostic gospels.* New York: Random House.

Paglia, C. (1990). *Sexual personae: Art and decadence from Nefertiti to Emily Dickinson.* New Haven, CT: Yale University Press.

Paglia, C. (1992). *Sex, art, and American culture.* New York: Vintage Books.

Pally, R., (2000). *The mind-brain relationship.* London: Karnac Press.

Pally, R., (2005). A neuroscience perspective on forms of intersubjective infant research and adult treatment. In B. Beebe, S. Knoblauch, J. Rustin, & D. Sorter (Eds.), *Forms of intersubjectively in infant research and adult treatment* (pp. 191–241). New York: Other Press.

Paris, B.J. (1994). *Karen Horney: A psychoanalyst's search for self-understanding.* New Haven, CT: Yale University Press.

Peebles-Kleiger, M.J. (2002). *Beginnings: The art and science of beginning psychotherapy.* Hillsdale, NJ: Analytic Press.

Pennebaker, J.W. (1991). *Opening Up: The healing power of confiding in others.* New York: Morrow.

Pennebaker, J.W. (1997). *Opening Up: The healing power of expressing emotions.* New York: Morrow.

Person, E.S. (1988). *Dreams of love and fateful encounters: The power of romantic passion.* New York: W.W. Norton.

Person, E.S. (2002). *Feeling strong: The achievement of authentic power.* New York: William Morrow.

Petrucelli, J. (2001). Close encounters of the regulatory kind: An interpersonal/relational look at self-regulation. In J. Petrucelli & C. Stuart (Eds.), *Hungers and compulsions: The psychodynamic treatment of eating disorders and addictions* (pp. 97–112). Northvale, NJ: Aronson.

Petrucelli, J., & Stuart, C. (Eds.) (2001). *Hungers and compulsion: The psychodynamic treatment of eating disorders and addictions.* Northvale, NJ: Jason Aronson.

Pettinati, H., Kogan, L.G., Margolis, C., Shrier, L., & Wade, J.H. (1989). Hypnosis, hypnotizability and the bulimic patient. In L.M. Hornyak & E.K. Baker (Eds.), *Experiential therapies for eating disorders* (pp. 34–60). New York: Guilford.

Pipher, M. (1994). *Reviving Ophelia: Saving the selves of adolescent girls.* New York, Ballantine.

Pike, K.M. (1998). Long-term course of anorexia nervosa: Response, relapse, remission, and recovery. *Clinical Psychology Review,* 18(4), 447–475.

Pike, K.M., & Borovoy, A. (2004). The rise of eating disorders in Japan: Issues of culture and limitations of the model of "Westernization." *Culture, Medicine and Psychiatry,* 28, 493–531.

Pines, D. (1993). *A woman's unconscious use of her body.* New Haven, CT: Yale University Press.

Piran, N. (1996). The reduction of preoccupation with body weight and shape in schools: A feminist approach. *Eating Disorders: The Journal of Treatment and Prevention,* 4(4), 323–333.

Piran, N. (2004). Teachers: On "being" (rather than doing) prevention. *Eating Disorders: The Journal of Treatment and Prevention,* 12(1), 1–10.

Polivy, J., & Herman, C.P. (1999). Distress and eating: why do dieters overeat? *International Journal of Eating Disorders, 26*(2), 153–164.

Pope, H.G. & Hudson, F.E. (2004). Bulimia nervosa: Persistent disorder requires equally persistent treatment. *Current Psychology, 3*(1), 13–22.

Pothos, E.N., Creese, I., & Hoebel, B.G. (1995). Restricted eating with weight loss selectively decreases extra cellular dopamine in the nucleus accumbens and alters dopamine response to amphetamine, morphine, and food intake. *Journal of Neuroscience, 15*(10), 6640–6650.

Powers, P.S., Bannon, Y., Eubanks, R., & McCormick, T. (2007). Quetiapine in anorexia nervosa patients: An open label outpatient pilot study. *International Journal of Eating Disorders, 40*(1), 21–26.

Powers, P., & Cloak, N. (2007). Medication-related weight changes: Impact on treatment of eating disorder patients. In J. Yager, & P. Powers (Eds.), *Clinical manual of eating disorders* (pp. 255–278). Washington, DC: American Psychiatric Press.

Powers, P., & Santana, C.A., (2002). Eating disorders: A guide for the primary care physician. *Primary Care: Clinics in Office Practice, 29*(1), 81–98.

Powers, P.S., Santana, C.A., & Bannon, Y.S. (2002). Olanzapine in the treatment of anorexia nervosa: An open label trial. *International Journal of Eating Disorders 32*(2), 146–154.

Powers, P. & Thompson, R.A. (2007). Athletes and eating disorders. In J. Yager & P. Powers (Eds.), *Clinical manual of eating disorders* (pp. 357–385). Washington, DC: American Psychiatric Press.

Price, W.A., Babai, M.R., & Torem, M.S., (1986). Anorexia nervosa in late life. *Hillside Journal of Clinical Psychiatry, 8*(2), 144–151.

Prochaska, J.O., & DiClemente, C.C., (1986). Toward a comprehensive model of change. In M.R. Miller, & N. Heather (Eds.). *Treating addictive behaviors: Processes of change* (pp. 3–27). New York: Plenum.

Prochaska, J.O., & DiClemente, C.C., (1992). The transtheoretical approach. In J.C. Norcross, & M.R. Goldfried (Eds.), *Handbook of psychotherapy integration* (pp. 300–334). New York: Basic Books.

Prozan, C.K. (1992). *Feminist psychoanalytic psychotherapy.* Northvale, NJ: Aronson.

Quadlfieg, N., & Fichter, M.M. (2003). The course and outcome of bulimia nervosa. *European Child and Adolescent Psychiatry, 12*(Suppl. 1), 99–109.

Rabinor, J.R. (1991). The process of recovery from an eating disorder: The use of journal writing in the initial phase of treatment. *Psychotherapy in Private Practice, 9,* 93–106.

Raboch, J., & Faltus, F. (1991). Sexuality of women with anorexia nervosa. *Acta Psychiatrica Scandinavia, 84,* 9–11.

Rako, S., & Mazer, H. (1980). *Semrad: The heart of a therapist.* New York: Jason Aronson.

Reid, I.C., & Stewart, C.A. (2001). How antidepressants work. New perspectives on the pathophysiology of depressive disorder. *British Journal of Psychiatry, 178,* 299–303.

Reindl, A.M. (2001). *Sensing the self: Women's recovery from bulimia.* Cambridge, MA: Harvard University Press.

Richard, M. (2005). Effective treatment of eating disorders in Europe: Treatment outcome and its predictors. *European Eating Disorders Review, 13,* 169–179.

Rigotti, N.A., Nussbaum, S.R., Herzog, D.B., & Neer, R.M. (1984). Osteoporosis in women with anorexia nervosa. *New England Journal of Medicine, 311,* 1601–1606.

Rinsley, D.B. (1980). *Treatment of the severely disturbed adolescent.* New York: Aronson.

Rinsley, D.B. (1982). *Borderline and other self disorders: A developmental and object relations perspective.* New York: Aronson.

Rinsley, D.B. (1989). *Developmental pathogenesis and treatment of borderline and narcissistic personalities.* Northvale, NJ: Aronson.

Rizzuto, A.M. (1988). Transference, language, and affect in the treatment of buli-marexia. *International Journal of Psycho-Analysis, 69*, 369–387.

Rodin, G.M. (1991). The etiology of eating disorders: Lessons from high risk groups. *Psychiatric Annals, 29*, 181–182.

Rodin, J., Silberstein, L., & Striegel-Moore, R. (1984). Women and weight: A nor-mative discontent. In T.B. Sonderegger (Ed.), *Psychology and gender: Nebraska Symposium on Motivation*. Lincoln, NB: University of Nebraska Press.

Rodin, J. (1993). Cultural and psychosocial determinants of weight concerns. *Annals of Internal Medicine, 199*(7), 643–645.

Roe, D., Dekel, R., Harel, G., Fennig, S., & Fennig, S., (2006). Clients' feelings dur-ing termination of psychodynamically oriented psychotherapy. *Bulletin of the Menninger Clinic, 70*(1), 68–81.

Romano, S.J., Halmi, K.A., Sarker, N.P., Koke, S.C., & Lee, J.S. (2002). A placebo-controlled study of fluoxetine in continued treatment of bulimia nervosa after successful acutefluoxetine treatment. *American Journal of Psychiatry, 159*(1), 96–102.

Romans, S.E., Gendall, K.A., Martin, J.L., & Mullen, P.E. (2001). Child sexual abuse and later disordered eating: A New Zealand epidemiological study. *International Journal of Eating Disorders, 29*(4), 380–392.

Root, M.P.P. (1990). Disordered eating in women of color. *Sex Roles, 22*(7, 8), 525–536.

Rorty, M., & Yager, J. (1993). Speculations on the role of childhood abuse in the development of eating disorders among women. *Eating Disorders: Journal of Treatment and Prevention, 1*, 199–210.

Rorty, M., Yager, J., & Rossotto, E. (1994). Childhood sexual, physical and psycho-logical abuse in bulimia nervosa. *American Journal of Psychiatry, 151*, 1122–1126.

Rose, M. (1990). *Healing hurt minds: The Peper Harow experience*. London: Tavistock/Routledge.

Rosen, I.C. (1993, October 14). *Relational masochism: The search for a "bad–enough object."* Paper presented to the Topeka Psychoanalytic Society.

Rosenberger, J.B. (1999). Foreword: Heightening cultural awareness in the psycho-analytic situation. *Psychoanalysis and Psychotherapy, 16*, 163–164.

Rossotto, E., Rorty-Greenfield, M., & Yager, J. (1996). What causes and maintains bulimia nervosa: Recorded and non-recorded women's reflections on the disorder. *Eating Disorders: The Journal of Treatment and Prevention, 4*(2), 115–127.

Russell, C.J., & Keel, P.K. (2002). Homosexuality as a specific risk factor for eating disorders in men. *International Journal of Eating Disorders, 31*(3), 300–306.

Russell, J. (2003). So much to learn and so little time. In M. Maj, K. Halmi, J.J. Lopez- Ibor, & N. Sartorius (Eds.), *Eating disorders* (pp. 204–206). Hove, UK: Wiley.

Russell, J. (2004). Management of anorexia nervosa revisited. *British Medical Journal, 328*, 479–480.

Russell, J., & Megan G. (1992). Is tardive anorexia a discrete diagnostic entity? *Australia and New Zealand Journal of Psychiatry, 26*, 263–272.

Russell, J., & Meares, R. (1997). Paradox, persecution, and the double game: Psychotherapy in anorexia nervosa. *Australian and New Zealand Journal of Psychiatry 31*, 691–699.

Sacksteder, J.L. (1989). Psychosomatic dissociation and false self development in anorexia nervosa. In M. G. Fromm & B. L. Smith (Eds.), *The facilitating environment: Clinical applications of Winnicott's theory* (pp. 365–393). Madison, CT: International Universities Press.

Sandler, J. (1987). *From safety to superego*. London: Karmac Books.

Sands, S. (1991). Bulimia, dissociation, and empathy; A self-psychological view. In C.L. Johnson (Ed.), *Psychodynamic treatment of anorexia nervosa and bulimia* (pp. 34–50). New York: Guilford.

Schafer, R. (1960). The loving and beloved superego in Freud's structural theory. *Psychoanalytic Study of the Child, 15* (pp. 163–188). New York: International Universities Press.

Schafer, R. (1983). *The analytic attitude.* New York: Aronson.

Schafer, R. (1992). *Retelling a life: Narration and dialogue in psychoanalysis.* New York: Basic Books.

Schafer, R. (Ed.) (1997). *The contemporary Kleinians of London.* Madison, CT: International Universities Press.

Schafer, R. (2003). *Bad feelings.* New York: Other Press.

Scharff, D.E. (1982). *The sexual relationship: An object relations view of sex and the family.* London: Routledge.

Schlesinger, H.J. (1995). The process of interpretation and the moment of change. *Journal of the American Psychoanalytic Association, 43*(3), 663–688.

Schlesinger, H.J. (1996). The fear of being left half-cured. *Bulletin of the Menninger Clinic, 60*(4), 420–448.

Schlesinger, H.J., (2005). *Endings and beginnings: On terminating psychotherapy and psychoanalysis.* Hillsdale, NJ: Analytic Press.

Schlundt, D.G., & Johnson, W.G. (1990). *Eating disorders: Assessment and treatment.* Boston: Allyn & Bacon.

Schmidt, U., Treasure, J. (1993). *A survival kit for sufferers of bulimia nervosa and binge eating disorder.* London: Psychology Press.

Schnarch, D. (1997). *Passionate marriage: Sex, love, and intimacy in emotionally committed relationships.* New York: W.W. Norton.

Schnarch, D. (2000). Desire problems: A systemic perspective. In S.R. Leiblum & R.C. Rosen (Eds.), *Principles and practices of sex therapy* (3rd ed., pp. 17–56) New York: Guilford.

Schneider, J.A. (1995). Eating disorders, addictions, and unconscious fantasy. *Bulletin of the Menninger Clinic 59*(2), 177–190.

Schore, A.N. (2001). The effects of a secure attachment relationship on right brain development, affect regulation, and infant mental health. *Infant Mental Health Journal 22,* 7–66.

Schore, A.N. (2003). *Affect dysregulation and disorders of the self.* New York: WW Norton.

Schore, A.N. (2005). Attachment, affect regulation, and the developing right brain: Linking developmental neuroscience to pediatrics. *Pediatrics in Review, 26*(8), 204–216.

Schover, L. (2000). Sexual problems in chronic illness. In S.R. Leiblum. & R.C. Rosen (Eds.), *Principles and practice of sex therapy* (3rd ed., pp. 398–422). New York: Guilford.

Schuker, E., & Levinson, N.A. (1991). *Female psychology: An annotated psychoanalytic bibliography.* Hillsdale, NJ: Analytic Press.

Schuyler, D. (1991). *A practical guide to cognitive therapy.* New York: W.W. Norton.

Schwam, J.S., Klass, E., Alonso, C., & Perry, R. (1998). Risperidone and refusal to eat [letter]. *Journal of American Academy of Child & Adolescent Psychiatry, 37*(6), 572–573.

Schwartz, J. (Ed.). (1988). *Bulimia: Psychoanalytic treatment and theory.* Madison, CT: International Universities Press.

Searles, H.F. (1986). *My work with borderline patients.* Northvale, NJ: Aronson.

Serpell, L., Livingstone, A., Neiderman, M., & Lask, B. (2002). Anorexia nervosa: Obsessive compulsive disorder, obsessive-compulsive personality disorder, or neither? *Clinical Psychology Review, 22,* 647–669.

Settlage, C.F. (1990). Childhood to adulthood: Structural change toward independence and autonomy. In R.A. Nemiroff, & C.A. Colarusso (Eds.), *New dimensions in adult development* (pp. 26–46). New York: Basic Books.

Shapiro, J.R., Berkman, N.D., Brownley, K.A., Sedway, J.A., Lohr, K.N., & Bulik, C.M. (2007). Bulimia nervosa treatment: A systematic review of randomized controlled trials. *International Journal of Eating Disorders*, 40(4), 321–336.

Shengold, L. (1989). *Soul murder: The effect of childhood abuse and deprivation*. New Haven CT: Yale University Press.

Shengold, L. (1999). *Soul murder revisited: Thoughts about therapy, hate, love and memory*. New Haven CT: Yale University Press.

Silverman, M.A. (1987). The analyst's response. *Psychoanalytic Inquiry*, 7, 277–287.

Silverman, M.A. (2006). Book review. *Psychoanalytic Quarterly*, 75(3), 898–907.

Simpson, W.S., & Ramberg, J.A. (1992). Sexual dysfunction in married female patients with anorexia and bulimia nervosa. *Journal of Sex & Marital Therapy*, 18(1), 44–54.

Smith, H. (2001). *Why religion matters*. New York: HarperCollins.

Smith, H. (2003). *The way things are*. Berkeley: University of California Press.

Smith, H.F. (2005). Dialogue in conflict: Toward an integration of methods. *Psychoanalytic Quarterly*, 74(1), 327–363.

Sokol, M.S., & Gray, N.S., (1997). Case Study: An infection triggered, autoimmune subtype of anorexia nervosa. *Journal of the American Academy of Child and Adolescent Psychiatry*, 36, 1128–1133.

Sokol, M.S., Gray, N.S., Goldstein, A., & Kaye, W., (1999). Methylphenidate treatment for bulimia nervosa associated with cluster B personality disorder. *International Journal of Eating Disorders*, 25(2), 233–237.

Sokol, M.S., Steinberg, D., & Zerbe, K.J. (1998). Childhood eating disorders. *Current Opinion in Pediatrics*, 10, 369–377.

Solms, M., & Turnbull, O (2002). *The brain and the inner world: And introduction to the neuroscience of subjective experience*. New York: Other Press.

Sontag, S. (2000). *In America*. New York: Farrar, Straus, & Giroux.

Sowell, E.R., Peterson, B.S., Thompson, P.M., Welcome, S.E., Henkenius, A.L., & Toga, A.W. (2003). Mapping cortical change across the human life span. *Nature Neuroscience*, 6(3), 309–315.

Spence, D. (1982). *Narrative truth and historical truth: Meaning and interpretation in psychoanalysis*. New York: Norton.

Spitz, R.A. (1957). *No and yes: On the genesis of human communication*. New York, International Universities Press.

Srinivasagam, N.M, Kaye, W., Plotnicov, K., Greeno, C., Welzin, T.E., & Rao, R. (1995). Persistent perfectionism, symmetry, and exactness after long-term recovery from anorexia nervosa. *American Journal of Psychiatry*, 152(11), 1603–1634.

Steiger, H., Goldstein, C., Mongrain, M., & Van der Feen, J. (1990). Description of eating disordered, psychiatric, and normal women along cognitive and psychodynamic dimensions. *International Journal of Eating Disorders*, 9(2), 129–140.

Stein, H., Fonagy, P. Ferguson, K.S. & Wisman, M. (2000). Lives through time. An ideographic approach to the study of resilience. *Bulletin of the Menninger Clinic*, 64(2), 281–305.

Steiner, H. (1990). Defense styles in eating disorders. *International Journal of Eating Disorders*, 9(2), 141–151.

Steiner-Adair, C. (1991a). When the body speaks: Girls, eating disorders, and psychotherapy. In A.G. Rogers (Ed.), *Women, girls and psychotherapy: Reframing resistance* (pp. 253–256). New York: Haworth Press.

Steiner-Adair, C. (1991b). New maps of development, new models of therapy: The psychology of women and the treatment of eating disorders. In C.L. Johnson (Ed.), *Psychodynamic treatment of anorexia nervosa and bulimia* (pp. 225–244). New York: Guilford.

Steiner-Adair, C., & Sjostrom, L. (2006). *Full of ourselves: A wellness program to advance girl power, health, and leadership.* New York: Teachers College Press.

Steinhausen, H.C. (2002) The outcome of anorexia nervosa in the 20th century. *American Journal of Psychiatry, 159,* 1284–1293.

Stern, D.N. (1985). *The interpersonal world of the infant.* New York: Basic Books.

Stern, D.N. (2004). *The present moment.* New York: WW Norton.

Stewart, D.E., Robinson, E., Goldbloom, D.S., & Wright, C. (1990). Infertility and eating disorders. *American Journal of Obstetrics and Gynecology, 157,* 627–630.

Stiver, I.P. (1991). *The meaning of care: Reframing treatment models.* In J.V. Jordan, A.E. Kaplan, J.B. Miller, I. Stiver, J. Surrey et al. (Eds.), *Women's growth in connection: Writings from the Stone Center* (pp. 250–267). New York: Guilford.

Stoller, R.J. (1979). *Sexual excitement: Dynamics of erotic life.* New York: Pantheon.

Stoller, R.J. (1985). *Observing the erotic imagination.* New Haven, CT: Yale University Press.

Stolorow, R.D., Brandchaft, B. & Atwood, G.E. (1987). *Psychoanalytic treatment: An intersubjective approach.* Hillsdale, NJ: Analytic Press.

Stone, L. (1961). *The psychoanalytic situation: An examination of its development and essential nature.* New York: International Universities Press.

Stoving, R.K., Brixen, K., & Hagen, C. (2003). Clinical impact on the endocrine alternations inpatients with eating disorders; Adaptations to inappropriate response. In M. Maj, K. Halmi, J.J. Lopez-Ibor, & N. Sartorius (Eds.), *Eating disorders* (pp. 201–204). London: Wiley.

Striegel-Moore, R. H. (1993). Homosexuality and eating disorders. *National Anorexic Aid Society Newsletter, 16,* 1–6.

Striegel-Moore, R.H., Tucker, N., & Hsu, J. (1990). Body image dissatisfaction and disordered eating in lesbian college students. *International Journal of Eating Disorders,* 9(5), 493–500.

Strober, M. (1980). Personality and symptomatic features in non-chronic anorexia nervosa patients. *Journal of Psychosomatic Research, 24,* 353–359.

Strober, M. (2004). Managing the chronic, treatment-resistant patient with anorexia nervosa. *International Journal of Eating Disorders, 36*(3), 245–255.

Strober, M. (2006). *Treatment of chronic anorexia.* Plenary Address at the Renfrew Foundation Conference, Philadelphia, Pa.

Strober, M., Freeman, R., & Morrell, W. (1997). The long term course of severe anorexia nervosa in adolescents: Survival analysis of recovery, relapse and outcome predictors over 10–15 years in a prospective study. *International Journal of Eating Disorders,* 22(4), 339–360.

Strober, M., Freeman, R., & Morrell, W. (1999). Atypical anorexia nervosa: Separation from typical case in course and outcome in a long-term prospective study. *International Journal of Eating Disorders, 25*(2), 135–142.

Strober M, Pataki, C., Freeman, R., & DeAntonio, M. (1999). No effect of adjunctive fluoxetine on eating behavior or weight phobia during the inpatient treatment of anorexia nervosa: An historical case-control study. *Journal of Child and Adolescent Psychopharmacology, 9,* 195–201.

Sullivan, H.S. (1953). *The interpersonal theory of psychiatry.* New York: W.W. Norton.

Sullivan, H.S. (1956). *Clinical studies in psychiatry.* New York: W.W. Norton.

Sullivan, P.F. (1995). Mortality in anorexia nervosa. *American Journal of Psychiatry, 152,* 1073–1074.

Sullivan, P.F., Bulik, C.M., Fear, J., & Pickering, A. (1998). Outcome of anorexia nervosa: A case-controlled study. *American Journal of Psychiatry, 155*(7), 939–946.

Sutherland, J.D. (1989). *Fairbairn's journey into the interior.* London: Free Association Books.

Swann, W.B., Jr. (1996). *Self-traps*. New York: Freeman.

Swift, W.J., & Letvin, R. (1984). Bulimia and the basic fault: A psychoanalytic interpretation of the bingeing-vomiting syndrome. *Journal of the American Academy of Child Psychiatry, 23*, 489–497.

Taylor, C.B, Bryson, S., Luce, K.H., Cunning, D., Doyle, A.C., Abascal, L.B., Rockwell, R., Dev, P., Winzelberg, A.J., Wilfrey, D.E. (2006). Prevention of eating disorders in at-risk college women. *Archives of General Psychiatry, 63*(8), 881–888.

Theander, S. (1970). Anorexia nervosa: A psychiatric investigation of 94 patients. *Acta Psychiatrica Scandinavica, 214*(Suppl.), 1–194.

Theander, S. (1983a). Long-term prognosis of anorexia nervosa: A preliminary report. In P.H. Darby, P.E. Garfinkel, D.M. Garner, & D.V. Coscina (Eds.), *Anorexia nervosa: Recent developments in research* (pp. 441–442). New York: Alan R. Liss.

Theander, S. (1983b). Research on outcome and prognosis of anorexia nervosa and some results from a Swedish long-term study. *International Journal of Eating Disorders, 2*(4), 167–174.

Theander, S. (1985). Outcome and prognosis in anorexia nervosa and bulimia: Some results of previous investigations, compared with those of a Swedish long-term study. *Journal of Psychiatric Research, 19*, 493–508.

Theander S. (1992) Chronicity in anorexia nervosa: Results from the Swedish long-term study. In W. Herzog, H.C. Deter, & W. Vandereycken (Eds.), *The Course of Eating Disorders: Long-term follow-up studies of anorexia and bulimia nervosa* (pp. 214–227). Berlin, Springer.

Thommen, M., Vallach, L., Kiencke, S. (1995). Prevalence of eating disorders in a Swiss family planning clinic: A pilot study. *Eating Disorders: The Journal of Treatment and Prevention, 3*, 324–331.

Thompson, B. (1994). Food, bodies, and growing up female: Childhood lessons about culture, race, and class. In P. Fallon, M.A. Katzman, & S. Wooley (Eds.), *Feminist perspectives on eating disorders* (pp. 355–377). New York, Guilford.

Thompson, C. (1964). *Interpersonal psychoanalysis: The selected papers of Clara Thompson*. New York: Basic Books.

Thompson-Brenner, H., & Westen, D. (2005a). A naturalistic study for bulimia nervosa, Part 1: Comorbidity and therapeutic outcomes. *Journal of Nervous and Mental Disease, 193*(9), 585–595.

Thompson-Brenner, H., & Westen, D. (2005b). A naturalistic study for bulimia nervosa, Part 2: Therapeutic interventions in the community. *Journal of Nervous and Mental Disease, 193*(9), 585–595.

Thompson-Brenner, H., & Westen, D. (2005c.). Personality subtypes in eating disorders: Validation of a classification in a naturalistic sample. *British Journal Psychiatry, 186*, 516–524.

Ticho, E. (1972). Termination of psychoanalysis: Treatment goals, life goals. *Psychoanalytic Quarterly, 41*, 315–333.

Tiggemann, M. (1999). Body image research summary: Body image and aging. *Body Image & Health Incorporated Research Summaries*, 1–9.

Tiggeman, M., & Lynch, J.E. (2001). Body image across the life span in adult women: The role of self objectification. *Developmental Psychology, 2*, 243–253.

Titus, M. (1982). Don't just do something, stand there: The role of action and will in psychotherapy. *Bulletin of the Menninger Clinic, 46*(5), 465–471.

Tobin, J.L., & Dobard, R.G. (1999). *Hidden in plain view: A secret story of quilts and the Underground Railroad*. New York: Random House.

Toga, A.W., Thompson, P.M., & Sowell, E.R. (2006). Mapping brain maturation. *Trends in Neuroscience, 29*(3), 148–159.

Tolkien, J.R.R (1977) *The Hobbit: On there and back again*. Boston: Houghton Mifflin. (Original work published 1937)

Tozzi, F., Sullivan, P.F., Fear, J.L., McKenzie, J., & Bulik, C. (2003). Causes and recovery in anorexia nervosa: The patient perspective. *International Journal of Eating Disorders*, 33(2), 143–154.

Treasure, J. (1989). Staged matched interventions for eating disorders. In P. Bria, A. Ciocca, & S. De Risio (Eds.), *Psychotherapeutic issues on eating disorders: Models, methods, and results* (pp. 59–66). Rome: Societa Editrice Universo.

Treasure, J. (1997). *Anorexia nervosa: A survival guide for families, friends, and sufferers*. London: Psychology Press.

Treasure, J., & Schmidt, U. (1999). Beyond effectiveness and efficiency lies quality in services for eating disorders. *European Eating Disorders Review*, 7, 162–178.

Treasure, J., & Ward, A. (1997). A practical guide to the use of motivational interviewing in anorexia nervosa. *European Eating Disorders Review*, 5(2), 102–114.

Treasure, J. (2003). Bringing the soma into psychosomatic aspects of eating disorders. In M. Maj, K. Halmi, J.J. Lopez-Ibor, & N. Sartorius (pp. 193–197). London: Wiley.

Tribole, E., & Resch, E. (1995). *Intuitive eating: A revolutionary program that works*. New York: St. Martins.

Troop, N.A., Holbrey, A., Trowler, R., & Treasure, J. (1994). Ways of coping in women with eating disorders. *Journal of Nervous and Mental Diseases*, 182(10), 535–546.

Tuiten, A., Panhuysen, G., Everaerd, W., Koppeschaar, H., Krabbe, P., & Zelissen, P. (1993). The paradoxical nature of sexuality in anorexia nervosa. *Journal of Sex & Marital Therapy*, 19, 259–275.

Tustin, F. (1986). *Autistic barriers in neurotic patients*. New Haven, CT: Yale University Press.

Tustin, F. (1990). *The protective shell in children and adults*. London: Karmac.

Tyson, P., & Tyson, R. (1990). *Psychoanalytic theories of development: An integration*. New Haven, CT: Yale University Press.

Vaillant, G.E. (1993). *The wisdom of the ego*. Cambridge, MA: Harvard University Press.

Vaillant, G.E. (2002). *Aging well. Surprising quideposts to a happier life from the landmark, Harvard Study of adult development*. Boston: Little, Brown.

Vaillant, G.E., & Mukamal, K. (2001). Successful aging. *American Journal of Psychiatry*, 158, 839–847.

Valla, A., Groenning, I.L., Syversen, U., & Hoeiseth, A. (2000). Anorexia nervosa: Slow regain of bone mass. *Osteoporosis International*, 11, 141–145.

Vandereycken, W., & vanDeth, R. (1994). *From fasting saints to anorexic girls: The history of self-starvation*. New York: New York University Press.

Vanderpost, L. (1982). *Yet being someone other*. London, Hogarth Press.

Vanderbroucke, S., Vandereycken, W., & Norre, J. (1997). *Eating disorders and marital relationships*. London: Routledge.

Viamontes, G.I., & Beitman, B.D. (2006) Neural substrates of psychotherapeutic change part II: Beyond default mode. *Psychiatric Annals*, 36(4), 238–245.

Viorst, J. (1986). *Necessary losses: The loves, illusions, dependencies, and impossible expectations that all of us have to give up in order to grow*. New York: Simon & Schuster.

Vitousek, K.B., Daly, J., Heiser, C. (1991). Reconstructing the internal world of the eating-disordered individual: Overcoming denial and distortion in self-report. *International Journal of Eating Disorders*, 10(6), 647–666.

Wallerstein, J.S. & Blakeslee, S. (1995). *The good marriage: How and why love lasts*. Boston: Houghton Mifflin.

Wallerstein, R.S. (1986). *Forty-two lives in treatment: A study of psychoanalysis and psychotherapy*. New York: Guilford.

Wallerstein, R.S., & Goldberger, I. (Eds.). (1998). *Ideas and identities: The life and work of Erik Erikson*. Madison, CT: International Universities Press.

Walsh, B.T., & Devlin, M.J. (1998). Eating disorders: progress and problems. *Science*, 280, 1387–1390.

Walsh, B.T., Agras, W.S., Devlin, M.J.,Fairburn, C., Wilson, T., Kahn, C. et al. (2000). Fluoxetine for bulimia nervosa following poor response to psychotherapy. *American Journal of Psychiatry*, 157(8), 1332–1334.

Walsh, B.T., Kaplan, A., Attia, E., Olmsted, M., Parides, M., Carter, J. et al. (2006). Fluoxetine after weight restoration in anorexia nervosa: A randomized controlled trial. *Journal of the American Medical Association*, 295(22), 2605–2612.

Wampold, B.E. (2001). *The great psychotherapy debate: Models, methods, and findings*. Mahwah, NJ, Lawrence Erlbaum.

Weaver, K., Wuest, J., & Ciliska, D. (2005). Understanding women's journey of recovery from anorexia nervosa. *Qualitative Health Research*, 15(2), 188–206.

Weiss, J., Sampson, H., & the Mount Zion Psychotherapy Research Group (1986). *The psychoanalytic process: Theory, clinical observations, and empirical research*. New York: Guilford.

Weissman, M.M., Markowitz, J.C., & Klerman, G. (2000). *Comprehensive guide to interpersonal psychotherapy*. New York: Basic Books.

Werne, J. (Ed.) (1996). *Treating eating disorders*. San Francisco: Jossey-Bass.

Westen, D. (2000). Integrative psychotherapy: Integrating psychodynamic and cognitive-behavioral therapy and technique. In C.R. Snyder & R. Ingram (Eds.), *Handbook of psychological change: Psychotherapy processes and practices for the 21st century* (pp. 217–242). New York: Wiley.

Westen, D., & Gabbard, G. (2002). Developments in cognitive neuroscience: II. Implications for theories of transference. *Journals of the American Psychoanalytic Association*, 50(1), 99–134.

Westen, D. & Harnden-Fischer, J. (2001). Personality profiles in eating disorders: Rethinking the distinction between Axis I and Axis II. *American Journal of Psychiatry*, 158, 247–255.

Westen, D., Novotny, C.M., & Thompson-Brenner, H. (2004). The empirical status of empirically supported psychotherapies: Assumptions, findings, and reporting in controlled clinical trials. *Psychological Bulletin*, 130, 631–663.

Wheelis, A. (1973). *How people change*. New York, Harper.

Wiederman, W.M. (1996). Women, sex and food: A review of research on eating disorders and sexuality. *The Journal of Sex Research*, 33, 301–311.

Wiesel, F. (1972). *Souls on fire: Portraits and legends of Hasidic Masters*. New York, Random House.

Wilson, C.P., Hogan, C.C., & Mintz, I.L. (1992). *Psychodynamic technique in the treatment of the eating disorders*. Northvale, NJ: Aronson.

Wilson, G.T. (1996). Treatment of bulimia nervosa: When CBT fails. *Behaviour Research Therapy*, 34(3), 197–212.

Winestine, M. (1973). Panel report: The experience of separation in infancy and its reverberations through the course of life: Infancy and childhood. *Journal of the American Psychoanalytic Association*, 21, 135–154.

Winnicott, D.W. (1958a). The capacity to be alone. *International Journal of Psycho-Analysis*, 39, 416–420.

Winnicott, D.W. (1958b). Primitive emotional development. In *Collected papers: Through pediatrics to psycho-analysis* (pp. 145–156). New York: Basic Books. (Original work published 1945)

Winnicott, D.W. (1965a). Ego distortion in terms of true and false self. In *The maturational processes and the facilitating environment: Studies in the theory of emotional development* (pp. 140–152). New York: International Universities Press. (Original work published in 1960)

Winnicott, D.W. (1965b). The development of the capacity for concern. In *The maturational processes and the facilitating environment: Studies in the theory of emotional development* (pp. 73–82). New York: International Universities Press. (Original work published in 1963)

Winnicott, D.W. (1965c). *The maturational processes and the facilitating environment: Studies in the theory of emotional development.* New York: International Universities Press.

Winnicott, D.W. (1971). Transitional objects and transitional phenomena: a study of the first not-me possession In *Playing and Reality* (pp. 1–25). New York: Basic Books. (Original work published 1953)

Winnicott, D.W. (1972). Basis for self in body. *International Journal of Child Psychotherapy, 1,* 7–16.

Winnicott, D.W. (1977). Hate in the counter-transference. In *Through paediatrics to psychoanalysis* (pp. 194–203). New York: Brunner-Mazel. (Original work published in 1949)

Winnicott, D.W. (1988). *Human nature.* London: Free Association Books.

Winters, N.C. (2002). Feeding problems in infancy and early childhood. *Primary Psychiatry, 10*(6), 30–34.

Wiseman, R. (2002). *Queen bees and wannabees: Helping your daughter survive cliques, gossip, boyfriends, and other realities of adolescence.* New York, Three Rivers Press.

Wittgenstein, L. (1969). *On certainty.* (G.E.M. Anscombe, & G.H. von Wright, Eds.). Oxford, UK, Blackwell Publishing LTD.

Wolf, N. (1991). *The beauty myth.* New York: Morrow.

Wonderlich, S.A., Crosby, J.E., Mitchell, J.E., Thompson, K.M., Redlin, J., Demuth, G. et al. (2001). Eating disturbance and sexual trauma in childhood and adulthood. *International Journal of Eating Disorders, 30*(4), 401–412.

Wooley, S.C. (1991). Use of countertransference in the treatment of eating disorders: A gender perspective. In C.L. Johnson (Ed.), *Psychodynamic treatment of anorexia nervosa and bulimia* (pp. 245–294). New York: Guilford.

Wooley, S.C. (1994). The female therapist as outlaw. In P. Fallon, M.A. Katzman, & S.C. Wooley (Eds.), *Feminist perspectives on eating disorders* (pp. 318–338). New York: Guilford.

Yager, J. (1988). The treatment of eating disorders. *Journal of Psychiatry 49* (Suppl. 9), 18–25.

Yager, J. (1992). Psychotherapeutic strategies for bulimia nervosa. *Journal of Psychotherapy Practice Research, 1*(2), 91–102.

Yager, J, (2003). Clinical computing: monitoring patients with eating disorders by using e-mail as an adjunct to clinical activities. *Psychiatric Services, 54,* 1586–1588.

Yager, J. (2007a). Cognitive-behavioral therapy for eating disorders. In J. Yager, & P. Powers (Eds.), *Clinical manual of eating disorders* (pp. 287–303). Washington, DC: American Psychiatric Press.

Yager, J. (2007b). Management of patients with chronic, intractable eating disorders. In Yager, J., Powers, P. (Eds.), *Clinical manual of eating disorders* (pp. 407–436). Washington, DC: American Psychiatric Press.

Yager, J., Devlin, M., Halmi, K., Herzog, D., Mitchell, J., Powers, P., & Zerbe, K. (2005). Eating disorders. *Focus 3*(4), 503–510.

Yager, J., Kurtzman, F., Landsverk, J., & Wiesmeier, E. (1988). Behaviors and attitudes related to eating disorders in homosexual male college students. *American Journal of Psychiatry, 145,* 495–497.

Yager, J., Landsverk, J., Edelstein, C.K., & Hyler, S.E. (1989). Screening for Axis II personality disorders in women with bulimic eating disorders. *Psychosomatics 30,* 255–262.

Young-Bruehl, E. (1993). On feminism and psychoanalysis—In the case of anorexia nervosa. *Psychoanalytic Psychology*, 10(3), 317–330.

Young-Bruehl, E. & Cummins, S. (1993). What happened to "anorexie hysterique"? *Annual of Psychoanalysis*, 21, 179–198.

Zerbe, K. J. (1988). Walking on the razor's edge: The use of consultation in the treatment of a self-mutilating patient. *Bulletin of the Menninger Clinic*, 52(6), 492–503.

Zerbe, K.J. (1990). Through the storm: Psychoanalytic theory in the psychotherapy of the anxiety disorders. *Bulletin of the Menninger Clinic*, 54(2), 171–183.

Zerbe, K.J. (1992a). Eating disorders in the 1990s: Clinical challenges and treatment implications. *Bulletin of the Menninger Clinic*, 56(2), 167–187.

Zerbe, K.J. (1992b). Why eating-disordered patients resist sex therapy: A response to Simpson and Ramberg. *Journal of Sex & Marital Therapy*, 18(1), 55–64.

Zerbe, K.J. (1992c). Recurrent pancreatitis presenting as fever of unknown origin in a recovering bulimic. *International Journal of Eating Disorders*, 12(3), 337–340.

Zerbe, K. (1993a). Whose body is it anyway? Understanding and treating psychosomatic aspects of eating disorders. *Bulletin of the Menninger Clinic*, 57(2), 161–177.

Zerbe, K. (1993b). Selves that starve and suffocate: The continuum of eating disorders and dissociative phenomena. *Bulletin of the Menninger Clinic*, 57(3), 319–327.

Zerbe, K. (1995a). *The body betrayed: Women, eating disorders, and treatment.* Carlsbad, CA: Gurze Books. (Original work published 1993)

Zerbe, K. (1995b) The emerging sexual self of the patient with an eating disorder: Implications for treatment. *Eating Disorders: Journal of Treatment and Prevention*, 3, 197–215.

Zerbe, K. (1995c). Integrating feminist and psychodynamic principals in the treatment of an eating disorder patient. Implications for using countertransference responses. *Bulletin of the Menninger Clinic*, 59(2), 160–176.

Zerbe, K.J. (1996a) Extending the frame: Working with managed care to support treatment for a refractory patient. In J. Werne (Ed.), *Treating eating disorders* (pp. 335–356). San Francisco: Jossey-Bass.

Zerbe, K. (1996b). Feminist psychodynamic psychotherapy of eating disorders: Theoretic integration informing clinical practice. *Psychiatric Clinics of North America*, 19(4), 811–827.

Zerbe, K. (1996c) Eating disorders: The apple doesn't fall far from the tree. *Contemporary Pediatrics*, 13, 65–76.

Zerbe, K. (1998) Knowable secrets, Transference and countertransference manifestations in eating disorder patients. In W. Vandereyken & P.J. Beaumont (Eds.), *Treating eating disorders* (pp. 30–55). London: Athlone Press.

Zerbe, K. (1999). *Women's mental health in primary care.* Philadelphia: Saunders.

Zerbe, K. (2001a). When the self starves. Alliance and outcome in the treatment of eating disorders. In J. Petrocelli, & C. Stuart (Eds.), *Hungers and compulsions: Contemporary perspectives in the psychoanalytic treatment of eating disorders and addictions* (pp. 185–206). Northvale, NJ: Aronson.

Zerbe, K. (2001b). The crucial role of psychodynamic understanding in the treatment of eating disorders. *Psychiatric Clinics of North America*, 24(2), 305–313.

Zerbe, K. (2002a). Eating disorders in midlife and beyond: Transition and transformation at a crucial developmental stage. *Psychoanalysis and Psychotherapy*, 19(1), 9–20.

Zerbe, K. (2002b). Giving birth to new dreams. *Bulletin of the Menninger Clinic*, 66(4), 369–377.

Zerbe, K.J. (Ed). (2002c). *Primary care: Women's mental health.* Philadelphia: W.B. Saunders.

Zerbe, K.J. (2003). Eating disorders in middle and late life: A neglected problem: *Primary Psychiatry*, 10(6), 80–82.

Zerbe, K.J. (2007a). Psychodynamic management of eating disorders. In J. Yager & P. Powers (Eds.), *Clinical manual of eating disorders* (pp. 349–379). Washington, DC: American Psychiatric Press.

Zerbe, K.J. (2007b). Eating disorders in the 21st century: Identification, management, and prevention in obstetrics and gynecology. *Best Practice & Research Clinical Obstetrics and Gynecology, 21*(2), 331–343.

Zerbe, K.J. (2007c). Panel report: Psychotherapy and psychoanalysis 50 years later. *Journal of the American Psychoanalytic Association, 55*(1), 229–238.

Zerbe, K.J., & Domnitei, D. (2004a). Eating disorders at middle age, Part I. *Eating Disorders Review, 15*(3), 1–3.

Zerbe, K.J., & Domnitei, D. (2004b). Eating disorders at middle age, Part II. *Eating Disorders Review, 15*(4), 1–4.

Zerbe, K.J., & Fabacher, J. (1989). Benefits and limitations of Bowen therapy with psychiatric inpatients. *Bulletin of the Menninger Clinic, 53*(6), 522–526.

Zerbe, K. J., Marsh, S. R., & Coyne, L. (1993). Comorbidity in an inpatient eating disordered population: Clinical characteristics and treatment implications. *Psychiatric Hospital, 24*(1/2), 3–8.

Zerbe, K.J., & Rosenberg, J. *Diagnosis and treatment of eating disorders in obstetrics and gynecology.* Washington, DC: American College of Obstetrics and Gynecology, 2008.

Zerbe, K.J., Yager, J., & Becker, A.E. (2002). Eating disorders: Update 2002. *Psychiatric Update, 22*(3), 1–9.

Zetzel, E. (1970). *The capacity for emotional growth.* London: Maresfield. (Original work published 1965)

Index